Bringing Peace Home

A
Hypatia
BOOK

Bringing
Peace
Home

FEMINISM, VIOLENCE, AND NATURE

edited by
Karen J. Warren and Duane L. Cady

INDIANA UNIVERSITY PRESS
Bloomington and Indianapolis

The paper used in this publication meets the minimum requirements of
American National Standard for Information Sciences—Permanence of Paper
for Printed Library Materials, ANSI Z39.48-1984.

Manufactured in the United States of America

Library of Congress Cataloging-in-Publication Data

Bringing peace home : feminism, violence, and nature / edited by Karen
J. Warren and Duane L. Cady.
    p.   cm. — (A Hypatia book)
Includes index.
    ISBN 0-253-33086-6 (cl : alk. paper) — ISBN-0-253-21015-1(pa : alk. paper)
    1. Women and peace. 2. Feminism. I. Warren, Karen, date.
II. Cady, Duane L. III. Series.
JX1965.B75 1996   95-49791
327.1′72′082—dc20

1 2 3 4 5 01 00 99 98 97 96

Contents

vii   Preface

ix   Introduction

1   Feminism and Peace: Seeing Connections
    Karen J. Warren and Duane L. Cady

16   The One Who Burns Herself for Peace
    Cheyney Ryan

33   Meditations on National Identity
    Bat-Ami Bar On

54   Making Peace with the Earth: Indigenous Agriculture
    and the Green Revolution
    Deane Curtin

68   Bringing Peace Home: A Feminist Philosophical Perspective on
    the Abuse of Women, Children, and Pet Animals
    Carol J. Adams

88   Mothering, Diversity, and Peace: Comments on
    Sara Ruddick's Feminist Maternal Peace Politics
    Alison Bailey

106   "Severed Heads": Susan Griffin's Account of War,
    Detachment, and Denial
    William Andrew Myers

118   The Psychology of Tyranny: Wollstonecraft and Woolf
    on the Gendered Dimension of War
    Barbara Andrew

133   Unthinkable Fathering: Connecting Incest and Nuclearism
    Jane Caputi

152   Onward Christian Soldiers: The War Talk of
    Beverly Davenport LaHaye
    Adrienne E. Christiansen

165   Woman as Caretaker: An Archetype That Supports
    Patriarchal Militarism
    Laura Duhan Kaplan

175   Men in Groups: Collective Responsibility for Rape
        Larry May and Robert Strikwerda

192   An Alternative to Pacifism? Feminism and Just-War Theory
        Lucinda J. Peach

211   Feminist Justice and the Pursuit of Peace
        James P. Sterba

225   Notes on Contributors

229   Index

Preface

This has been a very special project for us. It arose in conversations as we prepared for team-teaching a course on "Peace, Ecology and Feminism" in the MALS program at Hamline University in the spring of 1991. Our hope was to encourage and expand scholarship on feminism and peace broadly conceived. We wanted both to support colleagues working on the interconnections between these exciting and challenging areas of philosophy and also to make such work available for students and teachers. This anthology results from expanding the "feminism and peace" special issue of *Hypatia* (volume 9, number 2, Spring 1994) which we co-edited. For some, this collection of essays may seem too disparate, too various to be meaningfully captured by the notion of "feminism and peace." We think it would be a mistake to dismiss this volume in that way. Just as there is not one feminism, there is not one feminist conception of peace and not one feminist conception of the range of issues appropriately fitting the "feminism and peace" category. We see feminist peace issues along a continuum from feminist perspectives on intrapersonal violence (e.g., suicide, eating disorders), to interpersonal violence (e.g., rape, incest, sexual harassment), to covert institutional violence (e.g., racism, sexism, economic exploitation), to overt structural violence (e.g., militarism, warism). Whether or not one agrees that these issues, or the stance that a particular author takes on any of them, are defensible as legitimate feminist peace issues is an open question; that they deserve thoughtful consideration as candidates for feminist peace issues is beyond question. When issuing our "call for papers" we deliberately cast the net as widely as possible because we believe that recognition of interconnections among the various issues addressed in this volume is a crucial first step in developing informed positions on the nature and extent of feminist peace politics.

To all the authors who submitted manuscripts on the topic "feminism and peace," both those whose papers are included in this volume and those whose papers are not, we say "thank you." Thank you for daring to think through this difficult and relatively new terrain of feminist philosophy. We are grateful also to the many reviewers of manuscripts who gave generously of their time and energy, especially when the topic of feminism and peace was a stretch from their own philosophical scholarship. Thanks go to Kathryn Pyne Addelson, Joyce Berkman, Laurence Bove, Rita Nakashima Brock, Claudia Card, Eve Browning Cole, Jean Bethke Elshtain, Cynthia Enloe, Linda Forcey, William Gay, Trudy Govier, Lori Gruen, Lisa Heldke, Sara Hoagland, David Hoekema, Nancy Holland, Robert Hull, Amy Ihlan, David E. Johnson, Marti Kheel, Eve Feder Kittay, Mahnaz Kousha, Dina LeGall, Linda McAlister, Elizabeth Minnich, Linda Nicholson, Patricia Palmerton, Judith Pressler, Laura M. Purdy, Meredith Redlin, Sara Ruddick, Hammed Shahidian, Paula Smithka, Charlene Spretnak, Barbara Thiede, Jo Vellacott, Mary Ellen Waithe, Barbara Wall, Henry West, and Iris Marion Young.

We express special appreciation to our institutions, Macalester College and Hamline University, for needed secretarial and work-study assistance, and to our colleagues Nancy Holland and Henry West for reading drafts of our paper. Others deserve special mention: two Macalester students, Nisvan Erkal and Jessica Sundin; Mary C. Smith, the Hamline Humanities Division Secretary; and Hamline Philosophy Department Assistant Greg Swan; each of whom spent many hours making phone calls, generating correspondence, and finalizing details for this volume. The editorial staff of *Hypatia*, and especially editor Linda Lopez McAlister, believed in and supported this project from the start. Joan Catapano and LuAnne Holladay of Indiana University Press made the transition from journal to anthology smooth and efficient.

On a more personal level, we would like to thank our colleagues at both Macalester and Hamline, and our friends for their unwavering support of this project during a time when both of us were juggling several other projects with timetables: Marge Bails; Sandra, Annie, and Ton Cady; Charme Davidson; Fran Dunne; Betty Ivey; Karen Johnson; Mark Jones; Bruce Nordstrom; and Cortney Warren. Without their encouragement and support this project would not have been the joy it was to conceive and produce.

KJW and DLC

Introduction

This collection of essays on feminism and peace deliberately approaches the topic in a way which is novel for both feminist philosophy and peace studies scholarship. It does so through feature articles which address a broad range of issues concerning interconnections between feminist philosophy and peace scholarship.

In our own opening essay, "Feminism and Peace: Seeing Connections," we try to make visible the contributions of women even and especially when women cannot merely be added to mainstream, non-feminist accounts of peace. We argue that if feminism is taken seriously, then most philosophical discussions of peace must be updated, expanded, and reconceived in ways that centralize feminist insights into the interrelationships among women, nature, peace, and war. We do so by discussing six connections through which feminist scholarship informs mainstream philosophical discussions of peace: conceptual, empirical, historical, political, symbolic/linguistic, and psychological.

With "The One Who Burns Herself for Peace" Cheyney Ryan considers the case of Alice Hertz, an eighty-two-year-old woman who, in 1965, immolated herself in protest against the Vietnam War. Ryan's perspective is developed through his study of the writings of Dorothy Day, the founder of the Catholic Worker Movement and a central figure in the history of nonviolence. He reflects on how Alice Hertz's action and Dorothy Day's vision of nonviolent commitment can each illuminate the other.

Bat-Ami Bar On's "Meditations on National Identity" is about her coming to awareness of her national identity as a Jewish-Israeli while building a friendship with a Palestinian woman, Amal Kawar. She reflects on the place of such awareness in the process of the re-formation of identity, concluding that, at least in the Jewish-Israeli-Palestinian context, a peace that does not reproduce the past necessitates an ethico-politically based self-examination and change.

Since its inception in the years following World War II, the Green Revolution has been defended not just as a technical program designed to alleviate world hunger but as a moral program to achieve world peace. Deane Curtin's "Making Peace with the Earth: Indigenous Agriculture and the Green Revolution" disputes the moral claim to a politics of peace, arguing instead that the Green Revolution was designed to displace indigenous women's agriculture—forms of ecological peacemaking, akin to pacifism. Curtin argues that the warist intentions of the Green Revolution are characteristic of a form of domination he calls "developmentalism." A complete understanding of domination necessitates linking developmentalism with other forms of domination such as racism, sexism, and naturism.

In "Bringing Peace Home: A Feminist Philosophical Perspective on the Abuse of Women, Children, and Pet Animals," Carol J. Adams connects the sexual victimization of women, children, and pet animals with the violence manifest in patriarchal culture. After discussing these connections, Adams demonstrates the importance of taking them seriously because of their implications for conceptual analysis, epistemology, and political, environmental, and applied philosophy. Her goal is to broaden our understanding of issues relevant to creating peace and to suggest what must be included in any adequate feminist peace politics.

Alison Bailey's "Mothering, Diversity, and Peace: Comments on Sara Ruddick's Feminist Maternal Peace Politics" looks at Ruddick's groundbreaking *Maternal Thinking: Toward a Politics of Peace*. Beginning with Ruddick's "practicalist conception of truth" and her use of feminist standpoint theory, Bailey argues that neither component can adequately ground a feminist maternal peace politics without first answering the question, "Who speaks for mothers?" Bailey compares Ruddick's "maternal practice" with Patricia Hill Collins's account of African American women's "motherwork" to raise questions about the implications of differences among mothers—differences by virtue of class, race, and sex. She concludes that maternal arguments must address the variety of relationships mothers have to violence and military institutions for peace politics to be complete.

William Andrew Myers shows the feminist theme of embodied knowledge to be crucial to understanding our war history in " 'Severed Heads': Susan Griffin's Account of War, Detachment, and Denial." Griffin's account of technological distance in war-making exposes cultural strategies of detachment and denial that seek to hide the reality of human suffering. Myers takes Griffin's work to provide an indispensable diagnosis of this pervasive cultural pathology. Reflections on the history of aerial bombing and on the perpetrators of the Nazi Holocaust demonstrate these patterns on a large scale. Griffin's feminist reconstruction of consciousness as associative and integrative may point to a cure.

"The Psychology of Tyranny: Wollstonecraft and Woolf on the Gendered Dimension of War" is Barbara Andrew's discussion of the social construction of the soldier and gender hierarchy in the context of particular constructions of masculinity and femininity. Both Wollstonecraft and Woolf contend that private tyrannies lead to public ones, and that men's domination in families provides a model for public domination, thus revealing social and psychological conditions which replicate domination, violence, and war. Andrew examines how constructs of gender promote and participate in the psychological conditions necessary for war.

In "Unthinkable Fathering: Connecting Incest and Nuclearism," Jane Caputi examines cultural productions with nuclear themes to reveal a regular recurrence of the notion of incestuous fatherhood. Connections include a nuclear-father figure, one who threatens dependents while purportedly protecting them; the desecration of the future; the betrayal of trust; insidious long-term effects after initial harm; the shattering of safety; the cult of secrecy aided by psychological defenses of denial, numbing, and splitting (in both survivor and perpetrator); the violation of life-preservative taboos; and survival.

Adrienne E. Christiansen examines warist values reflected in the discourse of a prominent Christian proponent of traditional roles for women. "Onward Christian Soldiers: The War Talk of Beverly Davenport LaHaye" illuminates the consistent and extended use of military language and images to describe non-military events and to motivate Christian women to live submissive, domestic lives. Christiansen considers the complex, contested relationship between Christianity, femininity, and war in general along with LaHaye's mix of these concepts in particular, offering reasons why this metaphoric language is so difficult to dismantle and why it poses dangers to feminists, Christians, and peace activists.

Laura Duhan Kaplan's "Woman as Caretaker: An Archetype That Supports Patriarchal Militarism" challenges feminist peace theories that find hope for peace in the ideal of the caretaking woman. She finds such views to be founded in patriarchal gender distinctions and argues that they fail to critique adequately the patriarchal dualism that constitutes the self by devaluing the other. Kaplan claims that the practice of caretaking about which such views speak may easily be co-opted into the service of war. She wants feminist peace theory to address the devaluation of "others" in order to undermine this justification and motivation for war.

In "Men in Groups: Collective Responsibility for Rape," Larry May and Robert Strikwerda criticize several views on rape and responsibility: that only the rapist is responsible since only he committed the act; that no one is responsible since rape is a biological response to stimuli; that everyone is responsible since men and women contribute to the rape culture; and that patriarchy is responsible, but no one person or group. They develop and defend the thesis that, in some societies, men are collectively responsible for rape since most men benefit from rape and most men are similar to the rapist.

Lucinda J. Peach observes that only rarely have feminist theorists addressed the adequacy of the just-war tradition, a set of principles developed over hundreds of years to assess the justice of going to war and the morality of conduct in war. Her essay, "An Alternative to Pacifism? Feminism and Just-War Theory," takes up this task. Peach evaluates feminist contributions to just-war theorizing and suggests ways of strengthening, as opposed to abandoning, this moral approach to war.

With "Feminist Justice and the Pursuit of Peace," James P. Sterba argues that the achievement of feminist justice is centrally related to the pursuit of peace. To maintain consistency, those who oppose violence in international arenas must, according to Sterba, oppose violence against women as well. This requires putting an end to the overt violence against women that takes the distinctive form of rape, battering, sexual harassment, and sexual abuse, and to the structural violence that takes the form of inequalities suffered by women in their families and in the economic arena.

No collection of fourteen articles can exhaust the interrelationships between feminism and peace. We believe the essays collected here provide a rich and varied array of stimulating and thoughtful contributions to this important and growing field of study. Our hope is that they may suggest take-off points for students and researchers to put greater emphasis on work in this area and stimulate new ways to understand and reconcile the many complexities and tensions facing feminism and peace.

Bringing Peace Home

Feminism and Peace:
Seeing Connections

KAREN J. WARREN and DUANE L. CADY

Introduction

What do feminism and peace have to do with one another? What is peace, if it isn't just the absence of war? Do we get anywhere in a search for connections between feminism and peace if we ask, "Where do women fit in to concerns for peace?" What if we take conventional accounts of peace and just "add women and stir"?

We can add women to mainstream accounts of peace just to the extent that what we are adding about women is consonant with the basic presuppositions of mainstream accounts. Women are combatants and military personnel; women are political leaders, protesters, and grassroots organizers; some women believe in just-war theory and others are pacifists; women are hostage-takers and hostages —women "fit in" in many of the ways men fit in. Seeing these sorts of ways women fit in means making visible what is often invisible or undervalued, namely, the full extent of women's roles and participation in social structures. By "adding women and stirring," mainstream accounts of peace are reformed.

But many feminists argue that one cannot always fit women in by the "add and stir" method.[1] When the basic beliefs, attitudes, values or assumptions added conflict with those already in place, we are more likely to get a very different substance—or an explosion—than a simple mixture. This is because what one is adding challenges the very conceptual framework already in place.[2]

Our goal in this essay is to make visible the contributions of women even and especially when women do not "fit in." To do this, we must reframe the discussion by asking different questions: "Why don't women fit into mainstream accounts

Hypatia vol. 9, no. 2 (Spring 1994) © by Karen J. Warren and Duane L. Cady

of peace? How does the exclusion or marginalization of women bias those accounts? In what ways does a feminist perspective affect how we understand the nature of peace and what we entertain as solutions to conflicts?" Only if we ask questions like these will we begin to see the complexity and diversity a feminist perspective brings to thoughtful considerations of peace. And, only if we ask such questions are we in a position to take seriously connections between feminism and peace.

In what follows we argue that if feminism is taken seriously, then most philosophical discussions of peace must be updated, expanded, and reconceived in ways which centralize feminist insights into the interrelationships between women, nature, war, and peace. We do so by discussing six ways that feminist scholarship informs mainstream philosophical discussions of peace.

FEMINISM-PEACE CONNECTIONS

The scholarly literature suggests many of what we will call "woman-peace connections" relevant to feminism. We discuss six such connections: Conceptual, empirical/experiential, historical, political, symbolic/linguistic, and psychological connections. For our purposes, they provide numerous interrelated sorts of answers to the question "What has feminism to do with peace?" They thereby set the stage for showing something we do not explicitly argue for here, namely, the ethical and theoretical imperatives of including feminism in discussion of peace issues.

1. Conceptual Connections

Of special interest to feminist philosophers are "conceptual frameworks." A conceptual framework is a set of basic beliefs, values, attitudes, and assumptions that shape and reflect how we view ourselves and others. It is a socially constructed lens through which one views the world. When it explains, justifies, and maintains relationships of domination and subordination, a conceptual framework is oppressive. An oppressive conceptual framework is patriarchal when it explains, justifies, and maintains the subordination of women by men (Warren 1987, 1989, 1990, 1994).

Perhaps the most obvious connection between feminism and peace is that both are structured around the concept and logic of domination (see (5) below). Although there are a great many varieties of feminism, all feminists agree that the domination/subordination of women exists, is morally wrong, and must be eliminated. Most feminists agree that the social construction of gender is affected by such multiple factors as race/ethnicity, class, affectional preferences, age, religion, and geographic location. So, in fact, any feminist movement to end the oppression of women will also be a movement, for example, to end the multiple oppressions of racism, classism, heterosexism, ageism, ethnocentrism, anti-Semitism, imperialism, and so on (see Warren 1990).

War, the "decision by arms," the "final arbiter of disputes," "an act of force which theoretically has no limits" (Clausewitz 1976) amounts to domination pushed to the extreme: Imposition of will by one group onto another by means of threat, injury, and death. Genuine peace ("positive peace"), on the other hand, involves interaction between and among individuals and groups where such behavior is orderly from within, cooperative, and based on agreement. Genuine peace is not a mere absence of war ("negative peace"), where order is imposed from outside by domination (Cady 1989, 1991). It is the process and reality where life-affirming, self-determined, environmentally sustainable ends are sought and accomplished through coalitionary, interactive, cooperative means.

Feminism and peace share an important conceptual connection: Both are critical of, and committed to the elimination of, coercive power-over privilege systems of domination as a basis of interaction between individuals and groups. A feminist critique and development of any peace politics, therefore, ultimately is a critique of systems of unjustified domination.

What constitutes such systems of unjustified domination? Warren has explicitly argued elsewhere (Warren 1987, 1988, 1990, 1994, N.d.) that at the conceptual level they consist of at least five oppressive ways of interpreting the world and acting in it. These are five characteristics of an oppressive conceptual framework and the behaviors linked with their implementation: (1) value-hierarchical thinking, that is, Up-Down thinking which attributes higher value (status, prestige) to what is "Up" than to what is "Down"; (2) value dualisms, that is, disjunctive pairs in which the disjuncts are seen as oppositional (rather than as complementary) and as exclusive (rather than as inclusive); value dualisms include reason/emotion, mind/body, culture/nature, human/nature, and man/woman dichotomies; (3) conceptions of power as power-over (in contrast to power-with, power-within, power toward, and power-against power);[3] (4) conceptions of privilege which favor the interests of the "Ups"; and (5) a logic of domination, that is, a structure of argumentation which presumes that superiority justifies subordination.

In a patriarchal conceptual framework, higher status is attributed to what is male-gender-identified than to what is female-gender-identified. Many feminists claim that, at least in Western culture, emotion, body, and nature have been historically female-gender-identified and considered inferior to reason, mind, and culture, which have been male-gender-identified.

Conceptually, a feminist perspective suggests that patriarchal conceptual frameworks and the behavior they give rise to, are what sanction, maintain, and perpetuate "isms of domination"—sexism, racism, classism, warism,[4] naturism[5] and the coercive power-over institutions and practices necessary to maintain these "isms." If this is correct, then no account of peace is adequate which does not reveal patriarchal conceptual frameworks; they underlie and sustain war and conflict resolution strategies. (Examples of why we think this is correct are laced throughout the remainder of the paper.)

One glaring example of how the dominant cultural outlook manifests this oppressive conceptual framework is seen in macho, polarized, dichotomized attitudes toward war and peace. Pacifists are dismissed as naive, soft wimps;

warriors are realistic, hard heroes. War and peace are seen as opposites. In fact few individual warists or pacifists live up to these exaggerated extremes. This suggests a reconceptualization of values along a continuum which allows degrees of pacifism and degrees of justification for war (Cady 1989).

Feminist philosophers regard conceptual considerations to be at the core of peace issues because many of the other women-peace connections can be explained theoretically with an analysis of patriarchal conceptual frameworks in place. The evidence for the existence of such conceptual connections comes from a wide variety of sources: empirical data and history; art, literature, and religion; politics, ethics, and epistemology; language and science. Although we cannot discuss all of these sources here, we do consider several. They are evidence of woman-peace connections that, in turn, help to establish the nature and significance of the conceptual connections.

2. Empirical Connections

Empirical connections provide concrete data linking women, children, people of color, and the poor, with environmental destruction and various forms of violence, especially war. Military operations such as the Persian Gulf War not only kill humans; they wreak havoc on the environment by releasing toxics, pollutants, and radioactive materials into the air, water, and food. In the Middle East and in large portions of the southern hemisphere women and children bear the responsibilities, determined by gender and age roles, of collecting and distributing water; thus the women and the children are the ones who are disproportionally harmed by the presence of unsafe, or unpotable, water. Hence, the environmental effects of a war such as the Persian Gulf War threaten the lives and livelihood of those humans least able to escape the immediate effects—women, children, and the poor. A feminist perspective—especially an ecofeminist perspective that focuses on the interrelationships between the treatment of women and other subdominants, on the one hand, and the treatment of the nonhuman natural environment, on the other hand—shows how and where such effects will be borne disproportionately by women, children, racial minorities, and the poor.[6]

Consider chemical sensitivity. Persistent toxic chemicals, largely because of their ability to cross the placenta, to bioaccumulate, and to occur as mixtures, pose disproportionate serious health threats to infants, mothers, and the elderly. In the United States this is a crucial issue, for example, for Native Americans living on reservations, recognized by the federal government as "sovereign nations." Navajo Indians are the primary work force in the mining of uranium in the United States. According to a report, "Toxics and Minority Communities" (Center for Third World Organizing 1986), two million tons of radioactive uranium tailings have been dumped on Native American lands. Cancer of the reproductive organs occurs among Navaho teenagers at a rate seventeen times the national average. Indian reservations of the Kaibab Paiutes (Northern Arizona) and other tribes across the United States are targeted sites for hazardous waste incinerators, disposal and storage facilities. Many tribes, "faced with unemployment rates of eighty percent or higher, are desperate for both jobs and capital" (*The Christian Science Monitor* 1991). The infamous report *Toxic Wastes and Race in the United States* (Commission for Racial Justice of the United Church of Christ 1987) identified race as the primary factor in the location of uncontrolled, hazardous waste sites in the United States. Three out of every five African Americans and Hispanic Americans and more than half of all Asian Pacific Islanders and Native Americans live in communities with uncontrolled toxic waste sites.

Native American women face particular health risks. A survey of households and hospitals on the Pine Ridge Reservation in South Dakota revealed that in 1979 in one month thirty-eight percent of the pregnant women on the reservation suffered miscarriages, compared to the U.S. population rate of between ten and twenty percent. There were also extremely high rates of cleft palate and other birth defects, as well as hepatitis, jaundice, and serious diarrhea. Health officials confirmed that the Pine Ridge Reservation had higher than average rates of bone and gynecological cancers.

What does this have to do with peace? In addition to the obvious point that these toxics maim, harm, and kill their victims, the United States government plays a major role in the proliferation of these wastes. According to Seth Shulman's *The Threat at Home: Confronting the Toxic Legacy of the U.S. Military* (Shulman 1992), the U.S. military is one of the leading producers of unregulated toxic wastes, hidden from public view, control, and knowledge, at military and other installations in every state. For instance, Basin F, a phosphorescent toxic lake on the outskirts of Denver, is believed to be the earth's most toxic square mile (Shulman 1992, xi). The liquid filling this 100-acre lagoon contains "nearly 11 million gallons' worth of wastes, including by-products of the manufacture of nerve gas and mustard gas—chemical weapons whose lethality is normally measured in minute quantities such as milligrams" (xi). Most people associate the problem of toxic wastes with

> corporate industrial giants like Union Carbide, Exxon, or Du Pont. In fact, the Pentagon's vast enterprise produces well over a ton of toxic wastes every minute, a yearly output that some contend is greater than that of the top five U.S. chemical companies combined. To make matters considerably worse, the military branch of the federal government has for decades operated almost entirely unrestricted by environmental law. Billions of gallons of toxic wastes—a virtual ocean—have been dumped by the U.S. military directly into the ground at thousands of sites across the country over the past decades. (Shulman 1992, xiii)

According to Shulman, the national military toxic burden is "a figurative minefield. The nationwide military toxic waste problem is monumental—a nightmare of almost overwhelming proportion. And like JPG's [Jefferson Proving Ground in Madison, Indiana] bombs, the military's toxic legacy is sequestered from public view, waiting, politically at least, to explode" (Shulman 1992, 7).

The Pentagon's own account ranks it "among the worst violators of hazardous waste laws in the country" (Shulman 1992, 8). The Pentagon has already identified approximately 20,000 sites of suspected toxic contamination on land currently or formerly owned by the military worldwide; to date only 404 have been cleaned up (Shulman 1992, 8). The nearly unthinkable worry is whether a real cleanup of this toxic legacy is technically possible. These empirical examples show fundamental feminism/peace connections, namely, those involving the placement of uranium tailings and other toxic wastes, since the military bears primary responsibility for exposure to toxics in the United States.

Consider a different sort of case: In Somalia today, women, children, and the elderly are most in risk of starvation and violent death in part because they are least empowered and are most vulnerable to rape and disease in their war-torn country. Their defenselessness is cultural and political as well as practical. While men and boys are not immune to starvation and suffering, they have greater access to various means of self-defense and military protection.

In Bosnia-Herzegovina, women and girls have been raped and molested in horrific numbers in addition to the death, injury, and dislocation they have experienced as the "generic" victims of war. A recent article on war rape (gang rape by soldiers, beatings, and sexual enslavement) reports that victims are largely "being ignored in Croatia, where predominately male, Roman Catholic, and conservative health officials are too discomfited by the subject to provide care or compassion" (*Minneapolis Star/Tribune* 1992). Most of the victims will be ostracized in their tradition-bound societies once the war ends; many already have been cast out of their homes and left to fend for themselves. Their experiences are horrifying and legion. In the same article, Zorica Spoljar, a volunteer with the Kareta feminist organization who has been visiting refugee shelters to talk to rape victims, says, "Men rape during war because it is considered an act of the victors. In traditional societies, like those in the occupied areas [of Bosnia], women have always been considered property, so violating them is a way for the winners to show who now controls that property." Women's groups and antiwar organizations constantly protest that nothing is done for the innumerable victims of sexual violence which is viewed as a logical, predictable, rightful consequence of war. The Zagreb feminist movement has been making such appeals with virtually no success.

3. Historical Connections

Sadly, current reports of huge numbers of war rapes in Bosnia-Herzegovina and Rigoberta Menchú's recent testimony of rape and sexual violence against women by military oppressors in Guatemala (Menchú 1983) are just contemporary extensions of a patriarchal legacy documented by Susan Brownmiller in *Against Our Will: Men, Women, and Rape* (Brownmiller 1975). The history of rape shows it to be a "natural" part of war. Such empirical data itself establishes important historical connections between how one treats women, the poor, racial minorities, and the nonhuman environment, on the one hand, and engagement in military, war, and other violent conflict resolution strategies on the other. But one can look elsewhere as well.

Consider the actions of the Navy brass in the so-called Tailhook scandal, in which "officers and gentlemen" man-handled female officers at an annual fliers convention. The brass did nothing at first. According to journalist Amanda Smith, this is because "Naval officers knew perfectly well this behavior was quite ordinary" (Smith 1992). Carol Burke, a professor at the Naval Academy at Annapolis for seven years, describes woman-hating as deliberately taught at that tax-supported institution, often in marching songs and the way soldiers are penalized for unsoldier-like behavior. Examples of a marching song sets the stage for the depth and historical reality of this hatred: "My girl is a vegetable . . . my girl ain't got no eyes, just sockets full of flies." The song continues to boast of "cutting a woman in two with a chain saw or ramming an ice pick through her ears, then using the pick as a handlebar to ride her like a Harley motorcycle." Men keep "Hog Logs" of female visitors to the Academy reception office whom they deem unattractive, and "male midshipmen wear Chiquita and Dole banana stickers in their hats to mark each time they have sex with a date on the academy grounds" (Smith 1992).[7] As recently as October 4, 1993, *Time* magazine reported that "in heterosexual litigation, meanwhile, the Navy withdrew all charges against a pilot in one of the 120 sexual harassment cases stemming from the infamous Tailhook Association convention two years ago. Prosecutors abandoned the case against Lieutenant Cole Cowden after determining there wasn't sufficient evidence to go to court. The Navy has now dropped half of the Tailhook cases" (*Time* 1993). The Tailhook scandal is just one more piece of evidence of the historical connections between the military and the treatment of women as inferior subordinates. Any peace politics which fails to centralize the treatment of women in war and by the military in general will simply be male-gender-biased (if not blind) and, hence, grossly inadequate.

4. Political Connections (Praxis)

Françoise d'Eaubonne introduced the term *écoféminisme* in 1974 to bring attention to women's potential for bringing about an ecological revolution (d'Eaubonne 1974, 213–52). Ecofeminism has always been a grassroots political movement motivated by pressing pragmatic concerns (see Lahar 1991). These range from issues of women's and environmental health, to science, development, and technology, the treatment of animals, and peace, antinuclear, antimilitarism activism. The Seneca Falls and Greenham Commons Peace Camps, the 1981 Women's Pentagon Action, the Puget Sound Women's Peace Camp, FANG (a small all-women's feminist antinuclear action group), and Women's Strike for Peace (WSP) are just a few of the grassroots feminist peace groups. In addition, hundreds of grassroots environmental organizations and actions initiated by women and low-income minorities have emerged throughout the world. As Cynthia Hamilton claims, "Women often play a primary role in community action because it is about things they know best" (Hamilton 1991, 43).

Las Madres de la Plaza de Mayo, women who march every Thursday in the main square in Buenos Aires, Argentina, to commemorate the lives of "the disappeared" in the "Dirty War" (the *guerra sucia*), certainly illustrate the courageous peace politics of women. Week in and week out they protest the victimization of people, mostly between the ages of 17 and 25, who have been imprisoned, tortured, often shot. Over 30,000 have simply disappeared without a trace. For feminists, it is no wonder that a woman like Rigoberta Menchú wins the Nobel Peace Prize for similar activism in Guatemala.

A wonderful example of women as political agents of change that clearly shows woman-peace connections is provided by the Chipko movement. In 1974, twenty-seven women of Reni in Northern India took simple but effective action to stop tree felling. They threatened to hug the trees if the lumberjacks attempted to fell them. The women's protest, known as the Chipko (Hindi for "to embrace" or "hug") movement, saved 12,000 square kilometers of sensitive watershed.[8] The grassroots, nonviolent women-initiated Chipko movement was a *satyagraha* protest movement in the Gandhian tradition of nonviolence. It illustrates a peace action initiated by women which gives visibility to women's objections to the replacement of valuable indigenous forests by teak and eucalyptus monoculture (Center for Science and Environment 1984–85, 94).[9]

Water collection and distribution, food production, and forest management activities are precisely those which women engage in on a daily basis. They are also often "invisible" to mainstream theorists and policy-makers. Conceptually, this "invisibility" is significant: It accounts for the mistaken assumption that such accounts are not gender-biased. Failure to see these women and what they know —their epistemic privilege—results in misguided technologies, imposed development strategies, and the absence of women from most peace-initiative discussions at high-ranking decision-making levels. As an aside, it is interesting to note that one ecofeminist physicist, Vandana Shiva, a founding member of the Chipko movement, who, until recently, was probably best known for her book *Staying Alive: Women, Ecology, and Development* (Shiva 1988), won the Alternative Nobel Peace Prize for 1993.

5. Symbolic/Linguistic Connections

Much of feminist critique regarding war and violence focuses on language, particularly the symbolic connections between sexist-naturist-warist language, that is, language which inferiorizes women and nonhuman nature by naturalizing women and feminizing nature, and then gets used in discussions of war and nuclear issues. For example, naturist language describes women as cows, foxes, chicks, serpents, bitches, beavers, old bats, pussycats, cats, bird-brains, harebrains. Sexist language feminizes and sexualizes nature: Nature is raped, mastered, conquered, controlled, mined. "Her" "secrets" are "penetrated," and "her" "womb" is put into the service of the "man of science." "Virgin (not stud) timber" is felled, cut down. "Fertile (not potent) soil" is tilled, and land that lies "fallow" (not cultivated) is "barren," useless. Language which so feminizes nature and so naturalizes women describes, reflects, and perpetuates the domination and inferiorization of both by failing to see the extent to which the twin dominations of women and nature (including animals) are, in fact, culturally (and not merely figuratively) connected (Adams 1988, 61).

The adoption of sexist-naturist language in military and nuclear parlance carries the inequity to new heights (Warren N.d.). Nuclear missiles are on "farms," "in silos." That part of the submarine where twenty-four multiple warhead nuclear missiles are lined up, ready for launching, is called "the Christmas tree farm"; BAMBI is the acronym developed for an early version of an antiballistic missile system (for Ballistic Missile Boost Intercept). In her article "Sex and Death in the Rational World of Defense Intellectuals," Carol Cohn describes her one-year immersion in a university's center on defense technology and arms control. She relates a professor's explanation of why the MX missile is to be placed in the silos of the new Minuteman missiles, instead of replacing the older, less accurate ones "because they're in the nicest hole—you're not going to take the nicest missile you have and put it in a crummy hole." Cohn describes a linguistic world of vertical erector launchers, thrust-to-weight ratios, soft lay downs, deep penetration, penetration aids (also known as "penaids," devices that help bombers of missiles get past the "enemy's" defensive system), "the comparative advantages of protracted versus spasm attacks"—or what one military advisor to the National Security Council has called "releasing 70 to 80 percent of our megatonnage in one orgasmic whump"—where India's explosion of a nuclear bomb is spoken of as "losing her virginity" and New Zealand's refusal to allow nuclear-arms or nuclear-powered warships into its ports is described as "nuclear virginity" (Cohn 1989, 133–37). Such language and imagery creates, reinforces, and justifies nuclear weapons as a kind of male sexual dominance of females.

There are other examples of how sexist-naturist language in military contexts is both self-deceptive and symbolic of male-gendered dominance. Ronald Reagan dubbed the MX missile "the Peacekeeper." "Clean bombs" are those which announce that "radioactivity is the only 'dirty' part of killing people" (Cohn 1989, 132). Human deaths are only "collateral damage" (since bombs are targeted at buildings, not people). While a member of the Senate Armed Forces Committee, Senator Gary Hart recalled that during military lobbying efforts under the Carter administration, the central image was that of a "size race" which became "a macho issue." The American decision to drop the first atomic bomb into the centers of Hiroshima and Nagasaki, instead of rural areas, was based on the military's designation of those cities as "virgin targets," not to be subjected to conventional bombing (Spretnak 1989, 55).

As the Tailhook scandal reminded many, traditional military training reinforces sexist-naturist language and behaviors, with the attendant values of considering women a foul and lowly class (Cooke and Woollacott 1993; Ruddick 1993). Recruits and soldiers who fail to perform are addressed as faggot, girl, sissy, cunt, prissy, lays. The ultimate insult of being woman-like has been used throughout history against the vanquished (Spretnak 1989, 57). Even references to stereotypically female-gender-identified traits of childbearing and mothering are not free from patriarchal co-opting. In December 1942, Ernest Lawrence's telegram to the physicists at Chicago concerning the new "baby," the atom bomb, read, "Congratulations to the new parents. Can hardly wait to see the new arrival" (Cohn 1989, 140). As Carol Cohn shows, the idea of male birth, with its accompanying belittling of maternity, gets incorporated into the nuclear mentality. The "motherhood role" becomes that of "telemetry, tracking, and control" (Cohn 1989, 141). Once the sexism of the co-opted imagery is revealed, the naming of the bombs that destroyed Hiroshima and Nagasaki—"Little Boy" and "Fat Man"—seems only logical (even if perverse). As Carol Cohn claims, "These ultimate destroyers were . . . not just any progeny but male progeny. In early tests, before they were certain that the bombs would work, the scientists expressed their concern by saying that they hoped the baby was a boy, not a girl—that is, not a dud" (Cohn 1989, 141). Cohn concludes: "The entire history of the bomb project, in fact, seems permeated with imagery that confounds man's overwhelming technological power to destroy nature with the power to create—imagery that inverts men's destruction and asserts in its place the power to create new life and a new world. It converts men's destruction into their rebirth" (Cohn 1989, 142).

Lest one suppose this sexist-naturist language that informs military and nuclear parlance is an aberration of rational discourse, consider how well-entrenched sexist domination metaphors pervade the way rationality, rational or logical thinking, and rational behavior is described in Western philosophical contexts (Burtt 1969; Cady 1989; Cohn 1989; Cope-Kasten 1989; Warren 1989). Good reasoners knock down arguments; they tear, rip, chew, cut them up; attack them, try to beat, destroy, or annihilate them, preferably by nailing them to the wall. Good arguers are sharp, incisive, cutting, relentless, intimidating, brutal; those not good at giving arguments are wimpy, touchy, quarrelsome, irritable, nagging. Good arguments have a thrust to them: They are compelling, binding, air-tight, steel-trap, knock-down, dynamite, smashing and devastating bits of reasoning which lay things out and pin them down, overcoming any resistance. "Bad" arguments are described in metaphors of the dominated and powerless: They "fall flat on their face," are limp, lame, soft, fuzzy, silly, and "full of holes."

6. Psychological Connections

The imagery that domesticates nuclear and conventional weapons, naturalizes women, and feminizes nature comes at a high psychological cost. Many feminists claim that patriarchal conceptual frameworks generate what ecofeminist Susan Griffin calls "ideologies of madness" (Griffin 1989). Feminist scholarship abounds with discussions of "phallic worship," or what Helen Caldecott calls "missile envy," as a significant motivating force in the nuclear buildup (Cohn 1989, 133). Many feminists join psychiatrist R. J. Lifton in critiquing "nuclearism" as an addiction, characterized and maintained by "psychic numbing," a defense mechanism that enables us to deny the reality and threat of nuclear annihilation. *Denial* is the psychological process which makes possible the continuation of oppression by otherwise rational beings.

Setting aside complicated psychological issues, we can nonetheless ask, "Of what conceptual significance is the alleged psychological data on woman-nature-peace connections? What do feminist *philosophers* glean from such accounts?" We close our consideration of feminist/peace connections by proposing an answer: Such psychological accounts help us understand patriarchy as a dysfunctional social system which is grounded in a faulty belief system (or conceptual framework) (Warren 1993).

The notion of patriarchy as a socially dysfunctional system enables feminist philosophers to show why conceptual connections are so important and how conceptual connections are linked to the variety of other sorts of woman-nature-peace connections. In addition, the claim that patriarchy is a dysfunctional social system locates what ecofeminists see as various "dysfunctionalities" of patriarchy—the empirical invisibility of what women do, sexist-warist-naturist language, violence toward women, other cultures, and nature—in a historical, socioeconomic, cultural, and political context.[10]

To say that patriarchy is a dysfunctional system is to say that the fundamental beliefs, values, attitudes and assumptions (conceptual framework) of patriarchy give rise to impaired thinking, behaviors, and institutions which are unhealthy for humans, especially women, and the planet. The following diagram represents the features of patriarchy as a dysfunctional social system:

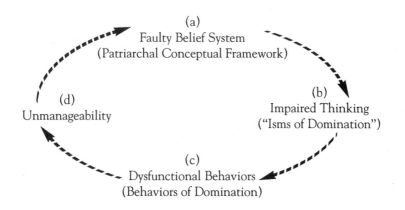

Fig. 1. Warren's Proposed Model of Patriarchy as a Dysfunctional Social System

Patriarchy, as an Up-Down system of power-over relationships of domination of women by men, is conceptually grounded in a faulty patriarchal belief and value system, (a), according to which (some) men are rational and women are not rational, or at least not rational in the more highly valued way (some) men are rational; reason and mind are more important than emotion and body; that humans are justified in using female nature simply to satisfy human consumptive needs. The discussion above of patriarchal conceptual frameworks describes the characteristics of this faulty belief system.

Patriarchal conceptual frameworks sanction, maintain, and perpetuate impaired thinking, (b): For example, that men can control women's inner lives, that it is men's role to determine women's choices, that human superiority over nature justifies human exploitation of nature, that women are closer to nature than men because they are less rational, more emotional, and respond in more instinctual ways than (dominant) men. The discussions above at (4) and (5) are examples of the linguistic and psychological forms such impaired thinking can take.

Operationalized, the evidence of patriarchy as a dysfunctional system is found in the behaviors to which it gives rise, (c), and the unmanageability, (d), which results. For example, in the United States, current estimates are that one out of every three or four women will be raped by someone she knows; globally, rape, sexual harassment, spouse-beating, and sado-masochistic pornography are examples of behaviors practiced, sanctioned, or tolerated within patriarchy. In the realm of environmentally destructive behaviors, strip-mining, factory farming, and pollution of the air, water, and soil are instances of behaviors maintained and sanctioned within patriarchy. They, too, rest on the faulty beliefs that it is okay to "rape the earth," that it is "man's God-given right" to have dominion (that is, domination) over the earth, that nature has only instrumental value, that environmental destruction is the acceptable price we pay for "progress." And the presumption of warism, that war is a natural, righteous, and ordinary way to impose dominion on a people or nation, goes hand in hand with patriarchy and leads to dysfunctional behaviors of nations and ultimately to international unmanageability.

Much of the current "unmanageability" of contemporary life in patriarchal societies, (d), is then viewed as a consequence of a patriarchal preoccupation with activities, events, and experiences that reflect historically male-gender-identified beliefs, values, attitudes, and assumptions. Included among these real-life consequences are precisely those concerns with nuclear proliferation, war, environmental destruction, and violence toward women, which many feminists see as the logical outgrowth of patriarchal thinking. In fact, it is often only through observing these dysfunctional behaviors—the symptoms of dysfunctionality—that one can truly see that and how patriarchy serves to maintain and perpetuate them. When patriarchy is understood as a dysfunctional system, this "unmanageability" can be seen for what it is—as a predictable and thus logical consequence of patriarchy.[11]

The theme that global environmental crises, war, and violence generally are predictable and logical consequences of sexism and patriarchal culture is pervasive in ecofeminist literature (see Russell 1989, 2). Ecofeminist Charlene Spretnak, for instance, argues that "a militarism and warfare are continual features of a patriarchal society because they reflect and instill patriarchal values and fulfill needs of such a system. Acknowledging the context of patriarchal conceptualizations that feed militarism is a first step toward reducing their impact and preserving life on Earth" (Spretnak 1989, 54). Stated in terms of the foregoing model of patriarchy as a dysfunctional social system, the claims by Spretnak and other feminists take on a clearer meaning: Patriarchal conceptual frameworks legitimate impaired thinking (about women, national and regional conflict, the environment) which is manifested in behaviors which, if continued, will make life on earth difficult, if not impossible. It is a stark message, but it is plausible. Its plausibility lies in understanding the conceptual roots of various woman-nature-peace connections in regional, national, and global contexts.

CONCLUSION

In this paper we have offered six sorts of women-peace connections provided by feminism and ecofeminism which suggest where and how women fit into discussions of peace. We suggested that if one takes feminism seriously, many current discussions of peace and war must be updated, expanded, and reconceived. They must be "updated" because feminist literature which points to women-nature-peace connections is currently available and, as such, needs to be addressed by any informed philosophical perspective. They must be "expanded" because the omission of such discussions will result in inadequate, because exclusionary, accounts of peace. And they must be "reconceived" because, once one looks at peace and war through a feminist lens, one sees things differently: Never again does one have the privilege or luxury of talking about nationalism, and regional conflict, militarism, war, and violence, as if women *and* nature didn't matter. They do. That's what is shown when one takes feminism and peace connections seriously.

NOTES

1. For a discussion of problems with the "add woman and stir" approach in curricular transformation projects, see Warren 1989.

2. Feminists also protest that the question "Where do women fit in?" misidentifies the problem as "the woman problem." One cannot understand white racism in the United States if one sees racism as "the Black problem": White-skin privilege and power are white phenomena that, as a consequence, create a Black condition. Similarly, one cannot understand sexism if one sees sexism as "the woman problem." And some feminists think this is what the question "Where do women fit in?" suggests, viz., that "fitting women in" is the problem.

3. For a discussion of these notions of power, see Warren 1994.

4. Warism is the view, often a cultural predisposition, that war is both morally justifiable in principle and often morally justified in fact. See "Warism" (Cady 1989, ch. 1).

5. Naturism is the view, often a social presumption, that the nonhuman natural environment may be destroyed without justification. Whether this includes warism is left an open question.

6. There is a discussion of a range of empirical issues, including chemical sensitivity issues, from an ecofeminist perspective in Warren (N.d.).

7. For an interesting account of the symbolic significance of Chiquita and Dole bananas, see Enloe (1990).

8. The discussion of the Chipko movement as an ecofeminist concern is taken from Warren (1988).

9. For an excellent discussion of the Chipko movement and its effectiveness as a resistance strategy to what she calls Western "maldevelopment"—first world development policies and practices aimed primarily at increasing productivity, capital accumulation, and the commercialization of third world economies for surplus and profit, see Shiva (1988).

10. The importance of this last point is twofold: Not only can patriarchy, conceived as a dysfunctional system, *not* be properly understood apart from the various historical and cultural contexts in which it is manifest; dysfunctional systems and addictions generally cannot be understood or treated as separate from any historical or cultural context. Any account of "dysfunctional systems" (or addictions) which suggests otherwise would be problematic from a feminist viewpoint.

11. This last point is crucial, for it suggests that the sort of dysfunctional behaviors which are rampant in, for instance, North Atlantic cultures—cultures which also are patriarchal—are a predictable, and, thus "logical," "natural," or "normal" consequence of patriarchy. Seen as predictable consequences of patriarchal values, beliefs, attitudes, and assumptions, these behaviors motivate and explain what we call the "*Of course* . . . " response: "*Of course*, you feel crazy when men don't acknowledge your contributions to the project." "*Of course*, you feel powerless to stop your boss's unwanted sexual advances toward you." "*Of course*, your life has become unmanageable; your work place is a male-dominated haven of exaggerated rationality." "*Of course*, you feel frightened to go out alone at night; rape is a very real threat!" "*Of course*, you feel confused and anxious; by standing up for yourself you're breaking all the rules, rocking the boat."

The "*Of course* . . . " response affirms that one who feels crazy, powerless, alone, confused, anxious within and under patriarchy is experiencing what one would expect someone trying to get one's needs met within a dysfunctional system to feel; the responses are *appropriate responses for one in a dysfunctional and patriarchal system* based on faulty beliefs—beliefs which recovering people are trying to shed! The "*Of course* . . . " response is a proper, descriptively accurate, reality-affirming response to people who suffer the ills and abuses of patriarchy. And the ecofeminist response is and must be that "*you are not* crazy, stupid, powerless, alone, or a sexual object."

REFERENCES

Adams, Carol. 1988. *The sexual politics of meat: A feminist-vegetarian critical theory.* New York: Continuum.

Brownmiller, Susan. 1975. *Against our will: Men, women and rape.* New York: Simon and Schuster.

Burtt, Edwin A. 1969. Philosophers as warriors. In *Critique of war*, ed. Robert Ginzberg. Chicago: Henry Regnery.

Cady, Duane L. 1991. War, gender, race, and class. Concerned Philosophers for Peace (CPP) Presidential Address, *Concerned Philosophers for Peace Newsletter* 11 (2): 4–10.

———. 1989. *From warism to pacifism: A moral continuum.* Philadelphia: Temple University Press.

Center for Science and Environment. 1984–85. *The state of India's environment: The second citizens' report.* New Delhi.

Center for Third World Organizing. 1986. *Toxics and minority communities.* Oakland, CA.

The Christian Science Monitor. 1991. February, 18: 18.

Clausewitz, Carl von. *On war.* Trans. Michael Howard and Peter Paret, 1976. Princeton: Princeton University Press.

Cohn, Carol. 1989. Sex and death in the rational world of defense intellectuals. In *Exposing nuclear phallacies*, ed. Diana E. H. Russell. New York: Pergamon Press.

Commission For Racial Justice of the United Church of Christ. 1987. *Toxic wastes and race in the United States: A national report on the racial and socioeconomic characteristics of communities with hazardous waste sites.* New York: United Church of Christ.

Cooke, Miriam, and Angela Woollacott 1993. *Gendering war talk.* Princeton: Princeton University Press.

Cope-Kasten, Vance. 1989. A portrait of dominating rationality. American Philosophical Association *Newsletter on Feminism and Philosophy* 88(2): 29–34.

d'Eaubonne, Françoise. 1974. *Le féminisme ou la mort.* Paris: Pierre Horay.

Enloe, Cynthia. 1990. *Bananas, beaches, and bases*. Berkeley: University of California Press.

Griffin, Susan. 1989. Ideologies of madness. In *Exposing nuclear phallacies*, ed. Diana E. H. Russell. New York: Pergamon Press.

Hamilton, Cynthia. 1991. Women, home, and community. *Woman of power: A magazine of feminism, spirituality, and politics* (20): 42–43.

Lahar, Stephanie. 1991. Ecofeminist theory and grassroots politics. *Hypatia* 6(1): 28–45.

Lifton, Robert Jay, and Richard Falk. 1982. *Indefensible weapons*. New York: Harper and Row.

Menchú, Rigoberta. 1983. *I, Rigoberta Menchú: An Indian woman in Guatemala*. Ed. Elisabeth Burgos-Debray. Trans. Ann Wright. New York: Verso.

Minneapolis Star/Tribune. 1992. War's rape victims have nowhere to turn in Croatia: Women's wounds largely ignored. (December 6).

Ruddick, Sara. 1993. Notes toward a feminist peace politics. In *Gendering war talk*, ed. Miriam Cooke and Angela Woollacott. Princeton: Princeton University Press.

Russell, Diana E. H. 1989. Introduction to *Exposing nuclear phallacies*, ed. Diana E. H. Russell. New York: Pergamon Press.

Shiva, Vandana. 1988. *Staying alive: Women, ecology, and development*. London: Zed Books.

Shulman, Seth. 1992. *The threat at home: Confronting the toxic legacy of the U.S. military*. Boston: Beacon Press.

Smith, Amanda. 1992. At naval academy, hatred toward women is part of life. *Minneapolis Star/Tribune*. November 13.

Spretnak, Charlene. 1989. Naming the cultural forces that push us toward war. In *Exposing Nuclear Phallacies*, ed. Diana E. H. Russell. New York: Pergamon Press.

Time. 1993. Another Tailhook pilot flies. October 4: 18.

Warren, Karen J. N.d. Taking empirical data seriously: An ecofeminist philosophical perspective. In *Ecofeminism: Multidisciplinary perspectives*. Forthcoming.

———. 1994. Toward an ecofeminist peace politics. In *Ecological feminist philosophies*, ed. Karen J. Warren. London: Routledge.

———. 1993. A feminist philosophical perspective on ecofeminist spiritualities. In *Ecofeminism and the sacred*. Boston: Crossroads/Continuum Books.

———. 1990. The power and promise of ecological feminism. *Environmental Ethics* 12(3): 125–46.

———. 1989. The feminist challenge to the malestream curriculum. *Feminist Teacher* 4(2/3): 46–52.

———. 1988. Toward an ecofeminist ethic. *Studies in the Humanities* 15(2): 140–56.

———. 1987. Feminism and ecology: Making connections. *Environmental Ethics* 9(1): 3–21.

The One Who Burns Herself for Peace

CHEYNEY RYAN

> Lit by a birth, I defend dark beginnings
> Waste that is never waste, most human giving
> Declared and clear as the mortal body of grace
> (Muriel Rukeyser, *The Body of Waking*)

Alice Hertz—do any of us remember her? How many of us ever knew her name?

A huge photograph of her hangs in the Revolutionary Museum in Hanoi, commemorating her act of martyrdom in protest of both the American involvement in Vietnam and (in her words) "the arms race all over the world." She said to her daughter that it was an act performed "not out of despair but out of hope." This is what she did:

In March of 1965, to protest "a great country trying to wipe out a small country for no reason," Alice Hertz stood on a street corner in Detroit, covered herself with gasoline, and set herself on fire. She was (self-described as) "part Jewish and part Christian," a refugee from Nazi Germany, an active member of both Women's Strike for Peace and Women's International League for Peace and Freedom. And she was eighty-two years old.

Until recently, I had never heard of Alice Hertz. I knew that there were men from the United States who had immolated themselves in protest against the war, most notably Norman Morrison (whose picture hangs with Alice Hertz's in Hanoi). But I did not know that Morrison's act, much publicized at the time, had followed Alice Hertz's by seven months and may have been partly inspired by it. Nor did I know, until I began exploring and reflecting on the conditions of Alice Hertz's death, of Florence Beaumont, a fifty-five-year-old La Puente, California, homemaker who immolated herself in protest of the war on October 15, 1967.[1]

Hypatia vol. 9, no. 2 (Spring 1994) © by Cheyney Ryan

When I first learned of them, I found my ignorance of these women surprising. Due to my Quaker background, I was active in the antiwar movement pretty much from its inception. So it seemed to me that I should have at least heard of Alice Hertz—who was herself a Quaker. But though surprising, my ignorance is apparently not exceptional. For some time now, I have been asking people I know who were active in the antiwar movement if they have heard of Alice Hertz, and only one has.[2] Like me, most people seem unaware that American women engaged in such acts of self-immolation during this period. For some time now, moreover, I have been combing the periodicals of that time, not just liberal ones like *The Nation* but more leftist ones like *The Progressive*, and the only reference to Alice Hertz that I have found is in an editorial by A. J. Muste in *Liberation* magazine, where she is mentioned, but only mentioned, in a discussion of Norman Morrison's act and the tactic of self-immolation.[3]

I continue to find the invisibility of Alice Hertz to be disturbing. Her actions, however we might respond to them, are an important part of the history of nonviolent resistance to war, and they should not be forgotten. Moreover, I find her invisibility to be perplexing. Admittedly, sexist culture and sexist peace movements have rarely accorded much recognition to women who have acted in the name of peace; but I still wonder whether this explains the total invisibility of Alice Hertz. Might there be something particularly troubling about an act of self-immolation when performed by a *woman* that explains the resistance to speak of it?[4] I am interested in such questions, and shall speak to them as I proceed. But over time, my concern has shifted to more general questions about self-immolation as a political act and its relation to nonviolence. My question has become: does the act of self-immolation represent (as Alice Hertz believed it represented) a right understanding of nonviolence?

I first became aware of Alice Hertz while exploring the life and writings of Dorothy Day, the co-founder and leading light of the Catholic Worker Movement. For forty-five years, until her death in 1980, Dorothy Day worked tirelessly and effectively to champion the cause of nonviolence. She was a driving force of the antinuclear weapons movement of the 1950s; she was a major inspiration to Philip and Daniel Berrigan, Elizabeth McAllister, Cesar Chavez, and other major proponents of nonviolent direct action in the 1960s; and she is credited with playing a major role in bringing about the more critical attitude toward war that the Catholic Church has evidenced in recent years.[5] I would add that she had a profound effect on my own life: I worked with her in the 1960s, albeit briefly; but that brief experience had an impact that resonates to this day. I would agree with those who regard Dorothy Day as the premier woman peace activist, if not the premier peace activist, of our time. (Cesar Chavez once said that he viewed her as more important to the nonviolent tradition than either Gandhi or Martin Luther King.)[6] She was not just an activist, though. For in her long life she wrote hundreds of articles and almost a dozen books articulating her vision of nonviolent commitment, its sources and its demands.

In this essay I want to reflect on Alice Hertz's action and its relation to nonviolence by reflecting on Dorothy Day's response to it. Much of what I say will be concerned with how that response helps us understand Dorothy Day's broader vision of nonviolence—a vision that possesses both historical and practical interest for students of nonviolence. But my ultimate interest is in how that vision can help us understand actions like Alice Hertz's and their place in a politics of nonviolence.

As I shall explain, Dorothy Day's response to actions like Alice Hertz's was both troubled and deeply ambivalent. She could not bring herself to *accept* such actions, in part because they contradicted her insistence that nonviolent commitment should be an essentially undramatic affair. That insistence stands at the heart of what she termed the "ordinariness" of nonviolent politics, which I shall explore in the first parts of this essay. Yet Dorothy Day could not bring herself to *condemn* such actions either, because she took them to be animated by the same logic of "identification" (with the victims of violence) that stood at the heart of the deepest commitment to nonviolence. I shall consider this logic of identification and its place in Dorothy Day's vision of nonviolence in the later parts of this essay.

Dorothy Day's response to self-immolation was not just troubled and ambivalent, it also remained very much at the level of suggestion. She was not a "systematic" thinker. She liked to say that she responded to things primarily from the heart. Hence the value of her work lies more in its provocations than its demonstrations. Some of its more provocative dimensions involve the deep connection that she always drew between her conception of nonviolent commitment and her experiences as a woman. Throughout her life, Dorothy Day always stood in a complex relation to feminism as a political movement. Indeed, as scholars like June O'Connor and Nancy Roberts have discussed, Dorothy Day's explicit statements on feminism (as she understood it) were consistently quite critical.[7] At the same time, though, she always claimed that her experiences as a woman, specifically her experiences as a single mother, were of profound importance to her vision of nonviolent commitment and her capacity to translate that vision into action. I believe that her views here are of interest in their own right, but I shall also suggest that they speak to an issue that I have raised above: whether there is something particularly troubling about an act of self-immolation performed by a woman.

I. IMMOLATION AND ORDINARINESS

When they occurred, acts of self-immolation by antiwar activists provoked strong reactions on all sides of the political spectrum. In an editorial titled "Ordeal of Pacifists," the *New York Times* of November 11, 1965, maintained that "as a matter of logic, they have contradicted their own principles of non-violence by turning upon themselves the full fury of the violence they condemn." Within the peace community, the reaction of some was equally as harsh. Thomas Merton, for example, was so "shocked" by such actions that he briefly disassociated himself from such antiwar groups as the Catholic Peace Fellowship, whose overzealousness (in his view) may have inspired such actions. To one of his friends in the Fellowship he wrote of the "spirit of irrationality" that such actions embodied; to another he wrote that such actions "lead me to make the regretful decision that I cannot accept the present spirit of the movement as it presents itself to me."[8] Prior to these events, Merton's growing concern with issues of war and peace had inspired him to seek out the friendship and counsel of Dorothy Day. But the actions of self-immolation put a strain on their relationship. "Do actions such as these represent a right understanding of nonviolence?" he wrote her. "I think not."[9]

Merton was responding specifically to the death of Roger LaPorte, a twenty-one-year-old philosophy student who on November 9, 1965, one week after Morrison's death, had burned himself in front of the United Nations' Dag Hammarskjold Library. "I am a Catholic Worker," he said in the hospital shortly before his death, "I'm against war, all wars. I did this as a religious action" (Zaroulis and Sullivan 1984, 5). But not all responses to LaPorte's actions, even within the Catholic community, were as strong as Merton's. Daniel Berrigan, for example, spoke of how LaPorte's death "could not but touch my life with fire." Though he viewed LaPorte's death as unquestionably "terrible," a "homing of disaster in the youthful Catholic Worker community," he could not bring himself to condemn it (see Berrigan 1987, 179). Indeed, against the orders of his church superiors, Berrigan spoke so sympathetically of LaPorte at a memorial service for him that his superiors exiled him to Latin America for a time (Meconis 1980, 12; Berrigan 1987).

The difference between Merton's harsher response and Berrigan's gentler response partly reflected a difference in how they *characterized* the act of self-immolation. Merton regarded it as clearly an act of suicide, an act of inflicting violence against oneself, and that is why he (like the *New York Times*) regarded the act as not just immoral but irrational—for one who espoused opposition to violence in all its forms.[10] Berrigan was less confident that actions such as these could be so easily dismissed. "Was the death of LaPorte, in fact, a suicide?" he wondered (Berrigan 1987, 180). I think that Berrigan's reticence at deeming such actions suicide can be understood if we invoke the distinction, important to a number of traditions of nonviolence, between doing violence to oneself and taking violence upon oneself. Consider for example a case in which the only way to prevent violence against a victim is to place one's own body between the aggressor and victim—in a manner that most certainly means the loss of one's own life. When they endorse a preventative act of this sort, proponents of nonviolence do not regard it as an act of "suicide" because they regard it as an act of taking violence upon oneself rather than doing violence to oneself.[11] Might acts of self-immolation be understood as acts of "taking on" violence, akin to placing one's body between aggressor and victim? (Note that the *New York Times* speaks of them as acts of "turning" violence against oneself, a term that strikes me as rather ambivalent on this matter.) To view acts of self-immolation in this way is, as Berrigan notes, to view them as acts of self-sacrifice (Berrigan's term is "self offering") *rather* then suicide; but obviously more must be said about the logic of viewing them in this way (Berrigan 1987, 180). I return to this issue in the later parts of this essay.

By all accounts, Dorothy Day was profoundly disturbed by LaPorte's action, and this led her to inquire into and reflect on his act and the act of others, such as Alice Hertz, who had given their lives in protest. Dorothy Day recorded her response in the pages of the Catholic Worker newspaper, most notably in her essay "A Brief Flame," and she spoke of self-immolation often to her friends and co-workers.[12]

Like Merton, Dorothy Day was troubled by the problem of suicide. But like Berrigan, she also wondered whether regarding self-immolation as *just* an act of suicide was adequate to understanding the act itself or the problems that it posed for commitment to nonviolence. There is a sense, after all, in which the problem of suicide can be rather easily dealt with: Dorothy Day notes that while Catholicism has always held that suicide is a sin, it has also held that "anyone who (takes) his life (is) temporarily unbalanced, not in full possession of his faculties . . . and so absolved of guilt."[13] The problem is that whereas this may relieve us of the burden of *judging* the person who commits self-immolation, it does nothing to help us *understand* that person—and why that person is moved to such an action. As Dorothy Day (like Berrigan) observes, suicide is typically the fruit of private despair; but the act of one who immolates herself in protest must, she writes, "be spoken of in a far deeper context" (Day 1992, 166). Judging the self-immolator as sinful also does little to help us assess self-immolation as a *political* act—specifically, as an act that means to be continuous with the deepest aspirations of nonviolent resistance. I shall explore the issue of assessment first, and then turn to Dorothy Day's efforts at understanding the self-immolator and her actions.

II. RESISTANCE AND THE DRAMATIC

Dorothy Day regarded nonviolent commitment, indeed she regarded all "true" commitment, as an importantly *undramatic* affair. I want to suggest that a central doubt she had about self-immolation as a political act involved that act's dramatic dimension.

The term "undramatic" is my term, not hers. But I think that it usefully captures two features of nonviolent commitment that Dorothy Day saw as essential. First of all, to say that such commitment should be undramatic is to say it should resist publicizing itself, drawing attention to itself; that it should resist undue concern with how it looks in the eyes of others; that it should resist, in these respects, what might be termed the impulse to "theatricality".[14] Second, to say that such commitment should be undramatic is to say that it should reject any notion that the transformations it desires will be brought about by a single decisive action. "Like Lord Jim, in Conrad's story," she writes, "we are all waiting for great opportunities to show heroism" (Day 1992, 105). But the deepest transformations, she maintains, are not the result of great opportunities properly seized. They are the result, rather, of thousands of "small steps"—those small opportunities that we may overlook while waiting for the big ones.

Both these senses of the undramatic are contained in what is perhaps the most recurrent phrase in all of Dorothy Day's writings, "by little and by little." When she speaks of how the nonviolent must proceed "by little and by little," she means that their actions must be "hidden" and "small." As such, the "martyrdom" to which the nonviolent should aspire is not that of "gallantly standing before a firing squad" but that of "losing a job because of not taking a loyalty oath, or buying a war bond, or paying a tax." Or, "if it is a bloody martyrdom, it is the cry in the dark, the terror, the shame, the loneliness, nobody to hear, nobody to suffer with, let alone save" (Day 1992, 105). Her commitment to the undramatic in both these senses is further embodied in her veneration of the nineteenth century Catholic saint, Therese of Lisieux—whose life of unpretentious but unrelenting religious commitment served as a model and inspiration to Dorothy Day throughout her adult life.[15] Indeed, Dorothy Day wrote an entire book about her, which she began by contrasting Therese of Lisieux with Joan of Arc, and suggesting that the former's life provides a more compelling model of passionate commitment (Day 1979, v). But mightn't the valorization of the undramatic contained in this veneration of Therese easily become a veneration of obsequiousness and subservience?

It might. To some extent it does in George Eliot's *Middlemarch*. That work begins with a panegyric to Therese and her qualities that anticipates, in notable respects, the words of Dorothy Day. The life of a Therese, Eliot writes, is "no epic life wherein there (is) a constant unfolding of far-resonant action"; it is not a life that centers "in some long-recognizable deed." And yet, she writes at the novel's conclusion, "the world is partly dependent on unhistoric acts," and "things are not so ill as they might have been" because of those "who lived faithfully a hidden life, and rest in unvisited tombs" (Eliot 1921, 2–3, 621). But there is in fact a world of difference between what George Eliot and Dorothy Day are recommending. What Eliot seems to be endorsing is the life of small kindnesses, a life that we identify with a certain bourgeois domesticity, a life that achieves invisibility through the fact that it never offends anyone—for it always aims to please. What Dorothy Day is endorsing is a life of what she calls (in a phrase I love) "gentle sabotage." It is a life of endless personal resistances, of refusals to participate in any institution or arrangement that implicates one in the practices of violence. And it achieves its invisibility in part through the fact that those it opposes wish that it would just go away.

In explaining Dorothy Day's picture of commitment to my students, I have found it useful to reflect on the *images* that are often associated with oppositional politics. In the waning days of the antiwar movement, for example, it was common to liken radical political activity to starting a *fire*. A popular slogan within the Left was "It only takes a single match to start a prairie fire." To start a fire is to do something dramatic: it is something that is apparent to all, and it aspires to be decisive. But for that reason, the fire image is one that Dorothy Day would tend to avoid. Hence she is suspicious of saints, like Joan of Arc, who are burned at the stake, as (I am suggesting) she is suspicious of activists like Alice Hertz who bring fire upon themselves. Her images of political commitment tend to be liquid—nonviolent commitment as akin to the stream that unobtrusively but relentlessly transforms the landscape around it. Her images also tend to be vegetative. Dorothy Day liked to think of practitioners of nonviolence as flowers (Therese of Lisieux is commonly known as the "Little Flower")—not because the flower is delicate, retiring, and easily trod upon, but because in its endurance it has the power that all plants have to crack in time the rocks that they seek root in.

These images suggest that Dorothy Day regards nonviolent commitment as a profoundly *prosaic* matter. In her words, the politics that it animates and expresses is a politics of "ordinariness" (Day 1992, 174). Now I have yet to say anything about *why* nonviolent commitment should possess this characteristic in her view. But first, let me say a word about the relation of Dorothy Day's view to other conceptions of nonviolence. The notion that nonviolent commitment should be undramatic—in the sense of not unduly concerned with appearances —was of the greatest importance to the vision of Martin Luther King, Jr. Indeed, this notion was a central theme of the last speech that King ever delivered as well as the speech of his that was read at his funeral.[16] But unlike Dorothy Day, King was deeply convinced of both the possibility and importance of the single decisive action to the achievement of nonviolence's goals. It is action of just that sort that he has in mind, I think, when he speaks in his "Letter from Birmingham Jail" of "creating crises"; and it is because of his belief in the value of such action that his political practice (in contrast to Dorothy Day's) was so oriented to *confrontation*.

Why was Dorothy Day so skeptical of the dramatic? There are a variety of reasons. She was generally suspicious of the impulse to self-publication because she regarded it as deeply implicated in our penchant for violence, specifically warfare. She felt, as Simone Weil also felt, that the penchant to commit large-scale acts of violence was often animated by the desire to distinguish oneself in the eyes of others.[17] Dorothy Day also believed that the avoidance of the dramatic was important for nonviolent commitment to achieve the influence on people it desired: most people's lives are prosaic and ordinary, she always insisted. If we would speak to them, we must not distance ourselves from them. But over and above these, there is a reason for her suspicion of the dramatic that refers us to a central and to some extent distinctive feature of her vision of nonviolence. What I have in mind is her deep and enduring concern with how nonviolent commitment can be *sustained*—how we can maintain our attachment to the methods and goals of nonviolence so that "nonviolent" will characterize not just our particular actions in the pursuit of particular goals but also our entire lives. This was, it should be noted, a concern of Martin Luther King, Jr., as well. King liked to observe that being "militant" meant being not only "demanding" but "persistent," and his speeches from the very start often alluded to the problem of "durability."[18]

But more so than King, Dorothy Day was concerned with the virtues that are

necessary to sustain commitment and the forms of practice that are in turn necessary to sustain those virtues. There were several reasons why she regarded the
undramatic "little way" (as she termed it) as essential to making nonviolent commitment a permanent rather than episodic part of our lives. A nonviolent commitment that is unduly concerned with appearances too easily succumbs to a
paralyzing sense of marginality—given the extent to which public recognition in
our world is linked to the manifestation of violence. Moreover, a nonviolent commitment that is unduly concerned with the single decisive action too easily succumbs to a paralyzing sense of ineffectiveness—given that the violence of today's
world is too pervasive to be transformed in any appreciable way by a single deed.
In Dorothy Day's view, the failure to take these truths to heart could only lead
to what Merton called "the fetishism of immediate visible results," a fetishism
that, because it is characteristic of "the power structure itself," would invariably
result in the rejection of nonviolence for the ways of the power structure.[19]

III. Commitment and endurance

I find a great deal of value in both the general problem that Dorothy Day
raises, the problem of how to sustain nonviolent commitment, and her particular
response to it. The problem of how to sustain commitment is a problem that any
oppositional politics must confront. And the experiences of the 1960s and 1970s
lend a good deal of credence to Dorothy Day's views about the threat to nonviolent commitment posed by "the fetishism of immediate visible results." An important but very complex case in this regard is the waning of the commitment
to nonviolence in the civil rights movement in general, and the Student Non-
Violent Coordinating Committee in particular (I find Clayborne Carson's excellent history of that group essential here; see Carson 1981). At the same time, I
worry that Dorothy Day's feelings on these matters render her a bit too unrespon-
sive to the ways in which, in the history of nonviolent struggle, activists have
sought to move others through the dramatic dimension of their actions. For the
same suspicions of the theatrical that animated her doubts about self-immolation
underlay her reservations about draft-card burning (despite the fact that the earliest perpetrators of that act were Catholic Workers). These suspicions also underlay her serious criticisms of acts of "ultra-resistance," for example, acts of property destruction such as the destruction of draft-board files (see Klejment 1988).

As I understand acts of draft-card burning, ultra-resistance, and perhaps self-
immolation too, they are premised on the fact that public recognition in our
world is linked to the manifestation of violence. But instead of rejecting the goal
of public recognition, such acts seek such recognition through a violence that is
directed against things—or against oneself. Choosing such an action does not
imply that a single decisive action will achieve ultimate goals. Those who choose
such actions may believe, however, that through being publicly recognized their
actions will inspire others to adopt and sustain the life of small resistances. But
did such actions in fact have these consequences? I like to believe that acts of
draft-card burning and ultra-resistance did, but I suspect that the influence of

acts of self-immolation was deeply compromised by the very rashness of the act, a rashness that rendered its meaning for others obscure. I suspect that this is why those actions fail to live on in our memory as other acts of dramatic antiwar resistance do.

The question of memory raises again the problem of Alice Hertz's invisibility. For reasons that will become clear, I want to approach it by considering how Dorothy Day connected her view of nonviolent commitment to her experiences as a mother.

Dorothy Day became a mother at about the same time that she decided to join the Catholic church. She decided to become a Catholic, it should be noted, after a long period of intense involvement with anarchist and Marxist organizations. Consequently, her decision was met with a certain astonishment by most of her friends and political comrades. It was also met with rejection by her partner, the father of her child, who said that he would not stay with her if she did not forsake her convictions. When she refused to do that, he left; and she proceeded to raise the child by herself. She was aided throughout the years by those who lived near her in the Catholic Worker's communal "house of hospitality" in downtown Manhattan, but apparently Dorothy Day did not feel that what she viewed as the burdens of single motherhood could be appreciably lifted by more collective child-rearing arrangements.

Dorothy Day's writings on motherhood and its political meaning are notable for the importance that she accords to the experience of giving birth. Indeed, she tells us in her autobiography that soon after giving birth she sat up in her hospital bed and wrote an article about it for the *New Masses*! (She reports that the article was widely reprinted in workers' papers throughout the world, and that when she met Diego Rivera some years later he greeted her as the author of that piece.)[20] She felt that the experience of giving birth provided her with a deep understanding of our connections with one another—yet both the experience and the understanding it provided were marginalized in political discussion. I have found some interesting parallels between Dorothy Day's outlook here and that of the poet Muriel Rukeyser (a women whose life and politics were in many ways similar to Dorothy Day's). For Muriel Rukeyser too felt that the experience of giving birth was accorded too little significance in politics as well as poetry. And for Muriel Rukeyser as for Dorothy Day, its political significance lay in the deep identification with others that she experienced in giving birth. Muriel Rukeyser's interesting term for this sense of identification is "the green wave" (Kertesz 1980, 224–229). In her autobiography, Dorothy Day speaks of how bringing a child into the world was one of the occasions when the self experienced the deepest sense of "oneness" with others.[21] I shall have more to say about the issue of identification when I consider its relation to nonviolent commitment.

It was in the period immediately preceding her giving birth, as she was wrestling not just with the impending tasks of motherhood but the prospect of bearing those tasks alone, that Dorothy Day first encountered the writings of Therese of Lisieux. From that point on there was a deep connection in her mind between

the picture of commitment that she associated with Therese and her own experiences of life as a single mother, a connection that expressed itself in the con-
viction that women like her were somehow more capable of understanding and
enduring the rigors of nonviolent commitment. For her, motherhood involved
"deep moments of happiness" that invariably "gave way to a feeling of struggle,
of a long silent fight still to be gone through" (Day 1981, 138, 158). Muriel
Rukeyser, I would note again, speaks of her own experiences in a similar way—for
the father of her child also abandoned her just prior to her giving birth, leaving her to years of "fierce loneliness and fine well-being." (She speaks of child-
rearing as "green pain.") Through these experiences of personal struggle, both
Dorothy Day and Muriel Rukeyser felt that they were rendered both more open
to and more equipped for a politics of "unchanging endurance/Under the skies
of war" (Rukeyser 1982, 570, 524).

Obviously it is a matter of deep controversy how universal or invariable these
felt connections might be. Moreover, I am uncertain myself how strongly we
should take Dorothy Day's own pronouncements on these matters: her views are
stated quite generally, and emphatically—but so too are Muriel Rukeyser's, and
"arguing" with Dorothy Day's pronouncements may make about as much sense
as "arguing" with Muriel Rukeyser's poetry. I am also aware that Dorothy Day's
insistence on the virtue of "endurance" could be construed as potentially sanc-
tioning the worst forms of slavishness. She is aware of this too. In fact, she quotes
approvingly Bakunin's view that Christianity's valorization of suffering has in the
past rationalized the worst forms of "enslavement and the annihilation of humanity" (Day 1981, 149). In arguing for endurance she is not asking us to accept
enslavement and annihilation. She is suggesting that the struggle against such
evils requires its own endurance.

But there is no question that, despite the political purposes for which she
would employ it, the picture of women that Dorothy Day adopts is a deeply traditional one. Because it is so traditional, though, it may help us reflect on the
question that I posed at the start: whether there is something particularly troubling about an act of self-immolation performed by a woman. (That Dorothy Day
herself found it particularly troubling is evidenced in the fact that she found it
easier to speak of LaPorte's or Morrison's actions than of Alice Hertz's.) Here is
one speculation: the stereotype has it that women are creatures of self-sacrifice.
But the problem with Alice Hertz's act of self-sacrifice is that it contradicts the
kind of self-sacrifice to which women are supposed to be inclined: in childbirth
and motherhood (the stereotype has it), a woman not only gives her body to
others, laboring thereby for the endurance of the race, in a manner that itself
requires endurance, but the endurance that it requires is itself connected to the
effects on the woman's body of childbirth and motherhood: her body is opened
and enlarged, filled and stretched—so that the endurance of the mother's body
is associated with its expansiveness. This is how the stereotype has it. The problem with Alice Hertz's action then is not just in the fact that it destroys the
maternal body, quickly and finally, but in the *manner* that it destroys it: through

a death by fire that shrivels the body and folds it into itself. In the name of a maternal-type concern for others, she may thus be felt to have violated the conditions of her maternal status.

IV. IMMOLATION AND IDENTIFICATION

Questions about the propriety of self-immolation as a tactic still leave unaddressed the question of what impels someone, Alice Hertz for example, to choose such an action.

As I've already noted, Dorothy Day does not dwell on the issue of suicide because suicide, as she understands it, is the expression of private despair and the kind of mental "imbalance" that despair can bring about, whereas the act of self-immolation must "be spoken of in a far deeper context" (Day 1992, 166). Thus Dorothy Day is led to frame the problem posed by Alice Hertz, Norman Morrison, and Roger LaPorte not as one of judgment but as one of *comprehension*: "I want to understand what (they) must have been thinking," she writes, as they set about to immolate themselves. It strikes me that her project is remarkably like Kierkegaard's attempt in *Fear and Trembling* to understand what must have been going on in Abraham's mind as he moved toward the sacrifice of Isaac. Like Kierkegaard, Dorothy Day is sensitive to the problem of incomprehensibility: she is mindful that the task of comprehending such "sad and terrible acts" in all their sublimity must necessarily withstand a vertigo of silence or silences—of both awe and shock. And like Kierkegaard, she is sensitive to the problem of presumptuousness: she is aware that the object of her comprehension is a person, or in this case persons, who can no longer speak for themselves; so her interpretation of their actions is meant to speak with them rather than for them.

This (I suggest) is how she understands the act of the self-immolators:

What Alice Hertz and Norman Morrison and Roger LaPorte were all trying to do, Dorothy Day writes, was "to endure the sufferings that their nation was inflicting on others" (Day 1992, 167). At the start, it is significant that Dorothy Day does not speak of someone like Alice Hertz as suffering *for* the Vietnamese—a phrase that would suggest that her actions were animated primarily by a kind of compassion. Rather, she speaks of her as *sharing* their sufferings, so that their sufferings just *are* her sufferings too. And she speaks this way because she regards Alice Hertz's actions as animated less by compassion for others than by a kind of *identification* with them. And it is because she regards such actions in this way that Dorothy Day regards them as embodying some of the deepest impulses of nonviolence as she understands those impulses, for throughout her life Dorothy Day regarded such identification as essential to nonviolent commitment and the kind of sacrifice that it involves. "Sin is separateness" was one of Roger LaPorte's favorite sayings—echoing Thomas Merton's claim that "Christian nonviolence is not built on a presupposed division, but on the basic unity of man."[22]

But there are serious philosophical issues raised by such talk of taking on the sufferings and taking on the identity of another—issues that concern both the intelligibility and the desirability of such (apparently extreme) moral identifications. These issues have been at the heart of the important writings on moral identification produced in recent years by Marilyn Frye (1983, 52–83), María Lugones (1987), Karen J. Warren (1990), and Val Plumwood (1991) among others. Obviously I cannot address here all the issues they have raised. But I can try to explicate Dorothy Day's views a bit more—in ways that may speak to some of their concerns.

To begin with, I think it is significant that Dorothy Day speaks of sharing another's *suffering*. For another's suffering, as she understands it, is distinct from another's "viewpoint" or "outlook," and sharing another's suffering is distinct from seeing the world through their eyes. What is shared here is not something spectral. I stress this, because it seems to me that there is a uniqueness to our "outlooks" that may be effaced by talk of "assuming their viewpoint," whereas the uniqueness of our suffering may be neither as pronounced nor as important. For one of the evils of deep suffering can be the dreary sameness of its instances; it is a sameness that can make suffering insufferable. Dorothy Day's first writings on shared suffering were prompted by her experience in jail, and she seems to have felt that suffering the experience of jail with the other inmates revealed to her the affinities of their respective sufferings outside of jail. When I was in jail for resisting the Vietnam War, I often wondered whether there was something about the sheer monotony of jail that might illuminate a certain monotony in all suffering. A further point is that in Dorothy Day's view sharing another's suffering seems to be distinct from sharing the physical sensations that the suffering involves. We might think of suffering as an *experience* (broadly conceived) rather than a sensation. I stress this because there seems to be a privacy to sensations that would be effaced by talk of "sharing their sensations," whereas experiences like suffering seem to me to be more accessible to others. Over the past year, for example, I have been helping my partner cope with breast cancer. I have certainly never felt that I could share her *physical* pain, but I have felt that I could share, and when successful I have shared, (some of) her suffering.

More problematic, though, is Dorothy Day's talk of identifying with others through sharing their suffering. June O'Connor, in a work that I have already recommended, observes that the experience of identification with others (O'Connor's term is "oneness" with others) "pre-dated Dorothy Day's Christian conversion and may be the key to understanding and assessing her contribution to our understanding of the moral life" (O'Connor 1991, 59). How should we construe Dorothy Day's notion of identification?

Quite strongly, it seems. In one of her first reflections on the conditions of radical commitment, for example, she describes a result of her experiences in jail: "I suffered not only my own sorrow but the sorrows of those about me. I was no longer myself. I was mankind. I was no longer a young girl, part of a radical movement seeking justice for those oppressed; I *was* the oppressed. I was that drug addict, screaming and tossing in her cell, beating her head against the wall. I was that shoplifter who, for rebellion, was sentenced to solitary. I was that woman who had killed her child, who had murdered her lover" (Day 1992, 5). This sounds a lot like Walt Whitman ("I do not ask the wounded person how he feels . . . I myself/become the wounded person . . . ").[23] And it invites the same incredulity: are we to believe that we can somehow inhabit another individual, that our persons can somehow merge?

On one level, obviously not. What is inhabited is not the other's person, but the other's identity; or more precisely: *one* of their identities—the identity that is constituted by their suffering. I stress this last point because an important worry in talk of identifying with another is that it seems to efface our important differences from one another. But it needn't, as long as each of us is taken to possess multiple identities; for then the sharing of one of them is perfectly compatible with a difference grounded in the identities that we do not share. On another level, though, Dorothy Day does believe that there is a sense in which we can and do "inhabit" another person, the sense that is evoked in talk of how we all begin our lives within our mothers. She does not believe that in sharing another's suffering our relation to that person becomes literally or metaphorically akin to the relation with our mothers. But she does believe, and this point harkens back to my earlier remarks on the significance of childbirth, that there is something in the experience of giving birth and mothering that renders one more open to the possibility of deep identifications with another, hence something in that experience that renders us more open to the possibilities of identifying with another by sharing their suffering.

When Dorothy Day herself articulates what she means by the identification that animates her nonviolent commitment, she does so in terms of the religious doctrine of the "Mystical Body of Christ," which holds (for her) that we possess a oneness with one another by virtue of our oneness with that "body." Now the meaning of this doctrine is obviously far from clear. Moreover, it is one that even Christian-minded thinkers like Simone Weil have found objectionable. Echoing the worries of contemporary philosophers about identification, Weil suggests that to regard our relation to one another as akin to sharing the same "Mystical Body" seems to *reduce* us to parts of some larger whole—in a manner that discounts our "true dignity" (Weil, as quoted in Frye 1982, 100). I think that my remarks on suffering may help illuminate at least part of what this doctrine means to Dorothy Day. For insofar as Christian mystical thinking regards the "Mystical Body of Christ" as itself the embodiment of human suffering, then to say that we are one through that "body" is to say that we are identified through our shared suffering.[24] And this allows us to construe the doctrine "Mystical Body of Christ" in a less totalitarian and more decentralized way. In Dorothy Day's views, our oneness consists not in being appendages of the same "body" but in instantiating the same "body."[25] To say that we each instantiate the same "body" is to say that each of our lives can exemplify the fact of human suffering.

I hope that these remarks do something to clarify the notion of identification with those who suffer. But returning to the act of self-immolation a major question remains: assuming that we can make sense of "enduring another's suffering," how does this idea in turn enable us to make sense of *sacrificing* oneself as an expression of "enduring another's suffering"?

One answer lies in the further meanings of "endure." For "enduring" can connote not just the suffering of something but the resisting of it. This is the sense in which we speak of enduring "through" a bad situation, or of a bad situation's being the "test" of our endurance: by this we mean that we survived the situation in a manner that bespeaks of our not yielding to it, of our holding out against it; in so doing, we demonstrated a capacity for resistance. It would seem though that Alice Hertz does anything but "resist" the suffering inflicted on the Vietnamese, for rather than survive that suffering she wills that suffering upon herself in a manner that means her own death. But I think that there is another way to look at it if we set aside the matter of survival and focus on the matter of resistance. For consider: a Jew who could escape from the Warsaw Ghetto but chooses not to escape could in some sense be regarded as willing that suffering upon herself. (To invoke an earlier distinction: while such a person certainly does not commit violence against herself she might be seen as taking violence upon herself.) Yet that person's choice to stay and share that suffering with those with whom she identifies, the choice to share that suffering to and through the end, could be viewed as an act of *defiance*—and an inspiration.

If ascribing a similar logic to Alice Hertz and others sounds farfetched, I would note that this is the spirit in which the Vietnamese themselves seem to have taken it. Their peace committee spoke of the "holiness and nobility" of death by self-immolation, while acknowledging the inherent mystery of such actions (Zaroulis and Sullivan 1984, 3).

V. Conclusion

I have considered how Dorothy Day's vision of nonviolence and Alice Hertz's action may each illuminate the other, but I have been all too aware of the incompleteness of my endeavor. My discussion of Dorothy Day's views has been not just sketchy but extremely selective. I have focused on particular aspects of her views that seem to be particularly illuminated by the topic of self-immolation. These are also aspects that particularly engage experiences in my own life. But a great deal more remains to be said about Dorothy Day's ideas on nonviolence, their place in her life, and their meaning for all of our lives.

I am also aware of how little we have come to know of Alice Hertz. Her actions are important because they serve to remind us that nonviolent commitment is not always the comfortable and complacent doctrine that it can sometimes seem to be, that it sometimes demands as much as it consoles—which is just to say that nonviolence has its martyrs as well as its saints. A full account of nonviolence must acknowledge and understand both figures. But Alice Hertz's own voice is lost to us, and so Alice Hertz herself remains a mystery. We can speak to that mystery, but we cannot dispel it. Because Alice Hertz's voice is lost to us,

I conclude with the words of Nhat Chi Mai (1981), "an ordinary Vietnamese woman," as she herself put it, "without talent or ability," who wrote in a letter (explaining her own act of self-immolation):

> I offer my body as a torch
> to dissipate the dark
> to waken love among men
> to give peace to Vietnam
> (the one who burns herself for peace)

NOTES

This essay has benefited greatly from the comments of Sandra Ehsan, Leslie Scott, and Claudia Yuckman. The suggestions of Karen J. Warren and various anonymous reviewers of this essay were also of great help. I thank Robert Gould, Betty Reardon, Irene Diamond, Jeff Land, and Diana Sheridan for their wisdom, and the University of Oregon Humanities Center for a grant supporting my work on this essay.

1. My information on Alice Hertz and Florence Beaumont comes primarily from Nancy Zaroulis and Gerald Sullivan (1984, 2–5). They observe that at least nine Americans burned themselves to death or otherwise committed suicide in opposition to the Vietnam War; these include one other woman (who is not named by Zaroulis and Sullivan). In addition, the New York Times of November 12, 1965, reported that Celene Jankowski, "despondent over casualty reports from Vietnam," attempted self-immolation—stating that "all the world's problems are my problems." She went on to survive.

2. That one is David Miller, a former Catholic Worker who some may remember as one of the first to burn his draft card in protest against the Vietnam War.

3. Liberation (December 1965, 7). Alice Hertz is mentioned in the New York Times articles of November 11 and November 12, 1965 on the death of Roger LaPorte, to be discussed below. But the paper did not report her death at the time.

4. I have found some provocative parallels between my concerns and some of Gayatri Spivak's concerns with the self-immolation of widows in India, though they are too complex to be addressed in this essay. See Spivak (1988).

5. On Dorothy Day's life and influence, see Miller (1982). There is a good discussion of Dorothy Day's religious and political influence in Piehl (1982, 241–50).

6. He said this to me in personal conversation in the spring of 1991.

7. There are various reasons for her critical view: some of them involve her very conservative views on sexuality, an expression of her Catholicism; but they also involve her associations, rooted in her own experience, of feminist politics with the suffrage movement, linked with her suspicions, as an anarchist, about the value of electoral politics as a tool for meaningful change. See O'Connor (1991) and Roberts (1984).

8. See Merton, letters to John C. Heidbrink and James Forrest (1985, 425 and 286, respectively).

9. Merton's response is cited and discussed in Piehl (1982, 232). On the response of the Quaker community (to Roger Morrison's death, in particular), see "Colleagues Stunned by Self-Immolation," New York Times November 4, 1965.

10. The charge of irrationality is reminiscent of Jan Narveson's well-known argument against pacifism, except that the point here concerns the logic of a pacifist's inflicting violence on himself or herself whereas Narveson's point concerns the logic of not resisting violence inflicted on oneself. See Narveson (1975, 439–451). See Ryan (1983) for my response to Narveson.

11. Dorothy Day raises a similar problem when she asks whether the act of soldiers who lay down their arms in war is "suicide" if it means their certain death. See Day (1992, 168).

12. "A Brief Flame" is reprinted in Day (1992, 165–168). Dorothy Day's personal reaction to LaPorte's death is described in Miller (1982, 482–83). My understanding of her thoughts about self-immolation is informed in part by personal discussions with those who worked with her at the time.

13. Day (1992, 166). Note that the characterization of Catholic doctrine is Dorothy Day's; the accuracy of this characterization need not concern us here.

14. The term "theatricality" is one that I have taken from the art critic Michael Fried, who contrasts it with the quality of "absorption." See Fried (1980).

15. There is a great deal of literature on St. Therese, though much of it is written from a rather doctrinaire Catholic perspective. The book that had the greatest influence on Dorothy Day was the *Autobiography of St. Therese of Lisieux* (1958); one might also consult Sackville-West (1944). On the importance of St. Therese to Dorothy Day, see Coles (1973).

16. Clearly King was wrestling with the problems of celebrity. See "The Drum Major Instinct" and "I See the Promised Land," in King (1991, 259–67, 279–86).

17. What I have termed "self-publication" Weil discusses in terms of the Hegelian notion, "prestige." See Weil (1976, 25) where she, too, questions the figure of Joan of Arc.

18. See "Conversation with Martin Luther King, Jr.," "Our God Is Marching On," and "The Most Durable Power," in King (1991).

19. Merton (1968, 22). The remark is from Merton's essay, "Blessed Are the Meek," which he wrote in response to Roger LaPorte's actions.

20. On the circumstances of her writing the article, see Day (1981, 137). Portions of the article are found in Day (1992, 27–32).

21. See in particular "Love Overflows," in Day (1981, 138–151). Sara Ruddick (1989, 210) has an important discussion of the sense of oneness involved in the birthing experience.

22. LaPorte's views are reported in the *New York Times* story of November 11, 1965. The quote from Merton is from Merton (1968, 15).

23. I found these lines, from Whitman's "Song of Myself," in Sanchez-Eppler (1989, 944).

24. A useful introduction to thinking on these matters is Dupre (1981).

25. As Northrop Frye puts it, each of us is not so much identified *with* the "Mystical Body of Christ" as identified *as* that body. He also speaks of the body's being "complete within each of us" (Frye 1982, 100).

REFERENCES

Berrigan, Daniel. 1987. *To dwell in peace—An autobiography*. San Francisco: Harper and Row.

Carson, Clayborne. 1981. *In struggle: SNCC and the black awakening of the 1960s*. Cambridge: Harvard University Press.

Coles, Robert. 1973. *A spectacle unto this world*. New York: Viking.

Day, Dorothy. 1979. *Theresa*. Springfield: Templegate Publishers.

———. 1981. *The long loneliness*. San Francisco: Harper and Row.

———. 1992. *Selected writings*. New York: Orbis Books.

Dupre, Lotus. 1981. *The deeper life—An introduction to Christian mysticism*. New York: Crossroad.

Eliot, George. 1921. *Middlemarch*. New York: Thomas Nelson and Sons.

Fried, Michael. 1980. *Absorption and theatricality—painting and beholder in the age of Diderot*. Chicago: University of Chicago Press.

Frye, Marilyn. 1983. *The politics of reality*. Trumansburg, NY: The Crossing Press.

Frye, Northrop. 1982. *The great code*. San Diego: Harcourt Brace Jovanovich.

Kertesz, Louise. 1980. *The poetic vision of Muriel Rukeyser*. Baton Rouge: Louisiana State University Press.

King, Martin Luther, Jr. 1991. *A testament of hope: The essential writings of Martin Luther King, Jr.* San Francisco: Harper.

Klejment, Anne. 1988. War resistance and property destruction. In *A revolution of the heart*, ed. P. Coy. Philadelphia: Temple University Press.

Lugones, María. 1987. Playfulness, 'world'-travelling, and loving perception. *Hypatia* 2(2): 3–19.

Nhat Chi Mai. 1981. One who burns herself for peace. In *My country is the whole world*, ed. Cambridge Women's Peace Collective. London: Pandora Press.

Meconis, Charles. 1980. *With clumsy grace—The American Catholic left 1961–1975*. New York: Seabury Press.

Merton, Thomas. 1968. *Faith and violence*. South Bend: University of Notre Dame Press.

Merton, Thomas. 1985. *The hidden ground of love—The letters of Thomas Merton*, ed. William H. Shannon. New York: Farrar, Straus, Giroux.

Miller, William. 1982. *Dorothy Day: A biography*. San Francisco: Harper and Row.

Narveson, Jan. 1975. Pacifism: A philosophical analysis. In *Today's moral problems*, ed. Richard Wasserstrom. New York: Macmillan.

O'Connor, June. 1991. *The moral vision of Dorothy Day—A feminist perspective*. New York: Crossroad.

Piehl, Mel. 1982. *Breaking bread*. Philadelphia: Temple University Press.

Plumwood, Val. 1991. Nature, self, and gender: Feminism, environmental philosophy, and the critique of rationalism. *Hypatia* 6(1): 3–27.

Roberts, Nancy L. 1984. *Dorothy Day and the Catholic worker*. Albany: SUNY Press.

Ruddick, Sara. 1989. *Maternal thinking*. New York: Ballantine Books.

Rukeyser, Muriel. 1982. *Collected poems*. New York: McGraw Hill.

Ryan, Cheyney. 1983. Pacifism, self defense, and the possibility of killing. *Ethics* 93(3): 508–24.

Sackville-West, Victoria. 1944. *The eagle and the dove*. New York: Doubleday.

Sanchez-Eppler, Karen. 1989. To stand between: A political perspective on Whitman's poetics of merger and embodiment. *English Literary History* 56(4): 944.

Spivak, Gayatri. 1988. Can the subaltern speak? In *Marxism and the interpretation of culture*, ed. Cary Nelson and Lawrence Grossberg. Chicago: University of Illinois.

Therese of Lisieux, St. 1958. *Autobiography of St. Therese of Lisieux*. Trans. Ronald Knox. New York: P. J. Kennedy and Sons.

Warren, Karen J. 1990. The power and promise of ecological feminism. *Environmental Ethics* 12: 125–45.

Weil, Simone. 1976. *The notebooks of Simone Weil*. Trans. Arthur Wills. London: Routledge and Kegan Paul.

Zaroulis, Nancy, and Gerald Sullivan. 1984. *Who spoke up?* New York: Doubleday.

Meditations on National Identity

BAT-AMI BAR ON

On September 13, 1993, Shimon Peres, Israel's Minister of Foreign Affairs, and Mahmoud Abbas, the Palestinian Liberation Organization's negotiator, signed an agreement that committed Israel and the PLO to work toward peaceful coexistence. This agreement, one of the agreements expected to transform the relations between Israel, its neighboring Arab states, and the Palestinians, and replace hostility with cooperation, is being hailed, as it cautiously should be, as setting the foundations for a new era for the Middle East, or more precisely, Southwest Asia and North Africa.

It would take more than formal agreements to bring about peace, especially in the case of Jewish-Israelis[1] and Palestinians. Our national identities have been co-formed. Peace makes it possible to re-form, hence re-fashion our identities consciously, a re-fashioning that must happen if Jewish-Israelis and Palestinians are to try to avoid the reproduction of a peacetime version of connected national identities that were forged mostly in opposition to each other and in a relation that for the past forty-five years has been one of dominance by the State of Israel and its Jewish-Israeli citizens.

I do not know what kind of process Palestinians have to undertake in order to refashion their identities. My essay is about the process that I have undertaken, thus about my encounters with my Jewish-Israeli identity, a process that I hope is relevant to other Jewish-Israelis if not also Jews who are not Israeli.[2] The context of the specific encounters that I discuss in this essay has been my friendship with Amal Kawar, a Palestinian woman whom I met in the summer of 1988, at that year's meeting of the National Women's Studies Association. We were introduced to each other by a mutual friend in a public and thus, for us at that point in time, a rather safe space. Since then Amal and I have seen each other a few

Hypatia vol. 9, no. 2 (Spring 1994) © by Bat-Ami Bar On

times, and we correspond and talk with each other often and regularly. So we, who could have been enemies, have become friends.

If Amal and I were to adopt, for example, Janice Raymond's view of women as "having no state or geographical homeland" (1986, 152), our friendship might have been made possible by a realization that our sense of ourselves as belonging to different nations depends on false beliefs. But both Amal and I, like many women who belong to groups for whom national independence is new or not yet a reality, see women as socially multiply marked by, both class and sexuality, for example, and as deeply embedded in national groups and, therefore, as possessing national identities.[3] Women's national identities may not be conscious, especially for established members of states and societies at the metropolitan core of the world system, where immigrant nationalities tend to turn into the ethnicities of a multicultural nation and create "hyphenated" identities such as those of the Arab-American or Jewish-American. But for some women, even within the metropolitan core, national identities are important. In Amal's and my case national identities could, but did not, become an obstacle to friendship. And for me the friendship became a space and an incentive for a critical assessment of both my ideas about and my sense of national identity.

I use the term "national identity" in this essay even though I am not certain what an identity is and I am even less certain about what a nation may be. I believe that one may have more than one identity.[4] I think that identity is a product of membership in some imagined community[5] of which the nation is one. I think that phenomenologically it is a sort of a temporary ensemble of both uncritically learned as well as critically adopted mental and bodily dispositions and sensibilities, thus images, beliefs, feelings, emotions, body postures, facial expressions, and movements, many of these connected in patterns that are not necessarily at the forefront of one's awareness of oneself. What one is aware of as being a part of an identity is probably a function of a pragmatic necessity in either a deliberative context or a context of differences.[6]

It is not only that I think that one is not aware of an identity as such but only of elements of it; I also think that at times one is not aware of any of the elements of an identity and, therefore, has no sense of oneself as possessing that identity. When I sit in my study reading a text, perhaps a text such as Plato's *Symposium*, I usually do not think of or feel myself as a Jewish-Israeli. I begin to feel something of this sort in relation to Plato's *Symposium* when I contextualize it and think of it as the work of an ancient Greek philosopher, a person whose culture I imagine as both radically different from mine and as familiarly intertwined with my culture, even where the two do not coexist easily.[7]

Because I live in the United States, I have a heightened awareness of myself as a Jewish-Israeli when I am in public. Almost everywhere outside of my apartment I am in the context of differences of a kind that focus my attention on my Jewish-Israeliness. Perhaps the simplest example of my sense of an awareness of my Jewish-Israeliness in a context of difference has to do with language. The language of the U.S. public is American English, which is a culturally entwined English and in some important respects different from other culturally entwined

English languages, for example, British-English. Reading a text in English in my apartment, I do something that I began doing in elementary school in Israel when I began studying English. But in Israel, if and when I step into the Jewish-Israeli public, I step into a mostly Israeli-Hebrew-speaking space. To step outside of my apartment in the United States is to step into a mostly American-English-speaking space.

By now I move in the American-English-speaking space with the ease of a bicultural fluent English speaker though, despite my understanding of American culture, not with the ease of a fluent American-English speaker, hence, not effortlessly. In the American-English-speaking space, my English speech is always accented; I pronounce some words and word combinations as an Israeli-Hebrew speaker, my speech sometimes follows the grammatical rules of Hebrew or is peppered with Hebrew words; and I speak according to a version of the Jewish-Israeli public rules of communication and conversation. I am aware of my accent and of its being an Israeli-Hebrew speaker's accent that does not fit well into the American-English-speaking space though others may just be aware of my foreignness.[8] And being aware of my Israeli-Hebrew speaker's accent, I am thereby aware of my Jewish-Israeliness.

Being aware of my Jewish-Israeliness in the context of the differences between me and Amal is not the same kind of thing. As a Jewish-Israeli in the United States, I am both an alien, which is what my example above emphasizes, and a member of a minority with a history of oppression, as well as success, including, nationalist success. My relationship with Amal, though occurring in the United States where both of us reside, is a relationship between members of antagonistic groups that are still engaged in the process of nation-state formation but are not at the same place along its trajectory. In this latter context, becoming aware of myself as a Jewish-Israeli, I became aware of myself as a member of a sociopolitical hegemonic and dominant group.[9]

I have been aware of myself as a member of the Israeli sociopolitical hegemonic and dominant group in relation to the Palestinians many times before I met Amal. I was taught not only hegemonic but also counterhegemonic lessons even as a child. For example, while, on the one hand, I studied official stories about Israel according to which it was a state that aspires to egalitarianism, on the other hand, my father took me to visit Arab villages and towns and discussed with me the oppression of the Palestinians following Israeli independence. And yet in the context of the first steps in making an adult friendship with a Palestinian woman who was personally hurt by the injustices of conquest, curfews, dispossession, and cultural repression, my awareness of myself as a Jewish-Israeli was disquieting. This is particularly so because Amal and I became friends quickly and easily.

Amal and I liked each other from the first awkward moments when it was not yet clear whether we could trust each other, and we have a lot in common. We are women and feminists. We are of approximately the same age. And we are both academics in the United States, where she has been residing since she was eighteen and I since I was twenty-four. We also have something deeper and more atavistic in common. We spent our youth only about 75 kilometers apart in small Middle-Eastern Mediterranean coastal towns. Perhaps as a consequence, we validate for each other that we have a similar sensual connection with our environment, that we are moved quite similarly by colors, smells, and sounds, taking certain combinations as natural and feeling ourselves as strangers when encountering others. We construct our living spaces with what for each other seem like familiar patterns of furnishing and decoration. We consider certain foods, such as the small chopped vegetable salad, eggplant salad, and majadaras, a lentils and rice dish with medieval origins, as home foods. And we move and gesture in ways that resemble each other.

I.

Yoram Binur, a Jewish-Israeli investigative reporter, aware of the similarities between Jewish-Israelis and Palestinians, disguised himself in 1986 as a Palestinian laborer from the West Bank in order to approximate the current West Bank or Gaza Palestinian experience of a man his age. When I read about his preparations to present himself in public as a Palestinian laborer, I was struck by how little he had to do. He writes about them in his book *My Enemy, My Self*:

> In order to carry out my project, I first had to give myself the appearance of a typical Palestinian laborer. This was easily accomplished with the aid of suitable clothes and accessories. . . . I purchased several pairs of big, very old black pants as well as a few patched shirts. My new wardrobe was completed when I took down from the top shelf of my father's closet an old striped jacket which had been worn years before the State of Israel was established. I also gathered some of the typical paraphernalia of an Arab laborer. First, I borrowed a cheap plastic shopping basket from my mother, the type of basket elderly housewives take with them to the open market. . . . I then bought several copies of the illustrated weekly newspaper *Al Biader Al Siasi*. . . . Finally, I bought three cartons of Farid cigarettes; manufactured in East Jerusalem, they have a strong bitter taste and are never smoked by Jews. To complete the image I left my face unshaven and brought along my worn and trusty red keffiyeh, the traditional Arab headdress. (Binur 1989, xiv–xv)

Binur spent several months in disguise. While fluent in Palestinian-Arabic, his Arabic would not mislead a linguist, and because he is not of Middle-Eastern or North-African Jewish descent, he lacks the darker olive skin and dark hair and eyes associated with the Palestinians, as well as some shared cultural elements. He could pass as a Palestinian laborer and be accepted as such by both Israeli Jews and Palestinians, because while members of the two sociocultures imagine themselves as radically different from each other, in some important ways they are quite alike, and because he had the right props and acted in conformity with the expectations of each group. It is that easy.

But is it really?

Binur did not grow up as a Palestinian. He was not formed and molded by the historically specific Palestinian socioculture, which, even if similar in some important ways to the Jewish-Israeli socioculture, nonetheless, according to some scholars, differs sufficiently from it for them to be considered two distinct ethnicities.[10] The two sociocultures have been developed both separately and in relation to each other. As a modern socioculture, the Jewish-Israeli socioculture developed as a form of, and in relation to, Zionist responses to, first, the European Jewish experience and, second, the Palestinian response to Zionism. This response has as its quest not only to shelter Jews from anti-semitism but also to construct a redemptive utopian future for the Jews, a future for which national autonomy and a life in Israel were seen as necessary catalysts (see Shapira 1992). As a modern socioculture, the Palestinian socioculture developed as a Muslim and Christian Arab culture under Turkish rule. It had growing contact with Europe as Europe began its colonial move into the Middle East and, from the end of the nineteenth century, Palestinian socioculture developed in relation to Zionism.[11]

The relation between the Jewish-Israeli and Palestinian sociocultures has been both mutually productive[12] and conflictual. Moreover, since 1948, part of the Palestinian population and, since 1967, an additional part of that population have experienced the Palestinian socioculture not merely in the context of a conflict with but also in the context of subordination to the Jewish-Israeli socioculture, with formative consequences to both groups.[13] Thus, for example, at the extreme, members of both groups have othered each other so much that not being the other has become a mark of one's own national identity, a situation that in the case of Jewish-Israelis may resemble that of whites in the United States as this is described by Toni Morrison in *Playing in the Dark* (1992).

II.

Amal and I do not constitute the negation of each other as a necessary condition of our identities. That would make friendship impossible. But we are aware of our dissimilarities or differences. We had some significantly different growing-up experiences even insofar as our environments were concerned. While her small Middle Eastern Mediterranean coastal town is an old Arab town at the edge of a new Jewish town, built to surround the old Arab town and ensure Jewish-Israeli control of the area, my town is a new Jewish town, which is a market center for neighboring Arab villages and towns. She is from the old part of Acre, a city with roots in the ancient Middle East, which was conquered by the Egyptian sultan in 1291 and was under Arab control (mostly Muslim, either Egyptian, Bedouin, or Turkish) until its conquest by the British in 1918 and by the Jewish-Israeli Hagana forces in 1948. Amal's family moved to Acre from

Haifa, another Middle Eastern Mediterranean coastal town, about 25 kilometers south of Acre, with a similar history to that of Acre. I was born in Barkai, a Jewish-Israeli kibbutz that was settled in 1947, and I grew up in Hadera, a Jewish-Israeli town that came into being in 1890.

Thirty-two thousand dunams or eight thousand acres of Barkai's land were confiscated from Abdul Hadi, a local Palestinian landlord, in 1949. Hadera's land was bought from Palestinian, mostly absentee, landlords. It was swampland, and the Palestinians called it El-Hadra, "The Green", the origin of the name Hadera, which makes no sense in Hebrew. Calling their settlement Hadera, the Jewish settlers did not merely name their settlement. They got rid of the Arabic name and renamed the area with a Hebrew-sounding, even if meaningless, name.

Settling is always accompanied by naming, which is among the means that the settler uses to create an environment in which she or he moves connectedly. A conquering-settling seems to be accompanied by a renaming that is a process of both naming and a forgetfulness of the previous names. Due to the forgetfulness involved in the settler-conqueror's renaming, the renaming connects her or him to the environment without connecting her or him to its conquered people.

In *The Question of Palestine*, Edward Said describes the Jewish-Israeli renaming that occurred in relation to Palestine as a relation between an interpretation and a presence that denies that presence (Said 1980, 3–15). The workings of such a denial and how it facilitates forgetfulness cut rather deep, as the following example by Meyron Benbenishti suggests. He writes:

> The tallest mountain peak in Israel is, as everyone knows, Meyron. Its historical name is Germak. . . . But, Germak is an Arabic (or Turkish) name and the "names committee" decided that the tallest Israeli mountain peak cannot have an Arabic name; so, they renamed it after a [Jewish-Israeli] village at the bottom of the mountain. At the end of a generation everyone has forgotten the old name referring to the mountain by its Hebrew name as if this were a biblical name rather than a new invention. Anton Shmas, a native of a [Palestinian] village at the bottom of the mountain, has no choice but to refer to the mountain by its Hebrew name, even when he translates the poems of a Palestinian poet. (Benbenishti 1988, 133; my translation)

Benbenishti's example is particularly poignant because it shows how a Jewish-Israeli renaming forces its linguistic reality and implied forgetfulness on the Palestinians. The example becomes even more poignant when one realizes that the settlement of the Jewish-Israeli village of Meyron, after which the mountain is renamed, began in 1949, a year following Israeli independence and the renaming of a portion of Palestine as Israel. In some cases renaming followed the banishing and transfer of the Palestinian population, hence, a physical and not only linguistic erasure of the past. One such case is that of the Jewish-Israeli town of Ashkelon, named after a biblical town of the same name which seems to have existed in approximately the same location. According to a travel guide to Israel which tells the official new geography, Jewish settlers who came to the area after 1948 were placed in the buildings of the deserted Arab village Mag'dal which was renamed Migdal Ashkelon (Israeli Department of Defense 1985, 43). But, the Palestinian villagers did not abandon it. On August 17, 1949, they received an expulsion order and were transported to the border of the Gaza strip (Jiryis 1976, 82).

Acre, Amal's hometown, was renamed too. In Hebrew it is called Akko, and this is how I, inscribed just like the land and the maps with the Jewish-Israeli conqueror-settler's new geography, think about it. What this means for us is something that Amal and I have explored together just a little since our first meeting, usually cautiously and very gingerly. This exploration focused on the names "Palestine" and "Israel"—what it means for each of us to have the same piece of land named by the other's name and possible naming alternatives. Some of the questions that I began to pose to myself are questions about interiorized nationality, about having a subjectivity that was and is constructed in such a way that among the right answers to the question of identity is the one that says "I am a Jewish-Israeli."

III.

It is because of my conversations with Amal that I have come to think about myself as a Jewish-Israeli. I used to think about myself as an Israeli who also happened to be of Jewish descent and who has adopted some elements of the Jewish tradition to give a certain meaning to my life. But I also adopted elements of other traditions, both philosophical and political, and they too give my life meaning, directing my actions and helping me make sense of things. My Jewishness, therefore, did not seem essential to my sense of myself as an Israeli. It was more like an herb that flavored my Israeliness, which was flavored by other herbs as well.

From the point of view of the Zionist leadership, especially the Jewish-Israeli Zionist leadership, my pre-Amal perception of myself is something that could be considered a successful outcome of a complex set of policies.[14] This is how I, the daughter of socialist-Zionist Romanian Jews—who immigrated to Palestine in 1947 while it was still a British Mandate yet contained the promise of imminent Jewish national determination, hence, the promise of Israel—was supposed to come to perceive myself. I was supposed to perceive myself first and foremost as an Israeli. Everything else that may give meaning to my life was to be as inessential as a Cartesian secondary quality. It could colorize but not define who I am, because to be defined in any other way meant that I was not defined first and foremost as a member of the new Jewish nation.

Yet, what is it that defined and still defines me? What is it that made and still makes me an Israeli and in that kind of primary fundamental way?

The Palestinian Intifada and its repressive handling by the Jewish-Israeli regime for seven years, a repression involving curfews, the demolition of houses, house arrests, detainments, expulsions, and just daily harassment which, according to Israeli news reports, has continued into the first month of the Israeli-Palestinian Liberation Organization agreement, has brought other Jewish-Israelis around to attempt to make sense of Israeliness. In a 1989 popular song, Chava Alberstein, an established Jewish-Israeli folk singer, uses "Chad-Gadia," a children's song that is sung at the end of the first night of Pesach, which is the biblically decreed celebration of Jewish independence, to talk about the confusion she feels about her Israeliness (Alberstein 1989).

The traditional "Chad-Gadia" is about violence and its violent punishment. The violence in question is attributed to animals (who I believe cannot act violently), people, angels, and god. The first act of violence is a cat's; it consists of the cat's killing and eating a young goat, a kid. The last act of violence is god's, who kills the angel of death, that killed the butcher, that killed the ox, that drank the water, that extinguished the fire, that burnt the stick, that hit the dog, that bit the cat, the first violator in this chain of violent events. After singing most of the verses of the traditional "Chad-Gadia," Alberstein sings:

> And why are you suddenly singing "Chad-Gadia"
> since it is neither Spring nor Pesach?
> And what has changed for you,
> what has changed?
> I have changed this year.
>
> That each night, each night,
> I have asked only four questions
> and this night I have one more—
> Until when will the cycle of terror continue?
>
> Chaser and chased,
> Hitter and hit.
> When will this insanity end?
>
> And what has changed for you,
> what has changed?
> I have changed this year.
>
> I was once a lamb and a quiet kid.
> Today, I am a tiger and a hunting wolf.
> I was a dove.
> I was a deer.
> Today, I do not know who I am.

Alberstein's "Chad-Gadia" is a subtle protest song. The first night of Pesach is celebrated with a ritual that is a structured teaching of the young, who are assigned specific questions about the events commemorated by the celebration—the exodus of the Hebrew or Israelite tribes from Egypt, ending in the settling of Canaan and the formation of the biblical period's first federated tribal and later, unified state of Israel, which becomes a divided kingdom after Solomon's death and was ultimately destroyed in 70 CE. Of all the biblically decreed holidays, Pesach is the only one that is celebrated with attention to the first night's ritual by most of the secular Jewish-Israeli population, simultaneously gaining meaning from and giving meaning to the formation of the modern state of Israel.

Though ending as it does with a statement of confusion about identity, Alberstein's "Chad-Gadia" points out two elements that are crucial to Jewish-Israeli identity and are alluded to with a biblically oriented metaphorical language—an innocent peacefulness, like the lamb's, deer's, and dove's, and a violent, possibly merciless, fierceness, like the tiger's and wolf's. These elements were taken by most of the Jewish-Israeli population as capable of coexisting with little, if any, tension. They were exposed as contradictory by the conquest and occupation that followed the 1967 Six Days War and mostly by the conquest and the Intifada and its repression.

IV.

Until 1967, but less and less so since, the tension between peacefulness and violence was muted through a multidiscoursed official, and officially encouraged, presentation of all pre-statehood violent clashes between Jewish settlers and Arabs and all Jewish-Israeli-Arab wars, as having been participated in against Jewish or Jewish-Israeli will. According to this presentation, which was and still is common to history books, literature and poetry, as well as governmental pronouncements, Jewish or Jewish-Israeli violence had been forced on the pre-state Jewish settlers or on the state of Israel by the Palestinians and other Arabs. It was an extracted response by a peaceful nation to a threat of destruction.[15]

After the Six Day War, which, like the War of Independence, was celebrated as a victorious war of defense by a small nation against incredible odds, year after year passed, and the conquered new territories of the West Bank, the Golan Heights, the Sinai, and the Gaza strip were not used to negotiate a peace with the neighboring Arab nations. They were connected more and more to the pre-1967 Israel with new roads and telephone and electric lines, and through the confiscation of land and water resources and their distribution among Jewish-Israeli settlers. The exploitative employment of the newly conquered Palestinian population transformed them into exporters of goods produced in Israel, and it was hard not to suspect the official national self-image. It was particularly hard not to suspect this national self-image in the light of growing evidence that the civil rights of the newly conquered Palestinians were being tampered with through the imposition of stiff censorship that made it impossible for Palestinians to voice any kind of nationalist intentions, aspirations, or longings. Other civil rights violations included detention and house arrest for prolonged periods of time and without trial; abusive treatment, including torture, by the military and secret service investigators; and deportation as punishment.

The Israeli (mostly but not totally Jewish) New Left organized to call attention to these growing doubts. Its most extreme factions claimed that the official

national self-image was totally fabricated and absolutely false and that Israel was
an aggressor state that came into being through aggression (see for example,
Bober 1972). These claims resemble the Israeli Communist Party's position, and
moderate versions of these claims have been advanced by the Old Zionist Left.
The less extreme factions focused on the Six Days War and claimed that it was
initially a defensive war that was transformed into a war of aggression by subsequent Jewish-Israeli governments that have institutionalized the war's con-
quests. This analysis has been adopted by most of the moderate Old Zionist Left
and by Liberals and Libertarians, all of whom believe that what has happened
since 1967 is a test of the nation's moral fiber.[16]

What has worried most of the moderate old and new Left, Liberal, and Lib-
ertarian critics, is that the Jewish-Israeli population would choose to win its
peace with the Palestinians, that is, impose a certain kind of peaceful existence
for its citizens through domination of and the use of force against the Palestinians, especially those in the areas conquered in the 1967 war. The moderate old
and new Left, consequently, did not celebrate Sharon's 1982 invasion of and war
in Lebanon, but rather criticized it from the outset, seeing it as suggestive of the
possible future they feared. Still, they expected the war to teach a lesson about
the need for a different kind of future. Thus Jacobo Timerman, who at the time
was living in Israel and seems to identify himself as a Jewish-Israeli in his book
The Longest War, says:

> What is actually creating this state of general disgust with ourselves, of
> nostalgia for something we seem to have lost only a brief while ago, is the
> realization that the most perfect expression of our national will, our mili-
> tary might, will not resolve the Palestinian problem, which is our biggest
> national issue. (Timerman 1982, 89)

By the time the Intifada started, on December 9, 1987, twenty years and a
half after the Six Day War and five and a half years after the invasion of Lebanon,
the lesson about the need for a different future which such critics as Timerman
expected Jewish-Israelis to learn, has not been learned. Speaking as always of its
commitment to peace, the Jewish-Israeli government of Begin and Shamir, with
the consensual support and approval of about half of the Jewish-Israeli population and the acquiescence of more, tried to win its peace, often, with draconian
measures. The Israeli Defense Forces' soldiers executed and enforced these measures. Though some objected and even refused to carry out some orders, too
many have gone even further than commanded, humiliating, beating, and even
unnecessarily shooting at Palestinians. While the last elections in Israel brought
in the Rabin government, which has worked out an agreement with the Palestinians, the Rabin government too professed an iron-fist approach to the Intifada.
As it attempts to negotiate peace with the Palestinians, the Rabin government
seems willing to concede to the Palestinians only as little as it can at a time and
refuses to deal with claims about the importance and extreme violations of civil
rights by Jewish-Israeli soldiers and civilians.[17]

Si Hi-Man, a young, popular, Jewish-Israeli rock singer, was shocked by the brutal conduct of some soldiers. She wrote "Shooting and Crying" (1988), an unpopular song that was censored by the Israeli Defense Forces radio station. The song laments and protests the soldiers' brutality, seeing it as a direct result of a struggle to win. Si Hi-Man sings:

> The street cleaner told me
> that in his village everything has changed
> and life seems different to me
> in the shadow of the filth.
> And in my house, the window is broken
> Tel-Aviv is bursting in
> even its smell has changed
> I feel the danger.
>
> Boys playing with lead
> girls with steel dolls
> life seems different to me
> in the shadow of the filth.
> And it does not matter to me at all
> who will win now,
> my world is gone now
> and the big light was put out.
>
> Shooting and crying
> burning and laughing
> when did we learn at all
> to bury people alive?
>
> Shooting and crying
> burning and laughing
> when did we forget
> that our children were also killed?
>
> On both sides, people only want to live
> in this fear, it is impossible to see
> looking for shelter, from the struggle
> it does not matter to me, who—is the strongest.

V.

For me, the conquest and occupation that followed the 1967 Six Days War did not have the myth-exploding quality that it had for some of my peers. As I pointed out before, I learned both hegemonic and counterhegemonic lessons when I was growing up. By the time I was drafted, at the end of 1966, I was a pacifist, in part since I was suspicious of the Israeli government, because I could not make sense of the official self-image. Failing to see how it is that a peace-loving nation must always be prepared and ready for war and is unable to have the peace that it sought, I thought that the Jewish-Israeli story was incoherent. Nonetheless, I lost my initial pacifism to the Six Days War, and the conquest and occupation that followed it affected me profoundly. Slowly I have come to feel and see it as a betrayal, a violation of the trust that as a critical but not yet too cynical, as well as a rather idealistic, young person, I had in Israel.

I say "a trust in Israel" because what I believed was that there were Israeli ethical principles and moral commitments to democracy and social justice that were and ought to be embodied in the conduct of the national collectivity vis-à-vis its own members and vis-à-vis other collectivities and their members. I knew that there were many cases in which these principles and commitments were violated. I knew about social, economic, and political discrimination against Jewish segments of the population, the Palestinians, and other minorities, such as the Druze, and against women. I knew about the military rule imposed on the Palestinian population within the 1948 disengagement lines, including the permanent and temporary curfews prohibiting movement between 10 p.m. and 4 a.m. I knew about the massacre in Kfar Kassim in 1956. But I construed each case as a case of abuse explainable by the youth of Israel. And Israel, I believed, was a country that had the right kind of ethico-political potential; it was perfectible, just like a Rawlsian reasonably good society.

In A *Theory of Justice* (1971),[18] John Rawls argues that a reasonably good society, which is, among other things, a society that can change for the better, deserves its members' loyalty. His argument, developed while the United States was being torn by internal conflicts about race, gender, class, and the Vietnam War, in the midst of talk about revolution and the need for a radical transformation of the United States, and when acts of civil disobedience abounded, provides the most current version of the philosophical underpinnings for what I used to believe. Believing as I did that Israel is fundamentally a just, democratic society committed to the substantive equality and freedom of all its members, independent of national origin, race, religion, or sex, just as its declaration of independence says, I was basically a loyal Rawlsian daughter to Israel.

I am not a loyal Rawlsian daughter anymore, and I have not been one for many years.[19] While I am slightly more optimistic now that Israel is negotiating with the Palestinian Liberation Organization, I am still distrustful of the Jewish-Israeli will to engage seriously in peace-making with the Palestinians, not just those in the areas conquered in and occupied since 1967, but also those who have been living with the Jewish-Israeli population since 1948, as well as the Palestinian refugees and the Palestinian exiles. What I took as discrete cases of abuse were mostly forms of the implementation of policy or cases condoned by policy. By 1967 the national habit with regard to the Palestinians has been one of a won peace, a peace imposed through domination and by force. The official treatment of the Palestinians in the territories conquered and occupied in 1967 has been nothing but a transfer of existing forms, an extension of the just-beginning-to-come-to-an-end official treatment of the Palestinians within the 1948 disengagement lines. The repressive measures that have been adopted since the Intifada began, including the intimidation of the Palestinians within the 1948 disengagement lines, are only the extreme of what has been much too ordinary for the Palestinians under Jewish-Israeli rule.[20]

While I stopped being a loyal Rawlsian daughter because I lost my naive trust as I came to realize how systemic injustice is in Israel, I do not see myself as disloyal to Israel, at least insofar as my affections are concerned.[21] I still see myself as an Israeli, trying as I do to learn to see myself as just a Jewish-Israeli, a member of one of the two primary ethnic or national sociocultures in Israel. I still feel emotionally connected to the country. I still miss it as one only misses one's home.

I do not know if I could ever feel differently. Among the values with which have been inscribed most thoroughly is the love of Israel, and I was brought up to love Israel in a variety of ways. I was brought up to love it by knowing its geography, topography, zoology, as well as history, and by appreciating its natural and archaeological beauty. But, most important, I was brought up to love it in a very material, physical way, through the work of the land, and through extensive travel throughout the country and especially rigorous hiking in its valleys and on its mountains, at its seashore, and in its desert. These have connected me to the country through my body. It is as if they grafted it onto my body so that I have a feel for the land and its seasonal changes that runs through my hands and my feet and vivid body-memories of adjusting myself to fit the curves of the land while asleep under the open sky just as one adjusts oneself to fit the curves of a lover's body.[22]

Talking once with Amal, I found out that extensive travel in Israel was not part of her curriculum, nor part of her extracurricular activities. Knowing what I know, I was not surprised, but I was very sad. I did not want her to have been deprived of the deep body-connected-sense that the whole country was hers and not just the little enclave that she was confined to. I wanted her to have had, through her body, more than the Mediterranean seashore and wind and the sound of the waves breaking during a winter storm. I wanted her to have had everything I had and have.

Wanting this for Amal would make me disloyal to Israel according to official and quite popular Jewish-Israeli dogma, because to want this for a Palestinian is to want to share the country fully, and a fully shared country would not be the Jewish-Israel that the dogma decrees Israel must be.[23] According to some deviations from the dogma, wanting anything for the Palestinians, even civil-rights, but especially their own state, is an act of treason.

VI.

When participating in some demonstrations against the Jewish-Israeli government and standing with the Women in Black on the northern edge of Tel-Aviv in November 1988, about a week before the Palestinian Liberation Organization's declaration of Palestinian independence, some of the Jewish-Israeli men passing by yelled at us that we were traitors, called us whores and accused us of sleeping with the enemy. Young soldiers in a military bus added threats to our lives, pointing their automatic rifles through the windows and pretending to shoot.

This was not my first experience of men's violent response to women demonstrating, and members of Women in Black told me that the curses, the anger, and the threats were routine, as I expected, due to my experiences in even "Take Back the Night" demonstrations. Members of other Jewish-Israeli peace organizations say the same. And the harassment of women in Israel, whether women demonstrating on their own or with men, is always in the form of an attack that connects treason with sex. It is always some variation of an accusation of whoring sluttishness and of sleeping with the enemy.

Women who are seen as belonging to one group—for example, Jewish-Israeli women who voluntarily have sex with members of another group that is considered as an enemy group, for example, Arabs in general in the Israeli case, and do not exchange their sex for money—violate a sexual taboo. Violating it, the women indicate that members of the group in question are desirable, that they can be loved and loved erotically, that one could have a shared life with them. Indicating this, they destabilize the idea of the enemy because the taboo does not simply assume the existence of enemies but also constitutes people as enemies. The taboo is essential to the idea of deep animosity, an idea that seems to have become necessary for a strict separation of Israeli Jews and Palestinians and seems needed for the maintenance of Jewish-Israeli control of the Palestinians.[24]

The separation of Israeli Jews from Palestinians has assured a Jewish-Israeli control of the Palestinians since 1948. It also assured that members of both groups would have mostly book knowledge of each other, which, even if not biased (a rather unlikely case where Palestinians are concerned [see Said 1978, 1980, and Kabbani 1986]) still does not endow the other with a full reality, due to the lack of direct interactions. To the extent that I had firsthand childhood experiences of Palestinian culture it was because my father's politics took him, and he took me with him, to Palestinian towns and villages where I played with children my age, ate with them, heard Arabic speech, and listened and danced to Arabic music. But I never had a Palestinian friend to grow up with, be it a neighbor or a schoolmate.

In the few mixed Palestinian-Jewish-Israeli towns, like Jaffa, Haifa, and Acre, some people do befriend each other across the ethnic divides. According to a 1980 poll, 43.6 percent of the Israeli Jews polled said that they were ready, without any qualification, to be friends with Palestinians.[25] But 1980 was before the Intifada, and given my 1993 summer's visit to an Israel that seemed to wish mostly to distance itself from the Palestinians, I doubt that in the seventh year of the Intifada the results of a similar poll would be the same. Even now that an agreement has been signed between Israel and the Palestinian Liberation Organization, the national aspirations of the Palestinians alarm and frighten Israeli Jews, as is evident from the Israeli newspapers. Fear does not motivate friendship. Fear motivates withdrawal and closure. A Jewish-Israeli-Palestinian friendship has to overcome this and it must do so on both sides because the Palestinians have their very justified share of fear.[26]

Amal grew up afraid of the Jewish-Israeli police and soldiers. Sometimes police officers and soldiers still frighten her.

VII.

Sometimes I am frightened by sights and sounds that remind me of the possibility of terrorist/guerrilla attacks or sabotage of the kind that happened while I grew up, like the night attack on a house in a neighboring village which left only one young girl alive, or the mined roads that killed and injured passengers in buses on their way to work. Sometimes I am also frightened by sights and sounds that remind me of the possibility of war. At times I have flashbacks and at other times hallucinations that can transform an American countryside into a silent battlefield. At times, following the siren of an ambulance or a fire truck, I freeze and shake. And I have nights burdened with nightmares in which I am in charge of people's safety while under attack and am just about to fail.[27]

In 1979, when I heard about the signing of the Camp David agreements between Israel and Egypt, I suddenly sensed my body with a rifle on my right shoulder feeling so much like a part of me, and I wondered what kind of peace is possible between people whose bodies, like mine, were formed to such a great extent by military training. Though mine was just a woman's military training, nonetheless, I was trained since I was fourteen, and the training extended the survival training I had in the youth movement and fit perfectly with my childhood tomboyish games.

I still train myself, re-creating some version of the body I was expected to have, a body that belongs to a world if not at war, then prepared for war. I was not aware of the extent to which I had a ready-to-fight body until about ten years ago when Elaine Rubin told me that watching me, even when I am absolutely motionless, she senses me as a ready-to-fight body. I do not know how she sensed it. But I thought then about that minute in 1979 when I experienced the unity of a rifle and my body in the middle of a living room in Columbus, Ohio, and this after seven years in the United States away from Israel where the tension of readiness-to-fight has been a constant of the Jewish-Israeli ordinary life. It was four years later and the peace with Egypt did not advance very far. It has not advanced much further since though the comprehensive negotiations of peace in the Middle East may change the situation.[28]

How far could peace with the Palestinians go? In the case of Jewish-Israelis and Palestinians it is not merely ready-to-fight bodies that may be in the way, nor just the fears that engender a mutual mistrust (see Gordon and Gordon 1991). The Palestinians have been dealt with unjustly. They will have to forgive so much, and they would not want and should not have to forget in order to forgive. But, if they do not forget, how could Israeli Jews live with our shame?

I feel shame. I feel it about the past and the present. I feel it when I read an

Amnesty International report about the use of high-velocity bullets against dem-onstrators in the West Bank. I feel it when I read in the *New York Times* about the detention camps in the Negev and the abusive treatment of the detainees, about wounded Palestinian girls and women, about the demolition of houses, and about the destruction of olive groves. I feel it as well when I read a Jewish-Israeli newspaper's account of West Bank settlers who threaten Israel with a civil war as a response to the news about the agreement between Israel and the Palestinian Liberation Organization, of Jewish-Israeli demands for revenge as a response to a killing of a Jewish-Israeli by a Palestinian, or of an Air Force general who con-fesses to be moved more by pictures of destroyed houses in Kiriat Shmone than those of Lebanese villages attacked by the units that he commands.

Dalia Elkana, who was assigned to searching Palestinian women crossing from Jordan to the West Bank at the Allenby Bridge, said about her work:

> In my first week I was embarrassed, ashamed, and disgusted. I used to speak in a quiet voice. I tried to be kind, but slowly I lost my human-ity. . . . Gradually that job takes you over. You have difficulty remembering that these are women like yourself. But there are people who actually en-joy doing it, especially among those who search the men. We, the girls, tried to retain some of our sanity, to observe certain limits whenever pos-sible, but I cannot say that we succeeded. (Elkana quoted in Lipman 1988, 40)

I do not want to lose what Elkana refers to as "humanity," and what I see in terms of certain dispositions, such as a courage to face the truth, and certain sensibilities, such as the openness to witness another's pain, which I value be-cause of the place that I believe they have in moral psychology, and because they enable me to feel shame. I believe that the experience of shame in the face of wrongdoing, because shame is a certain kind of moral feeling, is an essential ex-perience for maintaining a sense of myself as a moral agent. Uncomfortable as shame is, I need it, and I need it more than I need the anger that I feel at the governments that have formulated and dictated the Jewish-Israeli policy in rela-tion to the Palestinians. Although anger too presupposes horror at what hap-pens, and it too is a moral feeling and thus motivates action, it allows me to separate myself from what becomes posited as the origin of the repression, for example, the Israeli government. In this respect anger is a self-assuring and pu-rifying feeling. Shame, on the other hand, does not separate but includes. It is a feeling entailing the taking of personal responsibility, of seeing oneself implicated in the wrongdoing.

In addition, shame is not only different from anger but also from guilt. Guilt is appropriate where one is personally and actively involved in a wrongdoing; it is not a feeling one can have because of another's wrongdoing. Yet, because of the relation between integrity, dignity, and shame, one can feel shamed by another's wrongdoing if one sees one's own integrity and dignity as diminished by the wrongdoing. I cannot feel guilty for being a Jewish-Israeli, but I can feel ashamed of the systemic injustice toward the Palestinians. My life has been intertwined with it even if I personally did not contribute to it in any but inescapably complicit ways and even if, as I should, I protest it, and I contribute to its elimination by whatever means I can.[29]

Perhaps the most important thing about shame is what Zygmunt Bauman points out in *Modernity and the Holocaust* (1989/91, 210–17) and that is that shame liberates and can aid the process of recovering the moral significance of an event. And if Bauman is right, then for Jewish-Israelis, many of whom have numbed themselves to the injustices inflicted by Jewish-Israelis on the Palestinians[30] and would prefer to go along with and even celebrate the agreement between Israel and the Palestinian Liberation Organization, yet without acknowledging Palestinian suffering, shame would be a healing antidote to de-moralization.

NOTES

I began this essay in 1990 following an invitation to speak about my friendship with Amal at the University of Minnesota's Center for Advanced Feminist Studies. I read another version of this essay at the Fall, 1992 meeting of SOPHIA, the feminist philosophy graduate student group there. The current version of the essay has benefitted from the comments of Karen J. Warren and the shock of my latest summer stay in Israel in 1993. Amal read this essay with understanding.

1. I use "Jewish-Israeli" in order to emphasize the multinational character of the state of Israel in which Jews are a majority and Palestinians a substantial minority. I believe that the emphasis is important because it disrupts the projected image of Israel as a one-people state, something that many have been claiming is far from the reality of any modern nation-state. An early commentator on the subject is Ernest Renan, whose 1888 address "What is a Nation?" is included in Bhaba (1990, 8–23). I also recommend McNeill (1986).

2. I have been criticized by Jewish-Israelis and other Jews for my positions regarding the Jewish-Israeli-Palestinian relation on the ground that I do not live in Israel and consequently do not have certain daily experiences which, according to my critics, are the foundation for the right kind of positions regarding the Jewish-Israeli-Palestinian relation. I do think that not living in Israel has facilitated some of my changes by giving me an opportunity to think and feel away from the local pressures. I do not think that what follows from this is that my position is, therefore, irrelevant to other Jewish-Israelis and other Jews. The relationship between experiences and beliefs and attitudes is much more dialectical than my critics believe.

3. Feminists in the United States and most of Western Europe have had a hard time understanding the importance of national identity for women belonging to nations that have just gained national independence or have not yet gained it. While I do not want to defend nationalism, I do sympathize with the sense that national independence creates conditions for the production of local and unique feminisms which are a little less colonized. This, at least, is Amal's sense, and what she always points out to me is that I have a nationally independent state, which is something that may free me to see things differently. For a recent discussion of the relation between feminism and nationalism in the Middle Eastern context, see Mervat (1993, 29–48). Among earlier responses to the perceived conflict between nationalism and feminism is Jayawardena (1986). For a nonfeminist debate on the subject of nationalism see, for example, Twining (1991).

4. Ann Ferguson offers a theory of an aspectual self that suggests the possibility of a multifaceted yet single identity whose elements are not necessarily bundled in coherent groups. It is one of the few theories of identity I am aware of that promises the possibility of conceptualizing identity not as multiple or fractured (Ferguson 1987, 339–56).

5. I use the term "imagined community" in the way that Benedict Anderson uses it (Anderson

1983) although I do not restrict it to the "nation" as he does because the nation is not the only kind of identity forming imagined community.

6. For the notion of an identity that is a function of pragmatic necessity see Korsgaard (1989). For a context of difference dependent on the awareness of identity see, for example, Riley (1988).

7. Reading, in particular a contextualizing reading that situates the reader and what is read, can be a form of what María Lugones calls "world travelling" (Lugones 1987).

8. Americans respond to my accent by asking me where I am from and attributing a specific foreignness to me as they ask their question, thus saying things such as "Are you from Germany or France?" or "Are you from India?" They correct my pronunciation and grammar as well as my linguistic conduct. They respond to their sense of my foreignness by bonding through the things that seem like a real common denominator to them, such as television programs they used to watch as children, making sure as they do that these are not television programs I had available to me as a child.

9. Neither Israeli Jews nor Palestinians constitute homogeneous groups. But in our relation with each other the heterogeneous Jewish-Israeli socioculture is hegemonic.

10. See part 3, "The Israeli Scene and the Palestinians", in Esman and Rabinovich (1986).

11. See Khlidi (1991) for a description of the Palestinians and their culture prior to the modern Jewish arrival and settling.

12. An interesting view of the Jewish-Arab relation, including the Jewish-Israeli-Palestinian relation is developed by Alcalay (1993).

13. Franz Fanon's discussions of this (1967 and 1968) are the classical references for analyses of the formative effects of oppression on the oppressed and the oppressors. Two other classical references are Memmi (1991) and Césaire (1972). But one could use Hegel's analysis of the master and slave relationship and Marx's analysis of alienation as well. For documentation of the effects on the Jewish-Israeli-Palestinian relation see, for example, Grossman (1987 and 1992).

14. For a discussion of the formation of the Jewish-Israeli see Elon (1971) and Evron (1988, esp. chap. 9, 308–23).

15. Shapira (1992), which belongs to Israel's revisionist history, describes the formation of the Jewish-Israeli official self-presentation. For examples of such a presentation see Eban (1972), Herzog (1982), and Schiff (1985). The extent to which the presentation is a Jewish-Israeli myth is made very clear by Simha Flapan (1987). The book's chapters address seven myths: (1) the Zionists accepted the UN partition and planned for peace; (2) the Arabs rejected the UN partition and launched a war; (3) the Palestinians fled voluntarily, intending reconquest; (4) all the Arab states united to expel the Jews from Palestine; (5) the Arab invasion made war inevitable; (6) defenseless Israel faced destruction by the Arab Goliath; (7) Israel always sought peace, but no Arab leader has responded.

16. See, for example, Avineri (1981, 217–27), Leibowitz (1988, 17–42), and Merhav (1980, 250–333).

17. The Rabin government's "Iron-Fist" commitments have manifested themselves most clearly for outsiders in the deportation of 415 Palestinians as punishment for a murder of an Israeli, the destruction of houses in retaliation for demonstrations, and the violent suppression of these demonstrations. The deportees have returned, but most of them have been put in detention camps.

18. See especially Chap. 6, "Duty and Obligation," where Rawls discusses civil disobedience and conscientious objection.

19. One of the ways in which the question of loyalty has been debated among Jewish-Israelis (mostly men) is by focusing it on the issue of a refusal to be stationed in the occupied territories when drafted to the military or called for reserve duty. Examples of some of the discussions of this question can be found in newsletters of organizations such as Yesh Gvul. An Israeli philosophical paper by Royal Netz (1990) articulates some of the questions faced by draftees in relation to Socrates' conduct and arguments in the *Crito*, a move that resembles that of U.S. philosophers when addressing questions regarding the draft during and after the Vietnam War. A feminist view on loyalty, which still uses a kind of Socratic/Liberal contractual framework, but does not focus on military service, can be gleaned from Rich (1979, 275–310).

20. For detailed analyses see Benziman and Mansour (1992) and Shehadeh (1985) as well as Benbenishti (1988) and Jiryis (1976).

21. The question of loyalty is particularly hard for Jewish-Israelis like me who have chosen to emigrate, since emigration is considered as betrayal and is stigmatized. For the conflictual emotional life it creates see Shoked (1988).

22. I was both surprised and angry to find out while reading Keren (1989) that the material inscription was intended and built into the Jewish-Israeli educational program from kindergarten to grade 12.

23. One would have expected the Jewish-Israeli peace activists to understand it. Yet while a few do, from the Palestinian point of view the picture is more revealing. In her interview with Penny Rosenwasser, Nabila Espanioli, a Palestinian-Israeli woman from Haifa, describes herself as fighting for a democratic Israel which cannot be Jewish dominated and says, "I want to be fully a partner. . . . " She goes on to point out that insofar as the Israeli left, Peace Now, and Women and Peace are still uncritical of the Zionist dogma, they do not yet want her as their partner (Rosenwasser 1992, 148–56).

24. The 1990 Israeli film *Hide and Seek*, which addresses the formation of identity in the case of a young Jewish boy in the just pre-independence days of Israel, uses homosexual erotic connectedness between a Jew and a Palestinian to address the construction of the Palestinian as an enemy, the betrayal that is associated with eroticism, and the violence that the deconstruction of the enemy through love evokes in men. Accad (1990) is an instructive study of the relationship of sexuality and violence in Lebanese literature which brings out some of the aspects of the relationship between sexuality, animosity, and taboo for Lebanon yet is suggestive for some generalizations on the subject. Another instructive study is Cypress (1991) whose chapter on the nationalist view of La Malinche points out how sexual taboos and their violations worked for Mexico's nation-building literature. Like Accad's work, Cypress' work too is specific, and it is also suggestive for some generalizations on the subject. A more general yet suggestive work whose specific focus is Latin-American nation-building literature, is Franco (1989). Parker et al. (1992) offers a comparative kaleidoscopic view of possible relations between national identities and sexualities and their constitution by taboos, as well as breakdown through the violation of taboos.

25. Shipler (1986, 277) provides, in addition to statistics, extensive information about Jewish-Israeli-Palestinian personal relations and about the attitudes of the two groups toward each other.

26. Although addressing male friendship, May and Strikwerda (1992) is instructive in its discussion of trust.

27. I have fairly classical symptoms of PTSD (Post Traumatic Stress Disorder). I doubt that many Jewish-Israeli and Palestinian children and adults are free from the trauma of a daily life intertwined with violence.

28. I see the possibility of a better future when I read about economic and cultural agreements among multiple countries in the Middle East. The latest issue of the *Middle East Report* (1993) is careful in its discussion of a possible better future yet optimistic in its vision of a regional kind of economic integration.

29. Authors like Oren (1992) would probably respond to my discussion of shame as springing out of a fear of an Israeli identity. To the extent that an Israeli identity is intertwined in the oppressive erasure of the Palestinians as I believe that it is, I think that it should be feared and reformed.

30. For an informative and suggestive collection of studies on the subject see Gal (1990).

References

Accad, Evelyne. 1990. *Sexuality and war: Literary masks of the Middle East*. New York: New York University Press.

Alberstein, Chava. 1989. Chad-Gadia. In *London* (phonograph record). Holon, Israel: NMC Music.

Alcalay, Ammiel. 1993. *After Jews and Arabs: Remaking Levantine culture*. Minneapolis: University of Minnesota Press.

Anderson, Benedict. 1983. *Imagined communities: Reflections on the origins and spread of nationalism*. London: Verso.

Avineri, Shlomo. 1981. *The making of modern Zionism: Intellectual origins of the Jewish state.* New York: Basic Books.

Bauman, Zygmunt. 1989. *Modernity and the Holocaust.* Ithaca: Cornell University Press.

Benbenishti, Meyron. 1988. *The sling and the club: Territories, Jews, and Arabs* (in Hebrew). Jerusalem: Keter.

Benziman, Uzi, and Atallah Mansour. 1992. *Subtenants* (in Hebrew). Jerusalem: Keter.

Bhaba, Homi K., ed. 1990. *Nation and narration.* London: Routledge.

Binur, Yoram. 1989. *My enemy, my self.* New York: Doubleday.

Bober, Arie, ed. 1972. *The other Israel: The radical case against Zionism.* New York: Doubleday.

Césaire, Aimé. 1972. *Discourse on colonialism.* New York: Monthly Review.

Cypress, Sandra Messinger. 1991. *La Malinche in Mexican literature: From history to myth.* Austin: University of Texas Press.

Eban, Abba. 1972. *My country: The story of modern Israel.* New York: Random House.

Elon, Amos. 1971. *The Israelis: Founders and sons.* New York: Holt, Rinehart and Winston.

Esman, Milton J., and Itamar Rabinovich, eds. 1986. *Ethnicity, pluralism and the state in the Middle East.* Ithaca: Cornell University Press.

Evron, Boaz. 1988. *A national reckoning* (in Hebrew). Tel Aviv: Dvir.

Fanon, Franz. 1967. *Black skin white masks.* New York: Grove.

———. 1968. *The wretched of the earth.* New York: Grove.

Ferguson, Ann. 1987. A feminist aspect theory of the self. *Science, morality, and feminist theory,* ed. Marsha Hanen and Kai Nielson. Calgary: University of Calgary Press.

Flapan, Simha. 1987. *The birth of Israel: Myths and reality.* New York: Pantheon.

Franco, Jean. 1989. *Plotting women.* New York: New York University Press.

Gal, Reuven. 1990. *The seventh war: The effects of the Intifada on Israeli Society* (in Hebrew). Tel Aviv: Hakibbutz Hameuhad.

Gordon, Haim, and Rivca Gordon, eds. 1991. *Israel/Palestine: The quest for dialogue.* Maryknoll, NY: Orbis Books.

Grossman, David. 1987. *The yellow wind* (in Hebrew). Tel Aviv: Hakibbuz Hameuchad.

———. 1992. *Sleeping on a wire* (in Hebrew). Tel Aviv: Hakibbuz Hameuchad.

Herzog, Chaim. 1982. *The Arab-Israeli wars: War and peace in the Middle East.* New York: Random House.

Hi-Man, Si. 1988. Shooting and Crying. In *The second album* (phonograph record). Tel Aviv: CBS.

Israeli Department of Defense. 1985. *Israel—sites and places.*

Jayawardena, Kumari. 1986. *Feminism and nationalism in the third world.* London: Zed Books.

Jiryis, Sabri. 1976. *The Arabs in Israel.* New York: Monthly Review Press.

Kabbani, Rana. 1986. *Europe's myths of the orient.* Bloomington: Indiana University Press.

Keren, Michael. 1989. *The pen and the sword: Israeli intellectuals and the making of the nation-state.* Boulder, CO: Westview.

Khlidi, Walid. 1991. *Before their diaspora: A photographic history of the Palestinians, 1876–1948.* Washington, D.C.: Institute for Palestinian Studies.

Korsgaard, Christine M. 1989. Personal identity and the unity of agency: A Kantian response to Parfit. *Philosophy and Public Affairs* 18(2): 101–32.

Leibowitz, Yeshayau. 1988. *On just about everything: Talks with Michael Shashar.* Jerusalem: Keter.

Lipman, Beata. 1988. *Israel: The embattled land: Jewish and Palestinian women talk about their lives.* London: Pandora.

Lugones, María. 1987. Playfulness, "world" travelling, and loving perception. *Hypatia* 2(2): 3–19.

May, Larry, and Robert Strikwerda. 1992. Male friendship and intimacy. *Hypatia* 7(3): 110–25.

McNeill, William H. 1986. *Polyethnicity and national unity in world history.* Toronto: University of Toronto.

Memmi, Albert. 1991. *The colonizer and the colonized.* Boston: Beacon Press.

Merhav, Peretz. 1980. *The Israeli left: History, problems, documents.* San Diego: A. S. Barnes and Company.

Mervat, Hatem. 1993. Toward the development of post-Islamic and post-nationalist feminist discourses in the Middle East. In *Arab women: Old boundaries, new frontiers,* ed. Judith E. Tucker. Bloomington: Indiana University Press.

Morrison, Toni. 1992. *Playing in the dark: Whiteness and the literary imagination.* Cambridge: Harvard University Press.

Netz, Royal. 1990. Socrates and the high school seniors. *Metaphora: Philosophical Journal* ?(??): 43–60.

Oren, Yoseph. 1992. *The pen as a political trumpet* (in Hebrew). Rishon Lezion: Yated.

Parker, Andrew, Mary Russo, Dorris Sommer, and Patricia Yaeger. 1992. *Nationalisms and sexualities.* New York: Routledge.

Rawls, John. 1971. *A theory of justice.* Cambridge: Harvard University Press.

Raymond, Janice G. 1986. *A passion for friends.* Boston: Beacon.

Renan, Ernest. [1888] 1990. What is a nation? See Bhaba 1990.

Rich, Adrienne. 1979. Disloyal to civilization: Feminism, racism, gynephobia. In *On lies, secrets, and silence: Selected prose 1966–1978.* New York: W. W. Norton.

Riley, Denise. 1988. *"Am I that name?" Feminism and the category of 'women' in history.* Minneapolis: University of Minnesota Press.

Rosenwasser, Penny. 1992. *Voices from a promised land: Palestinian and Israeli peace activists speak their hearts in conversations with Penny Rosenwasser.* Willimantic, CT: Curbstone.

Said, Edward. 1978. *Orientalism.* New York: Random House.

———. 1980. *The question of Palestine.* New York: Vintage.

Schiff, Zeev. 1985. *A history of the Israeli army: 1874 to the present.* New York: Macmillan.

Shapira, Anita. 1992. *The dove's sword: Zionism and force 1881–1948* (in Hebrew). Tel Aviv: Am Oved.

Shehadeh, Raja. 1985. *Occupier's law: Israel and the West Bank.* Washington, D.C.: Institute for Palestinian Studies.

Shipler, David K. 1986. *Arab and Jew: Wounded spirits in a promised land.* New York: Times Books.

Shoked, Moshe. 1988. *Children of circumstances: Israeli emigrants in New York.* Ithaca: Cornell University Press.

Timerman, Jacobo. 1982. *The longest war: Israel in Lebanon.* New York: Alfred A. Knopf.

Twining, William, ed. 1991. *Issues of self-determination.* Aberdeen: Aberdeen University Press.

Making Peace with the Earth: Indigenous Agriculture and the Green Revolution

DEANE CURTIN

1. INTRODUCTION

In 1970 Norman Borlaug won the Nobel Prize recognizing his role as father of the Green Revolution. While Borlaug's work was on plant genetics, he did not win for biology. He won the prize for *peace*. Thus culminated the effort of two decades and more to represent the Green Revolution as a peace program. According to narrowly defined criteria, the Green Revolution has been proclaimed a success: yields on all the major seeds produced by Green Revolution research have at least doubled since World War II. Yet, the claim that it is a peace program demands a broader assessment in terms of its social, political, and environmental impact.

The assessment I propose here has two dimensions. Both are intended to understand the characteristic *violence* of the Green Revolution despite its explicit peace agenda. The Green Revolution's violence is, I believe, enabled by a set of "First World" attitudes toward the so-called Third World that puts the First World at the center ethically and conceptually, spinning out other "worlds" from that center to ethical and conceptual margins.[1] This system of marginalization, which I call developmentalism, is a system of domination that connects with, and benefits from, other forms of domination such as racism, sexism, classism, castism, and naturism. Any analysis of domination that is not linked to developmentalism risks a conceptual bias toward the First World.

Second, to address the peace claims of the Green Revolution specifically, I characterize developmentalism as an ideology that is akin to what Duane Cady

Reprinted by permission of *Environmental Ethics* (from vol. 17, no. 1, Spring 1995)

has called warism (Cady 1989). It is structurally committed to violence in its treatment of indigenous communities and the earth, violence that is justified as a moral good. If the Green Revolution is a peace program, therefore, it must defend the claim that peace comes through violence. This, I believe, confuses peace with pacification.

Since women have been the Third World's principal food producers, the Green Revolution was designed to displace women's agriculture. These agricultural practices, ironically, tend to be forms of ecological peacemaking, akin to pacifism. I do not intend these remarks to romanticize indigenous women's agriculture. Violence does exist within indigenous communities. This violence, however, is immeasurably worsened by the effects of the Green Revolution. Furthermore, in speaking of "women's agriculture," I am not essentializing their typical practices. My approach is nonessentialist. Women are not inherently closer to nature than men. Men are not the sole perpetrators of environmental violence. For complex reasons, women's practices do tend toward peacemaking with the earth, but in fragmented cultures all practices are distorted.

I am concerned, as well, about overgeneralization. Any generalization, however nuanced, risks losing sight of the diversity of women's lives.[2] Yet this concern generates a dilemma: women's practices are often invisible to development experts. Without some degree of generalization, they will remain invisible. I focus on the effects of the Green Revolution in India, therefore, because of personal experience with Indian agriculture, and because India was one of the original test sites for the success of the Green Revolution. Even within India, generalization can be difficult. The state of Kerala, for example, has a matrilineal social structure that may be seen as having affected agricultural practice (and success) there. While granting these important points of diversity, I believe my generalizations—as qualified as they must be, even limited to a country like India—can be useful in understanding the condition of women's agriculture elsewhere. Here I will be content to suggest some of the connections that might be taken up at a later time.

2. DEVELOPMENTALISM AND THE GREEN REVOLUTION

In *Principles of Political Economy* John Stuart Mill described the British Empire's colonies as,

> . . . hardly to be looked upon as countries, . . . but more properly as outlying agricultural or manufacturing estates belonging to a larger community. Our West Indian colonies, for example, cannot be regarded as countries with a productive capital of their own . . . [but are rather] the place where England finds it convenient to carry on the production of sugar, coffee and a few other tropical commodities. (Mill 1965, 693)

Mill's colonialist ideas have hardly become outmoded in an age when agricultural multinationals have replaced the East India Company. The sense that the Third

World is "outlying," distant from, dependent on, and defined by the center is at the heart of contemporary developmentalism.

Richard Levins captures the dynamic of center and margin through "seven developmentalist myths in agriculture":

(1) *Backward is labor-intensive, modern is capital-intensive agriculture.*

(2) *Diversity is backward, uniform monoculture is modern.*

(3) *Small scale is backward, large scale is modern.*

(4) *Backward is subjection to nature, modern implies increasingly complete control over everything that happens in the field or orchard or pasture.*

(5) *Folk knowledge is backward, scientific knowledge is modern.*

(6) *Specialists are modern, generalists backward.*

(7) *The smaller the object of study, the more modern.* (Levins 1986, 13–20)

Developmentalism is defined by a complex set of attitudes including issues of economic scale, reductionism, relationship of the person and community to the land, and the epistemic status of the outside "expert" as against the insider to a practice. In this section I use these myths to characterize the Green Revolution historically as a form of developmentalism.

The Green Revolution began in 1944 when the Rockefeller Foundation invited Borlaug to leave his wartime job in a Du Pont laboratory to direct the wheat breeding program at the International Maize and Wheat Improvement Center in Mexico. Under Borlaug's direction, the center produced the so-called High Yielding Variety (HYV) of wheat that was initially targeted for two areas, northwest Mexico, and the Punjab region of what are now India and Pakistan.

In principle, Borlaug's accomplishment was simple. Inorganic nitrogen fertilizer, when applied to traditional varieties of wheat, made the whole plant grow larger. Tall varieties, top-heavy with grain, had the tendency to topple over (called "lodging"), thus reducing the yield. Borlaug genetically engineered a dwarf variety of wheat to concentrate fertilizer in the grain (and profit) producing part of the plant. The Green Revolution was possible because HYVs can accept very high doses of fertilizer.

While the core of the Green Revolution is simple, the broader impact is complex. As Borlaug himself explained, a whole package of technologies was transferred to the Punjab, including " . . . seeds, fertilizers, insecticides, weed killers, and machinery—and the credit with which to buy them" (Borlaug 1971, 231).

High doses of fertilizer require much greater reserves of water to be effective. Green Revolution crops therefore require massive irrigation.[3] In contrast to traditional agriculture, which is based on crop rotation, the Green Revolution involves plant monoculture. This makes HYVs especially susceptible to pests and diseases, thus the Green Revolution's dependence on pesticides (Chabousson 1986). In contrast to agriculture based on the principle of recycling inputs, the Green Revolution depends on external sources for seeds, chemicals, and machinery. Green Revolution hybrid seeds are not self-pollinating, so they must be purchased each year from a seed company. The biotechnology revolution now occurring in agriculture carries plant monoculture further, to the level of individual brand names. Agrochemical companies are now engineering seeds to respond (or not respond) only to their particular commercial brand of fertilizer, herbicide, or pesticide[4] (see Kloppenburg 1988).

Though brief, this summary of Green Revolution technology is sufficient to illustrate the impact it has had on indigenous women's agriculture. The Green Revolution does not depend on replenishing the soil, the peasant's traditional source of security. It does not depend on conserving water, but on the assumption that access to water is unlimited. It demands political and economic dependence on a small number of seed and agrochemical companies rather than building on local self-reliance. Since its economy of scale depends on bigger being better, it depends on loans—and the ability to repay loans—from Western-dominated international agencies, such as the World Bank.

The ideology of the Green Revolution is replete with the developmentalist myth. Everything that characterizes traditional agriculture—agriculture that is labor-intensive, diverse, small-scale, and responsive to the cycles of nature—is represented as backward and primitive. Indigenous knowledge is reduced to folk tale or superstition. Only the outside expert "knows."

3. INDIGENOUS WOMEN'S AGRICULTURE

What are the agricultural practices that needed "development"? Anthropological research helps to explain the gendered roles of traditional farmers. The hunter/gatherer paradigm, according to which the hunters provide most of the food, has been dismissed as a sexist myth. In such societies, up to 80 percent of food is gathered by women. Women's roles as gatherers, in turn, led to the invention of agriculture as predominantly a women's practice. On the assumption that "the workers invented their tools" (Stanley 1982) most anthropologists now agree that women invented the important agricultural tools. Because women have also been the traditional plant breeders, they bred most of the world's grains, including wheat, rice, maize, barely, oats, sorghum, millet, and rye. These cereals still supply 75 percent of all human food energy (Stanley, 293–94).

In Africa and many parts of Asia, agriculture is still disproportionately women's work. According to a recent Worldwatch Paper, "Gender Bias: Roadblock to Sustainable Development," women in sub-Saharan Africa grow 80 percent of household food. Women's labor produces 70 to 80 percent of food on the Indian subcontinent, and 50 percent of food consumed in Latin America and the Caribbean (Jacobson 1993, 19).

This is much the situation Sir Albert Howard encountered in the late 1800s when he was dispatched to India by the British government to investigate methods of improving Indian agriculture. He found, much to his surprise, that their crops were free of pests, and that insecticides and fungicides had no place in their system of agriculture. Impressed, he decided " . . . I could not do better than watch the operations of these peasants, and acquire their traditional knowledge as rapidly as possible. For the time being, therefore, I regarded them as my professor of agriculture. Another group of instructors were obviously the insects and fungi themselves" (Howard 1943, 160).

The best agriculture, Howard would later write, is modeled on "nature's agriculture":

> The main characteristic of Nature's farming can therefore be summed up in a few words. Mother earth never attempts to farm without live stock: she always raises mixed crops; great pains are taken to preserve the soil and to prevent erosion; the mixed vegetable and animal wastes are converted into humus; there is no waste; the processes of growth and the processes of decay balance one another; ample provision is made to maintain large reserves of fertility; the greatest care is taken to store the rainfall; both plants and animals are left to protect themselves against disease. (23 and 14)

The cyclical principle made Howard's book, *An Agricultural Testament*, a classic in the organic, sustainable agriculture movement. It is not often recognized that this movement owes a great debt to Third World women's agricultural knowledge.[5]

The foremost commitment of cyclical agriculture is to biological diversity. In a healthy ecosystem, decay balances growth. Soil regenerates through recycling plant and animal matter. Plant agriculture, therefore, requires animals for fertilizer. Crops that use nitrogen, such as wheat and rice, must rotate with plants that return nitrogen to the soil, such as pulses (beans, peas, and lentils).

The cyclical principle also embraces water conservation, which begins with healthy soil that retains moisture. Water depends on mixed land use as well. Agricultural land must be mixed with forested land. Trees prevent flooding and are a self-regenerating resource for fodder that retains water. Forests are also necessary for food, building materials, and traditional medicines.

Traditional agriculture does not depend on pesticides. It lets biological diversity do the work. As any agriculturist knows, it is not true that everything is connected in nature. If that were the case, Dutch Elm disease would have wiped out oak and other species. Traditional agriculture takes advantage of the disjunctions in nature to control pests. Corn rootworm will not eat soybean roots, for example, so crop rotation removes the rootworm's source of food.

Traditional agriculture is also cyclical and localized in the genetics of its seeds. It is typical for each family to maintain its own stock of seeds from year to year. Women usually are responsible for selecting the best seeds for cultivation the next season. Village-based genetic breeding means that seeds are developed to meet the needs of widely diverse growing conditions. Seeds are bred to "meet the expectations of the land," in the words of Wes Jackson; land is not altered to meet the demands of the seed (Jackson 1987). The genetic diversity of traditional agriculture is a safeguard against widespread devastation of crops due to climatic change or pests. Village plant breeding is also a political issue. When women control plant breeding, they are at the nexus of activities that most determine family and community survival. It is just this sense of what is appropriate to a place, the refusal to dominate a place, I will contend, that developmentalism reads as backward.

4. WARISM, WOMEN, AND THE ENVIRONMENT

I will not argue directly against warism. Rather, my purpose here is to clarify what would have to go into a defense of a warist environmental ideology. In keeping the argument "close to the ground," in focusing, that is, on the actual impact of the Green Revolution on Third World peoples, I hope to show how *difficult* it would be to defend the violence of the Green Revolution as moral.

Duane Cady coined the term "warism" as a parallel term to "pacifism." Warism is the view " . . . that war is both morally justifiable in principle and often morally justified in fact." Pacifism holds that, " . . . war, by its very nature, is morally wrong and . . . humans should work for peaceful resolution of conflict" (Cady 1989, 3–4). Cady was thinking in terms of explicit military violence rather than the covert political violence of the Green Revolution. Recently, however, Cady has connected warism with other forms of domination: sexism, racism, and classism (Cady 1991, 4–10). As a reminder that I am stretching Cady's meaning beyond military violence, I say that the ideology of the Green Revolution is *akin* to warism, that developmentalism is warist.

In connecting warism with other forms of domination, Cady draws on Marilyn Frye's insight that "arrogant perception" underlies the structures of oppression. According to Frye, Western civilization's answer to the question of man's place in nature is " . . . everything that is, is resource for man's exploitation. With this world view, men see with arrogant eyes which organize everything seen with reference to themselves and their own interests" (Frye 1983, 67).

Developmentalism and warism both perceive the world arrogantly. Like racism, sexism, classism and naturism, they construct a moral pecking order. Those at the top "know," "act," "develop," and enjoy the moral prerogative. Those at the bottom are ignorant, passive recipients of the actions of others. Recently, for example, former Harvard economist and World Bank official, now Assistant Secretary of the Treasury Lawrence Summers argued in a World Bank memo that the Third World may be "underpolluted" and that it would make sense to shift highly polluting industries from the First World to the Third World[6] (Summers 1992). The arrogance of this suggestion—reminiscent of John Stuart Mill—is unusual today only for its candor.

While the dominations of women and nature are connected in the Green Revolution, they are not identical. Nature is entirely outside the moral sphere for the developmentalist; it is something to be controlled as a "resource for man's exploitation." Since it lacks moral standing, the developmentalist's impact on nature is regarded as nonmoral. While developmentalism itself is a moral crusade, applications of science to nature are understood as morally neutral technical improvements.

Women and indigenous cultures are morally unlike nature in this respect.

They do have moral standing for the developmentalist. We see this in the very fact that they are constructed as needing "development." While different, the connection between the domination of women and the domination of nature is that developmentalism operates in the mode of "control over" indigenous communities through controlling their natural "resources." I will consider, first, the warist domination of women and indigenous communities in the Green Revolution, then the warist domination of nature.

Warism and Indigenous Peoples

It would be inviting to think that the effects of the Green Revolution on women, their communities, and their environments, were unfortunate side effects of well-intentioned development programs. However, that is not true. Before the Green Revolution, there were important research programs in both Mexico (Lappé and Collins 1978, 112–16; Pearse 1980, 33–37) and India on a wide variety of self-pollinating seeds traditionally cultivated by peasants. These programs were consciously undermined by the politics of the Green Revolution.

In India, the Cuttack Institute was investigating techniques to increase yields on traditional varieties of rice based on the indigenous knowledge of tribal peoples. The institute had collected and preserved 20,000 indigenous varieties of rice, a storehouse of genetic information patiently developed over centuries by village women. Unlike the genetically uniform rice developed by the IRRI in the Philippines—another Rockefeller/Ford Food for Peace program—these indigenous species were genetically diverse, having been bred over the entire Indian subcontinent. Nevertheless, for political reasons the Indian minister of agriculture, who had been trained in Mexico, demanded to have the Cuttack Institute's germplasm turned over to IRRI. When the director resisted, he was fired[7] (Shiva 1991, 43–44).

There were elements in Mexico and India that resisted the Green Revolution as an assault against national autonomy. They were often silenced when food was used as a political weapon. In 1966, for example, Lyndon Johnson refused to commit food aid to India until it adopted the Green Revolution as national agricultural policy (Shiva 1991, 31). U.S. AID was also involved in subverting the Allende administration in Chile by withholding food aid (Lappé and Collins 1978, 357–60).

There was no scientific reason for directing research exclusively toward improving seeds that undercut the political control of the world's poor. Such programs already existed, as I have noted; Richard Lewontin has argued that open-pollinated varieties of seed could have been as productive as HYV hybrids (Lewontin 1982, 16). In fact, under less than ideal conditions, traditional seeds are often *more* productive than HYVs. Since most Third World farmers work small plots of marginal land with irregular access to water, less than ideal conditions are the norm, not the exception. The fact that HYVs were chosen for development, therefore, while programs on open-pollinated varieties were forcibly shut down, reflects the class and gender interests of the Green Revolution. HYVs are genetically engineered to be a privately owned commodity.

In addition to the attempt by multinationals to control indigenous communities through genetic research, control is also increasing as courts in the United States and its industrialized allies are now recognizing the legal right to patent genetic information, thus privatizing the seed. American companies often claim that the Third World steals intellectual property from the First World. However, this conveniently narrow argument only applies to items that are defined by the First World as commodities. Resources taken from the Third World are defined (by the First World) as "the common heritage of mankind."

Most of the world's sources of genetic diversity, upon which First World research depends, are in the Third World. Colonialism has always depended on exploitation of this diversity to produce commodities that are sold back to the Third World on credit provided by the First World. As early as 1848, for example, the East India Company was collecting plant species in India. In 1853, when Admiral Perry colonized Japan, he collected plant species, including rice (Kloppenburg 1988, 14 and 55). That this kind of treatment is warist is not news to many residents of the Third World. Recently, for example, 500 farmers in Bangalore, India, stormed and ransacked the office of Cargill, Inc., to protest the intellectual property provisions of the General Agreement on Tariffs and Trades (Khor 1993; Shiva 1993; Shiva and Radha 1993).

The effects of this "top-down" ideology on indigenous people are both predictable and tragic. Vandana Shiva and Maria Mies have challenged the claim that so-called ethnic conflict is responsible for recent violence in India's Punjab region (Mies and others 1988, 134; Shiva 1991, 189–92). Religious conflict, they argue, is the effect. The cause is the Green Revolution. The same system of irrigation that caused the Punjab to be chosen in the first place as the test site for Green Revolution techniques is now causing violence over water rights. Farmers who had the means to mechanize and repay foreign loans have benefited, their acreages increasing rapidly as small farmers are driven out of business. Small farmers—women and men—have been displaced, cut off from their traditional source of security. Men who are displaced by this process seek wage-labor jobs on the large farms, or they migrate to the cities leaving their families behind. Women who are displaced often are expected to work as an unpaid adjunct to their husband's wage-labor. As is almost always the case in such situations, violence against women has increased in the form of sati, "kitchen accidents," and female infanticide.[8] In many cultures, the same women who grow and prepare the food are the last to eat, even in the best of times.

Warism and Nature

The Green Revolution's vision of agriculture is the violent conquest of nature. This begins with a reductionist, noncontextual conception of science. A Harvard botanist said, "We now operationally have a kind of world gene pool . . .

Darwin aside, speciation aside, we can now envision moving any gene, in principal at least, out of any organism and into any organism." Nobel laureate David Baltimore put it even more succinctly. He said, "We can outdo evolution" (Kloppenburg, 3). The desire to outdo evolution in the control of nature reveals the dualistic intentions of Green Revolution ideology. Science is not a romance *with* nature, it is a race *against* nature, and science is winning.

Most revealing are the conceptual and empirical connections between Green Revolution techniques and the technology of war. Vandana Shiva has pointed out that, "Violence was part of the very context of discovery of pesticides during World War I. The manufacture of explosives had a direct spin-off on the development of synthetic insecticides. The tear gas, chloropicrin, was found to be insecticidal in 1916 and thus changed from a wartime product to a peacetime one"[9] (Shiva 1988, 156). Organophosphates, such as malathion, are designed to destroy the central nervous system. Insecticides and herbicides are tested by their "kill ratios." Broad spectrum herbicides kill all vegetation, leaving the earth biologically neutral. Agent Orange, used as a defoliant during the war in Vietnam, is one such product.

The infamous 1984 disaster in Bhopal, India, summarizes the impact of developmentalism. It was caused by a leak of methyl-isocyanate from a Union Carbide plant that produced nitrogen fertilizer. More than 3000 people died; roughly 500,000 were injured. A 1989 survey found that 50 percent of women in the affected area were experiencing menstrual problems, and there had been a marked increase in stillbirths, spontaneous abortions, and genetic defects in infants. Fifty-seven percent of those examined suffered from post-traumatic stress disorder, the same disorder that affects many veterans of war. Union Carbide has refused to admit any liability, claiming it was a terrorist act by a disgruntled employee (Crump 1991, 32).

It is often claimed that science and technology are morally neutral, and that only political judgments about the applications of science are open to moral scrutiny. The Green Revolution makes this distinction between technology and gender bias difficult to sustain. Class, race, and gender biases have been genetically engineered into the "miracle seeds" of the Green Revolution. Research such as the Cuttack Institute's that is sensitive to local traditions shows that women's agriculture is not at all opposed, in principle, to culturally sensitive development or to scientific research. It is opposed to the political genetics of the Green Revolution.

I do not doubt the sincerity of some participants in the Green Revolution, such as Borlaug, who believed that the Green Revolution would bring world peace. Nevertheless, the Green Revolution succeeded to a much greater degree than any overt form of militarism in reducing Third World peasants to political and economic dependence on northern industrial and scientific powers. A recent survey of sustainable Third World development concluded that, "There is much merit to the argument that if given the choice between the present system of international assistance and no assistance at all, the Third World's poor would be better off with none" (Korten 1991, 177).

5. Women's agriculture as ecological pacifism

In stark contrast to the ideology of the Green Revolution, Third World women's agriculture is structurally akin to pacifism in its commitment to ecological peacemaking. Its mode is "collaboration with" nature. Unlike the universalism of the developmentalist, which regards everything that is different as needing "development" in its own image, women's cyclical practices reveal a sense of what is appropriate to and sustainable in a particular place. Nature is not on the far side of the moral divide. The community includes the land as much as its people. Treatment of the land, therefore, reveals the moral self.

The sense of the deep relation of person and place is often expressed in moral or mythological terms. Consider, for example, the arrogant perception in the following passage from the *Journal of the Indian Pesticide Industry* as the author struggles to explain the peasant's relationship to the land:

> [A] more important [difficulty in marketing products in India] is the mental attitude of the agriculturalist about killing. Pesticides spell killing, maybe small and perhaps invisible insects. But it is killing that they are used for. This killing is anathema to the majority of the agriculturalists, be they Hindu, Jain or others. By nature, the agriculturalist is generous, wanting to bestow on others what he reaps out of Mother Earth. He [sic] does not think that he alone should enjoy the fruits of his labor . . . to kill those unseen and unknown lives, though they were thriving on what Mother Earth yields, is foreign to his nature. . . . It takes some time for the simple folk to get acclimatized to the very conception of killing tiny helpless and unarmed creatures. (Lappé and Collins 1978, 61)

The Indian idea of "ahimsa," or nonharming, puts the violence of the Green Revolution, and its cultural specificity, into sharp relief. Ahimsa requires a moral universe that includes insects in the moral cycle of life and death. Nature is seen in moral relationship to human beings. We are defined morally by our conduct with nature.

It is telling how often, in practice, development experts fail to perceive this deep relationship between women, indigenous cultures, and place. Third World women, for example, have long depended on grasses that grow along the borders of fields to make baskets and mats. When development experts decide that these grasses have no market value and plan programs that kill them with herbicide, this is arrogant perception. When these same experts decide that public, forested land is "undeveloped," and has value only when it is privatized and "developed" for profit, this too is arrogant perception.

Of Richard Levins' seven developmentalist myths, one seems most powerful in explaining the developmentalist's inability to appreciate place: "Backward is subjection to nature, modern implies increasingly complete control over everything that happens in the field or orchard or pasture." In the developmentalist's moral pecking order, one is either dominant over nature, or subject to it, either master or slave. The sense of living with nature in a particular place, which is neither subjugation nor dominance, is misread by the developmentalist as backwardness, as a life fit for a slave.

Far from defending the world's poor, the Green Revolution sought to defeat communism by destroying the world's peasant class. It did this by dividing the peasant economically, politically, and spiritually from the sense of place. Conversely, one could understand much about peasant resistance movements by considering them to be localized defenses of the connection between person and place. It is no accident that Liberation Theology in Central America, or Dalit Theology in India are perspectives that express the particular conditions of peoples.[10] They reject the universalizing tendencies of traditional theology.

Finally, it cannot be insisted often enough that pacifism is not passivism. Characterizing typically women's farming as pacifist does not mean that women must simply accept the violence perpetrated against them and their communities. On the contrary, pacifism is a form of resistance. The Chipko Movement in India, the Green Belt Movement in Africa,[11] and countless other small-scale women's movements the world over testify to the fact that women are not passive in defending the integrity of their communities and their environments.

6. CONCLUSION

Out of a concern to recognize the diversity of women's labor, I have confined the majority of my remarks to women's agriculture in India. I do believe, however, that these insights can be expanded to other contexts. Having begun with the 1970 Nobel Peace Prize, I want to mention the recipient of the 1992 prize in closing as a way of indicating how these connections might be made.

Rigoberta Menchu was born to a Mayan family in the highlands of Guatemala. She is the sixth of nine children. At the age of eight she began working on a plantation picking coffee and cotton. In her autobiography she describes a system of near slavery in which she and her family were forced to buy food and medicines from the landowner's store, work the fields for endless hours, only to find at the end of the growing season that they owed the landowner more than they had made.

Menchu's father, and later other family members, joined the Peasant Unity Committee in their struggle to prevent these plantation owners from removing Mayan families from their homelands. In 1979 Menchu's brother was detained by government troops supporting the wealthy landowners; he was publicly tortured and executed. Two months later her father joined a march that occupied the Spanish embassy to protest abuses of indigenous peoples. He and 37 others died when security forces set fire to the embassy. Menchu's mother was later kidnapped, raped, mutilated, and killed. Roughly 40,000 people, mostly indigenous people, have been killed or "disappeared" in Guatemala, and 45,000 others live in Mexico in refugee camps, where Menchu herself has lived since 1981.

The Green Revolution is inscribed in the details of Menchu's life. Because it depends on expensive technologies that increase political and economic dependence, and because its economic scale requires control of enormous numbers of acres, the wealthy, rather than indigenous owners of land, have benefited. As in Guatemala, local governments are generally all too happy to side with wealthy interests who promise to increase exports—exports like coffee and cotton.

Since the end of World War II, peace has been understood as the absence of military violence. Its language has been the language of nuclear deterrence, and "mutually assured destruction." Perhaps in keeping our eyes trained on the skies we have neglected to see the earth. Menchu's life and the lives of other women of the Third World argue for a frankly agrarian vision of peace.

Notes

1. The First/Third distinction marks this marginalization, and is, of course, part of the problem. I do not address the linguistic issue here.

2. In a separate paper (Curtin, forthcoming) I argue for a nonessentialist account of women's agriculture in terms of the actual practices in which women engage and the forms of knowledge that are generated by those practices. This provides a context-sensitive way of making women's practices visible which reclaims the concept of expertise for those who have been defined in opposition to the concept of expertise.

3. One reason the Punjab was chosen as the site for transfer of Green Revolution technology is that it already had a system of irrigation based on partial diversion of rivers (see Shiva 1991, 122).

4. The impact of these technologies is suggested by the juxtaposition of two facts: in five years, during the latter half of the 1960s, consumption of inorganic nitrogen fertilizer in India increased from 58,000 metric tons to 1.2 million metric tons. During that decade, India's currency was devalued by 37.5 percent as a result of its rising foreign debt (see Borlaug 1971, 233; Shiva 1991, 30).

5. The Rodale system of organic gardening is a direct result of peasant women's farming. Rodale was a student of Howard's.

6. *The Economist* published an except from an internal memo Summers wrote while at the World Bank. After the memo was revealed, Summers said that he was only trying to stimulate discussion within the World Bank.

7. The fragility of such genetic information cannot be overstated. As one observer commented, "The genetic heritage of a millennium in a particular valley can disappear in a single bowl of porridge." Once lost, it is lost forever. This has, in fact, happened. A cache of wheat germplasm stored at the Maize and Wheat Institute in Mexico was destroyed when an institute refrigerator shut down during a power outage (Lappé and Collins 1978, 174).

8. Sati is the practice of burning the widow on the husband's funeral pyre. The euphemism "kitchen accident" refers to situations in which women are doused with kerosene in the family kitchen and burned to death, often by the husband's relatives. The cause is often disappointment over a dowry. Female infanticide has become a subject of national debate in India with the advent of genetic testing for sex before birth.

9. At a political level, Green Revolution techniques marginalize Third World countries in other ways. Products such as DDT, that have long been banned in the First World because of their known damage to human health and the environment, are still widely sold in the Third World. Pesticide accidents among people who are illiterate and cannot read directions for recommended use are responsible for 40,000 deaths each year.

10. See Guha 1990 for a detailed account of the relation of person and place in the Himalaya foothills. Dalit means "the oppressed." It is often preferred as a more descriptive term than either Untouchable or Harajin (Gandhi's term meaning "children of God").

11. Founded by Wangari Maathi, the Green Belt Movement is run by women. It provides tree seedlings for planting in green belts in rural and urban areas. The women who plant the trees receive

25 cents for each tree that survives for at least three months. This generates income for women, who are generally excluded from the wage labor market. It also generates self-esteem: these plantings have a success rate of over 80 percent. 50,000 women and children have planted over 10 million trees since the movement began. Maathi recently won the alternative Nobel Prize.

The Chipko Movement is a movement of indigenous women in the Himalayan foothills which began when they hugged trees to prevent deforestation at the hands of lumber companies. The movement has grown into a comprehensive development program that addresses the environment, health, education, and political justice.

REFERENCES

Borlaug, Norman. 1971. The Green Revolution, Peace, and Humanity. In *Les Prix Nobel en 1970*, ed. anon. Stockholm: Imprimerieal Royal P. A. Norstedt & Söner.

Cady, Duane. 1989. *From Warism to Pacifism: A Moral Continuum*. Philadelphia: Temple University Press.

Cady, Duane. 1991. War, Gender, Race & Class. *Concerned Philosophers for Peace Newsletter* 11(2): 4–10.

Chabousson, F. 1986. How Pesticides Increase Pests. *Ecologist* 16(1): 29–36.

Crump, Andy. 1991. *Dictionary of Environment and Development*. London: Earthscan Publications Ltd.

Curtin, Deane. n.d. Women's Knowledge as Expert Knowledge: Indian Women and Ecodevelopment. Forthcoming in *Ecofeminism: Multidisciplinary Perspectives*, ed. Karen J. Warren. Bloomington: Indiana University Press.

Frye, Marilyn. 1983. *The Politics of Reality: Essays in Feminist Theory*. Trumansburg, NY: Crossings Press.

Guha, Ramachandra. 1990. *The Unquiet Woods: Ecological Change and Peasant Resistance in the Himalaya*. Berkeley: University of California Press.

Howard, Sir Albert. 1943. *An Agricultural Testament*. Rodale Press Edition, 1972 ed., London: Oxford University Press.

Jackson, Wes. 1987. Meeting the Expectations of the Land. In *Altars of Unhewn Stone: Science and the Earth*. San Francisco: North Point Press.

Jacobson, Jodi. 1993. *Gender Bias: Roadblock to Sustainable Development*. Vol. 110. Washington, DC: Worldwatch Institute.

Khor, Martin. 1993. 500,000 Indian Farmers Rally against GATT and Patenting of Seeds. *Third World Resurgence* (39): 20–22.

Kloppenburg, Jack Ralph. 1988. *First the Seed: The Political Economy of Plant Biotechnology: 1492–2000*. Cambridge: Cambridge University Press.

Korten, David C. 1991. Sustainable Development. *World Policy Journal* 9(1): 157–90.

Lappé, Frances Moore, and Joseph Collins. 1978. *Food First: Beyond the Myth of Scarcity*. New York: Ballantine.

Levins, Richard. 1986. Science and Progress: Seven Developmentalist Myths in Agriculture. *Monthly Review* 38(3): 13–20.

Lewontin, Richard. 1982. Agricultural Research and the Penetration of Capital. *Science for the People* 14(1): 12–17.

Mies, Maria, Veronika Bennholdt-Thomsen, and Claudia von Werlhof. 1988. *Women: The Last Colony*. London: Zed Books.

Mill, John Stuart. 1965. Vol. 3. *Principles of Political Economy*, ed. J. M. Robinson. Toronto: University of Toronto Press.

Pearse, Andrew. 1980. *Seeds of Plenty, Seeds of Want: Social and Economic Implications of the Green Revolution*. Oxford: Oxford University Press.

Shiva, Vandana. 1988. *Staying Alive: Women, Ecology and Development*. London: Zed Books.

———. 1991. *The Violence of the Green Revolution: Third World Agriculture, Ecology and Politics*. London and Penang: Zed Books, and Third World Network.

————. 1993. Farmers' Rights, Biodiversity and International Treaties. *Economic and Political Weekly* XXVIII(14): 555–60.

Shiva, Vandana, and Holla-Bhar Radha. 1993. The Rise of the Farmers' Seed Movement. *Third World Resurgence* (39): 24–27.

Stanley, Autumn. 1982. Daughters of Isis, Daughters of Demeter: When Women Sowed and Reaped. In *Women, Technology and Innovation*, ed. Joan Rothschild. New York: Pergamon.

Summers, Lawrence. 1992. Let Them Eat Pollution. *The Economist* 322(7745): 66(1).

Bringing Peace Home: A Feminist Philosophical Perspective on the Abuse of Women, Children, and Pet Animals

CAROL J. ADAMS

I. INTRODUCTION

I have been a vegetarian since 1974. In 1978, I started a hotline for battered women in rural upstate New York where I lived at that time. Because my vegetarianism was motivated by a concern for animals, I began to notice that animals—as well as the batterer's female sexual partner—were often victimized by violent men. For instance, one day a woman whom we had been helping to leave her violent husband called to report what had happened when he returned the children after his visitation was over. The children, the husband, and the wife were all sitting in his pickup truck in the driveway. Something occurred that enraged him. Simultaneously, the family dog appeared in the driveway. He plunged the truck forward so that it ran over the dog. He then threw the truck in reverse and backed over the dog. He repeated this forward-backward motion many times. Then he got out of the truck, grabbed his shotgun, and, in front of his devastated family, shot the dog several times.

Empirical evidence indicates that acts of sexual exploitation, including physical battering of sex partners, often involve violence against other animals as well. Drawing on a model provided by Karen J. Warren (Warren 1992, Warren forthcoming) I will make explicit the variety of connections between sexual violence and injury to animals which I will call the woman-animal abuse connections. I will then demonstrate the importance to feminist philosophy of taking seriously these empirical connections because of their implications for conceptual analysis, epistemology, political philosophy, environmental philosophy, and applied philosophy. In doing this, I hope to set a standard and provide a set of suggestions

Hypatia vol. 9, no. 2 (Spring 1994) © by Carol J. Adams

about what must be included in any adequate feminist peace politics. It is not my goal in what follows to use the examples of the abuse of animals solely to illustrate how women and children are made to suffer. Then I would recapitulate on a philosophical level what the abuser actually does, using animals instrumentally. Instead, I seek to broaden the reader's worldview about what counts as "feminist peace issues" to include concern about the connections between abuse of animals and abuse of women.

This essay takes Elizabeth Spelman's (1982) implicit understanding that somatophobia—hostility to the body—is symptomatic of sexism, racism, classism, *and* speciesism, and demonstrates how hostility to despised and disenfranchised bodies, that is, those of animals, children, women, and nondominant men, becomes interwoven. To avoid somatophobia, feminist philosophy must take the connections between abuse of animals and abuse of women seriously.

II. TERMINOLOGY

Several terms which feature in my argument deserve attention up front. I will use the conventional term "pet" to describe animals who are a part of a household.[1] Those involved in the movement to free animals from human oppression prefer the term "companion animal." While I find this term helpful, the word "pet" suggests some commonalities between sexualized behavior and animals: the term "pet" also connotes sexual activity, specifically, fondling and caressing.

Battering is a component or kind of sexual violation, since it occurs against one's sexual partner. Catharine MacKinnon's insights on this matter are helpful: battering "is sexually done to women. Not only in where it is done—over half of the incidents are in the bedroom. Or the surrounding events—precipitating sexual jealousy. . . . If women as gender female are defined as sexual beings, and violence is eroticized, then men violating women has a sexual component" (MacKinnon 1987, 92).[2]

One might suggest that the violence examined in this essay is really "male violence." But the minute we widen the scope of inquiry to include the other animals, we must proceed with sensitivity to the way language may be inaccurate. The anthropocentric presumption that "male" and "female" can be used interchangeably with "men" and "women" is erroneous. What is actually being discussed is human-male violence. While in what follows I am vigilant in using the adjective human to qualify male, I will abide with convention in discussing animal abuse, allowing that meaning to exclude human animals. Moreover, personally and philosophically I find the use of the pronoun "its" disturbing when used to refer to nonhuman animals. However, again, for the purpose of continuity of narratives when providing the empirical information, I will not intercede with [sic]s when "its" is used.

III. EMPIRICAL EVIDENCE

Karen J. Warren argues that understanding the empirical connections between women and nature improves our understanding of the subordination of women while also establishing the practical significance of ecofeminist philosophy (Warren 1992). Empirical connections that reveal connections between the abuse of animals and the abuse of women expose another layer of intentional infliction of suffering by violent men, another way of comprehending the phenomenology of sexual violation. I am concerned about what this control and terror means for women and our subordination, *and* for animals and their subordination.

Testimony from survivors and their advocates indicate two significant configurations in which sexually violent men harm women, children, and animals. There is a threat or actual killing of an animal, usually a pet, as a way of establishing or maintaining control over women and children who are being sexually victimized. And, there is a use of animals in sexually violating women or children, or the use of animals to gain some sort of sexual gratification. Of concern is a third way in which sexual exploitation influences behavior toward animals: anecdotal evidence suggests that child victims of sexual abuse injure animals. These configurations will be discussed under the specific forms that the sexual exploitation takes: battering, marital rape, pornography, child sexual abuse, ritual abuse, serial killing, and sexual harassment. Taken together, this evidence, as we will see, has striking implications for feminist philosophical considerations.

Battering is one form of human male sexual violence that victimizes women, children, and animals. Threats and abuse (often fatal) of pets by a woman's sexual partner occur in his attempts to establish control. As with other forms of battering, the killing of a pet is "done to show control and domination" (Ganley [1981] 1985, 16). Lenore Walker points out, "As a way to terrorize and control their women, batterers have even been known to hold pets hostage" (Walker 1989, 76). According to guides on identifying a batterer, the following are warning signs: he hunts; he own guns; he has threatened, harmed or killed a pet (Statman 1990). "Abusers are often cruel to animals. Many kill them for sport, and this should not be minimized. Anyone who beats a dog or other pets should be considered a potential batterer" (Pope-Lance and Engelsman 1987, 40). Bonnie Burstow, a radical feminist and therapist, warns that the killing of a pet by a human male heterosexual partner is one of the signs that "the woman is in an imminently life-threatening situation and immediate action is called for" (Burstow 1992, 149). For instance, one man slashed two pet cats to death and then threatened to turn the butcher knife on his wife and her dog (*Dallas Times Herald*, June 15, 1991). In another incident, Molly, after a brutal battering by her husband that lasted several hours, "realized he was laughing. Molly had seen him beat a dog like that once, slowly until it died. She remembered that he had laughed then, too." Shortly after that, Molly killed her husband in self-defense (Browne 1987, 133; see also Walker 1989, 20–21).

Diana Russell describes an incident that occurred in California: "[Michael] Lowe casually pumped a shot into the dog. The sheepdog ran under the family's truck, cowering in pain as Lowe went back into the house and returned with a .30-.30 Winchester rifle. He called to the animal and made her sit in front of him as he fired five more shots, killing the family pet [in front of the family].

Three months later he did the same to his wife. Then he killed himself" (Russell [1982] 1990, 296). Anne Ganley, a psychologist who has pioneered in victim-based counseling for batterers, identifies "the destruction of property and/or pets" as one of four forms of battering (along with physical, sexual, and psychological battering). She observes that: "typically, the offender and the victim do not iden-tify the destruction of property/pets as part of the battering; yet it is. The of-fender's purpose in destroying the property/pets is the same as in his physically attacking his partner. He is simply attacking another object to accomplish his battering of her. Sometimes we minimize the seriousness of this form of battering by saying that at least it is better than hitting her. Unfortunately, it often has the same psychological impact on the victim as a physical attack" (Ganley [1981] 1985, 15). (And we need to remember that pet battering *does* injure someone.)

Angela Browne found that many of the women she interviewed who had killed their husbands in self-defense frequently reported destruction of animals: "These incidents often seemed to the women a representation of their own death" (Browne 1987, 157). The killing of pets often resulted in the loss of a battered woman's last hope.

> The kitten was sitting in the yard. Billy got his rifle, walked up to it, and shot it. Then he hunted down the other two cats and shot them. Kim was hysterical—following him around, tugging on him, jumping up and down and screaming. She begged him not to kill the cats, and after he had, she begged him not to leave them there. So he picked them up and threw them over the fence. After Billy went to sleep that night, Kim crept out, found the cats, and buried them. Then she laid down in the field and cried. (Browne 1987, 153–54)

When the husband destroys a pet, he may be destroying the woman's only source of comfort and affection.[3]

A little-studied form of battering involves the use of animals for humiliation and sexual exploitation by batterers and/or marital rapists. This is the second form of sexual violence victimizing women and animals. Batterers and *marital rapists* (and the two groups are neither mutually exclusive nor completely inclu-sive of each other) may train dogs to "have sex with" their wives (Russell [1982] 1990, xii) or force their wives to have sex with a dog: "He would tie me up and force me to have intercourse with our family dog. . . . He would get on top of me, holding the dog, and he would like hump the dog, while the dog had its penis inside me" (Walker 1979, 120). The batterer's/rapist's control is amplified by requiring humiliating acts of his victim. Linda Marchiano ("Linda Lovelace") threatened by her batterer, Chuck, with death, was subjected to sex with a dog ("Lovelace" 1980, 105–13; see also 206): "Now I felt totally defeated. There were no greater humiliations left for me" (113). She explained, "From then on if I didn't do something he wanted, he'd bring me a pet, a dog" (112). As with the preceding cases, the threat or actual use of a pet to intimidate, coerce, control, or violate a woman is a form of sexual control or mastery over women by men.

A third linking of violence against women, children, and animals to human male sexual violence is *pornography*. One genre of pornography features sexual activity "between" humans and animals. (I qualify this term since I believe this activity to be coercive.) Bears, snakes, and dogs—to name just a few of the species of animals incorporated into pornographic films—are shown in a variety of sexual and sexualized positions with women. Linda "Lovelace's" sexual violation with a dog was filmed and became a popular pornographic loop. This loop—often cited by reporters and others in response to *Ordeal* ("Many who have seen *Deep Throat* or another, even sleazier film in which her co-star was a dog, will argue that Linda Lovelace liked what she was doing, and liked it a lot." ["Lovelace" 1986, 141, quoting Chip Visci of the Detroit *Free Press*])—depicts what Marchiano considers "the worst moment of my life" ("Lovelace" 1986, 194). There is some evidence that some viewers of pornography have attempted to duplicate such scenes in abusing their partners (see Russell 1984, 126).

My fourth case-in-point concerns *child sexual abuse*. The testimony of survivors of child sexual abuse reveal that threats and abuse of their pets were often used to establish control over them, while also ensuring their silence, by forcing them to decide between their victimization or the pet's death. Sylvia Fraser poignantly describes the dilemma this threat by her father-rapist presented to her as a child:

> Desperation makes me bold. At last I say the won't-love-me words: "I'm going to tell my mommy on you!"
>
> My father needs a permanent seal for my lips, one that will murder all defiance. "If you say once more that you're going to tell, I'm sending that cat of yours to the pound for gassing!"
>
> "I'll . . . I'll . . . I'll . . ."
>
> The air swooshes out of me as if I have been punched. My heart is broken. My resistance is broken. Smoky's life is in my hands. This is no longer a game, however desperate. Our bargain is sealed in blood. (Fraser 1987, 11–12)

This type of threat is not restricted to father-daughter rape. Alice Vachss, formerly a prosecutor of sex crimes, reports on this phenomenon in *Sex Crimes*: children "are threatened with huge, child-oriented consequences if they tell. The molester kills a kitten and says the same thing will happen to the child" (Vachss 1993, 465). One chilling case example involved a two-and-a-half-year-old girl whose abuser claimed to have killed the pet rabbit, cooked it, and forced her to eat it, warning her that if she reported the abuse, the rabbit's fate would be hers (see Faller 1990, 196).

Besides physical abuse of animals by child sexual abusers, there is the sexual use of animals by some child sexual abusers. In these cases, the sexual use of animals seems to enhance or expand or extend the abuse of the genuinely powerless and unsuspecting victim. For instance, one colleague reported a case in which a veterinarian, upon discovering that the dog had a sexually transmitted disease, made a referral that resulted in the discovery that the father was also sexually abusing his two pre-adolescent daughters. And there are other cases (see Faller 1990, 56–57).

A child may injure animals or pets or "stuffed animals" as a sign or signal or expression that something is very wrong. Abuse of animals is recognized in the most recent revision of the *Diagnostic and Statistical Manual of Mental Disorders of the American Psychiatric Association* (DSMRIII 1987) as one of the symptoms indicative of Conduct Disorder (see Ascione 1993). A pre-adolescent boy who had been brutally raped by his father described how he would tie a firecracker around a cat and watch as it exploded. Brohl reports that "an adult survivor tearfully related that when she was seven years old she drowned her cat" (Brohl 1991, 24). While Ascione cautions that "much of the information on the relation between sexual abuse of children and children's cruelty toward animals is derived from retrospective research," he is also able to provide some information drawn from a more reliable methodology:

> William Friedrich (April, 1992, personal communication) has generously provided data from a large-scale study of *substantiated* cases of sexual abuse in children 2–12 years of age. Most of these children had been victimized within twelve months of data collection that included administration of the Child Behavior Checklist (Achenbach 1988). Parental reports of cruelty to animals were 35% for abused boys and 27% for abused girls; the percentages were 5% for nonabused boys and 3% for nonabused girls, a highly significant difference based on clinical status. (Ascione 1993, 238–39)

Though the existence of *ritual abuse* continues to be debated in the social science literature and in the popular press, mutilated animals have been found in various parts of the country, and victims and some perpetrators describe the central role that killing animals has in ritual abuse (see for instance Raschke 1990, 39–41, 61, and passim). Consequently, reports of ritual abuse indicate a fifth pattern of patriarchal violence against women and other disenfranchised adults, children, and animals in which all aspects of abuse of animals is evident (see Hudson 1991, Anonymous 1992, Gould 1992, Young 1992, Smith 1993). To review, there are threats, abuse, torture, and killing of pets and other animals to establish control. Additionally, there is the use of animals for humiliation and further sexual exploitation. For instance, Elizabeth Rose reports forced sexual contact with animals as one aspect of ritual abuse (Rose 1993, 44). Last, injury to animals is one way that a child signals that something is wrong. Psychologists who have worked with survivors of ritual abuse indicate that, along with several other specific actions, physical symptoms, and preoccupations, harming animals or describing animals that have been hurt can be a warning sign that a child has been a victim of ritual abuse.

A sixth linking of violence against women, children, nondominant men, and animals to human male sexual violence is the *killing of animals by serial murderers* and other murderers who rape and mutilate. Serial killers share some common features: they are likely to report their crimes, are almost always male and usually younger than 35, and "the earliest acting out of sadistic impulses often occurs in the early teens in the form of torturing and killing animals such as cats and dogs" (Lunde 1976, 53). For instance, as a child, serial killer Jeffrey Dahmer searched the neighborhood for roadkills that he kept in a toolshed; kept the bones of racoons, dogs, cats, groundhogs, squirrels, and chipmunks inside formaldehydefilled pickle jars; kept an animal graveyard with skulls on top of crosses; and collected stuffed owls, rabbits, and small birds. According to one psychologist, David Silber, "His behavior didn't change. The objects changed" (quoted in Dvorchak 1991). Cruelty to animals in childhood was one of the significant differences in behavioral indicators between sexual murderers who were themselves abused before they became abusers and murderers without such a history (see Ressler et al. 1986).

Last, *sexual harassment* often includes pornographic material involving explicit depictions of human-animal sexual activity or reference to this material. Since an adequate discussion of sexual harassment takes me beyond the scope of the essay, I mention it here only to be sure it is included in the patterns of ways human male sexual violence has operated to subordinate women, children, and animals in interconnected ways. According to the testimony of their victims, sexual harassers incorporate this pornography that depicts animals with women into their victimization activities. Moreover, again according to victims and akin to Marchiano's experience, it is this aspect of sexual harassment that is the most humiliating. For instance, during the hearings to review the nomination of Clarence Thomas to the Supreme Court, held in October 1991 before the Senate Judiciary Committee, we heard from Anita Hill of Thomas's references to pornography: "I think the one that was the most embarrassing was his discussion of pornography involving these women with large breasts and engaged in a variety of sex with different people or animals. That was the thing that embarrassed me the most and made me feel the most humiliated" (Phelps and Winternitz 1993, 315).

IV. PHILOSOPHICAL IMPLICATIONS OF THE EMPIRICAL EVIDENCE

We have seen how animals are victims, too, through a variety of acts of sexual violence and exploitation. Truly this material on the connection between abuse of women, children and nondominant men and abuse of animals is painful to encounter. But only by taking this material seriously can we expand our knowledge about sexual violation and recognize its implications for feminist philosophy. In this section, I will show the importance of the connections of abuse of women and animals for feminist philosophy by examining the specific areas of conceptual analysis, epistemology, political philosophy, environmental philosophy, and applied philosophy.

V. CONCEPTUAL ANALYSIS

The empirical evidence cited above details a shocking hostility to the bodies of disenfranchised others—women, children, nondominant men, and animals. As Elizabeth Spelman recognized when she proposed the concept of somatophobia (hostility to the body), one of the important reasons for feminists to recognize somatophobia is to see the context for women's oppression and the relationship it has with other forms of oppression. Clearly, women's oppression is interwoven with that of animals, so that women and animals are both trapped by the control exercised over their own *and* each other's bodies (i.e., women and children who stay silent because of abusers' threats to their pets; pets who are killed to establish a climate of terror).

Spelman believes that it is important for feminists to recognize the legacy of the soul/body distinction and its use in denigrating women, children, animals, and "the natural," who are guilty by association with one another and with the bodily (Spelman 1982, 120, 127). The problem is not only that women are equated with animals' bodies, for instance in pornography, but also that *animals are equated with their bodies.* The soul/body split that concerns Spelman and that she identifies as a part of Western philosophical tradition is acutely evident in notions of animals having no soul, and in our current secular period, of animals having no consciousness, undergirding the instrumental ontology of animals as usable.

Spelman recognized that somatophobia is enacted in relationships such as men to women, masters to slaves, fathers to children, humans to animals (127); now we see that it is actually often enacted in relationships such as men to women *and* animals, fathers to children *and* animals. The connections between the abuse of women and the abuse of animals make explicit that somatophobia applies to species as well as gender, race, and class interactions. It also requires that we rethink philosophical arguments which rely on anthropocentric notions of harm from sexual objectification (see, for instance, LeMoncheck 1985, esp. 14–21).

The testimony of Anita Hill about the humiliating experience of hearing about pornography that included women with animals illuminates Spelman's formulation of somatophobia, particularly the insights that it applies to gender, race, class, and species, and that oppression is interwoven. Consider, for instance, Kimberlé Crenshaw's brilliant article on how feminist and antiracist narratives are structured in such a way as to exclude understanding the experience of a black woman such as Anita Hill. Crenshaw describes the working of interwoven oppressions of race and sex in the racializing of sexual harassment: "While black women share with white women the experience of being objectified as 'cunts,' 'beavers,' or 'pieces,' for them those insults are many times prefaced with 'black' or 'nigger' or 'jungle' " (Crenshaw 1992, 412). The sexual aggression experienced by women of color will often simultaneously represent their subordinate racial status.

In her discussion of the representation of African American women in pornography and the way such representation enabled the pornographic treatment of white women, Patricia Hill Collins ties together the racialization of sexual aggression against black women with the racist view that equated black women with animals:

> within the mind/body, culture/nature, male/female oppositional dichotomies in Western social thought, objects occupy an uncertain interim position. As objects white women become creations of culture—in this case, the mind of white men—using the materials of nature—in this case, uncontrolled female sexuality. In contrast, as animals Black women receive no such redeeming dose of culture and remain open to the type of exploitation visited on nature overall. Race becomes the distinguishing feature in determining the type of objectification women will encounter. Whiteness as symbolic of both civilization and culture is used to separate objects from animals. . . . The treatment of all women in contemporary pornography has strong ties to the portrayal of Black women as animals. . . . This linking of animals and white women within pornography becomes feasible when grounded in the earlier denigration of Black women as animals. (Collins 1990, 170–71, 172)

As Collins points out, race and gender have been inscribed *onto* species: the pre-existing division upon which pornography imposes its images is of animals—beasts, bodies not redeemed by souls—and animal nature, the notion that there is some pure, unmediated bodily sexuality that is not socially constructed. Sander Gilman writes that Buffon, for instance, "stated that this animal-like sexual appetite went so far as to lead black women to copulate with apes" (see Gilman 1985, 212). Pornography that features black women and animals together may function specifically as a racializing of both sex and species hierarchies. In fact, it appears that women of color are more likely to be used in pornography that shows bestiality (see Mayall and Russell 1992). Thus, sexual harassment of women of color by reference to such pornography will carry an added dimension to its demeaning and controlling message. In other words, given the association of black women's bodies and bestiality, Anita Hill may have experienced a specific form of racialized sexual harassment. Only by including animals within the lens of feminist philosophy can the extent and effect of somatophobia in a culture be made visible.

VI. Epistemological issues

If something is invisible we do not have access to it for knowledge. Much of the sexual victimization of women, children, and animals takes place in such a way as to be invisible to most people. In addition, there is the general invisibility of culturally accepted forms of animal abuse, such as flesh-eating, hunting, animal experimentation.[4] What will overcome the invisibility of animal abuse and of the connection between abuse of animals and abuse of women? A relational epistemology helps overcome this culturally structured invisibility. To the person who has a relational epistemology, who has significant relationships with animals, *and* who values these interactive relationships, animal abuse will be less invisible. A relational epistemology also means that a woman experiencing abuse does not isolate her experience, but empathetically may see one's experience as like, rather then radically different from, another's.

As a feminist speaker in the national animal rights movement, I have been approached by many sexual abuse survivors throughout the country who tell of how they made connections between their own sexual abuse and the use and abuse of animals. In 1990, one woman told me how the experience of being choked by her abusive husband transformed her relationship with animals. Suddenly she realized that just as her husband claimed to love her yet was trying to kill her, she claimed to love animals yet she ate them. She survived his attack, left the marriage and became active in vegetarian and animal rights activities in her community. A relational epistemology, in itself, does not automatically result in concern for animals. Aspects of animals' lives and their experience of oppression may remain invisible because of a dominant metaphysics that views animals instrumentally and accepts a value hierarchy. But if one starts to extend out a relational epistemology, this value hierarchy breaks down a little more and a metaphysical shift may occur.[5]

Second-person relationships provide the foundation for such a metaphysical shift. The concept of second persons, introduced by Annette Baier and amplified by Lorraine Code, recognizes that our knowledge is never atomistically individualistic or "self-made." Instead we become persons through our dependence upon other persons from whom we "acquire the essential arts of personhood" (Baier, qtd. in Code 1991, 82). In other words, lives begin in commonality and interdependence; thus in our acquisition of knowledge, "persons are essentially second persons" (Code 1991, 85). The connections between the abuse of animals and the abuse of women suggests that second-person relationships exist between humans and animals as well as between humans and humans. Women and children victimized by abusers reveal intense second-person relationships with animals as well as humans. Otherwise how could control be so inexorably established by the brutalization of pets? How else could they see their death prefigured in the death of the pet?

This second-person relationship can serve as a catalyst to change one's metaphysical stance vis-à-vis the other animals. As happened with the woman being choked by her husband, she suddenly recognized through second-person relations that she had accepted a value hierarchy that failed to protect or value animals. As Code explains: "Imposing meaning on someone else's existence from a position removed from it and ignorant of, or indifferent to, its specificities is at the furthest remove from second-person relations in their normative dimension" (Code 1991, 86). Second-person relations enable second-person thinking, from which the metaphysical shift evolves. With second-person thinking "knowledge claims are forms of address, speech acts, moments in a dialogue that assume and rely on the participation of (an) other subject(s)" (Code 1991, 121). Significantly, for the battered woman and many others, these other subjects are/include animals.

A relational epistemology paves the way for a metaphysical shift because it acknowledges the value of relationships, and of thinking relationally. Given this position, it is harder to say that our relationships are only with human beings, because many of us have significant relationships with animals. Thus seeing ourselves as born into relationships rather than as atomistic, self-made individuals allows for an important metaphysical shift too: no longer seeing humans as radically other than nonhuman life forms, no longer erecting a boundary between the presumably "self-made human" and the presumably "nature-made animal." Someone who has a relational epistemology is in a position to see what the dominant culture in its metaphysics has constructed as invisible and acceptable; the relational epistemology disables the functioning of somatophobia and its undergirding of animal oppression. This metaphysical shift involves valuing animals as other than objects or bodies and repudiating a subject-object relationship premised on domination rather than respect. It acknowledges that animals have a biography, not just a biology (Regan 1983), and that what is required is an anthropology, not an ethology, of animals (Noske 1989).

Feminist philosophers may distrust "animal rights" activism because "animal rights" philosophy is not based on a relational epistemology. However, what may be going on is that many animal rights activists (80 percent of whom are estimated to be women) join the animal rights movement based on a relational epistemology that enables a metaphysical shift that repudiates somatophobia. However, in the absence of a well-developed and popularized defense of animals based on a relational epistemology, they seek for a way to verbalize that which has not been bridged—their knowledge stance with an activist language. Rights (and interest) language has so far gained currency in the animal advocacy movement as the appropriate activist language. The result is that because the animal rights movement has been thought to have been begotten in the image of its "fathers" (Tom Regan and Peter Singer), feminist philosophy may have misread what is happening epistemologically.

VII. POLITICAL PHILOSOPHY

The gender-specific public/private distinction is a conceptually flawed one. Historically, in Western culture, female-gender-identified traits have been associated with the private ("domestic," "home") sphere, while male-gender-identified traits have been associated with the public ("civic," "political") sphere. The private sphere is, for women, "the distinctive sphere of intimate violation and abuse, neither free nor particularly personal" (MacKinnon 1989, 168). Pateman argues further that the subordination of women in the private sphere ("the sexual contract"), is what enables the construction of modern political theory ("the social contract"). Not only does the public/private distinction inscribe sexual difference and domination, it keeps invisible the empirical connections between human male sexual violence and violence toward women, children, and animals which this essay identifies. This prevents feminist philosophy from recognizing the importance of ecofeminist insights into what Karen J. Warren calls "women-nature connections" as being at the heart of feminist philosophy.

If we review the features of an oppressive conceptual framework that Warren has identified (1987, 1990), the way that the public/private distinction operates in the abuse of women and animals will become clearer. Among the features of an oppressive conceptual framework is value-hierarchical thinking or "up-down thinking" that places higher value, status, or prestige on what is up rather than what is down. Abuse enacts a value hierarchy—through abusive behavior a person establishes control, becoming "up" rather than "down"—while originating in value hierarchies: those who are "down" in terms of (public) status—women, children, nondominant men, and animals—are more likely to be victimized.

Warren also identifies value dualisms as part of an oppressive conceptual framework. Disjunctive pairs such as human/animal, male/female, adult/child, white/"non-white" are seen as oppositional rather than as complementary, and exclusive rather than inclusive. Higher value is accorded the first item in each dyad. Until recently, violence in the "private" home was not closely scrutinized by the public sphere (women, children, and animals having less value than men, adults, and humans). Feminist peace politics seeks to change this. As Sara Ruddick observes, "As there is no sharp division between the violences of domestic, civic, and military life, there is also no sharp division between the practices and thinking of private and public peace" (Ruddick 1993, 118). It is essential for feminist peace politics to recognize the human/animal dualism central to public/private distinctions. From Aristotle on, the conception of "manhood"— the public, civic man—depended heavily on seeing women not merely as "lesser humans than men but less-than-human": "it was precisely the sharpness of the Athenian conception of manhood that bore with it a necessary degradation and oppression of women, a denial of the status of 'human' to women" (see Brown 1988, 56). Thus, women were devalued through association with devalued animals. While we have progressed from this theoretical equation of women with animals, we have not eliminated the value dualism that undergirded such public/private separations, the value dualism by which biology determines who is "mind" and who is "body." We have just removed the human species from this debate. Whereas biology is no longer acceptable for determining human value, it remains acceptable for determining animals' less-than-human value. The role of biology as a central determining factor in the perpetuation of the human/animal dualism is similar to and interrelated with the way that privacy perpetuates the male/female dualism: that is, "biology" and "privacy" provide alibis for abuse.[6]

Finally, the "glue that holds it all together" (Warren, correspondence July 1993) is a logic of domination: "a value-hierarchical way of thinking which explains, justifies, and maintains the subordination of an 'inferior' group by a 'superior' group on the grounds of the (alleged) inferiority or superiority of the

respective group" (Warren 1987, 6). The idea of the private/public division protects the private domain from being the focus of certain ethical and philosophical concerns, concerns such as justice, that are often presumed to pertain only
to the public realm (Okin 1989). This private/public division functions as a part
of the logic of domination: the "I-have-a-right-to-do-what-I-want-in-my-own-
home" patriarchal justification for abusive behavior against those constructed as
"inferior"—adult female partners, children, and animals.

Through the operation of value hierarchies, value dualisms, and the logic
of domination, the public/private distinction has functioned historically within
patriarchal oppressive contexts to keep human male sexual violence toward
women, children, and pets out of the higher-status "political" areas and in the
inferior, out-of-police-concern private arena. This is to the detriment of women,
children, pets, and the entire culture.

VIII. Environmental philosophy

One could argue that environmental abuse is a form of somatophobia, that abuse
of the earth is an expression of the hatred of the earth's body. For this reason
alone environmental philosophy should be attentive to the conceptual issues
raised by the connection between the abuse of animals and the abuse of women.
In addition, and very specifically, information about the association between
guns, hunting, and battering suggests that any environmental philosophy that
defends hunting or offers a hunting model must be re-evaluated.[7] Environmental
and ecofeminist philosophers who appeal to a hunting model of any culture need
to rethink the implications of applying it to the dominant Western cultures where
battering is the major cause of injury to adult women, and hunting and owning
guns is implicated in this battering. In fact, some advocates for battered women
argue that battering incidents increase just prior to hunting season. Moreover, at
least one batterer's program requires batterers to relinquish all their guns and fire-
arms in order to participate in the program (see Stordeur and Stille, 1989).

IX. Applied philosophy

Several areas of applied philosophy are affected by these empirical connections between human male sexual violence toward women, children, and animals. In what follows I touch on a few of these areas.

A. Public Policy

Because of Health Department regulations, shelters for battered women cannot generally allow pets in the shelters. The movement to protect battered women
needs to establish relationships with local veterinarians and animal advocates so
that pets can be sheltered. Shelters need to inquire: "Do you have a pet that lives
with you? Are you afraid to leave the animal? Do you need shelter for your pet?"[8]

Training humane society workers and animal control officers to check for child abuse when following up on animal abuse has begun in some places, such as Florida, Ohio, Washington, D.C., and parts of California. But humane society workers and animal control officers should also be trained about woman-battering since injury to pets occurs not only in relationship to child abuse and neglect but also in cases of battering. Veterinarians, too, need to be trained along these lines, and the question of mandatory reporting of animal abuse needs to be addressed by the veterinary profession. But I am in no way advocating that a woman's decisions about whether to remain or leave should be overridden by intervention by these professionals. Instead, their role as allies should be established. And information about pet injury as itself being a form of battering needs to be publicized.

Homeless shelters and battered women's shelters are often offered surplus animal flesh from hunters. In fact, hunters, including the well-known celebrity bow-hunter Ted Nugent, often organize giveaways to these shelters. (We should be reminded that battered women make up about 40 percent of homeless people [see Zorza 1991].) But given the association of hunting and violence against humans, and batterer programs that require batterers to stop using any guns, accepting flesh from hunters to feed battered women and other homeless individuals presents ethical problems. (I know of at least one battered women's shelter that refused to accept flesh from hunters and of some animal activist and vegetarian organizations who adopt a battered women's shelter at which they periodically serve vegetarian meals.)

B. Biomedical Ethics

The relationship between being a survivor of child sexual abuse and anorexia (which is receiving more attention, see Root 1991, and Sloan and Leichner 1986) needs more exploration by those sensitive to the ethical legitimacy of vegetarian claims. One private-practice dietitian and counselor observed that "the animalistic nature of meat and dairy might seem particularly disgusting to patients recovering from sexual abuse" (Krizmanic 1992, 58). This is, in fact, one of the symptom clusters associated with ritual abuse survivors: "Did the child suddenly develop an eating disorder, e.g., refuse meat, catsup, spaghetti, tomatoes?" (Hudson 1991, 32; see also Gould 1992, 214). I have argued elsewhere that young girls might have a problem with food while also being vegetarians for ethical reasons (see Adams 1990, 159–62). In one location in Los Angeles, 90 percent of the anorexics being counseled were vegetarian (with 50 percent considered to have good reasons for their vegetarianism, i.e., they are not doing it solely to diet or restrict their fat intake because of "obsessive" concern for calories), while another program in Indiana estimated that 25 percent of "patients" at its program were vegetarian. Interestingly, "some dietitians and counselors insist that eating meat is integral to recovery" (Krizmanic 1992, 59). Rather than having their motives for vegetarianism pathologized, anorexic young women could benefit from a recognition that a relational epistemology may have catalyzed a metaphysical shift regarding "meat" animals.

C. Philosophical Psychology

Some programs offer healing to survivors of sexual victimization, including formerly battered women, through "animal-assisted therapy." Alice Vachss describes the comforting presence of a dog she brought to work at the sex crimes prosecutors' offices; some child victims only testified on videotape with the dog present: "With Sheba there to make her feel safe enough, the little girl was able to tell what had been done to her" (Vachss 1993, 172). A social worker at a battered women's shelter in Boston told Jay McDaniel, "The more my clients learn to trust animals and the Earth . . . the more they begin to trust themselves. And the more they trust themselves, the better they can free themselves from exploitive relationships" (McDaniel 1992, 1).

X. CONCLUSION: IMPLICATIONS FOR FEMINIST PEACE POLITICS

The connections between the abuse of animals and the abuse of women have important implications for a feminist peace politics. In conclusion I sketch some of the variety of ways of integrating the woman-animal abuse connections into evolving feminist peace politics and philosophy.

The connections between the abuse of animals and the abuse of women call attention to the effect of war and patriarchal militarism on relations between humans and animals and on the lives of animals. Like abusers, occupying forces may kill animals as an expression of control, to instill terror, and to ensure compliance. I have been told such stories: in one case, in the 1970s, after capturing the adult men in a household, the occupying military force very deliberately shot the pet canary in the assembled presence of the family. Just as with battery, such actions are reminders of how mastery is both instilled and exhibited. In addition, the destruction of animals, like rape, is a part of wartime actions (see, for instance, Brownmiller 1975, 39). Moreover, as Ascione reports (drawing on the work of Jonathan Randal and Nora Boustany), anecdotal evidence suggests that "children exposed to chronic war-time violence display violent and cruel behavior toward animals" (Ascione 1993, 232).

Sexualized violence takes on new dimensions in the light of the connections between the abuse of animals and the abuse of women. "The sadistic murderer derives sexual pleasure from the killing and mutilation or abuse of his victim. . . . The act of killing itself produces very powerful sexual arousal in these individuals" (Lunde 1976, 53, 56).[9] Thus, sex-crime offenders might relive their crime through animal surrogates. Arthur Gary Bishop, a child molester and murderer of five boys, relived his first murder by buying and killing as many as twenty puppies. (Most frequently the movement is in the other direction.) After doing an extensive literature review of children who are cruel to animals, Frank Ascione queries "What is the effect on the child who sexually abuses an animal and that animal dies (such as boys having intercourse with chickens)?" (conversation, September 1993). That the sadistic attacks on horses, often involving sexual mutilation, that have occurred in southern England since the mid-1980s are called "horse-ripping" suggests the sexualizing of animal abuse (see Doniger 1993, 25).

Making animal abuse visible expands feminist peace politics. Instead of the glorification of anonymous death in massive numbers that we encounter in heroic war writings, the connections between the abuse of animals and the abuse of women remind us of the specific embodiedness and agonizing painfulness of every single death. In the place of unnamed troops, there are named individuals, including animals. These names remind us that all victims—the pets as well as the troops —have a biography. In addition, we now see that biologisms, and the racism such biologisms give rise to, are involved in attitudes toward "animals" and "the enemy" (see Kappeler, forthcoming). The militaristic identity, like the abuser's control, is dependent on others as objects, rather than subjects. Moreover, it has been observed that "women are more likely to be permanently injured, scarred, or even killed by their husbands in societies in which animals are treated cruelly" (Levinson 1989, 45, cited in Ascione 1993). Finally, our growing understanding of the commodification of bodies in conjunction with militarism (Enloe 1989) can benefit from insights into the commodification of animals' bodies (Noske 1989). Dismantling somatophobia involves respecting the bodily integrity of all who have been equated with bodies.

In response to the conceptual connections between women and animals, feminism has often attempted theoretically to sever these connections (e.g., Wollstonecraft [1792] 1967, Beauvoir [1953] 1974). Clearly, in the light of the connections between the abuse of animals and the abuse of women, this theoretical response is inadequate because it presumes the acceptability of the human/animal value dualism while moving women from the disempowered side of the dyad to the dominating side. Any adequate feminist peace politics will be nonanthropocentric, rejecting value dualisms that are oppositional and hierarchical, such as the human/animal dualism.

In her discussion of feminism and militarism, bell hooks refers to "cultures of war, cultures of peace" (hooks 1989, 97). We have seen how the connections between the abuse of women and the abuse of animals both enact and occur within cultures of war. It remains for feminists to define clearly and specifically how animals will be included in cultures of peace.

NOTES

Thanks to Karen J. Warren for encouraging me to explore the philosophical implications of this subject and for her attentive readings of previous versions of this essay, as well as Duane Cady, the reviewers for *Hypatia*, and Frank Ascione, Bruce Buchanan, Jane Caputi, Kathleen Carlin, Pat Davis, Josephine Donovan, Leigh Nachman Hofheimer, Jennifer Manlowe, Drorah O'Donnell Setel, Ken Shapiro, Marjorie Procter-Smith, and Nancy Tuana for valuable discussions and promptings. Thanks also to Greta Gaard and Melinda Vadas, careful critics of an earlier draft, and DeLora Frederickson and Pam Willhoite, valued colleagues involved both in the movement against violence against women and Feminists for Animal Rights.

1. Just how humans should relate to other animals in any intimate way, that is, the feminist

implications of "pet" keeping and whether domestication of animals is consistent with a nonhierar-chical feminist theory, is beyond the scope of this paper, but see in general Noske (1989), Tuan (1984), Serpell (1986), and Mason (1993).

2. I am uncomfortable with the term "battered woman" although it is one that the movement against violence against women has itself adopted. I agree with Sarah Hoagland (1988) that the term elides the agency of the batterer, while also ascribing an unchanging status to his victim. However, because it is the commonly adopted term, and is used by the scholars and activists from whom I draw my empirical data, I will use the term in this essay.

3. These same acts of battering occur in some lesbian relationships. While human male violence is responsible for most of the damage to women and the other animals in cases of battering, a patri-archal, hierarchical culture will find expressions of this form of violence in some women's same-sex relationships. Where there is an acceptance of a patriarchal value hierarchy, some will wish to estab-lish control (and be on top in terms of the hierarchy) through violence: "38% of the respondents who had pets reported that their partners had abused the animals" (Renzetti 1992, 21). These acts of battering are considered violent and coercive behavior (see Hart 1986, 188). The battered lesbian whose partner injures or destroys a pet faces a double burden: overcoming the invisibility or trivial-izing of lesbian battering and the invisibility or trivializing of abuse to animals.

4. I do not argue for these claims here, for ecofeminist or feminist defenses of vegetarianism, or for the interconnections between human male sexual violence and flesh eating. I do so elsewhere (Adams 1990, 1991, 1993). Furthermore, whether or not one accepts such arguments does not di-rectly affect the argument of this piece. My point here is simply to show that eating, hunting, and dissecting animals certainly belong on the table for discussion of interconnecting forms of violence which are relevant to any feminist peace politics or any (eco)feminist analysis of violence.

5. This discussion of epistemological issues was worked out with the supportive insights and pa-tient prodding of Nancy Tuana.

6. Challenges to the ways by which we draw the line between "human" and "animal" can be found in Haraway (1992), Birke (1991 a&b), Midgley (1979, 1983), and Noske (1989) among others.

7. See for instance Foster et al. (1989) on the presence of a firearm in the home as one of the factors present in battering relationships that end in homicide.

8. I acknowledge the logistical problem this issue presents, and the concern that women might abandon the animals, not because of cruelty or insensitivity, but because they are overwhelmed with reshaping their own lives and feel that the animals are safer removed from the batterer's presence. Still, I believe it is an important step to make in protecting women and animals. I am indebted to DeLora Frederickson and Pam Willhoite for their advocacy of this program. For information on set-ting up such a program (developed for a workshop that DeLora and I gave at the 1993 Texas Council on Family Violence Conference), please send a stamped (55 cent) self-addressed envelope to me at 814 Grinnell Dr., Richardson, TX 75081.

9. Jane Caputi (1987) challenges Lunde's assertion that this occurs only in rare individuals; she sees it instead as constitutive of "the age of sex crime."

References

Achenbach, T. M. 1988. *Child behavior checklist (for ages 2–3, for ages 4–16)*. Burlington, Vermont: Center for Children, Youth, and Families.

Adams, Carol. 1990. *The sexual politics of meat: A feminist-vegetarian critical theory*. New York: Con-tinuum.

———. 1991. Ecofeminism and the eating of animals. *Hypatia* 6(1): 125–45.

———. 1993. The feminist traffic in animals. In *Ecofeminism: Woman, animal, nature*, ed. Greta Gaard. Philadelphia: Temple University Press.

American Psychiatric Association. 1987. *Diagnostic and statistical manual of mental disorders*. 3rd ed. rev. Washington, D.C.: American Psychiatric Association.

Anonymous. 1992. *Ritual abuse: A broad overview*. Baltimore, MD: Survivors of Incest Anonymous, P.O. Box 21817.

Ascione, Frank R. 1993. Children who are cruel to animals: A review of research and implications for developmental psychopathology. *Anthrozoos* 6(4): 226–47.

Baier, Annette. 1985. Cartesian persons. In *Postures of the mind: Essays on mind and morals*. Minneapolis: University of Minnesota Press.

Birke, Lynda. 1991a. Science, feminism and animal natures I: Extending the boundaries. *Woman's Studies International Forum* 14(5): 443–50.

———. 1991b. Science, feminism and animal natures II: Feminist critiques and the place of animals in science. *Women's Studies International Forum* 14(5): 451–58.

Brohl, Kathryn. 1991. *Pockets of craziness: Examining suspected incest*. Lexington, MA: Lexington Books.

Brown, Wendy. 1988. *Manhood and politics: A feminist reading in political theory*. Totowa, N.J.: Rowman and Littlefield.

Browne, Angela. 1987. *When battered women kill*. New York: Free Press.

Brownmiller, Susan. 1975. *Against our will: Men, women and rape*. New York: Simon and Schuster.

Burstow, Bonnie. 1992. *Radical feminist therapy: Working in the context of violence*. Newbury Park, CA: Sage.

Caputi, Jane. 1987. *The age of sex crime*. Bowling Green, OH: Bowling Green State University Popular Press.

Code, Lorraine. 1991. *What can she know? Feminist theory and the construction of knowledge*. Ithaca: Cornell University Press.

Collins, Patricia Hill. 1990. *Black feminist thought: Knowledge consciousness and the politics of empowerment*. Boston: Unwin Hyman.

Crenshaw, Kimberlé. 1992. Whose story is it anyway? Feminist and antiracist appropriations of Anita Hill. In *Race-ing justice, engendering power: Essays on Anita Hill, Clarence Thomas and the construction of social reality*, ed. Toni Morrison. New York: Pantheon Books.

de Beauvoir, Simone. [1953] 1974. *The second sex*. Trans. and ed. H. M. Parshley. New York: Vintage.

Doniger, Wendy. 1993. Diary. *London Review of Books*. 23 September: 25.

Dvorchak, Robert. 1991. Dahmer's troubled childhood offers clues but no simple answers. *Dallas Times Herald* August 11.

Enloe, Cynthia. 1989. *Bananas, beaches and bases: Making sense of international politics*. Berkeley: University of California Press.

Faller, Kathleen Coulborn. 1990. *Understanding child sexual maltreatment*. Newbury Park, CA: Sage.

Foster, Lynne A., Christine Mann Veale, and Catherine Ingram Fogel. 1989. Factors present when battered women kill. *Issues in Mental Health Nursing* 10: 273–84.

Fraser, Sylvia. 1987. *My father's house: A memoir of incest and of healing*. New York: Harper and Row.

Ganley, Anne L. [1981] 1985. *Court-mandated counseling for men who batter: A three-day workshop for mental health professionals*. Washington, D.C.: Center for Women Policy Studies.

Gilman, Sander L. 1985. Black bodies, white bodies: Toward an iconography of female sexuality in late nineteenth-century art, medicine, and literature. *Critical Inquiry* 12: 204–42.

Gould, Catherine. 1992. Diagnosis and treatment of ritually abused children. In *Out of darkness: Exploring satanism and ritual abuse*. See Sakheim and Devine 1992.

Haraway, Donna. 1992. Otherworldly conversations; terran topics; local terms. *Science as Culture* 3(14): 64–98.

Hart, Barbara. 1986. Lesbian battering: An examination. In *Naming the violence: Speaking out about lesbian battering*. See Lobel 1986.

Hoagland, Sarah Lucia. 1988. *Lesbian ethics: Toward new values*. Palo Alto: Institute for Lesbian Studies.

hooks, bell. 1989. Feminism and militarism: A comment. In *Talking back*. Boston: South End Press.

Hudson, Pamela S. 1991. *Ritual child abuse: Discovery, diagnosis and treatment*. Saratoga, CA: R & E Publishers.

Kappeler, Susanne. forthcoming. Animal conservationism and human conservationism. In *Animals and women: Feminist theoretical explorations*, ed. Carol J. Adams, Josephine Donovan, and Susanne Kappeler.

Krizmanic, Judy. 1992. Perfect obsession: Can vegetarianism cover up an eating disorder? *Vegetarian Times* (June): 52–60.

LeMoncheck, Linda. 1985. *Dehumanizing women: Treating persons as sex objects.* Totowa, N.J.: Rowman & Allanheld.

Levinson, David. 1989. *Family violence in cross-cultural perspective.* Newbury Park, CA: Sage.

Lobel, Kerry. 1986. *Naming the violence: Speaking out about lesbian battering.* Seattle: Seal Press.

"Lovelace," Linda [Linda Marchiano]. With Mike McGrady. 1980. *Ordeal.* New York: Berkeley Books.

———. 1986. *Out of bondage.* Secaucus, N.J.: Lyle Stuart Inc.

Lunde, Donald T. 1976. *Murder and madness.* San Francisco: San Francisco Book Co.

MacKinnon, Catharine A. 1987. *Feminism unmodified.* Cambridge: Harvard University Press.

———. 1989. *Toward a feminist theory of the state.* Cambridge: Harvard University Press.

McDaniel, Jay. 1992. Green grace. *Earth ethics: Evolving values for an earth community* 3(4): 1–4.

Mason, Jim. 1993. *An unnatural order: Uncovering the roots of our domination of nature and each other.* New York: Simon and Schuster.

Mayall, Alice, and Diana E. H. Russell. 1992. Racism in pornography. In *Making violence sexy*, ed. Diana E. H. Russell. New York: Teachers College.

Midgley, Mary. 1979. *Beast and man: The roots of human nature.* Ithaca: Cornell University Press.

———. 1983. *Animals and why they matter.* Athens: University of Georgia Press.

Noske, Barbara. 1989. *Humans and other animals: Beyond the boundaries of anthropology.* Winchester, MA: Unwin Human.

Okin, Susan Moller. 1989. *Justice, gender, and the family.* New York: Basic Books.

Pateman, Carole. 1988. *The sexual contract.* Stanford: Stanford University Press.

Phelps, Timothy M., and Helen Winternitz. 1993. *Capitol games: The inside story of Clarence Thomas, Anita Hill and a Supreme Court nomination.* New York: Harper Perennial.

Pope-Lance, Deborah J., and Joan Chamberlain Engelsman. 1987. *A guide for clergy on the problems of domestic violence.* Trenton: New Jersey Department of Community Affairs Division on Women.

Randal, Jonathan, and Nora Boustany. 1990. Children of war in Lebanon. In *Betrayal: A report on violence toward children in today's world*, ed. Caroline Moorehead. New York: Doubleday.

Raschke, Carl A. 1990. *Painted black: From drug killings to heavy metal—the alarming true story of how satanism is terrorizing our communities.* New York: Harper and Row.

Regan, Tom. 1983. *The case for animal rights.* Berkeley: University of California Press.

Renzetti, Claire M. 1992. *Violent betrayal: Partner abuse in lesbian relationships.* Newbury Park, CA: Sage.

Ressler, Robert K., Ann W. Burgess, Carol R. Hartman, John E. Douglas, and Arlene McCormack. 1986. Murderers who rape and mutilate. *Journal of Interpersonal Violence* 1(3): 273–87.

Root, Maria P. 1991. Persistent, disordered eating as a gender-specific, post-traumatic stress response to sexual assault. *Psychotherapy* 28(1): 96–102.

Rose, Elizabeth S. 1993. Surviving the unbelievable: A first-person account of cult ritual abuse. *Ms* (January/February): 404–450.

Ruddick, Sara. 1993. Notes toward a feminist peace politics. In *Gendering war talk*, ed. Miriam Cooke and Angela Woollacott. Princeton: Princeton University Press.

Russell, Diana E. H. 1984. *Sexual exploitation: Rape, child sexual abuse, and workplace harassment.* Newbury Park, CA: Sage.

———. [1982] 1990. *Rape in marriage: Expanded and revised edition with a new introduction.* Bloomington: Indiana University Press.

Sakheim, David K., and Susan E. Devine. 1992. *Out of darkness: Exploring satanism and ritual abuse.* New York: Lexington Books.

Serpell, James. 1986. *In the company of animals: A study of human-animal relationships.* New York: Basil Blackwell.

Sloan, G., and P. Leichner. 1986. Is there a relationship between sexual abuse or incest and eating disorders? *Canadian Journal of Psychiatry* 31(7): 656–60.

Smith, Margaret. 1993. *Ritual abuse: What it is. Why it happens. How to help.* San Francisco: Harper San Francisco.

Spelman, Elizabeth V. 1982. Woman as body: Ancient and contemporary views. *Feminist Studies* 8(1): 109–131.

Statman, Jan Berliner. 1990. Life doesn't have to be like this: How to spot a batterer before an abusive relationship begins. In *The battered woman's survival guide: Breaking the cycle.* Dallas: Taylor Publishing Co.

Stordeur, Richard A., and Richard Stille. 1989. *Ending men's violence against their partners: One road to peace.* Newbury Park, CA: Sage.

Tuan, Yi-Fu. 1984. *Dominance and affection: The making of pets.* New Haven: Yale University Press.

Vachss, Alice. 1993. *Sex crimes.* New York: Random House.

Walker, Lenore. 1979. *The battered woman.* New York: Harper and Row.

———. 1989. *Terrifying love: Why battered women kill and how society responds.* New York: Harper & Row.

Warren, Karen J. 1987. Feminism and ecology: Making connections. *Environmental Ethics* 9(1): 3–20.

———. 1990. The power and the promise of ecological feminism. *Environmental Ethics* 12(3): 125–46.

———. 1992. Women, nature, and technology: An ecofeminist philosophical perspective. *Research in Philosophy and Technology* 13: 13–29.

———. Forthcoming. *Ecofeminism: Multidisciplinary perspectives.* Bloomington: Indiana University Press.

Wollstonecraft, Mary. [1792] 1967. *A vindication of the rights of woman,* ed. Charles W. Hagelman, Jr. New York: W. W. Norton.

Young, Walter C. 1992. Recognition and treatment of survivors reporting ritual abuse. See Sakheim and Devine 1992.

Zorza, Joan. 1991. Woman-battering: A major cause of homelessness. *Clearinghouse Review* (special issue): 421–29.

Mothering, Diversity, and Peace: Comments on Sara Ruddick's Feminist Maternal Peace Politics

ALISON BAILEY

Differences of sex and gender are embedded in philosophical discussions of the sources of war and peacefulness. The women's peace movements of the late nineteenth and early twentieth centuries grounded their arguments for women's peacefulness in an appeal to differences of sex and gender. Yesterday's liberals emphasized women's lack of participation in politics and public life as an explanation of militarism. More recently radical feminists have appealed to biological arguments that link male hormones and aggression. The most common argument in the literature on women and peace, however, grounds women's pacifism in their roles as mothers.

The Moral Mothers, the upper- and middle-class feminists who opposed World War I, filled their speeches and pamphlets with appeals to women's special differences. Today's fascination with women's abilities for "contextual thinking," particular "ways of knowing," and "caring ethic" revives the language and concerns of these so-called Moral Mothers. So much so that Susan Faludi has asked whether these "different voices" are not, in fact, really "Victorian echoes" (Faludi 1991, 325–32).

Sara Ruddick's contemporary philosophical account of mothering reconsiders

Reprinted by permission of the *Journal of Social Philosophy* (from vol. 20, no. 1, Spring 1995).

the maternal arguments used in the women's peace movements of the earlier part of this century. Ruddick devoted nearly a decade to her philosophical analysis of mothering. The culmination of this project is her 1989 book, *Maternal Thinking: Toward a Politics of Peace*. In *Maternal Thinking*, Ruddick honors maternal work but also attempts to transform it. Ruddick believes there is a real basis for the traditional association between women and peace. She argues that those engaged in mothering work have distinct motives for rejecting war, distinct abilities for resolving conflicts nonviolently, and a unique perspective from which to criticize military thinking. If Ruddick is correct, her maternal thinking does not just echo Victorian accounts of women's special differences. It provides a philosophical foundation for a feminist peace politics.

Ruddick's project is ground-breaking work in both academic philosophy and feminist theory. In traditional Western philosophical thought, femaleness, womanly activity, birth giving, bodies, and emotions are seen as conflicting with rationality. While feminist epistemologists are addressing the general question of how gender and other social identities affect knowledge, few have specifically addressed the political and epistemic implications of maternal work. None have suggested that maternal activities give rise to unique ways of thinking. Within contemporary feminist epistemology, Ruddick's analysis of maternal thinking constitutes a radical and new claim. Already widely cited and reprinted within philosophy, *Maternal Thinking* has also attracted the attention of other disciplines. Even feminists who are skeptical about the implications of Ruddick's work have derived new articulations of problems, complexities, and ambiguities from the conceptual space Ruddick's analysis has created.

In this chapter, I first look at the relationship between the two basic components of Ruddick's argument in *Maternal Thinking*: the "practicalist conception of truth" (PCT) and feminist standpoint theory (FST). I argue that Ruddick is never clear about the exact relation between the two components of her argument and that this lack of clarity is the source of serious tensions in her work. I argue that, while there are ways Ruddick can *relieve* these tensions, none of these refinements will *resolve* them. These tensions point to a deeper problem in Ruddick's discussion of the critical power of maternal thinking.

While individually the practicalist conception of truth and feminist standpoint theory each furthers Ruddick's overall project, taken together they make her argument inconsistent. Resolving the inconsistency costs Ruddick the claims about maternal thinking essential to her overall project. In addition to this fundamental problem in the structure of her argument, I argue next that neither of the components of Ruddick's argument can adequately ground a feminist peace politics without first answering the question of who speaks for mothers. My analysis of Ruddick's construction of maternal practice shows that the move from maternal practice to a feminist peace politics is more complex than Ruddick presents it to be. While I can suggest ways to make Ruddick's argument consistent, she still faces—despite her claims of universality—the deeper problem of reconciling her account of maternal practice with the genuine diversity of actual maternal practices. Gender, race, and class all shape what counts as peace for mothers. Any effort to develop a feminist *maternal* peace politics must recognize and allow for the diversity among mothers before it can claim to provide a common critical perspective.

Part I

MATERNAL THINKING, PRACTICALISM, AND FEMINIST STANDPOINT THEORY

1. The Practicalist Conception of Truth: What Is It?

Ruddick's account has two central components: (1) The theoretical development of what she calls "maternal thinking," which she grounds in maternal practice and explains in terms of what she calls the "practicalist conception of truth" (PCT); and (2) the case for her claim that maternal thinking can ground a feminist peace politics, based on Nancy Hartsock's version of feminist standpoint theory (FST).

The practicalist conception of truth—the idea that truths arise from practices—is nothing new. Ruddick reports that her practicalism is rooted in the work of writers like Habermas, Winch, and Rorty whose views of truth derive from one reading of what Wittgenstein may have meant by "facts of living" and "forms of life" in his discussion of language as an activity.[1] Social constructivists interpret Wittgenstein's "forms of life" as social activities and argue for the existence of many truths, each arising from a particular social context.[2] Ruddick reports that, according to the philosophers she regards as practicalists, "Truth is perspectival, relative to the practices in which it is made" (Ruddick 1989, 16).

Ruddick, describing herself as following these practicalists, presents mothering activity as a "form of life."[3] She regards mothers' work as a function of a social practice rather than as a consequence of biological destiny. For Ruddick, "mothering" designates a conscious social practice that gives rise to its own way of thinking. In her view, the PCT holds that "distinctive ways of knowing and criteria of truth arise out of practices" and that "there is no truth by which all truths can be judged nor any total and inclusive narrative of all true statements." Instead, distinctive ways of knowing and criteria of truth arise out of their respective practices (Ruddick 1989, 13).[4] Practices are "collective human activities distinguished by the aims that identify them and by the consequent demands made on practitioners committed to those aims" (Ruddick 1989, 13–14).

Ruddick uses horse racing to illustrate. Horse racing is a practice defined by the goal of winning a race by riding a horse across a finish line ahead of the other racers. "A horse galloping riderless across the line, or a rider turning around to wave to the crowd before she reaches the finish line, are not engaged in the practice of horse racing." To engage in a practice is "to be committed to meeting its demands" or goals (1989, 14). According to Ruddick, these goals are so central to the practice that in their absence the practice would not exist. If truth, or standards of evaluation, are defined within particular practices or activities, then "mothering," which arises from, is tested against, and is honed and refined by the work mothers do, gives rise to its own set of standards. The goals of the practice of mothering—keeping children healthy and safe—shape and determine what is reasonable within mothering. Although mothers are also simultaneously involved in other practices—they are desktop publishers, bluegrass fiddlers, dog trainers, etc.—*as mothers*, they participate in an "identifiable practice" (Ruddick 1985, 98–100; and 1989, 17–29). Ruddick defines the practice of mothering in terms of three activities: preservative love, fostering growth, and social training.

Preservative love is the interest in preserving and protecting the life of a child.
Fostering growth involves nurturing a child's developing spirit.
Social training involves training a child to become acceptable to the mother's social group.

A primary feature of the PCT is that it prohibits any "privileged" practice from judging all other practices. In Ruddick's practicalist view, thought does not transcend its social origins. "There is no truth to be apprehended from a transcendental perspective" (Ruddick 1989, 15). For Ruddick this means that, "There is no truth by which all truths can be judged nor any foundation of truths nor any total and inclusive narrative of all true statements: instead distinctive ways of knowing and criteria for truth arise out of practices" (1989, 13). The criteria for truth are perspectival, relative to the practices in which it is made.

The PCT has limited critical power. But to have *limited* critical power is not the same as having *no* critical power. If there exists "no truth by which all truths can be judged," then the only criticism which can be made of participants in a practice—maternal thinkers, for instance—is *self-criticism*. Ruddick puts it this way:

> It is sometimes said that only those who participate in a practice can criticize its thinking. . . . When mothers engage in self-criticism, their judgments presuppose a knowledge of the efforts required to respond to children's demands that those unpracticed in tending to children do not have. *Maternal criticisms are best left to those who know what it means to attempt to protect, nurture, and train, just as criticism of scientific [or] psychoanalytic thinking should be left to those who have engaged in these practices. . . . There are moral grounds for critical restraint. People who have not engaged in a practice or who have not lived closely with practitioners have no right to criticize.* (Ruddick 1989, 26, my emphasis)

Maternal practice under Ruddick's PCT is primarily descriptive. Its normative power is limited to its participants and those familiar with the practice.

Ruddick's reliance on the PCT in the first part of her book helps her to describe the work mothers do and how this work shapes maternal thinking. Ruddick's goal, however, is not just to account for maternal work and how it gives rise to maternal thinking. She wants to argue that maternal thinking is capable of criticizing military thought. But as a practice, maternal thinking is limited to self-criticism: it is not capable of cross-practice criticism. At this point in her narrative, Ruddick appears to recognize that for her purposes maternal thinking needs a stronger normative force than the PCT allows. To find it, Ruddick turns to Nancy Hartsock's idea of a feminist standpoint.[5]

2. Ruddick's Shift to Feminist Standpoint Theory

In developing her particular version of feminist standpoint theory, Nancy Hartsock (1983) explores the epistemological consequences of claiming that the lives of women differ structurally from those of men. Hartsock both develops and transforms the Marxist idea of a privileged political and epistemological standpoint. From a Marxist perspective, there are two social standpoints: the bourgeoisie and the proletariat. Each speaks from a different social location, which produces a different understanding or interpretation of the world. If the division of labor between these two social groups can create two distinct social perspectives, then a parallel argument, Hartsock holds, can be made from the perspective of men and women who are similarly divided according to the labor they do. Hartsock describes women's activity in terms of two disciplines: their contributions to subsistence and their contributions to childrearing (Hartsock 1983, 291). Under capitalism, women, like men, sell their labor power to produce commodities that have an exchange value. Unlike men, women are also defined by their abilities to produce use-value within the home and by their ability to reproduce and care for offspring. In Hartsock's view, we should expect that the division of labor by gender will have epistemological consequences, just as class divisions do. If Marx's understanding of the world from the standpoint of the proletariat helped him to undermine bourgeois ideology, then a feminist standpoint might help us to undermine patriarchal ideologies.

Although Hartsock's presentation of her feminist standpoint does not address military thinking in particular, it is a natural extension to include it as a form of patriarchal thought. Ruddick's reading of Hartsock's feminist standpoint theory offers a new, improved power for maternal thinking; in the second part of her book, Ruddick abandons the PCT and enthusiastically relocates maternal thinking within Hartsock's version of feminist standpoint theory.

Hartsock uses "women's work" as the basis for her feminist standpoint. Ruddick interprets "women's work" to mean "caring labor," although it is not clear that this is what Hartsock had in mind. Since maternal practices make up a central part of caring labor, maternal thinking and its many variations could be considered a constituent element of Hartsock's standpoint. Ruddick claims that including maternal thinking as part of the feminist standpoint gives it "a critical power [she] had not imagined." Ruddick abandons her earlier practicalist position (Ruddick 1989, 130–131). She says,

> Despite their rejection of dualisms and their respect of difference, these standpoint philosophers seem very different from the Wittgensteinian pluralist who imagined maternal thinking as one discipline among oth-

ers. Standpoint thinkers are ready, as the Wittgensteinian pluralist
would never be, to declare that dominant values are destructive and perverse and that the feminist standpoint represents the "real" appropriately
human order of life. (Ruddick 1989, 134)

With this statement, Ruddick relocates maternal thinking within the feminist
standpoint. In addition to the broadened cross-practice critical possibilities that
standpoint theory affords maternal thinking, Ruddick also argues that maternal
practice/thinking is no longer to be thought of as merely "one discipline among
many." We should regard it, she thinks, as "superior to dominant ways of thinking" (Ruddick 1989, 129). With this move, Ruddick's maternal thinking acquires
the ability to criticize other practices. In short, the shift is from a primarily descriptive account (with internal normative power, at best) to a strongly normative
one. This is a dramatic methodological shift. What accounts for it?

Ruddick describes her move away from the PCT as a developmental step
in her thinking. She reports that, after years of writing about maternal thinking, her "pluralism"—the idea that there are many perspectives and hence many
standards for truth—"began to give way to angry and insistent claims of superiority" (Ruddick 1989, 129). Reading Hartsock in this frame of mind, Ruddick
reports, she saw that feminist standpoint theory offered a superior vision to dominant ways of thinking, including military thinking. As she puts it,

> A standpoint is an engaged vision of the world opposed and superior to
> dominant ways of thinking. As a proletarian standpoint is a superior vi-
> sion produced by the experience and oppressive conditions of labor, a
> feminist standpoint is a superior vision produced by the political condi-
> tions and distinctive work of women. . . . Hartsock not only proclaimed
> the worth of caring labor; she substantiated her claim by detailing char-
> acteristics of caring labor that were responsible for the standpoint's supe-
> riority. (Ruddick 1989, 129–30)

Ruddick is no longer saying that maternal thinking is one standpoint among many.
She clearly regards maternal thinking, taken as a feminist standpoint, as epistemologically, morally, and even practically superior to dominant—and military
—ways of thinking. The aim of Ruddick's book, after all, is not just to make the
point that the work mothers do gives rise to *a* way of thinking, but that it gives
rise to *a better* way of thinking. As part of the feminist standpoint, Ruddick
writes, maternal thinking is an "engaged critical and visionary perspective"
which will "reveal incrementally the superiority of the rationality of care to the
abstract masculine ways of knowing that dominate our lives" (Ruddick 1989, 136).

3. Problems with the Relationship between the PCT and Feminist Standpoint
Theory

Ruddick's methodological shift moves her discussion of maternal thinking
from a descriptive perspective to one that is unabashedly normative. But the re-

lation between Ruddick's use of the PCT in Part I of *Maternal Thinking* and her use of feminist standpoint theory in Part II is unclear. At first, Ruddick appears to be presenting two distinct critical possibilities for maternal thinking: one (on the PCT) which holds that truths/standards of evaluation are always *internal*, or relative to a given practice, and another (within the feminist standpoint theory) which permits some practices privileged, *external* standpoints from which to judge other practices. Can Ruddick have it both ways? Can maternal thinking be in a position to judge other practices, and at the same time be immune to criticism from other practices?

Ruddick uses the PCT to argue that mothering as a practice is not open to external criticism. But Ruddick's overall project is to use maternal thinking as a foundation for a feminist peace politics. If the goal of maternal thinking is to be critical of military practice, maternal thinking must have the critical means to do so. The critical power of maternal thinking quickly runs up against the limits of the PCT. Because practicalists are suspicious of attributing a privileged understanding of reality to any one discipline, it follows that maternal practice should be in no privileged position for evaluating military practice. Since Ruddick's declared project is to develop maternal thinking as a critique of military thinking, why does she start with the PCT which *by her own definition* has limited critical power?

One answer is that Ruddick regards her book as a decade-long developmental narrative of her thoughts on maternal thinking. By Part II of her book, she has rejected her descriptive analysis of mothering in favor of a stronger, normative view. But this move means that Ruddick must open up maternal thinking to external criticism in exchange for the privilege of criticizing military thinking. Yet her desire to account for maternal practice/thinking demands that she ensure that only mothers and those familiar with mothering participate in this project. (Use of the PCT ensures that outsiders to mothering do not exploit maternal thinking to serve their own purposes, such as furthering the causes or bolstering the power of patriarchy.) Ruddick objects to external attempts to criticize or evaluate maternal thinking as attempts to control mothers. Her objections parallel the arguments feminist women of color make for the need to develop their views independent of mainstream white feminism.[6]

The PCT grew out of the desire to avoid the cultural imperialism that arose from cross-practice criticism. But, without the PCT, Ruddick's claim that those unfamiliar with mothering "have no right to criticize" simply dismisses the value of external criticism before the outsiders even have a chance to speak. If Ruddick's abandonment of the PCT is a developmental step, it is a step she cannot make without cost, for making it demands that she give up the amnesty from criticism that the PCT affords maternal thinking. On the other hand, if Ruddick's project is not essentially developmental and she wants to retain this critical amnesty, then her total theory is inconsistent.

Ruddick's vacillation between desire for critical amnesty, on the one hand, and an account of maternal thinking capable of cross-practice criticism, on the other, points to a more pressing problem: the relation between the two components of her argument. Maternal thinking may count as a critical perspective, but it is far from unified. Although Ruddick's examples indicate that she recognizes that mothers are not a homogeneous group, she never considers how this affects maternal critiques of the military. In particular, she does not consider how the differences among mothers attributable to race, ethnicity, and class might influence mothers' cross-practice criticisms. Ruddick does not address this problem in either the PCT or feminist standpoint theory stage of her developmental narrative. And the unclear relationship between the two components only exacerbates this difficulty. I will argue that it ultimately undermines Ruddick's project.

Part II

WHO SPEAKS FOR MOTHERS?: THE IMPORTANCE OF MATERNAL IDENTITY TO THE FORMATION OF FEMINIST PEACE POLITICS

1. The Two Voices of Maternal Thinking

As developmental steps, the two components of Ruddick's argument help her outline what counts as maternal practice, but Ruddick's outline of what mothers do presupposes that we know who these mothers are. Even if we accept Hartsock's claim that outsiders have valuable criticisms to make of dominant ideologies, we still have to know who these outsiders are. Who speaks for mothers? What gives them the right to do so?[7] Even if mothering is a gendered activity (as it may be under Hartsock's feminist standpoint theory), we still need to know from which locations on racial/ethnic and class hierarchies these mothers speak.[8] Do they live in rural or urban environments? Are their governments peaceful or hostile?

Answers to these questions are important if Ruddick is to maintain that maternal thinking is compatible with peacemaking. The context of the practice is extremely influential to the kind of thinking in which mothers will participate. Not all mothers nurture, protect, or socialize their children in the same way or under the same circumstances. As Patricia Hill Collins emphasizes, "No standpoint is neutral because no individual or group exists unembedded in the world" (Collins 1990, 33). There is no singular standpoint that can be labeled "*the* maternal standpoint." Ruddick does not address this problem.

I identify two maternal voices in Ruddick's text: the first is her own voice. It reflects her personal experience of being a mother, of being mothered, and of observing mothers. The other is a "nearly universal" voice in which Ruddick makes broader claims about maternal practice. In her own voice, Ruddick acknowledges that her writing on mothering unavoidably reflects who she is. She explains candidly that her ideas are drawn from her personal experience of mothering in white, middle-class, capitalist, Protestant, patriarchal America, and from her own experience of being mothered in a heterosexual nuclear family (Ruddick 1980, 215). In her own voice, Ruddick sets the social context of her writing in a "technocentric, property-oriented culture ambivalently obsessed with the bonds of biology" (Ruddick 1989, 54). In this personal voice, Ruddick's claims about mothering are empirical, although rather impressionistic, observations of particular mothers in particular social and cultural circumstances. Although she mentions the Madres movement in Argentina, some literary mothers, and a few mothers she knows personally, they provide examples of maternal practices. They are not necessarily extendible to mothering in general.

In her other voice, Ruddick makes the claim that because all children demand preservative love, fostering growth, and social training, mothering universally consists in meeting these demands. Ruddick insists that her own experience as a mother has much in common with the experiences of (all?) other mothers. Ruddick's second voice is easily recognizable in her initial thoughts on maternal thinking, where she sets out the similarities that count as the identifying marks of maternal practice.

> The demands of children and the interests in meeting those demands are always and only expressed by people in particular cultures and classes of their culture, living in specific geographical, technological, and historical settings. Some features of the mothering experience are *invariant and nearly unchangeable*; others, though changeable, are *nearly universal*. It is therefore possible to identify interests that seem to govern maternal practice throughout the species. (Ruddick 1980, 214–215, my emphasis)

Although it may be possible to identify characteristics that "govern maternal practice throughout the species," it is fair to ask whether Ruddick succeeds in doing so with the characteristics that matter most for her project. The difficulty for Ruddick lies in distinguishing those features of mothering that are "invariant and nearly unchangeable" (i.e., long gestation period, prolonged infant and child dependence, and the physical fragility of infancy) from the changeable though "nearly universal" features of mothering (i.e., the identification of childbearing with childrearing, delegation of child care to biological mothers and other women and the social subordination of women to men) (Ruddick 1980, 228).[9]

Preservative love, nurturing, and social training are the three "nearly universal" but changeable features that define maternal practice for Ruddick.[10] Yet Ruddick treats these three activities not as "nearly universal" but as though they were straightforwardly universal. Ruddick says they "govern maternal practice throughout the species." She even boldly asserts: "I make claims about *all* children and believe them" (Ruddick 1989, 54, original emphasis).

Ruddick's position is confusing here. She acknowledges that her accounts "make it seem as if mothering is ahistorical and transcultural" (1982, 6). While she seems to recognize the diversity of mothering, acknowledging that maternal work is shaped by race, ethnicity, class, culture, and sexual orientation, she also insists that all mothers are involved in the same "forms of life"—preservation of life, nurturing, and social training. Despite the many times Ruddick declares her pluralist intentions, she does not identify who these mothers are and she fails to appreciate the implications of the diversity of mothers for her argument. As a result, she presents all mothers as being cut from the same pattern, while mentioning frequently but in passing that they are from different kinds of cloth.

Ruddick does not clearly distinguish when she is speaking from her own experience and when she is speaking in the other, broader voice of maternal thinking. Because her two voices sound as one, Ruddick's mothering is constructed along white, Anglo-American, middle-class—her own—lines. Ruddick's discussion of mothers and maternal thinking is vulnerable to Elizabeth Spelman's (1988) criticism of the general treatment of women in Western feminist theory. Spelman argues that important differences among women have been eclipsed by feminist theorists' desires to focus on "womanness" rather than the diversity among women. For Spelman, this leads

> . . . to the paradox at the heart of feminism: Any attempt to talk about all women in terms of something we have in common undermines attempts to talk about the differences among us, and vice versa. Is it possible to give the things women have in common their full significance without thereby implying that the differences among us are less important? (Spelman 1988, 3)

Ruddick's project suffers from a similar paradox. While Ruddick acknowledges the differences among mothers, these differences are eclipsed by her search for a description of "maternal thinking" that will work as a neatly packaged critical tool for a feminist peace politics. Ruddick's construction of maternal practice around a common set of activities results in descriptions and criteria that frequently, if not always, reflect the experiences of the dominant (her own) race, ethnicity, and class. Even when Ruddick shifts from a practicalist construction of maternal thinking to maternal thinking as part of feminist standpoint theory, differences among mothers remain invisible within her governing theory. To translate Spelman's general conclusion to Ruddick's specific problem, any attempt to talk about mothering in terms of something *all* mothers have in common undermines attempts to talk about their differences.

The "nearly universal" activities that Ruddick presents as central to maternal work do not allow her to raise or address questions that emerge from differences among mothers. Ruddick's failure to address these points invites the following challenges: Would racial-ethnic mothers describe their interests in meeting children's demands in Ruddick's terms? Do Ruddick's "nearly universal" activities accurately describe or capture the actual work of racial-ethnic mothers? Is the maternal thinking that arises from these different mothers' work the same maternal thinking Ruddick describes? Do the answers to these sorts of questions match or challenge Ruddick's analysis of maternal thinking?

Even if Ruddick's general descriptions establish a set of (nearly) universal conditions under which children flourish, they do not address important questions about why some mothers are unable to meet the needs of their children satisfactorily. Ruddick's descriptions ignore important details about mothering among women who are less privileged because of their race, ethnicity, and/or class.

Ruddick's "nearly universal" demands of preservative love, fostering growth, and social training don't fit women mothering under hardship. Can the maternal interest in meeting children's demands be broadly stated to include these women's experiences? Is it more appropriate to fashion new descriptions that reflect the circumstances of these mothers' work? Would these mothers define their children's needs differently? Would they identify more specific, practical, and achievable demands to meet? If an alternative list of demands more accurately captures the circumstances of racial-ethnic mothers' work, then the foundation of Ruddick's argument—the "nearly universal" features of mothers—becomes a casualty of Spelman's paradox.

2. Patricia Hill Collins's Alternative Maternal Model

The challenges I've just raised question whether Ruddick's account of the characteristics she finds in these particular practices legitimately generalize to *all* maternal activities—to maternal practice in general. Now I want to go further, and present another maternal model. It is straightforwardly perspectival and a convincing alternative to Ruddick's broad characterization of maternal practice.

Sociologist Patricia Hill Collins's work provides an excellent instance of theorizing from a clearly identifiable location. In "Shifting the Center: Race, Class, and Feminist Theorizing about Motherhood," Collins bases her argument on the premise that when no neutral standpoint exists from which to theorize, attention to the locations from which theory is done becomes crucial.[11]

Collins uses the context in which contemporary African American mothering occurs as the location from which to theorize—a location that she believes "promises to shift our thinking about motherhood itself" (Collins 1992, 5). As a result of "shifting the center" and theorizing from an identified location, Collins produces a description of maternal practice that is tangibly distinct from Ruddick's "nearly universal" version.

Collins's construction of "motherwork," based on the lives of mothers of color, produces a different and more specific list of mothering activities than Ruddick's does. Collins argues that survival, identity, and empowerment "form the bedrock of women of color's mothering" (Collins 1992, 7). I will briefly sketch Collins's presentation of these three activities.

According to Collins, the physical [and psychological] survival of their children is central to daily activities of these mothers. Unlike the survival of most children born into white middle-class communities, the survival of children of color can not be taken for granted. Disproportionate rates of infant mortality, poor medical care, crime, and drugs require the daily attention of these mothers.

The second activity of Collins's motherwork is teaching children how to retain their identity in a dominant white culture, without "becoming willing participants in their own subordination" (Collins 1990, 123). Collins's mothers regard self-definition in constructing individual and collective racial identity as important for their children (Collins 1992, 21–29). Collins's motherwork means helping one's children develop a meaningful racial identity within a society that devalues their history, work, culture, and customs. Unlike white middle-class children, the children of these mothers must overcome the frequently negative portrayal of their identities by the dominant culture.

Finally, Collins's motherwork is structured by racial-ethnic mothers' struggle over the definition and control of their caring labor, to empower themselves so that they may meet the needs of their own children and their communities. Theirs is a struggle against economic exploitation and usurpation of their labor to meet the needs of the dominant culture for service employees: nannies, hospital aides, housekeepers, cooks, and the like. These mothers' activities also include the struggle to empower themselves to control the choice to become mothers and to be able to retain the children they choose to have.

Collins regards the physical separation of racial-ethnic mothers from children as the "basis of a systematic effort to disempower racial-ethnic communities . . . designed to disempower racial-ethnic individuals" (Collins 1992, 16). In addition to the evidence Collins cites in support of this demand on the work of African American mothers, there is also analogous evidence in the history of institutions such as the Bureau of Indian Affairs, social service agencies, welfare departments, and the policies of these agencies, which affect the fates of Native American, Latina, African American, and Asian American children.

Working from a particular, identified location, Collins constructs a model of maternal activity that is significantly different from Ruddick's general account. It is easy to imagine that working from other particular identified locations—such as the experiences of Native American, lesbian, Latina, Asian American—would also produce a series of convincing alternative models of maternal activity.

What implications does the construction of a convincing alternative model of maternal activity have for Ruddick and her construction of a feminist peace politics?

3. Are Maternal Practice and Motherwork Compatible?

Recall that Ruddick describes maternal practice as defined by preservative love, nurturing, and social training. Collins describes racial-ethnic mothering as defined by survival, identity, and empowerment. Ruddick's investigation of maternal practice is fueled by her desire to identify common features of mothering useful in the construction of a feminist peace politics. Collins's project, while it implies a response to contemporary feminist writings on motherhood, is primarily an attempt to explore new approaches to theorizing about motherhood by using identified, particular locations.

While both of Ruddick's voices speak in terms of mothers' commonalities, Collins speaks about specific mothers working in specific communities. Collins argues that maternal activity cannot be treated as autonomously or understood independently of its context. It occurs in distinctive racial, ethnic, and economic contexts that profoundly shape the ways particular mothers relate to their particular children's needs in particular circumstances.

Because Collins's construction of a model of maternal activity begins from a particular location, it is incapable of generating categories as broad as Ruddick's. Casting the maternal definition net wider from the theoretical location of white middle-class women to cover all women does not make sense. Likewise, casting the maternal net from Collins's theoretical location to all women makes no sense. The definitions of survival, identity, and empowerment can not be broadened to include more privileged mothers without losing the contextual perspective that Collins wants to keep by studying mothers of color on their own terms.

Are these two views compatible? I argue that we should resist the urge to reconcile them merely for the sake of comprehensiveness. It is tempting to place Collins's narrower claims into Ruddick's broad categories, but doing so disregards the purpose of Collins's project and obliterates the features of racial-ethnic mothering that Collins makes visible. Placing racial-ethnic mothering within more broadly constructed frameworks would allow it to be swallowed up and negated in the vastness of what Susan Bordo calls "the view from everywhere" (Bordo 1989, 20).

Treating survival, identity, and empowerment as variants of Ruddick's protection, nurturing, and training, is to regard the different experiences of racial-ethnic people as though they were evidence for theories that have already been carved out along white middle-class lines.[12] A variation on this theme is the way some Anglo American feminists recognize the unique positions of racial-ethnic peoples, but then negate them by using them only as further evidence for their own, more general theories about women. Moves toward universalization of women's experience are usually followed by attempts to place the experiences of racial-ethnic women into broad categories for interpretation. Frequently, these categories are based on the experiences of—tailored to the interests of—dominant groups. The categories structure debate and so make it difficult for the authors to free themselves from old definitions or to embrace alternative treatments of identity. This approach often leads to an insulting intellectual "division of labor": white middle-class women come up with the theories, leaving women of color to provide lively narratives and entertaining experiences to support them.

4. How Diversity Issues Shape the Construction of a Feminist Maternal Peace Politics

If Collins is right and the location from which one constructs a critical perspective does influence the content of the criticism, then the problem of whether maternal thinking as part of a feminist standpoint can reveal biases in abstract masculine ways of thinking (such as military thinking) is more complex than Ruddick believes. If Ruddick regards maternal thinking as part of feminist standpoint theory as morally, epistemologically, and practically superior to abstract masculinity without addressing the differences among maternal practitioners, she ignores the fact that not all mothers have the same relation to (white) abstract masculinity.

Both racial-ethnic mothers and white mothers may share their anger over the horrors and wastes of their government's preparations for war, but their critiques of dominant/military ways of thinking will be different because of their obviously dissimilar relationships to white men and political power structures. Unlike women of color, white women, as wives and mothers or as secretaries, occupy a political "spectator's seat," that gives them a distinct political relationship with white men. White women's "spectator's seat" accounts, in part, for their lack of attention to the racial aspects of the abstract masculine positions they often critique (Hurtado et al. 1989).

To the extent that white women participate in the dominant culture, they benefit from the racial-ethnic hierarchy from which their race as a whole benefits. The privileges most white women gain from their associations with white men do find a way into feminist critiques. Their existence is proof of an overlap between the white middle-class feminist views and white dominant ways of knowing. Even liberal whites, as bell hooks notes, " . . . cannot recognize the ways in which their actions support and affirm the very structure of racist domination and oppression they wish to see eradicated" (hooks 1989, 113).

In U.S. society, white middle-class mothers may share more with (white) abstract masculinity/military thinking than either Hartsock or Ruddick's views lead us to believe. The place of most white women in the dominant culture gives them a distinct outlook that shapes their selection of peace issues and approaches to militarism. For instance, what counts as threatening, warlike, or peaceful is often described in ways that do not reflect the concerns of most women of color. Barbara Omolade explains how mainstream peace activists frequently "want people of color to fear what they fear and define peace as they define it, [and] are unmindful that people of color and their lands have already been and are being destroyed as part of the 'final solution' to the 'color line' " (Omolade 1989, 172). Many women of color have not gotten involved in the mainstream peace movement because, as Zala Chandler argues, "the average African American person does not have the time to worry about the dangers of nuclear war when the mere survival of the African race in the United States is an issue. . . . [I]n too many instances black men, women, and children can be killed at any point, in any place in these United States by either civilians or those in uniforms" (Chandler, 1989, 30).

Peace is not just the absence of violence to the white middle-class, nor is it simply resistance to nuclear war and war machinery. For many persons of color the holocausts have already started in their neighborhoods and on their streets, where the threat of war is indistinguishable from the threats of poverty and institutional violence.[13]

If Ruddick's maternal standpoint does not account for the relationships different mothers have to (white) abstract masculinity and to the military, her peace

politics can only draw narrow, incomplete conclusions about the relationship between maternal thinking and peace.

The ultimate problem with Ruddick's account of maternal thinking is that, while
she mentions the diversity among mothers and its influence, she never accounts for
its implications in her argument. For maternal thinking to offer criticism of military
practices, we need to know much more about the standpoint from which diverse
mothers speak. If Ruddick's shift from maternal practices to maternal standpoint
does not encourage readers to explore the issues raised by Brown, Chandler, and
Omolade, then her peace politics will draw incomplete conclusions about the
relationship between maternal thinking and peace. Mothers cannot separate
their race from their work as mothers. Individual maternal standpoints will incorporate racial standpoints. But in Ruddick's description of maternal activity,
her generic mothers do not speak from social locations of race and class.

These paradoxes at the heart of mothering, like those at the heart of feminism, are not easily resolved. The fundamental problem in Ruddick's argument
is not the incompatibility of her two methodological components. Nor is it lo-
calizable to her abandonment of the PCT in favor of standpoint theory. Her
argument ultimately founders on her failure to explore the implications of racial-
ethnic forms of maternal practice for a feminist peace politics, despite her ac-
knowledgement of their existence.

Ruddick's project would benefit from some guidelines to direct cross-practice
criticisms and other refinements. But without addressing how the social location—race and class as well as gender—of maternal practitioners influences maternal thinking, she cannot construct a complete feminist peace politics. Her pluralism requires more than just recognizing the existence of diversity; she must
also be able to talk about it.

Notes

1. Wittgenstein's discussion of "forms of life" can be found in his *Philosophical Investigations*,
sections 19, 23, 241 (ed. G. E. M. Anscombe, 1953).

2. I owe this insight on social constructivism to a conversation with Don Gustafson.

3. Ruddick expresses the idea as follows. If the statement: "A child's life must be protected"
strikes us as immediately true, this is because we daily act protectively and our true statement expresses as it reveals our commitment. What the sentence expresses and the commitment reveals is not
only the truth that children are deserving of protection but also the form of life in which truth is
indubitable. Preservative love is a "form of life": What has to be accepted, the given, is—so one could
say—"forms of life" (Ruddick 1989, 128).

4. It is not clear to me what role "truth" plays in Ruddick's discussion of practices. She could
have just as easily borrowed Alasdair MacIntyre's definition, which appeals to "standards of ex-
cellence," instead of truth in its explanation of practices. What I think Ruddick is trying to establish here is that each practice gives rise to its own particular standards. If what she is really
concerned with is a moral evaluation of military practice by maternal practice, it would have been
just as easy to speak in terms of maternal practice giving rise to standards of moral or political
evaluation rather than "truths." See MacIntyre, 1981, 175.

5. A note of caution is required here. It is very easy to interpret feminist standpoint as meaning
a women's perspective; some of these authors use the terms interchangeably. Women's perspective

refers to what some women empirically think—what actual women actually see and experience. Be-cause women have to confront reality on men's terms, their views have been distorted by patriarchal social arrangements. Women's experiences alone do not provide reliable grounds for feminist knowl-edge claims about nature and social relations. As Alison Jaggar points out: ". . . [s]ocialist feminists recognize that women's perceptions of reality are distorted both by male-dominant ideology and by the male-dominated structure of everyday life. The standpoint of women, therefore, is not something that can be discovered through a survey of women's existing beliefs and attitudes. . . . Instead, the standpoint of women is discovered through a collective process of political and scientific struggle" (Jaggar 1983, 371). But a standpoint is not a perspective; it takes science and politics to achieve a standpoint. Feminist standpoint theory holds that it is not enough for women to describe their ex-periences. Because experiences must be redescribed, feminist standpoint theory cannot be expressed through a survey of women's unreflective world views alone. As the word "feminist" indicates, this position is political and can only be constructed, or redescribed, collectively through critical dialogue and political struggle. Harding argues that the need for struggle "emphasizes the fact that a feminist standpoint is not something that anyone can have simply by claiming it. It is an achievement. A standpoint differs in this respect from a perspective, which anyone can have simply by 'opening one's eyes' " (Harding 1991, 127).

6. The point that black women need to work on their own issues independently of white women is explored by Elizabeth Hood (1978). One reason Ruddick might have stressed the impor-tance of limiting criticism to those familiar with a discipline is that Ruddick may see her mothers as a powerless group which needs space to develop their own views independently of outside criticism. Since the work that mothers do is devalued or receives little recognition in most societies, Ruddick claims that maternal thinking "when it has been acknowledged at all, has most often been recognized by people interested in interpreting and controlling rather than in listening" (Ruddick 1989, 26).

7. The more general, related point about which women have spoken and who has been listened to in the formation of accounts of women's nature is addressed by Elizabeth Spelman's introduction to her *The Inessential Woman: Problems of Exclusion in Feminist Thought* (1988).

8. According to Ruddick, "There is no reason to believe that the difference between female and male mothers in themselves makes one sex a 'better' mother" (Ruddick 1985, 98). Because the term "mother" is used by Ruddick to designate a social category, mothers can be both male and female. But Ruddick does not mention the fact that male and female mothers may do their mothering work in gender specific ways. My issue with Ruddick is that her definition of mothering is drawn from the work women do and then assumed to apply to the way men mother. If Ruddick is willing to admit that class, race, and culture influence mothering work, then she must also be willing to admit that sex and gender play a role in mothering.

9. I am now fairly certain that Ruddick's distinction between the universal and nearly un-changeable and nearly universal and changeable is made in order to give her three demands nearly universal standing. "Although the view that children require training seems nearly universal, there are marked disagreements among individuals and cultures about human nature, moral values, and the extent to which mothers, rather than teachers, priests, fathers or even government officials are re-sponsible for training" (Ruddick 1989, 103).

10. See Susan Rae Petersen, "Against Parenting" in *Mothering*, ed. Joyce Trebilcot (1983), pp. 62–70. bell hooks has argued that emphasis on the maternal is shortsighted because the word "ma-ternal" is too closely tied to women's behavior and men will not identify in ways traditionally seen as feminine. For these reasons, she argues for "parenting" as the proper term for child care work. See also "Revolutionary Parenting" in *Feminist Theory from Margin to Center* (1984), pp. 133–47.

11. Patricia Hill Collins, "Shifting the Center: Race, Class, and Feminist Theorizing about Motherhood," Cincinnati, 1992. I am extremely grateful to Patricia Hill Collins for sharing and discussing her unpublished work with me. For clarity and to maintain the distinctions of both Ruddick's and Collins's views, I use "motherwork" to refer to the maternal labor of racial-ethnic women (described by the themes of survival, power, and identity). I use "maternal practice" to refer to the work of the mothers Ruddick describes, whom I take to be primarily white women.

12. In "The Costs of Exclusionary Practices in Women's Studies," Maxine Baca Zinn and her colleagues identify a number of problematic approaches to race and class in the writings of white

middle-class feminists working in the social sciences. Ruddick's descriptions of maternal practice have elements of Zinn's first and third categories. The first problem, what Elizabeth Spelman and others call the "additive" approach, argues that once the essential woman is identified, one can account for diversity by giving her a little color and adjusting (fine-tuning) her economic status accordingly. This additive approach can never give us an accurate picture of all women because it theorizes about all women from the same location. Politically, additive approaches typically establish a common feminist agenda and describe variations on that agenda as "special interests." As a result, female subordination is treated as the unifying and universal enemy of women. Racial and economic issues are treated as secondary. Ruddick's approach also focuses descriptively on the aspects of life, values, customs, and problems of women in subordinate races and classes, but fails to follow through. After describing differences, it fails to explain the sources of real and perceived differences or to explore the challenges these differences present to the initial set of beliefs.

13. See Willmette Brown, *Black Women and the Peace Movement*, London: Falling Wall Press, 1981. It is also worth noting that for some, nuclear war is not a distant threat. For the people of the Western Shoshone Nation whose ancestral lands have been used by the U.S. government since the 1940s for nuclear testing, the war has already begun. Historically, the Shoshone Nation is the most bombed nation on earth. See, *For Mother Earth Newsletter*, no. 5 (August 1992), published by American Peace Test, P.O. Box 26725, Las Vegas, Nevada, 89126.

REFERENCES

Bordo, Susan. 1989. "The View from Nowhere and the Dream of Everywhere." *American Philosophical Association Newsletter in Feminism and Philosophy*, March 1989, p. 20.

Brown, Willmette. 1983. *Black Women and the Peace Movement*. London: Falling Wall Press.

Chandler, Zala. 1989. "Antiracism, Antisexism, and Peace (Sapphire's Perspective)." In Adrienne Harris and Ynestra King, eds., *Rocking the Ship of State: Towards a Feminist Peace Politics*. Boulder, CO: Westview Press, pp. 25–34.

Collins, Patricia Hill. 1990. *Black Feminist Thought: Knowledge, Consciousness and the Politics of Empowerment*. Boston: Unwin Hyman.

———. 1992. "Shifting the Center: Race, Class and Feminist Theorizing about Motherhood." Cincinnati, unpublished.

Faludi, Susan. 1991. *Backlash: America's Undeclared War against Women*. New York: Crown Publishers.

Harding, Sandra. 1991. *Whose Science? Whose Knowledge?: Thinking from Women's Lives*. Ithaca: Cornell University Press.

Hartsock, Nancy. 1983. "The Feminist Standpoint: Developing the Ground for a Specifically Feminist Historical Materialism." In *Discovering Reality: Feminist Perspectives of Epistemology, Metaphysics, Methodology, and Philosophy of Science*. Sandra Harding and Merrill B. Hintikka, eds. Holland: D. Reidel, pp. 283–310.

Hood, Elizabeth. 1978. "Black Women, White Women: Separate Paths to Liberation." *Black Scholar* (April).

hooks, bell. 1984. *Feminist Theory from Margin to Center*. Boston: South End Press.

Hurtado, Aida, et al. 1989. "Relating to Privilege: Seduction and Rejection in the Subordination of White Women and Women of Color." *Signs: Journal of Women in Culture and Society*, 14(4): 833–55.

Jaggar, Alison. 1983. *Feminist Politics and Human Nature*. Totowa, N.J.: Rowman and Allenheld.

MacIntyre, Alasdair. 1981. *After Virtue*. Notre Dame: University of Notre Dame Press.

Omolade, Barbara. 1989. "We Speak for the Planet." In Adrienne Harris and Ynestra King, eds., *Rocking the Ship of State: Towards a Feminist Peace Politics*. Boulder, Co.: Westview Press, pp. 171–89.

Petersen, Susan Rae. 1983. "Against Parenting." In *Mothering: Essays in Feminist Theory*, ed. Joyce Trebilcot. Totowa, N.J.: Rowman and Allenheld, pp. 62–70.

Ruddick, Sara. 1983. "Thinking about Mothering: Putting Maternal Thinking to Use." *Women's Studies Quarterly* 11, no. 4, pp. 4–7.

———. 1985. "Maternal Thinking and the Practice of Peace." *Journal of Peace Education* (Boston University), no. 167, pp. 97–112.

———. 1989. *Maternal Thinking: Toward a Politics of Peace.* Boston: Beacon Press.

Spelman, Elizabeth V. 1988. *The Inessential Woman: Problems of Exclusion in Feminist Thought.* Boston: Beacon Press.

Winch, Peter. 1970. "Understanding a Primitive Society." In *Rationality*, ed. Bryan R. Wilson. Oxford: Basil Blackwell, pp. 78–111.

Wittgenstein, Ludwig. 1968. *The Philosophical Investigations*, 3rd edition, ed. G. E. M. Anscombe. New York: Macmillan.

Zinn, Maxine Baca, Lynn Weber Cannon, Elizabeth Higganbotham, and Bonnie Thornton Dill. 1986. "The Costs of Exclusionary Practices in Women's Studies." *Signs: Journal of Women in Culture and Society* 11(2): 290–303.

"Severed Heads": Susan Griffin's Account of War, Detachment, and Denial

WILLIAM ANDREW MYERS

It is by now a familiar story that embedded in the fabric of Western culture are validations of quantified knowledge that is detached from its subject, that is separate from the consequences of its application, that reduces what it studies to its seemingly independent parts. Another familiar story is the development in modern warfare of technologies which distance the warmakers from the effects of their actions. Recent work in feminist philosophy and literary criticism has begun to connect these stories as two facets of the same basic pattern of detachment. In this chapter I will show how Susan Griffin's account of the connections between the distancing structures of modern knowing and the patterns of denial pervading governments, societies, and dysfunctional families helps us to understand the forms of thought which have animated the development of modern military strategies, especially aerial bombing. The central feminist theme woven through much of Griffin's work is *embodied knowledge*, the idea that epistemological (and emotional) detachment and psychological denial are ultimately attempts to stand outside the body, to engage in the pretense that thought stands apart from the world. Indeed (mindful of the irony), we can read the history of recent military technology as the progressive *disembodiment* of war making, which a neurologist might call a generalized agnosia, an inability to recognize the world and our bodies as our own.

After a brief discussion of technological distancing, I will identify a structure of detachment in this history and show that Griffin's feminist treatment of some paradigm cases of such detachment point to empathetic imagination as an alternative. The experiences of the victims of bombing in this century reveal what is being kept out of sight, and provide a context for application of Griffin's idea of embodied knowledge. But I will end with a paradox: our own embeddedness in a war-making culture so implicates all of us in its forms of thought that to attempt to distance ourselves from these forms of thought is to practice the very thinking we seek to escape. Griffin's work is thus diagnostic of a pathology we all—to some degree—suffer; but she also demonstrates how a feminist reconstruction of consciousness as associative and integrative may point to a cure.

The technological history works like this: up through the middle of the nineteenth century the scope of warfare was limited by the range of the weapons. Soldiers had to be close to kill each other, and atrocities against civilians or unarmed prisoners were committed by hand. The development of rifling—machining grooves into the inner surfaces of gun barrels so that bullets spin as they travel their trajectories—greatly increased the range and accuracy of weapons carried, e.g., by soldiers in the American Civil War and in the Franco-Prussian War of 1870. The same wars saw the development of the Gatling gun, forerunner of the machine gun. The carnage of these wars shocked their societies, and that shock became a familiar experience in the twentieth century as the technology available for killing repeatedly outstripped the thinking of those who would employ it—the generals and politicians. This mismatch of technology and understanding was well established by World War I, a great turning point in the history of the West, and the development of technologies has accelerated since. The airplane was, from its very inception, perceived as a potential adjunct to military action. World War I saw the creation of a new kind of warrior hero—the fighter pilot—and also the beginnings of aerial bombing and strafing of civilians. Long range artillery, too, is part of this story, but it is the airplane that captured (and continues to this day to hold) the public imagination.

Indeed, in the midst of World War I South African Jan Smuts headed a British commission to investigate defenses against air attack and the future of airplanes in warfare; he reported in 1917 that,

> the day may not be far off when aerial operations, with their devastation of enemy lands and destruction of industrial and populace centres on a vast scale, may become the principal operations of war, to which the older forms of military and naval operations may become secondary and subordinate. . . . (Boyle 229)

The primitive and fragile airplanes of the early years of the war were severely limited in their capabilities, but their initial function of observation in support of ground troops quickly gave way to aggressive use in bombing and strafing trenches, roads and railroads, then factories and cities. Meanwhile, dirigibles had already dropped bombs on London, and in June 1917 a flight of 14 German bombers attacked London in daylight, killing or maiming 600 people and incidentally demonstrating the ineffectiveness of the British defenses. In the political aftermath of this attack, Hugh Trenchard, the chief of the Royal Flying Corps and early champion of air power, produced a report in which he noted,

> Reprisals on open towns are repugnant to British ideas but we may be forced to adopt them. It would be worse than useless to do so, however, unless we are determined that once adopted they will be carried through to the end. The enemy would almost certainly reply in kind. . . . (Boyle 222)

The point of Trenchard's report was not to question the morality or even the utility of such an escalation of violence, but to argue for more aircraft and an expanded role for the forces he commanded.

Once the concept of dropping bombs on cities is accepted, that is, once strategists and their governments and their publics agree that blowing up civilian populations is morally acceptable, or perhaps even necessary, incremental increases in violence become mere technical improvements. To the strategists, there is no categorical difference between the first bombs dropped from dirigibles on London and the firestorm which destroyed Dresden in 1945. And while we know that there is a very big moral gap between the bombing of Dresden and the potential omnicide which could result from large-scale use of nuclear devices, to the American decision-makers in 1945 the atomic bomb was simply a more efficient weapon to do the same job lots of smaller weapons had done before.

Freeman Dyson recapitulates in microcosm this moral erosion in his account of his work as a civilian mathematician during World War II:

> At the beginning of the war I believed fiercely in the brotherhood of man, called myself a follower of Gandhi, and was morally opposed to all violence. After a year of war I retreated, and said, Unfortunately, nonviolent resistance against Hitler is impracticable, but I am still morally opposed to bombing. A few years later I said, Unfortunately it seems that bombing is necessary to win the war, and so I am willing to work for Bomber Command, but I am still morally opposed to bombing cities indiscriminately. After I arrived at Bomber Command I said, Unfortunately it turns out that we are after all bombing cities indiscriminately, but this is morally justified because it is helping to win the war. A year later I said, Unfortunately it seems that our bombing is not really helping to win the war, but at least I am morally justified in working to save the lives of the bomber crews. In the last spring of the war I could no longer find any excuses . . . I had surrendered one moral principle after another, and in the end it was all for nothing. (Dyson 31–32)

Dyson later married a German woman, started a family, and once revisited his wife's former home, where she had as a child hidden in a bomb shelter:

> We tried without success to explain all this to the children. "You mean
> Mummy was down here because Daddy's friends were dropping bombs on
> the garden?" You really cannot explain things like that to a seven-year-
> old. (Dyson 32)

Whether or not "things like that" can make sense to *adults*, our history implicates us in a peculiar circularity which, for decades, we have been unable to
face as a society: we created a war system in which absolutely everyone on the
planet is—in the perverse jargon of the war planners—a "soft target." The logical extension of the bomber's insulation from the effects of his raid—button
pushers in underground bunkers thousands of miles from their target—brings the
violence of the war system back home to the bomber and makes even more acute
the perceived need to hide the potential for disaster inherent in Cold War deterrence. The breakup of the Soviet Union has not effectively changed the risks
of this system. We are simply more complacent about it.

Such complacency has an identifiable structure; it is not mere apathy or dull-
ness of spirit. It is rather that the normal human feeling response to suffering,
commonly evoked in the presence of people or animals in pain or distress (or
their images), requires empathetic imagination to arise in the abstract or at a
distance, and the socialization of a war society replaces that empathetic imagination with dehumanizing images of the "enemy," patriotic idealism, and pseudo-
rational calculations of military necessity. Griffin's approach to these strategies
leads me to term them *disembodiments*, because they cut us off as knowers from
what our bodies tell us about the world and suffering.

Thus Griffin, in a 1979 essay in which she criticizes the common belief that
pornography provides men with necessary catharsis, calls those, like Freud, who
believe this "severed heads," because to believe it requires one not to feel the
genuine suffering and victimization inherent in images of bondage and torture
(Griffin 1982b: 105). Her more recent work, especially *A Chorus of Stones: The
Private Life of War*, explores how the historical pattern of distancing through
technologies expresses a larger structure of insulation in government that employs document classification, stonewalling, systems of "plausible deniability,"
false claims of national security interests, planted news stories, disinformation,
and outright lies to protect the image of a benign government always acting in
the national interest.

Griffin interweaves various narrative voices, a method she used with powerful effect in *Woman and Nature: The Roaring Inside Her* (Griffin 1978). In *A
Chorus of Stones* we are shown, side by side, victims of atomic testing; frightened
whistle-blowers at a nuclear weapons plant; Hugh Trenchard; Heinrich Himmler;
the artists Charlotte Salomon—who died in Auschwitz, and Kathe Kollwitz—
who lost her son in World War I and a grandson in World War II; Werner
von Braun, whose passion to develop vehicles for space travel led him to work in
a German missile project where the laborers were slaves from a nearby concentration camp; physicist Enrico Fermi, who created the first controlled nuclear

reaction; and various members of Griffin's own family struggling with guilty knowledge and family secrets. She also inserts brief interruptions in italics: a "scientific" voice describing the evolution of life and the physics of radiation, or the history of weapons technology and deployment. These juxtapositions form a steady reiteration of the patterns of detached knowing and psychological denial and the damage these patterns do to people.

Through this integrative methodology Griffin shows how Himmler and Fermi and Von Braun and Trenchard all could be thought of in the same way: heads whose bodies—the full life of feeling and empathy and care and connection to the cycles of life—have gotten lost. This loss—the devaluing or outright denial of the body—is of course one of the oldest traditions in the West. These men are but extreme examples of an inheritance all of us share.

Its alternative is hinted at in Griffin's essay on ideology, where she says:

> . . . all original thought—political, scientific, poetic—shares one quality. That is the desire to know the whole truth, to understand and to know what is obscured or what has been forgotten, to take in the unknown. And this desire to know is perhaps finally a way of loving. It is intimately connected to an attitude which honours all that is living. For the desire to know deeply all that is, as part of our outrage over injustice and suffering, accepts the truth, the whole and compassionate being. (Griffin 1982a: 181)

Parker Palmer, in *To Know as We Are Known*, calls such full and engaged knowing "wholesight," and he describes the outcome of an ideal education a knower who "would become a person whose destiny is not to rule, but to raise to consciousness the interrelated quality of all of life, to enter into partnership with nature, history, society, and ourselves" (Palmer 38). And Palmer too identifies such knowing with love. This is only to hint at an epistemological and pedagogical alternative to the patterns our history so violently displays.

Empathetic imagination depends on embodied knowledge: to respond empathetically to others requires deep awareness of our selves as physical and emotional beings. Just as high-functioning autistic persons may understand intellectually the behavioral signs of suffering but be unable to feel the inner states of others, the rational "severed heads" Griffin discusses build—sometimes quite deliberately—patterns of life and thought that insulate them from the emotional lives of others. At the same time they become insulated from their own emotional lives.

Griffin shows how psychological denial and the epistemology of detachment stunts the lives of scientists like Von Braun and Fermi. Von Braun looks past the concentration camp victims at Dora on his way to work every day; later, trying to come to the US, he denies he saw them. Because of his useful knowledge of rocketry, US officials conspire in Von Braun's denials, and, to get around the awkward fact of his Nazi party membership, grant him an exception to the law which would have prohibited his immigration. It is the knowledge that counts, not the way it was obtained.

Fermi is even weirder, in Griffin's account. Asked what will prevent the first chain reaction from just going on to infinity, consuming Chicago and everything else, Fermi says the risk is negligible (note: not impossible!); but anyway, there are safeguards, including a man with an axe standing next to a rope which will release the rods that *should* stop the reaction, and two more men with buckets of a chemical which also should stop it just in case the axe fails (Griffin 1992: 74). Later, at Trinity Site, Fermi makes side bets "on the possibility that the whole state of New Mexico would be incinerated." Griffin comments wryly,

> Such a bet produces an obvious problem. But only for a mind that be-
> lieves itself to be a part of a body. Had the entire state of New Mexico
> been incinerated, Fermi, who was watching the test in New Mexico that
> day, would have perished. He would not have been able to collect his
> debt, or even understand that he had won. (80)

Fermi's scientific detachment was shaken by the force of the first atomic explosion, Griffin tells us, so much so that someone else had to drive his car away from the site afterwards, with Fermi a passenger; and he later told his wife that "during this journey it had seemed to him as if his car were jumping from curve to curve and skipping the straight stretches in between" (81). Fermi, discovering his own capacity to be shocked, "was able to confess this shock to his wife, and thus, knowing himself in this way, regain composure, as in the telling he wedded together two parts of his being" (81).

No such redeeming self-knowledge appears in Griffin's searching examination of Heinrich Himmler. Understanding this man's inner life is, I think, prerequisite to understanding the twentieth century's paradigm case of evil. But access is difficult. Of reading Himmler's boyhood diary Griffin says:

> I have begun to think of these words as ciphers. Repeat them to myself,
> hoping to find a door into the mind of this man, even as his character
> first forms so that I might learn how it is he becomes himself. (118)

One defining moment in Himmler's adult life came when he was shown Jews being shot at the edge of a pit they had been forced to dig themselves. Himmler worried that their killers would be brutalized by this work, would no longer be able to exemplify the Aryan warrior ideal. And so, as Griffin recounts, shaken by what he saw, Himmler ordered engineers to devise the infamous gas vans, precursors to the later gas chambers. These trucks piped their exhaust into the back where the prisoners died in terror and agony (but at least out of sight). Even so, the designers had to modify the trucks after early experiments, providing them with drains to make emptying them less revolting.

Here we encounter one of the most intriguing mysteries of the epistemology of detachment. In a different essay, Griffin observes that the people who design the machines of mass murder are intensely practical, at least in a technical sense; both Fermi and Himmler, she says, "had an intimate knowledge of nature" (Griffin 1990: 92).

I visited Auschwitz some years ago and found myself engrossed in the trolley mechanisms that pushed gassed corpses into the ovens. I used to earn my living as a mechanic and I still spend time with various tools in my hands. Decoding the machine, the literal nuts and bolts, is a lifelong habit. And what overwhelmed me about seeing these trolleys was: this was not an abstract idea couched in carefully deniable bureaucratic doublespeak. Somebody drew blueprints for this, wrote out specifications for the sizes of these bolts and wheels and springs, calculated exactly how wide and long the platform should be so that the mechanism would *work*. Some very practical engineer had to calculate how much fuel it would take to incinerate a human corpse—and then multiply.

What explains this human capacity to use reason (in the tradition, our "highest," most distinctly *human* capacity) to devise means of efficient mass murder? Hannah Arendt's analysis of Adolph Eichmann's radical thoughtlessness—his inability to recognize in its fullness the reality of his actions—is one way to account for it (Arendt 1963). Griffin adds to this picture. Of Fermi and Himmler she says, "their awareness of what existence is, no matter how practical, was not embedded in the cycle of life. They distanced themselves from the wholeness of experience" (Griffin 1990: 92). She notes that our culture has a number of institutions that help us in that distancing, such as the concept of "objectivity" in science and bureaucracy, "which keeps people from seeing the implications and direct consequences of their actions" (92–93). These institutions can do their work of distancing us from nature because we understand consciousness as *separate* from nature:

> It takes a bending of language at this point to speak of consciousness as embedded in the way we breathe, the way we stand, all the intricate numbers of relationships we have, where we live on the planet, the trees next to us.
>
> Yet all experience of material existence threatens the imaginary schism between nature and consciousness; even language, which is itself a natural experience, reflects the acoustical shape of mouth and tongue. The very word *culture* derives from the word for the cultivation of the soil. *Spirit* derives from the word for breath. (93)

In *A Chorus of Stones* Griffin looks to Himmler's upbringing to explain his character. Psychoanalyst Alice Miller has provided insight into the effects of the autocratic educational theories Himmler was raised under. Griffin sees the pointed effects of this background in the diary the boy is required to create by (and for!) his father. He learns to keep meticulous records, but also to reveal nothing he feels. These habits last his whole life. Griffin adds, with characteristic perception,

The religious tradition that shaped Heinrich's childhood argues that the soul is not part of flesh but is instead a prisoner of the body. But suppose the soul is meant to live in and through the body and to know itself in the heart of earthly existence? Then the soul is an integral part of the child's whole being, and its growth is thus part of the child's growth. It is for example, like a seed planted underground in the soil, naturally moving toward the light. And it comes into its fullest manifestation thus only when seen, especially when self meeting self returns a gaze. (Griffin 1992: 123)

This comment reminds me of the remark by Dr. Thomas More, the alcoholic, half-mad genius who narrates Walker Percy's *Love in the Ruins*: "When I left the hospital, I resolved not to lie. Lying cuts one off. Lying to someone is like blindfolding him: you cannot see the other's eyes to see how he sees you and so you do not know how it stands with yourself" (Percy 1981: 74).

Himmler's father, his education, and his religious background all abetted the production of a character whose reaction to witnessing naked men, women, and children being shot to death was concern for the feelings of their killers. And though he suffered psychosomatic ailments which both he and his physician could connect to the work he did, Himmler seems never to have been capable of knowing how it stood with himself.

And if we do not know how it stands with ourselves, we cannot effectively know others. In a culture that institutionalizes detachment it takes special effort to reclaim our empathetic imagination, but what is at stake is our very ability to respond to the claims of suffering humanity as whole persons. I would add that there is nothing unique or exotic or difficult to comprehend about the suffering that is kept out of sight by the distancing patterns of a war-making society. Indeed, when it is revealed by courageous reporting, there is a curious universality to the experience, for example, of being bombed. The dead may even look alike: Martha Gellhorn, reporting on the Russian bombing of Helsinki in 1939, writes,

> Close to a big filling station a bus lay on its side, already burned out, and beside it in the street was the first dead man I saw in this war. On my first morning in Madrid, three winters ago, I saw a man like this one. Now as then there was no identification left except the shoes, since the head and the arms had been destroyed. In Spain the small, dark, deformed bundle wore the rope-soled shoes of the poor, and here the used leather soles were carefully patched. Otherwise the two remnants of bodies were tragically the same. I thought it would be fine if the ones who order the bombing and the ones who do the bombing would walk on the ground some time and see what it is like. (Gellhorn 54)

Survivors become disoriented and uncomprehending, although they may temporarily rise to the challenge of putting out fires and attempting to rescue the injured. Nuha Al-Radi writes about her neighbors in Baghdad during the 1991–92 bombing. One elderly man is found riding his grandson's tricycle around and around in the garage, convinced he will never see his grandchildren again. Later, he dies in his sleep: "He had a bad heart and yesterday chased up nine floors to check the damage to our building. But he really died of sorrow: he could not comprehend why the world wanted to destroy us" (Al-Radi 219).

This theme of deep, uncomprehending sadness is common in survivor narratives, for bombing, besides killing people indiscriminately, destroys all that is familiar and valuable. "It's incredibly sad to see a bombed bridge—a murderous action, for it destroys a link," Al-Radi comments. "The sight affects everyone who sees it; many people cry" (Al-Radi 223). Sometimes the incomprehension amounts almost to an extreme inability to perceive the meaning of what is there. Gellhorn writes from Madrid in 1937,

> An old woman had been standing by the door. She came in now. She took my arm and pulled at me to come closer to hear her. She said, very softly, as if she were telling me a secret, "Look at that, look at that, do you see, that is my home, that's where I live, there, what you see there." She looked at me as if I should deny it, with wide, puzzled, frightened eyes. I did not know what to say. "I cannot understand," she said slowly, hoping I would understand and explain; after all I was a foreigner, I was younger than she, I had probably been to school, surely I could explain. "I do not understand," she said. "You see, it is my home." (Gellhorn 31)

Another woman, the front wall of her family's fifth floor apartment gone, the rooms exposed to wind and cold, the sewing machine and dishes smashed, the canary dead, was asked where they would live now. " 'But we will live here,' she said. 'Where else shall we go? This is our home, we have always lived here.' " (Gellhorn 30)

The disorientation affects animals, too. Al-Radi tells of stray dogs huddling together in her orchard during raids, howling plaintively; of birds flying upside down and in crazy patterns, dying by thousands; and of a huge number of dead flies one morning: "I wonder if the big explosions shocked them to death?" (Al-Radi 221).

These details are lost on strategists, of course. There would be no point to bomb cities if their inhabitants were *not* terrorized and demoralized. That is why it is done, after all. But the effectiveness of the strategy of bombing civilian centers depends not only on the victims being terrorized, but also on the bombers not engaging empathetically in their suffering. Strategists do indeed want to know what happens on the ground, to assess the effectiveness of their work. But the information they gather is filtered as military intelligence, not as empathetic engagement with the plight of the victims. The victims' reality indeed must be kept from sight. And so the history of warfare has a correlative history, that of techniques to prevent the perpetrators of the violence from truly seeing the results of their work. Making weapons effective at greater and greater distance is one such technique. Warrior comradeship is another. Trenchard's biographer comments on the feelings the early pilots had for the enemy:

> There was no malice in their ruthlessness. To see those one loved disappear or return dying and mutilated did not excite generosity; but hatred of the Germans was rare, and of this Trenchard approved. Values were changing with the increased mechanization of warfare; but while Trenchard remained in command wreaths and messages of condolence, which must read strangely to our later, more callous generation, continued to be dropped on either side of the line as spontaneous tributes to adversaries who had died bravely. (Boyle 215)

But such feeling extended only to other fliers. Trenchard himself wrote of the policy of having plenty of reserve pilots ready to take the place of casualties at once, so that there would never be empty chairs at meals:

> I always looked on the [Royal Flying Corps] as a family. I tried to put myself in the others' places and to consider the feelings of those who flew as if they had been my own. If as an ordinary pilot you see no vacant places around you, the tendency is to brood less on the fate of friends who have gone for ever. Instead your mind is taken up with buying drinks for the newcomers and making them feel at home. It was a matter of pride and human understanding. (Boyle 190)

Trenchard's pathologically limited ability to "consider the feelings" of others may make him an effective military leader, but it is a pathology nevertheless. Recognizing only the interests of your own group (of fliers or of fellow citizens) can lead to outright denial of the suffering of others. Al-Radi's diary contains this entry:

> I can't bear to hear the Voice of America going on about American children and how they are being affected by this war. Mrs Bush, the so-called humane partner in that marriage, had the gall to comfort a group of American school kids by saying, "Don't worry, it's far away." (Al-Radi 229)

Sometimes, though, it is not "far away": consider, for example, the revelation that government weapons testers in the 1940s and 1950s deliberately and repeatedly exposed soldiers and sailors to radiation and fallout from the nuclear weapons they set off in the southwestern deserts and Pacific Ocean. Griffin interviewed people who witnessed this testing close up, were injured, got sick, saw others die or disappear, and who now suffer the delayed injuries, the radiation and chemical-induced cancers which occur so long after exposure their causes cannot be proved—and then were disbelieved, discredited, denied compensation for health care. It has become one of our most familiar scripts: the reflexive denial by bureaucrats of any facts which might yield negative public perceptions or civil liability.

Perhaps worse is the fear engendered in those who would attempt to bring such matters to the public: Griffin interviewed a would-be whistle-blower who worked at the Oak Ridge weapons plant. She had discovered numerous safety violations and had been intimidated into suppressing her report. What could she do? She needed the job, she might not be believed if she went public, and she feared for her safety if she did. Was it the Nixon administration which contributed the word "coverup" to our public vocabulary? No matter: we have had the thing itself from time immemorial.

But government face-saving has a larger context. In Griffin's text the voices of warmakers and mass murderers merge with the voices of dysfunctional families; the impersonal, detached bureaucratic voice hiding behind plausible deniability works the same way as unspoken experience, atrocity carefully hidden from view, the gaps in family history or personal life.

"I do not see my life as separate from history," Griffin says. "In my mind family secrets mingle with the secrets of statesmen and bombers" (Griffin 1992: 4). Later she comments, "We are not used to associating our private lives with public events. Yet the histories of families cannot be separated from the histories of nations. To divide them is part of our denial" (11).

The private life of war means: the ways war-thinking, with its denials and avoidance of truth, pervades our own innermost lives when we do the same things as individuals. Griffin writes of her own family's secrets and their effects: her grandmother ostracized and abandoned and never spoken of for some transgression which broke up her father's family; secret alcoholism; dark hints of damaged relationships. The ways families and individuals face or refuse to face their most essential truths are the same as the ways whole communities, nations, face or refuse to face their reality.

But also: ideas of virtue, masculinity and femininity, courage, patriotism, and validated sacrifice display themselves in our literature, movies, and public spaces. Jean Bethke Elshtain speaks of this eloquently in her account of her growing up and education as a political theorist. The standard images of women as "beautiful souls" and men as "just warriors" work, she shows, to enforce the culture's dominant vision of warfare as a nasty but necessary masculine business carried out to protect those left behind—the women and children. But Elshtain also recounts her developing awareness of the disparity between so-called political realism as taught in political science departments and resistance to the militarism that defines patriotic duty exclusively as unquestioned obedience to government policy. Contemplating her son's resistance to militarism, yet "mindful of all the arguments concerning citizen duty and obligation and commitment to the common good," she struggles to find "a voice through which to traverse the terrain between particular loves and loyalties and public duties" (Elshtain 1987: 42). The cultural messages seem dichotomous, and ultimately, abstract, distanced from the experiences which could give them depth.

Our predicament is that to try to stand outside our history, to "be pacifist," and class ourselves as separate from the strategists and politicians and manufacturers, etc., creates another false standpoint. A central theme of Griffin's work is that we all, as members of a common culture, participate in these shared patterns of ideation: detachment, denial, domination. Our education systems, our public media, our political campaigns, all militate against embodied knowledge and construct an atomized social reality in which disconnection is normative. Thus to develop "wholesight" is first to discover our own individual participation in these shared patterns. Individual self-recognition is not enough, of course. The work of cultural reconstruction must follow if the forms of consciousness that make modern war-making possible and even perhaps inevitable are to be transcended.

Reading Griffin, I repeatedly meet myself in unexpected places, places I never thought to go. After all, I protest, I do not use pornography; I am not a rapist; I refused to go to war . . . but even as stones, Griffin tells us, record all that happens to them, the defacing flame and each drop of water, so do we all record denied experiences, covert patterns of thought, the subtle influences of our surroundings. We are all in this together. "Liberation" may help us to see what we are, but the idea that any of us is exempt from the tropes of culture and family is another denial.

REFERENCES

Al-Radi, Nuha. 1992. "Baghdad diary." *Granta* 42:211–37.

Arendt, Hannah. 1963. *Eichmann in Jerusalem: A report on the banality of evil.* New York: Viking.

Boyle, Andrew. 1962. *Trenchard.* London: Collins.

Dyson, Freeman. 1979. *Disturbing the universe.* New York: Harper and Row.

Elshtain, Jean Bethke. 1987. *Women and war.* New York: Basic Books.

Gellhorn, Martha. 1988. *The face of war.* Rev. ed. New York: Atlantic Monthly Press.

Griffin, Susan. 1978. *Woman and nature: The roaring inside her.* New York: Harper and Row.

———. 1981. *Pornography and silence: Culture's revenge against nature.* New York: Harper and Row.

———. 1982a. The way of all ideology. In *Made from this earth: An anthology of writings.* New York: Harper and Row.

———. 1982b. Sadism and catharsis: The treatment is the disease. In *Made from this earth: An anthology of writings.* New York: Harper and Row.

———. 1986. *Rape, the politics of consciousness.* 3rd. ed. rev. New York: Harper and Row.

———. 1990. Curves along the road. In *Reweaving the world,* ed. Irene Diamond and Gloria Feman Orenstein. San Francisco: Sierra Club.

———. 1992. *A chorus of stones: The private life of war.* New York: Doubleday.

Palmer, Parker J. 1983. *To Know as we are known: A spirituality of education.* San Francisco: Harper and Row.

Percy, Walker. 1981. *Love in the ruins.* New York: Avon/Bard.

The Psychology of Tyranny: Wollstonecraft and Woolf on the Gendered Dimension of War

BARBARA ANDREW

In this essay, by fixing initially on the critiques of war provided by Mary Wollstonecraft and Virginia Woolf, I examine how gender constructs promote and participate in the psychological conditions necessary for war. Wollstonecraft and Woolf focus not on the standard, macho image of the soldier, but on the effeminacy of the soldier. This disruptive reversal of the standard gender stereotype is part of the criticism of gender construction in which both authors engage. The disruption leads both writers to question all hierarchy, especially in the military and the family. With the aid of psychoanalytic theory, Woolf expands Wollstonecraft's criticism of hierarchy and relates the tyranny of the family to the tyranny of war. This analysis leads to an understanding of what I will define as the psychology of tyranny. The psychology of tyranny creates the psychological conditions necessary for war, a phenomenon that can be changed only through feminist reinterpretation of culture.

I. THE AUTHORS' SIMILARITIES

The connection between Wollstonecraft's and Woolf's work on war may initially seem unclear. When the two authors are compared, it is usually in regard to their arguments for women's education. Woolf wrote an essay about Wollstonecraft's life ("Four Figures" [1932] 1986), but this still does not lead to a connection in their political theories. Perhaps as a clue that she had Wollstonecraft's work in mind, Woolf, in *Three Guineas* ([1938] 1966), quotes but does not cite the well-known last line of Wollstonecraft's *Mary* ([1788]

Hypatia vol. 9, no. 2 (Spring 1994) © by Barbara Andrew

1976): In heaven "there is neither marrying, nor giving in marriage" (Wollstonecraft 1976, 68; Woolf 1966, 52).[1] Both authors are interested in women's freedom, rights and opportunities. My intention is to show that their political critiques of patriarchal virtue and domination coincide and that Wollstonecraft's work (in A Vindication of the Rights of Woman, [1792] 1988) launches some of Woolf's political themes (in Three Guineas and "Thoughts on Peace in an Air Raid" [1942] 1970).

The political theme of most importance for my purposes is Wollstonecraft's and Woolf's critiques of domination in the family and its relation to war. My phrase "the psychology of tyranny" designates what I identify in Wollstonecraft's and Woolf's work as a common claim concerning a major cause of war. Wollstonecraft and Woolf each claim that private life, its attachments and tyrannies, affects public life. Private tyranny provides an example or, perhaps, an unconscious paradigm for the domination and greed which lead to war. In addition, these private tyrannies reflect patriarchy and the cultural valuation of heroic virtues and war. Patriarchal families teach these virtues, and hence, create the psychological conditions that encourage war.

Women must act out femininity differently for families to change. Both Wollstonecraft and Woolf argue that femininity, for the most part, is socially constructed, and they see one's class as a determining factor in the construction of femininity. Each perceives her audience to be middle-class women and men. Both authors hope to convince middle-class women to change, and argue that middle-class women are responsible for furthering their own liberation and capable of reversing the destructiveness of patriarchal society. Wollstonecraft refers to her audience as "women of the middle classes." She desired a "revolution in female manners" from the women of her own class but undoubtedly wanted the men of her class to read her treatise as well. Woolf discusses how "the daughters of educated men," the daughters or sisters of bourgeois men, can prevent war. The daughters of educated men, Woolf points out, cannot be bourgeois themselves as they have little access to capital and lack the legal right to own property (Woolf 1966, 146). Woolf shows how women of her class can influence changes in social structure, through education, professional employment, and indifference to patriarchal heroism.

Both authors wrote their works in the historical contexts of war and revolution. A Vindication of the Rights of Woman is often characterized as a response to the reformation of the French educational system after the Revolution, or as a critique and expansion of liberal political arguments of the time.[2] Wollstonecraft also wanted more; she calls for a radical restructuring of society which would include women in all facets of public life. Although Wollstonecraft supported the French Revolution, she abhorred its violence. A war fought to defend one's country from invasion is the only justifiable war for Wollstonecraft. She writes that she wishes men would turn their bayonets into pruning hooks, that is, that men would give up war (Wollstonecraft 1988, 146). Analogously, war is a major theme in Woolf's work. Woolf intended to show that patriarchy, fascism, and war are related in motivation. Woolf saw herself as a cultural critic and saw her writing as counter to the patriarchal culture that surrounded her. Jane Marcus argues convincingly that Woolf sought to rewrite cultural myths, to reinterpret our understanding of culture through nonpatriarchal stories (Marcus 1987). For example, consider Woolf's use of the term "fascism." Woolf's argument is that the fascism of Mussolini and Hitler uses the same logic of domination as the fascism between the sexes: the fascism of the patriarchal family in which the father-husband rules completely and forcibly quells any signs of insurrection. *Three Guineas* responds directly to the fascism of Hitler and Mussolini as well as the fascism men display in oppressing women. Woolf's work tries to answer the question "How does fascism arise?" as well as the question "How can we prevent war?"

In some instances Wollstonecraft and Woolf develop similar arguments. In others, Woolf expands Wollstonecraft's arguments to the point where she comes to a different conclusion than Wollstonecraft. They are most in agreement in their discussion of the soldier.

II. SOLDIERS AND WOMEN: MASCULINE VIRTUE

Both Wollstonecraft and Woolf discuss masculine or "manly" virtues. For Wollstonecraft, manly virtues are positive, heroic virtues, such as reason, moral rectitude, strength, and courage. "Womanly" virtues are not virtues at all, but instead are sins or silliness, such as vanity and the love of physical beauty. The reversal Wollstonecraft makes is to accuse soldiers of acting womanly. Woolf will agree with this accusation but will take it further, accusing heroic virtues of being a cause of fascism between the sexes.

Wollstonecraft takes for granted that there is such a thing as true heroism and that it is desirable. She argues that one's character is actually formed, in part, by one's profession but denies that war educates men in heroic virtues. She asserts that most wars are fought for financial gain and so valorize greed. Such wars teach cunning and artifice, the skills women use to seduce men, not the strength of true heroism. Professional soldiers are taught to obey orders, just as women are taught to please. Standing armies therefore do not produce resolute, robust men, but vain, conniving ones. Wollstonecraft maintains that just as a soldier's air of fashion is a badge of slavery to a despotic profession (Wollstonecraft 1988, 17), so is beauty an illegitimate power a woman receives by debasing herself (Wollstonecraft 1988, 21). The professional military makes soldiers effeminate, not strong or independent.

According to Wollstonecraft, "Independence is the grand blessing of life" (1988, 5). Wollstonecraft here refers to both economic independence and independent opinion. Education is the key to both. Wollstonecraft argues for the necessity of education, but by education she means not only schooling, but social understanding or overall refinement. Soldiers, like middle-class women, lack education. Soldiers are sent into the world without amassing knowledge through intellectual pursuits which might develop into moral virtue, understanding, and judgment; instead, they collect information and mannerisms from casual observation.

Woolf, like Wollstonecraft, values independent thought. Woolf argues that only persons with independent thought can develop a critique of war. Formal education and economic independence are necessary for independent thought to develop, as is the aversion of false loyalties, that is, loyalties which encourage greed, territoriality, and the love of possession. Because men's schools and professions encourage false loyalties, Woolf argues that only educated, economically independent women who do not have such loyalties can hope to develop the independent opinion that will discourage war. This conclusion shows an interesting problem with Woolf's analysis: bourgeois men are socially situated so that it is practically impossible for them to discourage war, or to be pacifists. Yet, some bourgeois men were pacifists.

Woolf agrees with Wollstonecraft that soldiers use dress to display their physical achievements. She accuses soldiers of parading in uniform to excite envy, jealousy, and competition among men. Woolf goes further than Wollstonecraft when she asserts that all professional dress is a display of vanity and hierarchy. The soldier and the student, as well as the commanding officer and the professor, exhibit their rank through their dress.

Woolf is concerned with soldiers' internal motivations as well as their external displays of honor. In "Thoughts on Peace in an Air Raid," Woolf writes that getting rid of weapons will not be enough to change the young man who "is driven by voices in himself—ancient instincts, instincts fostered and cherished by education and tradition" (Woolf 1970, 246). Woolf does not mean that these ancient instincts are inherent, but rather that men's socialization, the determination of masculinity as an aggressive, judgmental, combative personality, is centuries old. What Woolf means by instinct is something more like cultural memory, the stereotypes defining masculinity reinforced by positive moral valuations in schools, professions, and literature. It is this cultural memory that Woolf wants to rewrite.

Both Wollstonecraft and Woolf see middle-class women and soldiers as co-conspirators in their own subordination because they embrace the illegitimate power afforded by beauty and gallantry. This power is illegitimate because it is not based on rights and when gained is part of the replication of the psychology of tyranny. Middle-class women and soldiers are more concerned with appearances, with being thought of as beautiful and virtuous, than with truth or freedom. Wollstonecraft, as an Enlightenment thinker, values truth and freedom as self-evidently good. Woolf values freedom because only free thought can discourage war. Vanity encourages soldiers and middle-class women to accept a dictator's kudos, thus also to accept the domination and power he wields.

III. SOCIETAL HIERARCHY: THE TYRANNY OF UNNATURAL DISTINCTIONS

The distinctions between women's and men's intellectual abilities and political rights are what Wollstonecraft calls "unnatural distinctions." Unnatural distinctions are those which are not inherent; they are historically and socially constructed, and they subordinate one group of persons to another. Unnatural distinctions include race, class, and rank (which wealthy families purchased for sons in the military). These unnatural distinctions separate people by hereditary factors rather than by merit, and are always harmful according to Wollstonecraft. "Natural distinctions" are inherent and do not subordinate one group of persons to another. A natural distinction between women and men according to Wollstonecraft is the role women play as mothers, especially providing physical care for infants, such as breast-feeding. This natural distinction does not subordinate women to men; it is a worthy, respectable fulfillment of a human duty. Like Socrates in Plato's *Republic*, Wollstonecraft claims that men and women may have different duties but not different virtues. Wollstonecraft allows that mothering is woman's most important role, but she also argues that women must be educated in order to perform it properly and produce patriotic children and that this role should not exclude women from other civic duties. Wollstonecraft's position, however, suggests that women and men properly have different functions, limiting the extent to which she can see femininity as a social construction and, ultimately, curtailing her criticism of social institutions.

Wollstonecraft locates political oppression in the hierarchical organization of society and the unnatural distinctions in hierarchy. She writes that "public spirit must be nurtured by private virtue, or it will resemble the factitious sentiment which makes women careful to preserve their reputation and men their honor" (Wollstonecraft 1988, 140). Private virtue, not a conceited show of sentiment for the sake of reputation, inspires a just society. Wollstonecraft attributes the lack of ethical integrity in her society to men's domination of women, another unnatural distinction. She contends that personal relationships, those between family members, friends, house owner and house servant, are a basic structure of society, and that these relationships also serve as a foundation or a model for public relationships and social institutions. But the public and private worlds are not as distinct as they seem. The private world educates us about how to form virtuous relationships. Without this education, we form unprincipled relationships in both realms, and will be especially susceptible to allowing public vice to corrupt our private actions. (Woolf will make a similar argument in *Three Guineas*.)

The relation of power among men in the military is an example of a lack of public virtue. Wollstonecraft asserts that the heads of government themselves do not fight and so never risk their own lives to maintain their power. Common men, however, can be conscripted against their will to fight wars to protect the interests of the wealthy (Wollstonecraft 1988, 143–4). This unequal relationship mirrors the power differences in men's relationships with women.

Wollstonecraft relates her concerns about war as a profession to her philosophical claims about economic and intellectual independence. Economic dependence fosters intellectual dependence because a dependent must agree with his provider to protect his livelihood. Oppressors want "meretricious slaves," not free thinkers. Wollstonecraft argues that all virtue is based on independence because of her Kantian notion that duties are binding only if developed through reason. Wollstonecraft, however, considers subordination itself to be an evil as it denies independence and consequently denies virtue from developing in the course of making moral decisions. A social status in life which refuses one this decision-making capacity effectively keeps one from being virtuous. She contends that "every profession, in which great subordination of rank constitutes its power, is highly injurious to morality. A standing army, for instance, is incompatible with freedom; because subordination and rigor are the very sinews of military discipline; and despotism is necessary to give vigor to enterprises that one will directs" (Wollstonecraft 1988, 17). Commanding soldiers behave as tyrants because their underlings must obey them and cannot act without their orders. A standing army, therefore, necessarily constitutes a group of people who practice and accept systematic tyranny, and this group of people is supported by the nation. For Wollstonecraft, any profession that operates with such vast power differentials corrupts society, and to hold such a system in esteem, as the government does with the military, is to sanction despotism.

Like Wollstonecraft, Woolf is also concerned with the way professions shape personalities. Bourgeois men's professions make them covetous of their wealth and territorial about the skills that make their money. Woolf identifies the professions as training grounds or arenas of exhibition for men's possessiveness, allegiances, selfishness, and pride: the same characteristics that perpetuate wars.

Wollstonecraft sees social hierarchies as interconnected systems of oppression, while Woolf argues that sexism is the root of oppression.[3] While Wollstonecraft argues that societal hierarchies are similar in form, and that sexism in the family is one model of domination and subordination, she does not claim that sexism *causes* other hierarchies. Rather, various examples of private domination teach public domination. Woolf, however, asserts that men's private tyrannies *cause* their public tyrannies. Woolf maintains that the paradigm of masculinity for educated men is the image of the tyrant, and that this image of man "suggests that the public and private worlds are inseparably connected; that the tyrannies and servilities of one are the tyrannies and servilities of the other" (Woolf 1966, 142). When this connection of worlds is misunderstood, Woolf's criticism of men's institutions is misconstrued. For example, Quentin Bell wrote of *Three Guineas*, "What really seemed wrong with the book—and I am speaking here of my own reaction at the time—was the attempt to involve a discussion of women's rights with the far more agonizing and immediate question of what we were to do in order to meet the ever-growing menace of Fascism and war" (Bell 1972 vol. 2, 205). One wants to ask, of course, more agonizing and immediate to whom? What Bell fails to understand is the central claim of *Three Guineas*: that the warring, fascist mentality explicitly operates in men's oppression of women, and that this mentality is a condition for war.[4]

IV. Linking women's oppression to war: the infantile fixation

Wollstonecraft provides an important first step in clarifying the relation between women's oppression and war with her characterization of natural and unnatural distinctions. She shows that unnatural distinctions of rank between men and women and among military men are based on the same corrupt notions. Her discussion of women's attempt to enslave men through seduction helps articulate a psychological understanding of tyranny. Wollstonecraft does not possess the insights of psychoanalytic thought, but she does argue that fathers are tyrants and that their oppression of their wives and daughters degrades both men and women and precludes the possibility of a free society.

Woolf's analysis goes further in explaining the psychology of tyranny. For Woolf, women's participation in any war efforts defeats women's long-term interests of gaining recognition as equals or of promoting Woolf's ideal of men and women working together. Men argue that they fight to protect women, the country we live in, and our bodies. Woolf argues that all of these claims are false (Woolf 1966, 107–9). Women have been treated as slaves for most of history by most countries. Women did not have the same citizenship status as men. Woolf calls the daughters of educated men who want to stop war "outsiders." Outsiders will not give in to men's claims about protecting women, but will instead respond with indifference. Woolf writes that an outsider would say

> "If you insist upon fighting to protect me, or 'our' country, let it be understood, soberly and rationally between us, that you are fighting to gratify a sex instinct which I cannot share; to procure benefits which I have not shared and probably will not share; but not to gratify my instincts, or to protect myself or my country. For," the outsider will say, "in fact, as a woman, I have no country. As a woman I want no country. As a woman my country is the whole world." (Woolf 1966, 108–9)

In this brilliant passage Woolf clearly demarcates the boundaries which men can no longer cross for her and for women who agree with her. Although women are affected by the hardships of war, war is never truly fought in our interest. Even when men do claim to protect us through war, in fact, they are only exercising their ownership over us through that protection. As Woolf suggests, by asking us to join them or to assent to their wars, men ask us to give up our own agency, to support an effort which makes us protected objects or a warrior's bounty, which makes us Other. Woolf refuses to be treated as a citizen or as a woman in need of protection, and, in doing so, refuses any justification for war based on protecting women. This is a strong rejection of the construction of femininity. Woolf rejects the patriarchal notion of femininity, of woman as coveted object and protected possession. Through this rejection, Woolf refuses to be subordinated to patriarchy, and she refuses to obey the patriarchal injunction to replicate the psychology of tyranny.

Woolf uses the Freudian notion of infantile fixation to explain how men's emotional need to keep women inferior is based on a unconscious, nonrational sex taboo (Woolf 1966, 126). By the term "infantile fixation" Woolf refers to an experience in infancy, usually during what Freud termed the Oedipus phase, that becomes unconsciously fixed in one's memory.[5] Here Woolf attempts to rewrite cultural history. The Oedipus complex is a masculinist, or a patriarchal, reading of Greek myth onto psychoanalytic theory; therefore, it is a patriarchal interpretation of culture. In Freud's reading of the Oedipus myth, the action is between father and son. The mother, Jocasta, is objectified, a possession the son wants but is denied by his father's superior strength (in the Oedipus complex). Woolf proposes that men's infantile fixations with their mothers motivate them to dominate and control women. This infantile fixation results in men's anger at women's attempts to be equal and women's fear of men's reprisal to their actions. Women fear men's criticism of or anger in response to women's independent actions, even if the women are financially independent from men. Consequently, women are less likely to state their independent opinions because they fear men's anger and violence.

To further Woolf's project of rewriting culture, I suggest using her implications regarding infantile fixation to name men's dominating response to women's independent opinions "the Creon complex." Sophocles' play *Antigone* seems to be a paradigm for how Woolf employs the concept of infantile fixation. Like Creon, the educated man is a dictator who sets his own laws and insists that they be followed regardless of their lack of wisdom or justice. The daughter who rebels against unjust or immoral laws must, like Antigone, be silenced. Antigone is Creon's niece and potential daughter-in-law, but she is Oedipus's daughter, and she provides the link for understanding the position of women and the independent opinion formed from the daughter's vantage point. Antigone acts against the laws of the state because those laws violate her human duties. Creon, overconfident with his power, ignores the significance of those human duties. In his subordination of women, the overconfident man's morality, his superego, adheres only to the power of the state and not to other moral codes or attachments. Boys' disappointments in their erotic attachments to their mothers lead them not only to form superegos (the Oedipus complex), but also to attempt to dominate and control women (the Creon complex). This system of hierarchy and repression is reminiscent of Wollstonecraft's description of the army. The commanding officer rules over the soldiers and squashes any sign of insurrection. Woolf implies that allegiance to this infantile fixation is part of what makes men fight wars.

> And Creon we read brought ruin on his house, and scattered the land with the bodies of the dead. It seems, Sir, as we listen to the voices of the past, as if we were looking at the photograph again, at the picture of dead bodies and ruined houses that the Spanish Government sends us almost weekly. Things repeat themselves it seems. Pictures and voices are the same today as they were 2,000 years ago. (Woolf 1966, 141)

Our cultural interpretation of masculinity has not evolved in the last two thousand years. Masculinity is equated with tyranny for men of power. Oedipus is unaware of his family, and Creon ignores his duty to them. Both cases bring destruction and create the psychological conditions necessary for war. Rather than listen to a daughter's wisdom, men fight wars to maintain masculine identity and independence. The Creon complex manifests itself in men's tyranny and dictatorships.[6] The need to control women, to not be ruled by them, results in women's deaths and sometimes in war. In Sophocles' play Creon, in his own eyes, can maintain his power only if it remains unchallenged. Creon considers any question of his judgment to be a challenge to his authority. Antigone is not the only one who attempts to tell Creon of his mistakes in judgment. The guard, Creon's son Haemon, and the prophet Tiresias also try to convince Creon of his mistake. Creon, the ruler who will not take counsel from women or from men he believes he should have power over, causes the ruin of his family and the death of those around him.

Fighting wars is an instantiation of the image of virility and masculinity bolstered by the nonrational sex taboo Woolf discusses. Hence, Woolf holds that patriarchal families are the nucleus of a fascist mentality. She suggests that war is part of the infantile fixation and that this fixation initiates habits in the family that lead to despotism. Woolf maintains that the desire to dominate, what I have defined as the Creon complex, is not only found in dictators such as Hitler and Mussolini but that it is found in "Man himself, the quintessence of virility, the perfect type of which all the others are imperfect adumbrations" (Woolf 1966, 142). Tyranny permeates the patriarchal paradigm of Man and our cultural interpretation of masculinity.

If the dictator is the patriarchal paradigm of Man, then the slave is the patriarchal paradigm of Woman. For Woolf (and for Wollstonecraft), the slave is the woman who attempts to dominate and control men through seduction but cannot dominate them because she has no legitimate power. Ismene, Antigone's sister, who did not bury her brother because she was afraid of Creon's wrath, is silenced and immobilized. She becomes what Wollstonecraft calls a meretricious slave. Antigone, the daughter who rebels against the tyrant, is a nonpatriarchal paradigm for woman.[7] Women must choose either to participate in tyranny by attempting to dominate men, to accept silence and inaction because of the Creon complex, or to risk death, because those who speak and act against men's dictatorship are killed. Women are silenced and enslaved by their fear of male violence.

V. THE ROLE OF MOTHERING IN GENDER CONSTRUCTION

Woolf specifically considers mothering and the emergence of fascism and dictators in "Thoughts on Peace in an Air Raid." She writes,

> Let us try to drag up into consciousness the subconscious Hitlerism that holds us down. It is the desire for aggression; the desire to dominate and enslave. Even in the darkness we can see that made visible. We can see shop windows blazing; and women gazing; painted women; dressed-up women; women with crimson lips and crimson fingernails. They are slaves who are trying to enslave. If we could free ourselves from slavery we should free men from tyranny. Hitlers are bred by slaves. (Woolf 1970, 245)

Here we see the replication of the psychology of tyranny. Woolf claims that patriarchal men become slaves to the desire of being a dictator. Men can only be free if women are emancipated, because it is only in giving up their domination of women that men will stop being tyrants. The tyrant is never free, according to Woolf (or Hegel or Plato). Women in patriarchal societies who do not rebel against patriarchy become slaves to their fear of men. Dictators, Woolf declares, are bred by slaves. Woolf points to the problem of mothering, the problem of the mother-child relationship and the dynamics of submission and oppression.

Men and women enact the roles of dictator and slaves because of what Woolf calls subconscious Hitlerism, the desire for aggression and domination. Subconscious Hitlerism is best understood in relation to infantile fixation. Woolf's novels often deal with the complex relation to the mother, the mother's generative and destructive powers. Woolf suggests that there is a solution to women's oppression, namely, that women should give up possessive mothering, or the exclusive right to the psychological bonding with children, for the sake of humanity and peace. Woolf claims that men who have more access to "creative feelings," the emotional bonding of the mother-infant relationship and the creative force of that bonding, the generative feelings expressed in art and through friendships, would be willing to give up being soldiers and fighting wars. Woolf argues that men need to be "man-womanly" and women need to be "woman-manly" (Woolf 1957, 102). Relinquishing patriarchal paradigms requires renouncing the desire for domination and possession exercised through patriarchal soldiering and mothering, and finding new ways to act out our genders.

Woolf's understanding of mothering foreshadows the theories of contemporary feminists. Like Dorothy Dinnerstein and Nancy Chodorow, Woolf suggests that women's exclusive charge over infants creates an immense need for the love of the mother (expressed through the nourishment of the breast) and hatred and fear of the mother because of her power and control.[8] Male children must separate from the mother, and this problematic process of separation creates a desire in adult males to dominate and control women, or to demand that women serve as mirrors reflecting men at twice their natural size (Woolf 1957, 35). These theories, and the ones they have inspired, are the future to which Woolf points, in which mothers give up possessive care and men learn to love creative teaching of children.

The connection between the role of Antigone, a nonpatriarchal notion of mothering, and peacemaking has developed in striking ways. Sara Ruddick argues that the practice of mothering teaches peacemaking skills that should be transferred to caring for the State. Jean Bethke Elshtain submits that Ruddick is one of "Antigone's Daughters,"[9] as she is a theorist who recognizes the importance of the vantage point of the private sphere and its relation to the civil society. Although Elshtain does not note this, Ruddick is profoundly influenced by Woolf.

Woolf indicates the complexity of mothering, the painful psychological processes of separation and union with the mother. I have argued that her reading of identity formation can be understood as a critique of patriarchal culture and leads to the Creon complex. The Creon complex is a psychological paradigm that explains how tyranny evolves. The psychology of tyranny is the unconscious desire to control one another which is initially formed in infancy or childhood. Men become tyrants out of fear of losing access to women. Women who do not rebel like Antigone become slaves who try to enslave. This circle of oppression and domination is what I call the psychology of tyranny.

There are at least two points in *Three Guineas* where Woolf explicitly compares soldiers and mothers. Early in the text, when discussing men's vanity in dress, Woolf mocks the wearing of ribbons or medals as signs of honor. "A woman who advertised her motherhood by a tuft of horsehair on the left shoulder would scarcely, you will agree, be a venerable object" (Woolf 1966, 21). Women are not allowed to advertise their prowess in producing children. Woolf's point is not that women should advertise, but that men do advertise their virility through their display of rank, and that this advertisement is ridiculous. In the second comparison Woolf argues that economic incentives should be provided for women to enter the field of mothering and compares this to recent pay increases for soldiers. If we want better mothers, we should give them higher rewards (Woolf 1966, 111). Woolf argues that paying women to bear children would make motherhood a more respectable profession and provide women with more opportunities for independence and hence a greater ability to form independent opinion. Woolf's comparison shows that soldiers and mothers are not given the same access to societal rewards. Mothering is a social, not a natural, role. For Woolf, women can refuse to mother and still be women, although the meaning of being a woman might change.

For Wollstonecraft, mothering has little to do with peace or war. Wollstonecraft values women's roles as mothers, although she argues forcefully against compelling women to be wives and mothers. Mothering is not problematic for Wollstonecraft; fathering is. She identifies men who participate in unnatural distinctions as dictators. She contends that children learn tyranny from the unequal relation their parents exhibit and from being allowed to treat tutors and servants with derision. According to Wollstonecraft, proper, virtuous mothering does not create the warring instinct; rather, it is the domination and subordination in men's relations to others that recycles those same instincts. She did not see, and could not see given her historical period, how mothering reproduces the psychology of tyranny. For Wollstonecraft, the psychology of tyranny is formulated by men's (fathers') oppression of women (mothers).

VI. Gender construction and styles of rebellion

Giving up mothering is not Woolf's only suggestion for defeating the psychology of tyranny. Another mode of rebellion is the transitional separatism Woolf creates with the Outsiders' Society, a hypothetical club for the daughters of educated men. Woolf claims that the daughters of educated men should not join men's societies for preventing war because to do so would mean merging women's identity with men's. Instead, the daughters of educated men should maintain the different vantage point subordination affords by being indifferent to men's war-ring actions. The Outsiders' Society names women as a political class, a step which allows women to argue for rights but can be discarded when no longer necessary. Though separatism is in conflict with the idea of men and women working together that we also see in *Three Guineas*, this separatism is a historical necessity, a transitional step meant to encourage men to throw off the limiting bonds of patriarchal masculinity. Women's indifference to men, just as a mother's indifference to a child, makes men question their identity. This is precisely the effect Woolf wants.

Woolf's suggestion that women separate from men and show indifference to men's vanity demonstrates her ambivalence to heterosexuality, or, at least, her doubt of the naturalness of heterosexuality. Woolf's criticism of gender construc-tion leads her to an idea of universal humanitarianism rather than to a "prolif-eration of genders."[10] (Although we are still situated in our sex; we are *woman-manly*.) Wollstonecraft does not have the same kind of gender criticism. It is clear that heterosexuality is the only natural state for Wollstonecraft, yet she wishes to see all differences between men and women eliminated besides those they show as lovers and as parents. For Wollstonecraft, some part of gender is biological, limiting her cultural criticism of social institutions and gender construction.

VII. Conclusion

Wollstonecraft needs to convince men to include women in the public realm of rights and makes her arguments based on her trust in reason. She uses male philosophers' accepted premises to conclude that women should be educated and expects men to be compelled by the logic of her argument. Woolf is much more elusive, and her arguments persuade or seduce rather than convince. While Woolf argues for women's inclusion in the professions and for women's education, she wants to maintain segregation in women's colleges and sometimes professes that women should keep their distance from men. We could say that these dif-ferences in presentation have to do with the fact that Woolf is simply a more sophisticated theorist than Wollstonecraft, or that it has to do with their cri-tiques of gender. Another possibility is that the authors' notions of reason differ because of the response each expects from her audience. In *A Vindication of the Rights of Men*, Wollstonecraft attacks Edmund Burke's use of seductive language and superficial wit, claiming that the attractiveness of the rhetoric hides the true meaning of his arguments. Wollstonecraft was committed to arguing straightfor-wardly and she expects men to take her arguments seriously as long as she argues well. Woolf is much more cynical and argues as if she knows that her readers must be seduced. With the advent of modernism and Freudianism, Woolf exists in a world that views reason with more complexity and less respect. Knowing that men will not be persuaded by her argument if she makes her most important claims first, she argues to those claims rather than from them. Her strongest claim, that patriarchal families are the nest of fascism, is never explicitly stated but is indicated by her comparison of Sophocles' Creon to the Spanish government and the implication that Woolf plays the part of Antigone in the analogy.

In their arguments, both Woolf and Wollstonecraft position themselves as Antigone in the sense that each addresses her essay to men and demands that these male authority figures rethink their laws, proclamations, and customs. Wollstonecraft begins her essay with a letter to Charles Maurice de Talleyrand-Périgord, who successfully convinced the French Assembly to create a compulsory, free system of national education for men. Woolf addresses *Three Guineas* to a man who requested a guinea for a society to prevent war. Wollstonecraft is participating in the common genre of letter-writing of her historical period.[11] Woolf uses the form of the letter to engage her reader in a dialogue, in which she takes on the patriarchal view point by point. The letter also allows her to be informal and ironic: a Platonic device. She engrosses the reader through the reader's participation in the argument and through her humor. Both Wollstonecraft and Woolf argue against male authority; we might think of each as Antigone arguing with Creon. Conversely, it might be claimed that in addressing their texts to men, both ask the father's permission to argue, instead of criticizing him. Wollstonecraft and Woolf, however, seem closer to demanding or even prescribing change than requesting permission to voice their dissent. Like Antigone, both authors are sure they are right.

Wollstonecraft and Woolf agree that tyranny begins at home. Both argue that the roots of oppression are in the patriarchal family. In looking at Wollstonecraft's and Woolf's comparisons of soldiers and women, it seems clear that the conditions for war rely on particular constructions of masculinity and femininity. Wollstonecraft criticizes most reasons for war and some aspects of masculinity and femininity, thus viewing war and masculinity as alterable constructions. Yet, she is still bound to natural roles and so does not explicitly link mothering to the conditions for war. Woolf's more radical criticism leads her away from the idea of any natural role for women or for men. From Woolf's theory, we can identify the Creon complex and the psychology of tyranny.

Freeing ourselves from the psychology of tyranny is the way to peace. Wollstonecraft and Woolf are examples of feminist theorists who have removed themselves from replicating the psychology of tyranny. Their criticism is the beginning of a cultural reinterpretation, of an alternative understanding of our world that frees us from the desire for possession and domination, and enables us to envision a feminist peace politics.

NOTES

An earlier version of this essay was presented at the Eastern Division of the Society for Women in Philosophy, March 19–21, 1993 in Tampa, Florida. I have benefitted greatly from the generous comments of the editors, Karen J. Warren and Duane Cady, and the anonymous reviewers. I also wish to thank Eva Feder Kittay, Susan Merrill Squier, Bruce Milem, Jean Keller, Ellen Feder, Barbara

Leclerc, and Shari Stone for reading various versions of this essay and providing many helpful comments.

1. This quotation is also a reference to the New Testament, Matt. 22: 30.

2. In her recent study of Wollstonecraft, Virginia Sapiro (1992) has argued convincingly that the text is more radical and original than a mere addendum to liberal arguments and should be treated as a more encompassing work on political and moral theory. I hope my analysis shows the wideranging effects of Wollstonecraft's theory that Sapiro indicates.

3. Wollstonecraft appears to be a socialist feminist. In *Three Guineas*, Woolf seems to be a radical feminist because she argues that sexism causes other forms of oppression. Woolf's claims in her other works are closer to seeing systems of oppression as connected, not ranked.

4. Woolf is not alone in making this claim. Klaus Theweleit (1989) argues that German fascism is based in hatred and fear of women. Theweleit analyzes the writings of the *Freikorpsmen*, defeated German soldiers from World War I who fought against the German workers movement. Many of these men later became commanding officers in Hitler's army.

5. Woolf does not refer to Freud but to a Professor Grensted who wrote a report for the archbishop of the English church outlining the psychological reasons against appointing women prelates. Grensted's report argued that men's inability to be psychologically comfortable with women priests, because of a nonrational sex taboo based on an infantile fixation, was the only psychological reason to maintain the prohibition (Woolf 1966, 125–7).

6. I hope to use the Creon complex to give an explication of men's personality development which better explains the fascism between the sexes. I am suggesting an alternative cultural interpretation, not a new theory for clinical practice. My aim in this essay is only to show how Woolf's and Wollstonecraft's analyses lead to such an interpretation.

7. Of course, Woolf is not the only theorist to suggest Antigone as a paradigm for Woman in relation to the state. Besides Hegel, Jean Bethke Elshtain has recommended Antigone. For a full portrait of Antigone in culture representation and literature see George Steiner (1984).

8. I am referring here to Dinnerstein's *The Mermaid and the Minotaur* (1976) and Chodorow's *The Reproduction of Mothering* (1978). Dinnerstein and Chodorow's arguments are by no means identical; however, they do share this general claim. These two texts inspired a great many more; rather than reviewing the literature, I suggest that Woolf foresaw this type of analysis and inspired some of it herself.

9. See Elshtain's article by that name (Elshtain 1982). In that article, Elshtain also calls Jane Addams one of Antigone's daughters. She later names the Mothers of the Plaza de Mayo in Buenos Aires, Argentina as Antigone's daughters (Elshtain 1989).

10. This phrase is used by Judith Butler (1987) to describe what she views as the opposite solution to a world without gender.

11. For example, Burke presents *Reflections on the Revolution in France* (1955) as a letter to a friend and Wollstonecraft, in turn, addressed *A Vindication of the Rights of Men* (1989) as a letter to Burke.

REFERENCES

Abel, Elizabeth. 1989. (En)gendering history. In *Virginia Woolf and the Fictions of Psychoanalysis*. Chicago: University of Chicago Press.

Bell, Quentin. 1972. *Virginia Woolf*. New York: Harcourt Brace Jovanovich.

Benjamin, Jessica. 1980. Rational violence and erotic domination. In *The future of difference*, ed. Hester Eisenstein and Alice Jardine. New Brunswick: Rutgers University Press.

Burke, Edmund. 1955. *Reflections on the revolution in France*. Indianapolis: Bobbs-Merrill.

Butler, Judith. 1987. Variations on sex and gender. In *Feminism as critique*, ed. Seyla Benhabib and Drucilla Cornell. Minneapolis: University of Minnesota Press.

Card, Claudia. 1990. Gender and moral luck. In *Character, identity and morality*, ed. Owen Flanagan and Amelie Oksenberg Rorty. Cambridge, Massachusetts: MIT Press.

Chodorow, Nancy. 1978. *The reproduction of mothering*. Berkeley: University of California Press.

———. 1989. *Feminism and psychoanalytic theory*. New Haven: Yale University Press.

Cooper, Helen M., Adrienne Auslander Munich, and Susan Merrill Squier. 1989. *Arms and the woman: War, gender and literary representation*. Chapel Hill: University of North Carolina Press.

Dinnerstein, Dorothy. 1976. *The mermaid and the minotaur*. New York: Harper Perennial.

Elshtain, Jean Bethke. 1982. Antigone's daughters. *Democracy* 2(2): 46–59.

———. 1989. Antigone's daughters reconsidered: Continuing reflections on women, politics and power. In *Life-world and politics: Between modernity and postmodernity*, ed. Stephen K. White. Notre Dame: University of Notre Dame Press.

Freud, Sigmund. 1954. *The origins of psycho-analysis*, ed. Marie Bonaparte, Anna Freud and Ernst Kris. Trans. Eric Mosbacher and James Strachey. New York: Basic Books, Inc.

———. 1969. *An outline of psycho-analysis*. Ed. and trans. James Strachey. New York: W. W. Norton & Company.

Grimshaw, Jean. 1990. Mary Wollstonecraft and the tensions in feminist philosophy. In *Socialism, feminism and philosophy*, ed. Sean Sayers and Peter Osborne. New York: Routledge.

Hummel, Madeline M. 1977. From the common reader to the uncommon critic: *Three guineas* and the epistolary form. *Bulletin of the New York Public Library* 80(2): 151–57.

Hussey, Mark, ed. 1991. *Virginia Woolf and war*. Syracuse, New York: Syracuse University Press.

Johnson, Pauline. 1990. From Virginia Woolf to the postmoderns: Developments in a feminist aesthetic. In *Socialism, feminism and philosophy*, ed. Sean Sayers and Peter Osborne. New York: Routledge.

Kaplan, Cora. 1986. *Sea changes*. London: Verso.

Kelley, Gary. 1992. *Revolutionary feminism: The mind and career of Mary Wollstonecraft*. New York: Macmillan.

Marcus, Jane. 1987. *Virginia Woolf and the languages of patriarchy*. Bloomington: Indiana University Press.

Ruddick, Sara. 1989. *Maternal thinking*. New York: Ballantine Books.

Sapiro, Virginia. 1992. *A vindication of political virtue: The political theory of Mary Wollstonecraft*. Chicago: University of Chicago Press.

Silver, Brenda R. 1983. *Three guineas* before and after: Further answers to correspondents. In *Virginia Woolf: A feminist slant*, ed. Jane Marcus. Lincoln: University of Nebraska Press.

Sophocles. 1982. Antigone. In *The complete plays of Sophocles*. Ed. Moses Hadas. Trans. Sir Richard Claverhouse Jebb. New York: Bantam Books.

Squier, Susan. 1981. Mirroring and mothering: Reflections on the mirror encounter metaphor in Virginia Woolf's works. *Twentieth Century Literature* 27(3): 272–88.

Steiner, George. 1984. *Antigones*. New York: Oxford University Press.

Theweleit, Klaus. 1989. *Male fantasies*. Trans. Erica Carter and Chris Turner. Minneapolis: University of Minnesota Press.

Wollstonecraft, Mary. [1788] 1976. *Mary*. In *Mary and The wrongs of women*, ed. Gary Kelley. New York: Oxford.

———. [1792] 1988. *A vindication of the rights of woman*, ed. Carol H. Poston. New York: W. W. Norton & Company.

———. [1790] 1989. *A vindication of the rights of men*. In *The works of Mary Wollstonecraft*, vol. 5, ed. Janet Todd and Marilyn Butler. New York: New York University Press.

Woolf, Virginia. [1928] 1951. *Orlando*. New York: Harcourt Brace Jovanovich.

———. [1929] 1957. *A room of one's own*. New York: Harcourt Brace Jovanovich.

———. [1937] 1965. *The years*. New York: Harcourt Brace Jovanovich.

———. [1932] 1986. Four figures. In *The second common reader*, ed. Andrew McNellie. New York: Harcourt Brace Jovanovich.

———. [1938] 1966. *Three guineas*. New York: Harcourt Brace Jovanovich, Publishers.

———. [1942] 1970. Thoughts on peace in an air raid. In *The death of the moth and other essays*. New York: Harcourt Brace Jovanovich.

Unthinkable Fathering:
Connecting Incest and Nuclearism

JANE CAPUTI

Like the arms race during the Cold War, the incestuous
father is also out of control. He fails to honor his most basic
responsibility as a parent—to protect the child. . . .
His fathering is unthinkable.

      (Amy Estelle, "Incest and the Bomb: Surviving in the Nuclear Age.")

The cover of *Newsweek*, October 7,1991, focuses on the post-Cold War nuclear world order. It features a mushroom cloud. Inscribed over that cloud are the words "The Future of the Bomb." Underneath this heading are three questions: "Will Bush's Plan Work? Can We Trust the Soviets? What is Saddam Hiding?" This is fairly ordinary, weekly-news-magazine matter. Yet, the whole meaning of this communique changes when we factor in the blurb at the top of the page. Above the *Newsweek* logo, referring to another inside story, is the headline "Surviving Incest. Can Memories Be Trusted?" Elsewhere, I have argued that media messages, broadcast and print, are constructed via a process of flow (Caputi 1991). By this I mean that in order to apprehend the full meaning of any media text, we have to see it, literally, in its context. We have to take into account the influence of whatever precedes and follows it, whatever surrounds it. Essentially, this, or any, magazine cover is a complex package of interconnecting items which often must be read together in order to comprehend a total message. The covert message here is that there are profound bonds between incest and the Bomb.

Normative discourse denies such a connection, rendering it unspeakable, even unthinkable. Yet, the repressed will return, the truth will out, if not in official channels then in unofficial ones. The *Newsweek* cover is by no means unique. My extensive examination of cultural productions with nuclear themes—popular

Hypatia vol. 9, no. 2 (Spring 1994) © by Jane Caputi

films, novels, visual artwork, songs, and so on—reveals the regular recurrence of the theme of incestuous fatherhood. Feminist theorists have long argued that there are profound interconnections between personal forms of patriarchal violences (such as rape and sexual murder) and institutional, frequently technological and militaristic, violences (see Caputi 1987; Daly 1978; Davis 1989; Griffin 1978; Russell 1989). In this essay, I extend this approach by using popular culture, incest survivors' accounts, scientific metaphor, and feminist theoretical writings to analyze the connections between the practices of incest and nuclearism.[1]

THE NUCLEAR FATHER: WARHEAD OF THE FAMILY

An uncanny image appears on the cover of a 1985 children's comic book *The Outsiders*. A band of tiny costumed heroes, ready for battle, approaches an enormous mushroom cloud, upon which is inscribed a face that is broadly reminiscent of a 1950s sitcom dad. A pipe juts from his mouth and his expression is a lordly know-it-all and sadistic smirk. Here is a prime portrait of the cultural figure whom I call the "nuclear father"—the quintessential patriarch, the man who nominally provides for and protects his dependents but who actually threatens and violates them. This "nuclear father" figure can be found ruling over a family, a laboratory, a corporation, a military force, a church, or a nation.

In his astute study *Fathering the Unthinkable* (1983) Brian Easlea, a physicist and historian, points to a predominance of metaphors of male birth and fatherhood in the language of the Manhattan Project, the U.S. government's mission to develop the atom bomb. He and Carol Cohn (1987) perceive these metaphors as indicators of the masculinist bias steering the development of nuclear weapons. For example, at Los Alamos in 1945, as scientists struggled to produce the bomb before the war ended, they took bets on whether they would produce a dud or a success—in their lingo, a "girl" or a "boy." Their project was a success, and the bomb dropped on Hiroshima was nicknamed "Little Boy." The National Baby Association reacted to this birth/explosion by naming J. Robert Oppenheimer "Father of the Year." Oppenheimer remains the paradigmatic father figure in a select nuclear club that includes such men as Edward Teller, "father of the U.S. H-bomb"; Glenn Seaborg, one of the "five fathers of plutonium"; Andrei Sakharov, "father of the Soviet H-bomb"; and Admiral Hyman B. Rickover, "father of America's nuclear navy."

Oppenheimer, Teller, and other such scientific nuclear fathers were widely heroized after World War II. Astutely, their colleague Leo Szilard observed, "It is remarkable that all these scientists . . . should be listened to, but mass murderers have always commanded the attention of the public, and atomic scientists are no exception to this rule" (cited in Boyer 1985, 61). This linkage of fatherhood and mass murder is eerily reflected in the contemporary nuclear family, where murderous mayhem is an increasingly common event.

Another kind of nuclear father was exemplified by forty-one-year-old Ernie Lasiter of Roswell, New Mexico, who in January 1992 strangled his wife and four of his children and then shot himself. A couple of days earlier, his seventeen-year-old daughter had been removed from the home by police, who were investigating her complaint of incestuous assault by Lasiter. In the aftermath of the atrocity, a number of friends confirmed, as is typical in such cases, that Lasiter was a "good guy" and fine family man. A secretary in the highway department where he worked added, "He was very conscientious and a hard worker. He was almost like a machine" (Jadrnak 1992, 3E). The machine that a family (war)head like Ernie Lasiter most resembles is the unendingly lethal nuclear weapon. Not only does the apocalyptically raging nuclear father have an immediate mass kill from his "blast," but the effects of his lethality linger forever in the bodies and psyches of his survivors. Eerily, the mass murder/suicide pattern of the nuclear father presages the probable fate of any nation that initiates nuclear war.

Nuclear-family men such as Lasiter seem omnipresent these days. Other recent family mass murderers include John List, Jeffrey MacDonald, Ramon Salcido, George Franklin, Gene Simmons, and even the god-identified, apocalyptically aimed, and allegedly sexually abusive father figure of the Branch Davidian Christian cult, David Koresh. This lethally abusive nuclear father is also represented by fictional "pop" figures such as Leland Palmer in "Twin Peaks" (1989–1990), Jerry Blake in *The Stepfather* (1988), "De-Fens" in the despicably racist *Falling Down* (1993), and Freddy Kruger in *A Nightmare on Elm Street* (1984).

Moreover, in all sorts of stories with explicit themes of nuclear weaponry and power—from comic books to popular films to elite literature—abusive fathers appear as prime metaphors for the Bomb. Examples include the novels *The Nuclear Age* by Tim O'Brien (1985), *Falling Angels* by Barbara Gowdy (1990), *The Mosquito Coast* by Paul Theroux (1982), *The Prince of Tides* by Pat Conroy (1986), the films *Star Wars* (1977), *Forbidden Planet* (1956), and *Desert Bloom* (1986), and even, humorously, the current hit television show "The Simpsons."

Of course, in his original mythic manifestations, primarily in television sitcoms, the fictionalized head of the nuclear family is the benevolent patriarch who always "knows best." During the 1950s, the heyday of atomic culture, fatherhood became a much valorized role, and Father's Day became for the first time a holiday of national significance (May 1988, 146). In *The Feminine Mystique* (1963) Betty Friedan connected the cult of the (white, middle-class) nuclear family with a national psyche scarred by "the loneliness of the war and the unspeakableness of the bomb." These conditions, she argued, made women particularly vulnerable to "the feminine mystique," the belief that the highest value for women was fulfillment in a femininity characterized by "sexual passivity, male domination, and nurturing maternal love" (37). At the same time, women and men also were vulnerable to a "masculine mystique," the illusion that a man's rightful position was head of the family, where he was all-powerful, protective, a provider, benevolent, omniscient, essentially godlike—attributes simultaneously ascribed to America's newest weapon.

In truth, the bomb, while purportedly protecting, actually threatens. So too does the nuclear father. Just as those seeking refuge in a fallout shelter from an atomic bomb attack might instead find themselves roasted alive, those seeking security in the nuclear family might instead find themselves under attack in the form of battery, rape, incest, and mass murder. Affirming the connection of the political to the personal, and in subliminal recognition of the often apocalyptic experience of American family life, the phrase "nuclear family" established itself firmly in the national vernacular by 1947.

The film *Atomic Cafe* (Rafferty, Loader, Rafferty 1982) is a witty compilation of clips from 1950s government and military disinformation. These clips demonstrate the efficacy of that inflated Great White Father image to such nuclearist propaganda. Over and over, they present heavily iconic white family images: dads coming home from work; moms in the kitchen, cooking and serving; and Dick and Jane-type kids in the living room, watching TV. Simultaneously, we see white governmental father figures blithely assuring us of the safety of radiation and indeed of nuclear war itself. This genuflection to paternal authority was equally apparent in mainstream popular culture. Television boasted popular shows with such masterfully subtle titles as "Father Knows Best" and "Make Room for Daddy." So dominant was the image of the white, middle-class, patriarchally ordered family that one critic claimed, "Dad's authority around the house appeared to be the whole point of the spectacle" (Miller 1986, 196). Of course, that televised paternal authority also served to legitimate and ordain "Dad's" authority around the globe.

Benevolent nuclear father imagery was resurrected with great vigor during the Reagan-Bush era when the federal government spent four billion dollars per year on the Strategic Defense Initiative or "Star Wars"—Reagan's proposed space-based nuclear "defense" system. In order to persuade Americans to place their trust in him and his utterly specious project, Reagan smoothly donned the mask of the father protector, promising that his plan would offer a "new hope for our children in the twenty-first century" (1983, 20).

Reagan's "good father" image continued in a 1985 television commercial produced by High Frontier, a pro-Star Wars lobbying group. The spot opened with a childlike drawing of a simple house: stick figures represented a family, and there was a gloomy-faced sun. A syrupy little girl voice chirped, "I asked my daddy what this Star Wars stuff is all about. He said that right now we can't protect ourselves from nuclear weapons, and that's why the president wants to build a Peace Shield." At this point, large red missiles appeared to threaten the house, but they harmlessly disintegrate when met by a blue arc in the sky. Like magic, the grumpy sun began to smile and the arc was transformed into a shimmering rainbow. This scenario was about as believable as Reagan's hair color. Yet, credibility was not really the point. The essential message of this little package was that we, the much vaunted "American people," are children, in need of the loving protection of the all-powerful father/president. See, he can even make the sun smile.

Reagan again assumed the mask of the benevolent nuclear father in his 1984 address to the peoples of Micronesia acknowledging the cessation of their "trust" relationship with the United States. In 1947, the United Nations had made the United States the administrator of Micronesia (which encompasses more than two thousand islands) as a "strategic trust." This action authorized the United States to use the area for military purposes. In exchange, the United States would "protect" the islands from invaders. Ironically, over the next eleven years, the real invader was the protector—the United States itself. The U.S. government tested sixty-nine atomic and hydrogen bombs on the islands, rendering some of them permanently uninhabitable. Diana Davenport (1989), a native of Rongelap Atoll, remembers witnessing the blast of the hydrogen bomb Bravo, dropped on neighboring Bikini Atoll in 1954:

> Electricity crackled through my father's body, and during the flash my mother saw all her bones, her arms and legs, and hips, glowing through her skin. Windows shattered, animals bled through their eyes. Bikini Atoll became debris. . . . Six hours after the "Bravo" blast, something rioted down on us, on our water and food. Like starflakes, or shavings of the moon. We danced in it, we played with it. It didn't go away. . . . We were caught in the fallout that scientists named "Bikini Snow." (61)

Within twenty-four hours, everyone on Rongelap showed signs of radiation sickness. The legacy of this contamination continues in the form of all sorts of health calamities, including "Blindness. Thyroid tumors. Miscarriages. Jellyfish babies. Mental retardation. Sterility. Lung cancer. Kidney cancer. Liver cancer. Sarcoma. Lymphoma. Leukemia. . . . Retardation. Infants born who leaked through one's fingers like breathing bags of jelly. Others with long, twisted pincers like crabs" (Davenport 1989, 62). More than 50 percent of the deaths on Rongelap each year are children under five.

Childbirth has become, in Davenport's word, a "metaphor" for the monstrosity of the future in a postnuclear world. With no sense of irony, nuclear father Reagan employed a metaphor of healthy children growing up and leaving home in his formal 1984 good-bye to the Marshall Islands:

> Greetings. For many years a very special relationship has existed between the United States and the people of the trust territory. . . . Under the trusteeship, we've come to know and respect you as members of our American family. And now, as happens to all families, members grow up and leave home. I want you to know that we wish you all the best. . . . We look forward to continuing our close relationship to you in your new status. But you'll always be family to us. (O'Rourke 1986)

Here Reagan revealed himself as the ultimate unthinking and unthinkable father. His own role and the "American family" to which he referred represented, on a global scale, the "toxic parenting" and "dysfunctional family" of scores of best-selling recovery books. The "family" he described is one afflicted by a se-

verely disordered and abusive father—one who more or less destroys the next
generation, physically and/or psychically, and then denies his own horrendous
behavior and tries to coerce everyone else into the denial as well.

Incest is the atrocity most paradigmatic of fatherly abuse. In her essay "The
Color of Holocaust," novelist Patricia A. Murphy (1985) uses nuclear metaphors
to describe both her incest experience and the interior self of her father/perpe-
trator:

> The nuclear winter resonates through our culture reaching into our global
> imagery as expressed through television. It extends into the secret heart
> of the family and finally into that private space inside our own skins. The
> color of this winter is ash, which seems to be the color of all holocausts
> public and private. My father and I were once children of the sky. That
> great blue bowl which hangs over the limitless prairie where we both ex-
> perienced our childhoods a generation apart. He is the color of ash now
> like a stain on that sky. He smudges life itself. . . . My father has surren-
> dered to the nuclear winter within. (Murphy 1985, unpaged)

Murphy reminds us that there would not be an external bomb unless a bomb
also existed in the hearts of men, and that the nuclear winter is a psychic state
of blight as well as a physical one. Her father, she tells us, is an artificial season, a
destroyed atmosphere, a stifler of breath, life, and color, a sorry substitute for that
older, original, nurturing father she simultaneously invokes: Father Sky. Barbara
Gowdy's *Falling Angels* (1990) also sets up a metaphoric link between nuclear
devastation and incest. This novel tells the story of a 1960s nuclear family con-
sisting of a tyrannical and crazed father, a nearly catatonic alcoholic mother, and
three daughters. One Christmas, the father bestows minimal and despised presents on his daughters, telling them that in the summer they will take a trip to
Disneyland. However, in the spring, heeding media messages of an imminent
Soviet attack, the father begins frenzied work on a basement A-bomb shelter.
When summer arrives, his daughters find that instead of going to one newly constructed, controlled environment, Disneyland, they are to spend two weeks together in another such environment—their father's brand-new bomb shelter.

The experience in the bomb shelter is, of course, hell on earth: the water supply is insufficient and everyone drinks whiskey incessantly; the oldest daughter gets her first period, to her unbearable shame; the tyrannical father grows
increasingly cranky, angry, and unpredictable; the air is foul; the toilet backs up,
and the stench is unbearable. The metaphor is unmistakable: nuclear family life,
while advertised like Disneyland, to be "the happiest place on earth," actually is
a lot more like life in a bomb shelter: waiting in cramped quarters amid insane
behavior for the "bomb" to drop. In Gowdy's novel, of course, some years later it
does: the father eventually makes incestuous advances toward the oldest daughter,
and the mother eventually kills herself by jumping off the roof of the house. The
daughters, with varying degrees of damage, manage to survive.

The incest-nuclear connection also appears in the 1986 film *Desert Bloom*, a movie that could easily be subtitled: *Or How I Learned to Stop Worrying and Love My Stepfather*. The setting of the film is Las Vegas in the early 1950s as the city awaits an impending bomb test. The film focuses on a family composed of a mother, Lilly, her three daughters, and a stepfather, Jack. Jack is a World War II veteran, wounded in both body and spirit, who desperately seeks esteem and power through possession of "secret" information obtained via his shortwave radio. Significantly, the family keeps a number of secrets of its own. Jack is an alcoholic and a bully, lording it over his stepdaughters and his wife, who placatingly calls him Daddy. Jack's relationship with Rose, the "blooming" pubescent oldest daughter, is charged with sexual tension: we see him verbally and physically abuse her. Moreover, Rose tells us that "Momma had a way of not seeing things." In these and other ways, the film strongly implies Jack's sexual abuse of Rose.

Eventually Rose, seeking safety, runs away. Ironically, she ends up at the eminently dangerous nuclear test site, where she is rounded up by the authorities and returned to Jack, who has followed her trail. As they drive back to the house, he tells her that he just wants to "protect" her. "From whom?" Rose asks pointedly. The film's parallel between the incestuous/abusive father and nuclear weapons is extremely persuasive. Each purportedly protects the family and yet each, in reality, invades it and threatens to destroy its members.

"TRUST ME"

> A world once divided into two armed camps now recognizes one sole and preeminent power, the United States of America. And they regard this with no dread. For the world trusts us with power, and the world is right. They trust us to be fair, and restrained. They trust us to be on the side of decency. They trust us to do what's right. . . . As long as I am president we will continue to lead in support of freedom everywhere, not out of arrogance and not out of altruism, but for the safety and security of our children.
>
> (State of the Union Address, George Bush, 1992)

> The incest survivor can be said to be incapable of experiencing trust. She has in fact learned that words don't mean what they say, that things are not always what they seem, and that what appears safe is generally not to be believed.
>
> (E. Sue Blume, *Secret Survivors: Uncovering Incest and its Aftereffects in Women*)

"Trust" is one of the key words linking incest and the Bomb on the *Newsweek* "Future of the Bomb" cover. Witness the similarity between the incest headline, "Can Memories Be Trusted?" and the bomb headline, "Can We Trust the Soviets?" Frankly, both of these questions desperately displace the really important concern about trust. That is: can we trust our fathers, grandfathers, uncles, brothers, priests, old family friends, neighbors, doctors, and teachers around issues of safety for children? At the same time, based on past deceptions by nuclear authorities, it is absurd to place much trust in the U.S. government, military, and associated nuclear facilities around issues of nuclear safety.

When I was about twelve, the older boys in my neighborhood used to sexually harass girls by playing a game called "Trust Me." A boy would put his hand on the top button of a girl's blouse, unbutton it, and ask "Trust me?" The girl was supposed to say "Yes," even as he proceeded to uncover her breasts or shove his hand down her pants, all the while reiterating, "Trust me?"

During the 1950s, United States military and government officials played "Trust Me" not only with the Pacific peoples of the United Nations "trust territory" but also with countless U.S. citizens, including: lower-echelon military personnel who, as part of their duties, were exposed to radiation from bomb tests; the residents of northern Arizona, Nevada, and Utah who regularly were hit with fallout from above-ground bomb tests; uranium miners (a great number of whom were Lakota, Kaibab Paiute, Navaho, and Pueblo Native Americans); and the residents of areas where nuclear production facilities like Hanford and Oak Ridge were located.

Throughout the era of above-ground testing (1951–1963), the Atomic Energy Commission and the United States government engaged in a "sustained and wide-ranging effort" (Boyer 1985, 318) to fool the public about the dangers associated with nuclear development and above-ground bomb testing. In the aftermath of the attacks on Japan, the U.S. government actually denied the lethal and disabling effects of the radiation from the Hiroshima and Nagasaki bombs by dismissing statements about them as "Japanese propaganda." By 1950, the Federal Civil Defense Agency was claiming that nuclear war survival was simply a matter of "keeping one's head" and making sure to "duck and cover." In 1953, President Eisenhower advised the Atomic Energy Commission to keep the public "confused" about any hazards associated with radiation. Despite warnings from scientists such as Linus Pauling, the official line was that "low" levels of radiation were perfectly safe, that people could trust the government to protect them, and that bomb tests were in our best interest. By and large, U.S. citizens believed the government, embraced the bomb through a million popular songs and artifacts, and accepted the notion of the "peaceful atom." Many of these people later developed cancer, sterility, and other serious and frequently lethal health problems in return for their trust (Gallagher 1993).

Now, after decades of enforced secrecy, information is beginning to be released about the massive extent of this betrayal of trust by the nuclear industry, the Atomic Energy Commission, and their supporters throughout the government. Tom Bailie (1990) is a resident of the desperately contaminated area in Washington state around the Hanford Nuclear Reservation. He characterizes his experience as a virtual rape since the day he was born:

As "downwinders," born and raised downwind of the Hanford Nuclear Reservation in Washington, we learned several years ago that the government decided—with cold deliberation—to use us as guinea pigs by releasing radioactivity into our food, water, milk and air without our consent. Now, we've learned that we can expect continuing cancer cases from our exposure in their "experiment." Is this what it feels like to be raped? The exposure began the same day our lives began. (Bailie 1990, 19)

Bailie observes that even after the government admitted that radioactivity had been released, residents were continually reassured there would be no "observable" health consequences. However, the reason that negative health effects were not observable was not because there was an absence of harm, but because the consequences of radioactive contamination were perceived as normal: "Unknowingly, we had been seeing the effects for a long time. For us, the unusual was the usual!" (19). Bailie recalls nuclear cleanup crews, "men dressed in space suits," wandering around his town throughout his childhood, nice guys who gave him candy. He remembers the "neck massages" he and other children received from the school nurse, who was actually looking for thyroid problems. He remembers farm animal mutations, a high rate of human and animal miscarriage, and a high local cancer rate. To Bailie, all of this was perceived as "normal," including his own horrific health consequences, starting with underdeveloped lungs and numerous birth defects. Eventually he "underwent multiple surgeries, endured paralysis, endured thyroid medication, a stint in an iron lung, loss of hair, sores all over my body, fevers, dizziness, poor hearing, asthma, teeth rotting out and, at age 18, a diagnosis of sterility."

Bailie's perception of the normalcy of abuse corresponds almost perfectly with testimony from people who literally were raped from birth. One incest survivor, Kyos Featherdancing, was raped by her father from the time she was a baby. Until she was nine years old, she thought that "every father did that with their daughter" (in Bass and Davis 1988, 395). Just as Bailie "thought all kids lived with death and deformity," Featherdancing assumed that all kids lived with incest. She too mistook the abnormal for the normal and suffered long-term damage from the normalized abuse. In her case, this included drug addiction, alcoholism, and self-hatred.

Lifton points to the shame of many Hiroshima survivors, their "sense of impaired body substance." He observes: "Radiation effects . . . are such that the experience has had no cutoff point. Survivors have the possibility of experiencing delayed but deadly radiation effects for the rest of their lives. That possibility extends to their children, to their children's children, indefinitely into the future" (Lifton and Falk 1992, 45–46). Like many survivors of Hiroshima, the survivors of incest often are frightened to have children, for the effects of incest, like the effects of radiation, are insidious, long term, and transmitted through generations. They, too, often lie harbored in the victim until they later erupt into disease or disorder. Some of the long-term effects of incest include fear, anxiety, anger, and hostility; eating disorders; allergies and asthma; shame; low self-esteem; guilt; depression; inability to trust or to establish relationships; phobias; multiple personality disorder; sexual dysfunction; a tendency toward revictimization through participating in such activities as prostitution; drug addiction; alcoholism; self-mutilation; and suicide (Wyatt and Powell 1988).

OFFICIAL SECRECY

Except possibly for the word "silence" and maybe the word "safety," the word "secret" recurs more than any other in feminist discussions of incest. Psychiatric social worker Florence Rush (1980) calls the sexual abuse of children patriarchy's "best-kept secret." Sociologist Diana Russell (1984) speaks of incest as "the secret trauma," marked by "a vicious cycle of betrayal, secrecy, unaccountability, repetition, and damaged lives" (16). Similarly, as any analyst of nuclear culture knows, an unprecedented and profoundly enforced official secrecy is the most prominent feature of the history of nuclear development (Lifton and Falk 1992, 26).

Secrecy is fundamental to the abuse of power—sexual and otherwise. Protected by the cult of secrecy, fathers molest their daughters; priests violate their flocks; governments test nuclear weapons on human populations, including their own; and weapons laboratories and defense contractors plan, manufacture, and mismanage weapons without public knowledge, scrutiny, or criticism. Secrecy in the nuclear world, moreover, creates a select club of those "in the know," bestows a sense of privilege, and fosters in-group loyalty. It encourages the arms race, allows safety problems to remain uninvestigated and unresolved at any number of nuclear weapons facilities in both the United States and the former Soviet Union, and has enabled disastrous accidents to be completely covered up.

So, too, the truth about child sexual abuse is covered up regularly, by individual perpetrators and the enabling culture. At the outset, children are told by abusers that their sexual activity is a secret that must never be told, frequently under threat of abandonment or death (for themselves or loved ones). If the children disregard that prohibition and tell the truth, they all too often are not believed. The invalidation of children's words, the characterization of their reports as fantasy, and massive community denial and resistance to believing in the abusive practices of paternal authorities (individual or institutional) have long histories in psychoanalytic theory and everyday practice (Summitt 1988).

This scenario of silence, secrecy, denial, avoidance, erasure, initial embrace of the trusted father-figure abuser, and victim blaming unerringly mirrors the typical responses of nuclear communities to complaints against the institutional abusers in their midst. Tom Bailie (1990) reveals what happened when his family blew the whistle on the devastation caused by Hanford:

> Our patriotism has been impugned, our credibility questioned. . . . We have been slandered as the "glow in the dark family" by friends and strangers alike. . . . Moscow was condemned for its three days of silence

after the Chernobyl nuclear accident. What about Washington's 40 years of silence? (Bailie 1990, 19)

Marylia Kelley is a resident of Livermore, California—home of the Lawrence Livermore Laboratory. She is also a founder of Tri-Valley CARE—Citizens Against a Radioactive Environment. When she moved to Livermore in 1976, she knew there was some "super-secret government facility" where almost everyone worked, but neither she nor anyone she spoke to seemed to have a clear idea about what went on there. There was some awareness that nuclear weapons work was occurring there, but most people dismissed it as constituting only a small proportion, maybe 10 percent, of the lab's actual endeavors. (In truth, weapons work accounted for about 90 percent of the lab's activities.) As antinuclear activists increasingly converged upon Livermore in the 1980s, local residents like Kelley became interested in finding out the truth. Yet local activism faced a certain measure of resistance since so many community members were economically dependent on the nuclear facility. After several years of deliberate non-cooperation, some of the churches agreed in 1989 to sponsor a series of talks entitled "Pathways to Peace," to be held in neighboring Pleasanton. Lectures were given over a six-week period, but, Kelley reports, not once did anyone mention Lawrence Livermore lab. As she told me in a 1993 conversation, "I felt like the community was keeping a dirty secret, and it was breaking a taboo to speak the name Livermore in a public way."

In other words, making genocidal bombs isn't taboo, but speaking out against them is. So too, as many observers note, incest is not really taboo in our culture, but speaking out against it is. The "dirty secret" scenario Kelley describes parallels the protection by family members of a trusted and/or economically powerful child abuser and the concomitant silencing of victims. Kelley concludes that one of the most important features of CARE's activism is to overcome this obeisance to secrecy and to get people to "name things by their true names, to find their voice." Indeed, in order to thwart both child sexual abuse and nuclearism, we must, in the phrase commonly used by survivors, "break silence." We must begin to spill those long held and closely guarded secrets and, concomitantly, believe the unbelievable, be it that a fine churchgoing family man is sexually abusing his daughter or that high rates of thyroid and brain cancer (such as those in Los Alamos) are due to radioactive contamination.

KEEPING SECRETS FROM ONESELF

"What was your family life like, Savannah?" I asked, pretending I was conducting an interview.

"Hiroshima," she whispered.

"And what has life been like since you left the warm, abiding bosom of your nurturing, close-knit family?"

"Nagasaki," she said, a bitter smile on her face.

(*The Prince of Tides*, Pat Conroy)

Victims of incest often seek temporary refuge in numbing, denial, and massive repression, keeping their worst secret even from themselves because confronting incest in their own lives is truly "thinking about the unthinkable." Pat Conroy's best-selling novel, *The Prince of Tides*, elaborates a complex narrative, encompassing nuclear devastations, the secrets of family life, and child rape. The book's narrator, Tom Wingo, tells us that he and his twin sister Savannah "entered the scene in the middle of a world war at the fearful dawning of the atomic age" (9). Their childhood was simultaneously haunted by a terror of their father's recurrent brutality, directed against them and their mother. While the world anticipated nuclear war, their "childhood was spent waiting for him to attack."

Tom further reveals that his is "a family of well-kept secrets and they all nearly end up killing us" (97). His father, Henry Wingo, relentlessly batters his family. His mother, Lila Wingo, adamantly forbids her three children to reveal their father's brutality. She also conceals the fact that she has been stalked by a rapist and murderer. Yet, the repressed returns, this time with apocalyptic virulence. The stalker and two other men escape from prison and come to the family's home while Henry is absent. They rape and try to kill Lila, Tom, and Savannah and are thwarted only because Luke, the oldest son, manages to disrupt the assaults and lead a lethal attack against the invaders. Lila orders everyone to render the event permanently unspeakable and unthinkable, meaning that everyone must wipe it from memory. Tom can't stop himself from remembering; still, he brackets that knowledge and refuses to deal with its implications or speak of it. Savannah completely expunges this and other horrific memories from her consciousness. She goes on to become an extraordinarily gifted poet, yet she regularly attempts suicide. Some years later, Lila conspires to sell off the Wingo family South Carolina island home to the U.S. government so that it can build a nuclear weapons facility there. Utterly opposed to nuclear weapons, Luke becomes a one-man guerrilla army, battling the construction of the plant. In a few months, he is shot and killed.

Savannah Wingo's name is not arbitrary. One of the United States' primary nuclear weapons facilities is the Savannah River Plant, located in South Carolina. For years, Savannah River was the major source of tritium for U.S. nuclear weapons, but it was closed for the first time in 1988 due to its unsafe practices. As recent investigations reveal, the Savannah River facility has a "long and shocking record of serious incidents of radioactive contamination and unsafe disposal of waste," hazards that the Department of Energy "has long attempted to keep . . . from public view" (Glenn 1988). The Savannah River, like the Columbia, is one of the most toxic bodies of water in the world.

Numbing, repression of memory, and denial characterize the Wingo family, patterns that serve as microcosmic mirrors for larger nuclearist abuse. Robert Jay Lifton and Eric Markusen (1990, 13) detail that denial, numbing, dissociation or splitting, and even "doubling" ("the formation of a functional second self") are not only classic responses of victims of genocidal practices but also characterize victimizer consciousness. In special circles, these ways of numbing are actually celebrated and encouraged. For example, General Curtis LeMay, who oversaw the Hiroshima bombing and the creation of the Strategic Air Command (SAC), was popularly portrayed, with no onus attached, as "more machine than man." Spencer Weart notes that in his capacity as head of SAC, "LeMay took care to select only officers like himself, men who kept their feelings under strict control" (Weart 1989, 149). Bombing, as one writer explained in the *Saturday Evening Post*, "had to be done 'mechanically, with swift, sure precision, undisturbed by emotion, either of fear . . . or pity' " (cited in Weart 1989, 149). LeMay himself recalled that when he flew bombers over Germany, "his imagination had caught a picture of a little girl down below, horribly burned and crying for her mother. 'You have to turn away from the picture,' he said, 'if you intend to keep on doing the work your Nation expects of you' " (cited in Weart 1989, 149).

I wager that unapologetic incestuous abusers might sound very much like LeMay—riveted on their own conquest or pleasure and steeling themselves to turn away from the "little girl down below," crying, injured, and annihilated. Just as the survivor splits into a "day child" and a "night child" (Atler 1991, 90), so does the abuser create a second self, enabling him to perform atrocities and to keep the secret of his depredations even from himself. With such abusers, psychic numbing means never having to say you're sorry.

Another method of inculcating nuclear numbing is to render weapons work an always unfinished jigsaw puzzle. General Leslie Groves, who was the military chief of the Manhattan Project, initiated a policy of "compartmentalization of knowledge." This policy ensured that "each man should know everything he needed to know about doing his job and nothing else" (Lifton and Falk 1992, 26). The internalization of this mentality among nuclear workers guarantees that none of them needs to face what he or she is doing. After living in Albuquerque for over ten years and speaking to scores of people who work at either Sandia or Los Alamos national laboratories, I rarely meet anyone who acknowledges working on nuclear weapons. Nearly everyone claims to perform some specialized, unrelated task. Even those technicians who acknowledge that they are making weapons often mute their awareness with truly stunning doublethink. As one weapons designer at Lawrence Livermore lab told an interviewer, "We're working on weapons of life, ones that will save people from weapons of death" (cited in Broad 1985, 47). Similarly, many incesters deny that they are grievously injuring children. In their minds, they are pleasuring the children, helping them to attain adulthood, loving them, giving them only what they want, responding to their initiation of sex play, and so on.

A January 1991 issue of *Time* magazine opted to name George Bush not "Man," but "Men of the Year" and actually depicted a two-faced presidential image on its cover. Such doubling nominally referred to Bush's disparate record on international and domestic affairs. Yet, this image simultaneously portrayed the "doubling" propensity of nuclear fathers and prepared the nation for Bush's role as commander in chief of the Persian Gulf War and mass murderous activities by the U.S. military. A similar construction appeared in a 1991 advertisement for the Army National Guard. It depicted a young man whose face was split precisely down the middle. On the right, it was a relatively normal face. On the left, the face was heavily painted camouflage style; the eye was widely opened and stared threateningly. This ad was stark testimony to the military's normative inculcation of a secret "killer self" within the soldier. It also portrayed the fissioned configurations of not only official femininity but also of official masculinity in the nuclear-fathered world.

TABOO VIOLATION: JUST DO IT

> Our mission: to boldly go where no man has gone before.
> *(Star Trek)*

In scores of nuclear movies such as the 1958 *Teenage Caveman* and the 1968 *Planet of the Apes*, there is a recurrent motif: the "forbidden zone," an area closely guarded by taboo that no one may enter. Usually, this area is contaminated by radiation from some long-ago nuclear war. In pro-technology films like *Teenage Caveman* the hero is the one who disregards the taboo and boldly strides into the proscribed area.

The 1956 film *Forbidden Planet* puts a different twist on this theme. A scientist, Morbius, lives alone on the paradisiacal planet Altair with his full-grown daughter, Altaira. Domestic chores are performed by a marvelously efficient robot named Robby. A spaceship from earth arrives to find out what happened to the original landing party that came to the planet twenty years ago. Morbius attempts to make them go away. He tells them that, in essence, the entire planet is taboo to them, for there is a deadly force on the planet that killed everyone in the landing party except himself and his daughter. Nevertheless, the captain of the ship refuses to leave.

As a sexual attraction develops between the captain and the daughter, the deadly planetary force again makes an appearance, threatening the men and their ship. Ultimately, we learn that the lethal force is generated by the jealous Morbius's own mind. The planet Altair formerly was inhabited by members of a technologically superior civilization, the Krell. Although they wiped themselves out years ago "in a single night," the Krell left behind the agent of their own destruction, a vast nuclear-powered machine. Morbius, lusting for the Krell's technological knowledge, has been able to tap into the machine's power, allowing him to produce externally all that he can imagine, such as the marvelous Robby. But, Morbius is operating under a serious mantle of denial. He is transgressing profoundly against self-, family-, and planetary-preservative taboos in his unbounded quest for both sexual and technological knowledge. The Krell machine manifests in material reality not only his conscious wishes but also his most awful unconscious thoughts and desires, unleashing "monsters from the id." The lethal planetary force, then, is actually an externalization of Morbius's unconscious. When his incestuous paradise with his "forbidden partner," his daughter, is threatened, his unconscious strikes out to eliminate the threat. In the film's climactic moment, Morbius faces his own evil self and the experience does indeed destroy him. Romance, however, manages to "save" Altaira. She and the captain escape into space, bringing Robby with them, while Morbius and the planet that shares Altaira's name are blown to bits.

The word forbidden in the film's title speaks not only to the archetypal "forbidden knowledge" that structures both ancient myths and mad-scientist movies, but also to the forbidden incestuous relationship that the father imposes on his daughter. *Forbidden Planet* is basically a conservative movie: it sets up pairs of false dichotomies and then in a tidy resolution replaces the "bad" heterosexual domination—incest with her father—with "good" heterosexual domination—marriage to the captain. Similarly, the "bad" nuclear technology—represented by the Krell machine—is replaced with "good" nuclear technology—in the form of Robby the Robot.

Yet, however conventional, *Forbidden Planet* once again holds up for view the connection between the incestuous father and nuclearism. If we look past the film's false oppositions, we can discern an unmistakable parallel between Morbius's unbounded quest for knowledge and his incestuous depredations. As Catharine MacKinnon sums it up, "Sexual metaphors for knowing are no coincidence. . . . Feminists are beginning to understand that to know has meant to fuck" (1983, 636). Manifestly, in the patriarchal tradition, knowledge is power (domination) just as space exists to be invaded. It was this reigning pornographic paradigm of knowledge that fired the drive to gain nuclear knowledge or, as the most common scientific metaphors put it, "to penetrate the hidden mysteries," to investigate "the most intimate properties of matter," and even to "smash resistant atoms" (Weart 1989, 58).

While social lip service is widely given to the incest taboo, Diana Russell (1986, 16) suggests that a minimum of one of every six women in the United States has been incestuously abused. The violation of life-preservative taboo[2] so characteristic of incestuous practice equally underwrites much technological adventuring. J. Robert Oppenheimer, for example, reflecting on the quest to split the atom, avowed, "It is my judgment in these things that when you see something that is technically sweet, you go ahead and do it, and you argue about what to do about it only after you have had your technical success" (cited in Lifton 1979, 425). Under the reigning ideologies of knowledge, power, and progress, there is no ethic of respect for others, no limit on phallic desires, no prudent calculation of future consequences. Whether advancing upon the "final frontier" of outer space, probing the "most intimate properties of matter," taking possession of desirable and colonizable "virgin land," or staking a claim on the body of a child, patriarchal men routinely disregard any notion of taboo or limitation and continually give themselves permission to "boldly go where no man has gone before."

FAMILY VALUES

The word "survivor" began to be used by incest victims sometime in the late 1970s or early 1980s. "Survivor" sheds some of the pain of the word "victim" and focuses on the time when the immediate danger is over and healing can begin. It also affirms a link between incest/child sexual abuse and what are, at least for the Western world, the two defining horrors of the twentieth century: the Nazi death camps and the use of atomic weaponry on Japan by the United States. While such an association may seem extreme, one medical expert, Dr. Judith Herman, who has been working on issues of incest and battery since 1976 affirms the profound connection (1992). She describes the link "between public and private worlds" and the commonalties "between rape survivors and combat veterans, between battered women and political prisoners, between the survivors of vast concentration camps created by tyrants who rule nations and the survivors of small, hidden concentration camps created by tyrants who rule their homes" (Herman 1992, 2–3). Just as neo-Nazis attempt to deny the reality of the Holocaust, so a confluence of forces consistently try to deny the reality and harm of incest. Most recently, there has been a growing movement to discredit memories that have been recovered by victims after years of forgetfulness (Tavris 1993). Survivors of incest must then bear witness to atrocity, renouncing numbing, and nurturing awareness. The word survivor as applied to incest also demands that we fathom the magnitude of the day-to-day inescapable devastations of this atrocity. We must understand its ongoing psychic and cultural consequences, its metaphorical enactment on the global scale, and its connection to other apocalyptic depredations.

A poem by Roseann Lloyd, "Not Even a Shadow on the Sidewalk" (1991, 84–87), makes the connection between incest and the bomb more powerfully than anything else I have encountered. The poem opens as Lloyd recalls her reaction to a PBS *Frontline* investigation of incest. In this televised news story, a woman returns to the room where she repeatedly was raped by her father, points to a wall, and describes how she would project herself into it during the assaults. Lloyd remembers that she was "jealous" when she heard this account:

> because I didn't go anywhere in particular
> when my dad climbed on my bed
> It's not that I can't remember where I went
> I didn't go anywhere
> I was just gone   like the people in Japan
> blown away by the atom-bomb
> Annihilated
> There wasn't even a shadow left
> on the sidewalk
> to say   someone's missing
> My symptoms developed   like the side-effects
> of nuclear war—numb hands   missing hands
> disconnected synapses
> wheezing chest
> damaged vision: staring at the white light
> weak limbs
> reamed out like the inside of a sewer pipe

aphasia   memory loss   splitting
headaches.

Lloyd and others tell us that incest is an apocalyptic, annihilating experience for the individual sufferer. Moreover, it signifies a greater apocalyptic event. For a society that fucks[3] and fucks over its children is not only acting out an extreme form of male supremacy, but it is also fucking its own future, eating up the next generation, and indulging in the grossest excesses of consumerism, individual gratification, and final-frontierism. Ellen Bass, a poet and counselor who has worked with incest survivors for decades, points to the apocalyptic significance of nuclear development (from war to toxic waste) and comments:

> It is not odd that men whose desire for profit has superseded their own instinct for survival should so abuse their young. To stunt a child's trust in people, in love, in her world, to instill a fear that may take a lifetime to overcome, may never be overcome, to force one's body into the body of a child, of a baby, to desecrate children so is consistent for people who desecrate all life and the possibility of future life. (Bass 1988, 43)

A stunning display of this desecrating dynamic occurred early in June 1992 at an oil recycling plant in California, during a speech by George Bush, the once self-proclaimed "environmental president." Some weeks earlier, the Bush administration had issued, in essence, a death sentence for many of the region's spotted owls by opening up a good portion of their Northwestern old-growth-forest home for logging. Bush referred to this during his speech, not by explicitly mentioning the owl, but by gesturing toward the sky and declaring that he cared as much as anyone else about those "little furry-feathery" things, but if those furry-feathery things got in the way of jobs and the mighty "family" (here a code word for corporate interests) they just had to go.

Mythically, the owl is a particularly powerful presence and the owl has long been regarded in many traditions, including the European and the Aztec, as the embodiment of wisdom and a favorite familiar of witches. In some Native American lore, particularly in the Northwest, the owl represents the powers of death. In his oration at the oil recycling plant, George Bush dared not speak the spotted owl's name, but the Owl is calling his name. For, in truth, the flagrantly witless leadership that Bush and his ilk have offered over the past century has resulted in widespread desecration and destruction of forests. The result is harm for both creatures and working-class humans whose jobs have been chainsawed out of existence due to unregulated corporate greed and mismanagement. Bush's foolish pronouncements sounded a death knell, not only for his failed administration, but also for the consummately wasteful, though much vaunted, "American way of life."

Despite all the 1992 Republican presidential campaign jabbering about an honoring of "family values," Bush's administration transgressed against the original and most essential "family values"—the equal sacredness of all life, a respect for future generations, and the commitment to what Carol Lee Sanchez calls humanity's "*familial* relationship with all creatures, elements, plants, and minerals, as well as humans" (1993, 213; italics mine). A multicultural feminist perspective might well concur with this Native American insight, realizing that the original theory of relativity is that *everything is a relative* . . . and one *never* fucks one's relatives.

Notes

1. "Nuclearism" is a word first used by Lifton (1979, 39) to mean "the passionate embrace of nuclear weapons as a solution to death anxiety and a way of restoring a lost sense of immortality." I use it to mean a world view combining disrespect for the atom with the exploitation, eroticization, and worship of nuclear technology as a means to extend elite men's domination over the elements and the earth.

2. By life-preservative or elemental taboos, I mean limits and prohibitions on exploitative, human-centered and/or individualist behaviors. Such taboos are based in the recognition not only that everything is alive but that all forms of life are interconnected, equally sacred, and deserving of respect, and, moreover, that we cannot destroy "nature" without destroying ourselves. Patriarchal taboos are based only in patriarchal self-preservation, protection, gain, self-gratification, and malice, e.g., taboos on lesbianism, taboos on speaking out against incest, taboos on standing in the way of "progress."

3. I use the word "fuck" deliberately. In common parlance, "fuck" can mean either to have sex (paradigmatically, a penis penetrating a vagina) or to destroy utterly. No other word conveys the eroticized domination and destruction so characteristic of patriarchal sex and patriarchal violences.

References

Atler, Marilyn Van Derbur. 1991. The darkest secret. *People Weekly* (June 10): 88–94.

Bailie, Tom. 1990. Growing up as a nuclear guinea pig. *New York Times* July 22, Sec. 4, 19.

Bass, Ellen. 1988. Introduction: In the truth itself, there is healing. In *I never told anyone: Writings by women survivors of child sexual abuse*, ed. Ellen Bass and Louise Thornton. New York: Harper and Row.

Bass, Ellen, and Laura Davis. 1988. *The courage to heal: A guide for women survivors of child sexual abuse*. New York: Harper and Row.

Blume, E. Sue. 1990. *Secret survivors: Uncovering incest and its aftereffects in women*. New York: Ballantine.

Boyer, Paul. 1985. *By the bomb's early light: American thought and culture at the dawn of the atomic age*. New York: Pantheon Books.

Broad, William J. 1985. *Star warriors*. New York: Simon and Schuster.

Caputi, Jane. 1987. *The age of sex crime*. Bowling Green, OH: Bowling Green State University Popular Press.

————. 1991. Charting the flow: The construction of meaning through juxtaposition in media texts. *Journal of Communication Inquiry* 15(2): 32–47.

Cohn, Carol. 1987. Sex and death in the rational world of defense intellectuals. *Signs: Journal of Women in Culture and Society* 12(4): 687–718.

Conroy, Pat. 1986. *The prince of tides*. New York: Bantam.

Davenport, Diana. 1989. Snow (Marshall Islands). *Ikon* 10, 60–64.

Davis, Angela. 1989. *Women, culture, and politics*. New York: Random House.

Easlea, Brian. 1983. *Fathering the unthinkable: Masculinity, scientists, and the nuclear arms race.* London: Pluto Press.

Estelle, Amy. 1991. Incest and the Bomb: Surviving in the nuclear age. Unpublished paper, University of New Mexico.

Featherdancing, Kyos. 1988. In *The courage to heal: A guide for women survivors of child sexual abuse,* ed. Ellen Bass and Laura Davis. New York: Harper and Row.

Friedan, Betty. 1963. *The feminine mystique.* New York: Dell.

Gallagher, Carole. 1993. *American ground zero: The secret nuclear war.* Cambridge: M.I.T. Press.

Glenn, John. 1988. Joint hearings on "Nuclear Reactor Safety at the DOE's Savannah River Plant," September 30. Opening statement to the *House of Representatives Environnmental, Energy, and Natural Resources subcommittee of the Committee on Government Operations and the Senate Committee on Government Affairs.*

Gowdy, Barbara. 1990. *Falling angels.* New York: Soho Press.

Griffin, Susan. 1978. *Woman and nature: The roaring inside her.* New York: Harper and Row.

Herman, Judith Lewis. 1992. *Trauma and recovery: The aftermath of violence from domestic abuse to political terror.* New York: Basic Books.

Jadrnak, Jackie. 1992. Social workers' actions proper in Roswell case. *Albuquerque Journal* January 24, 3E.

Lifton, Robert Jay. 1979. *The broken connection: On death and the continuity of life.* New York: Simon and Schuster.

Lifton, Robert Jay, and Richard Falk. 1992. *Indefensible weapons: The political and psychological case against nuclearism.* New York: Basic Books.

Lifton, Robert Jay, and Eric Markusen. 1990. *The genocidal mentality: Nazi holocaust and nuclear threat.* New York: Basic Books.

Lloyd, Roseann. 1991. Not even a shadow on the sidewalk. In *She who was lost is remembered: Healing from incest through creativity,* ed. Louise Wisechild. Seattle: The Seal Press.

May, Elaine Tyler. 1988. *Homeward bound: American families in the cold war era.* New York: Basic Books.

Miller, Mark Crispin. 1986. Deride and conquer. In *Watching television,* ed. Tod Gitlin. New York: Pantheon Books.

Murphy, Patricia A. 1985. The color of holocaust. Unpublished essay.

O'Brien, Tim. 1985. *The nuclear age.* New York: Dell Publishing, Laurel Trade.

O'Rourke, Dennis. 1986. *Half-Life* (film).

Rafferty, Kevin, Jayne Loader, and Pierce Rafferty. 1982. *Atomic cafe* (film).

Reagan, Ronald. 1983. Speech on a new defense. *New York Times* (March 24): 20.

Rush, Florence. 1980. *The best-kept secret: Sexual abuse of children.* New York: McGraw-Hill.

Russell, Diana E. H. 1986. *The secret trauma: Incest in the lives of girls—and women.* New York: Basic Books.

———. ed. 1989. *Exposing nuclear phallacies.* New York: Pergamon Press.

Sanchez, Carol Lee. 1993. Animal, vegetable and mineral: The sacred connection. In *Ecofeminism and the sacred,* ed. Carol Adams. New York: Continuum Publishing Company.

Summitt, Ronald. 1988. Hidden victims, hidden pain: Societal avoidance of child sexual abuse. In *Lasting effects of child abuse,* ed. Gail Elizabeth Wyatt and Gloria Johnson Powell. Newbury Park, CA: Sage Publications.

Tavris, Carol. 1993. Beware the incest-survivor machine. *New York Times Book Review* (January 3): 1, 16–17.

Theroux, Paul. 1982. *The mosquito coast.* New York: Avon Books.

Weart, Spencer. 1989. *Nuclear fear: A history of images.* Cambridge: Harvard University Press.

Wyatt, Gail Elizabeth, and Gloria Johnson Powell, eds. 1988. *Lasting effects of child sexual abuse.* Newbury Park, CA: Sage Publications.

Onward Christian Soldiers: The War Talk of Beverly Davenport LaHaye

ADRIENNE E. CHRISTIANSEN

As women make inroads into a variety of traditionally masculine occupations, including military service, scholars have become increasingly interested in questions about gender, war, and peace (Ruddick, 1989; Elshtain, 1987; Elshtain and Tobias, 1990; Enloe, 1988, 1989, 1993; Jeffords, 1989; Cohn, 1987; and Griffin, 1992). A 1990 National Endowment for the Humanities institute at Dartmouth College explored several of these questions, focusing particularly on how "warlike values are reinforced through the behavior normally expected of women . . . and men" (Cooke and Woollacott, 1993, preface). Language is one important form of behavior that reinforces warlike values. Cooke and Woollacott's anthology, *Gendering War Talk*, grew out of the Dartmouth College institute. It addresses the interconnections between war, language, and gender focusing largely on representations of war in movies, plays, and novels. Unlike most of the entries in that work, several scholars examine the war language of real individuals. Stanley Rosenberg's study (1993), "The Threshold of Thrill: Life Stories in the Skies Over Southeast Asia," compared the war stories of bomber pilots who flew during World War II and the Vietnam War. Carol Cohn's well-known (1987) analysis of the technostrategic rationality used by U.S. nuclear defense intellectuals and military strategists is extended in the anthology to include an analysis of their highly sexualized discourse.

While it is expected that military planners and personnel would use military-based language, the syndicated columnist Ellen Goodman has observed that war talk pervades the discourse of our elected officials, even when the subject has nothing to do with war. She writes:

> Nothing but war seems to have the same power to mobilize, to engage people in some communal effort against a perceived enemy, a named threat. Only a declaration of war stirs the juices enough to call us to sacrifice, to get civilians to join up. (1989)

So pervasive is a war mentality (and war language) in this society that one philosopher has coined the term "warism" to illustrate war's place as an "unconscious fundamental presupposition." He writes:

> The Western inclination to take warism for granted is so pervasive as to form an unexpressed attitude that is manifest in virtually all aspects of the culture from the obvious cases of politics and the popular media to business, education, and even religion. There is no conspiracy needed here; advertising, television, public and parochial school curricula, all tend to reflect the dominant outlook, the fundamental attitudes of the culture. (Cady, 1989)

These scholars and commentators share an understanding that war and organized violence are neither inevitable, nor genetically inherent, but have come to a central, ensconced place in American society through human agency. Their writings all suggest that war-like values are maintained and justified through language.

Although the provisional title of this anthology was *Feminism and Peace*, I will be discussing anti-feminism and war as they occur in the public discourse (especially the direct mail) of one highly successful, contemporary political activist. This approach is unusual, though conceptually justifiable. According to the rhetorical theorist Kenneth Burke, our ability to thoroughly understand the dimensions of concepts like "feminism" or "peace" is possible only through contextual juxtapositions to their negative referents (1969). He argues that to make a negative statement implies a positive statement.[1] For example, the concept of "anti-feminism" means little to us without understanding its negative referent— feminism. Likewise, to insist on the necessity for peace in our society presumes that we can conceptually distinguish it from its negation—"not peace," or war. Thus, in this chapter I try to comprehend the scope and values associated with feminism and peace by describing the machinations of their opposites.

This rhetorical analysis of war talk ought to be of interest to philosophers for reasons beyond the historically close relationship between rhetoric and philosophy in ancient and contemporary times. Indeed, the chapter seeks to illuminate warism as a fundamental and dangerous value in this society by noting its preeminence in the discourse of a female Christian leader who publicly advocates traditional sex roles. In an ideal world, political leaders would act in ways consistent with their values, principles, and policy goals. Christians, who claim to follow the "Prince of Peace," would not advocate war and women who advocate traditional sex roles would not speak in the language of military generals. Beverly LaHaye publicly claims to represent both Christians and submissive women, yet consistently utilizes a discourse of war to describe non-military events and to motivate her audiences. That she and her supporters see no contradiction between her stated ideals and her linguistic practices points to the need to carefully examine the relationships between Christianity, femininity, and war in general and LaHaye's mix of these concepts in particular. In what follows, I begin with a brief introduction to LaHaye and her public policy platform. I then describe the war-related metaphors in LaHaye's public rhetoric. In analyzing the ubiquity and centrality of the "war talk" trope,[2] I show that Beverly LaHaye's language reflects the contested, contradictory discourse about war by Christians and traditional women. I end by providing reasons why this metaphoric language is a danger to feminists and peace activists.

WHO IS BEVERLY LAHAYE?

For the past fifteen years, Beverly LaHaye has been the president of Concerned Women for America, the largest women's political organization in this country with a reputed 600,000 members.[3] CWA grew out of a gathering of 1,200 church women who came together in San Diego, CA, to protest against the Equal Rights Amendment.

Unlike many other conservative groups that came to prominence before and during the Reagan presidency, LaHaye's group has grown in strength and supporters. It operates a national office out of Washington, D.C., but has an interlocking network of state, local, and neighborhood affiliates. The organization's $12 million annual budget is financed almost entirely through individual contributions solicited through an innovative, tenacious, and brilliant direct mail program. LaHaye is often asked to share her opinions in the Pro/Con columns of *USA Today* and has many editorials printed in the *Washington Times*. Since 1990, LaHaye has had her own call-in radio talk show on Christian stations called "Beverly LaHaye Live," and now has her own television show on the conservative National Empowerment Television network. She is the author of ten books, some of which were written with her husband, Reverend Tim LaHaye.[4]

Primarily because of CWA's political lobbying and successful legal representation of conservative Christians, Beverly LaHaye and her organization have the respect and admiration of a host of conservative luminaries: Ronald Reagan, Oliver North, Dan Quayle, George Bush, and Clarence Thomas, to name but a few. Republican presidential aspirants and a plethora of congressional candidates have all wooed the group in order to win its backing. In 1987, Ronald Reagan said: "Beverly LaHaye is a powerhouse on the political scene today . . . [who] is changing the face of American politics" (10). His sentiments are echoed by scholars like Jim Reichley, a senior fellow at Georgetown University: "LaHaye and her organization are significant forces within the new religious right, which is itself a significant force" (Wilson, 1993:1).

CWA has seven broad goals: "1) to inform women of the erosion of our historical moral standards; 2) to expose movements that weaken the family; 3) to educate women in Godly principles for living; 4) to organize a united prayer network; 5) to train volunteer lobbyists; 6) to provide representation on family and moral concerns in Washington, D.C.; and, 7) to provide legal defense to preserve our religious freedoms, moral integrity, and the rights of the family" ("1979–1986: The CWA Story," 1986:4). These broad goals translate into support for a variety of conservative public policy initiatives, including prayer in schools, teaching creationism, educational voucher systems, increased military budgets and weapon systems, anti-homosexual legislation, and anti-abortion policies.

Christianity and political activism are integrally linked for CWA, a relationship best exemplified by the group's creation and sponsorship of 2,500 prayer/action chapters. These small groups embody LaHaye's efforts to create a mass movement of conservative "kitchen table lobbyists." In a typical prayer/action chapter, up to fifteen women meet weekly to pray for national and local political leaders, conservative legislation, and to plan local political activities or write letters to elected officials and corporate advertisers.

In spite of the group's impressive size, financing, political successes and media coverage, LaHaye and CWA are not well known to the average American. This is due, in part, to the group's own efforts—the women like to tout themselves as "God's best kept secret" (Eicher, 1987, 2A) and as "speaking softly, but with clout" (Cordray, 1985). LaHaye says she wants to have influence over public policy rather than power itself. It is this "stealth" quality of the organization that prompted one critic to opine: "If the Stepford Wives formed a hate group, it would look as normal—and be as terrifying—as Beverly LaHaye's Concerned Women for America" (Cone and Scheer, 1993).

Maintaining a credible image of femininity is important to LaHaye because it supports her *persona* as a concerned wife and mother. She creates this impression by smiling often and wearing a helmet of perfectly groomed, golden hair. She favors pink blush and wears matching fingernail polish. Softly colored dresses with lots of ruffles and lace are her personal trademark.

Beverly LaHaye enhances her physical appearance and demeanor by working tirelessly to promote public policies that reinforce traditional sex roles—what she calls "God's marvelous plan" for women. She believes that women should always be submissive to their husbands and that women's God-ordained roles are wife, homemaker, and mother. Rather than asserting that all women must be stay-at-home moms, LaHaye claims that she wants women to have choices about their lives:

> We must concentrate on stabilizing the economy and return to the conditions we had 20 and 30 years ago in which the average man's income

was sufficient to support his whole family. We need to return to women the choice between a career of homemaking and raising children or a career in business or the professions. A mother should not have to work outside the home if she does not choose to do so. (Rees, 1985)

In spite of her appropriation of feminists' language about creating choices for women, LaHaye repeatedly defines as selfish those women who do not choose the traditional life. She encourages CWA members to set aside their own selfish aspirations and to make sacrifices for their families:

We are letting women know that there are great satisfactions to being a homemaker, and there is nothing wrong with putting your top priority into raising your children during 20 years of your life. That is not really so many years if you look at your whole life span, which is about 75 years for American women. Really, what is 20 years devoted to raising and developing your children and sending them out to be godly and successful human beings? You can develop your own career after they are independent. (Rees, 1985)

CWA's determined commitment to traditional sex roles sets them apart from feminist organizations. CWA's members often claim that they are the women's group that *loves* men rather than hates them (Eicher, 1987). One CWA member enthused to a reporter: "Isn't it beautiful to see a feminine woman? I used to offend people when I got started, because I talked about . . . women being a little ball of fluff. And I kind of like that. I like softness, and I'll tell you something else: My husband loves it" (Henderson, 1986).

For our purposes, what is noteworthy about Beverly LaHaye is her ability to develop what seems, superficially, to be two contradictory rhetorical roles for herself and her supporters. In her speeches, writings, and direct mail, LaHaye proposes returning to a society where women serve domestic and submissive roles. Yet, in motivating her supporters to work for public policies that will bring about her vision of the ideal society, she draws heavily on a lexicon of war and military-related metaphors that place her in the metaphoric role of a military general or commander-in-chief. CWA members are not only encouraged to support real-world, male warriors, but also to become metaphorical warriors themselves. The next section of this paper illuminates the breadth and ubiquity of LaHaye's war talk and demonstrates how she adopts a military persona for herself.

LaHaye's war talk

Even though the United States currently is not involved in a declared war, LaHaye's rhetoric shows that she perceives herself and her supporters as engaged in a type of civil war. She says bluntly: "We are at war in America today" (n.d., ca. October 1992). Her most frequently used military metaphors are found in her speeches, articles, and direct mail appeals. They are like those described by Ellen Goodman: political disagreements recast as wars and battles. The natures of these wars are slightly different, but they share the qualities of being all-encompassing and posing dire threats to conservative Christians.

Whether she is taking the "aggressor" role or a defensive posture, LaHaye acts as a military leader and strategist in her rhetoric. Like a commander-in-chief, she declares war. In addition to joining the war on drugs, CWA has declared war on AIDS and flag burners. LaHaye also claims that her political opponents have declared war on CWA or its allies. In one abortion-related protest, she claimed that feminists have declared war on the Idaho potato farmer.[5] Eleanor Smeal, past president of NOW, was said to have declared war on Ronald Reagan; abortionists declared war on corporate America; the Legal Services Corporation declared war on the family; a war has been waged against the unborn; and, a cultural war currently rages in America. In one direct-mail letter, LaHaye implored her supporters to oppose an upcoming pro-choice march in Washington, D.C.:

> The radical feminists, abortionists and lesbians have declared war! . . . I have come up with a special "battle plan" which I believe is the only way to counter them. . . . Now you see why I say the radical feminists, abortionists and lesbians have declared war! They have declared war on you and me. . . . We will have to counter what this minority group of radicals is doing—or we will lose the war entirely. . . . I believe God has given us our Battle plan—and I am asking you to help me implement it. . . . Make no mistake about it my friend, we are coming under the most vicious attacks ever seen because of our pro-life and pro-family views. We will be maligned and persecuted but we must always stand up for what is right because we will win the war eventually. (n.d., ca. December 1989)

Even when LaHaye doesn't describe a public policy disagreement as war per se, her ritualistic use of the term "battle" implies the existence of a war. The battles "rage," are "crucial," "critical," and "fierce." LaHaye also issues battle plans, draws battle lines, distinguishes between moral battles, and loses some battles, but not wars. Most importantly, to LaHaye, "the hearts and minds of our children and grandchildren are the battleground" in the contemporary American cultural war (n.d., ca. July 1994).

CWA's warring opponents are often described as having immense destructive powers and are unable to resist using their "firepower." For example, ultraliberals are said to "bombard" Christian families, "raise weapons against us," and use "blitzkrieg" tactics. Feminists are really "feminazis" who use lobbying as a "secret weapon." Secular humanists "attack," make "frontal assaults," and "build financial war chests." Opponents "lead new assaults," "launch legal maneuvers," "slaughter unborn children," "destroy future generations of American children," "destroy families," "unleash radical policies," "unleash massive legislative attacks," plot "destructive reforms and curricula," and try to bring about the "wholesale destruction of parental authority and traditional families" (n.d., ca. July 1994). According to LaHaye, militant homosexuals and lesbians pose the worst danger because they "openly threatened to invade our schools and homes and desecrate our churches" (n.d., ca. September 1991).

Just as LaHaye uses war talk to describe her political opponents, she also uses a language of war to describe her own supporters. CWA members are referred to as "spiritual warriors" and "prayer warriors." She calls them "troops" and "ground troops." The women are called to "fight," "fight the good fight," "go on the defensive," "take the offensive," "occupy land," "move aggressively," "mount counter-strikes," "meet onslaughts head on" and go to the "front lines." The organization's national office in Washington, D.C., is described as a valuable "beachhead." CWA's different legislative, humanitarian, educational, and legal aid programs are described as "fronts" in the war. The spiritual warriors are also "in for the duration." She rallies her troops with claims that "Nor will we ever surrender in our fight to protect your authority to raise your children in a God-centered home and teach them moral absolutes" (n.d., ca. December 1992).

ANALYSIS

How may we best account for or explain Beverly LaHaye's extensive use of the war talk trope? Is her discourse anomalous or unexpected given her public commitments to traditional womanhood and Christianity? If so, then we can make claims about the extent to which the warist trope has permeated American society. In contrast, we also can argue that LaHaye's discourse is an entirely expectable rhetorical response to her environment, *specifically* reflecting the historical and intellectual traditions associated with Christianity. Both of these explanations provide unique insights into LaHaye's discourse, demonstrating that the relationships between traditional womanhood, war, and Christian belief are complex, contested, and fluid. I begin with the argument that LaHaye's warist discourse is inconsistent with her ideas about womanhood.

It is easy to show that Beverly LaHaye's war talk stands in stark contrast with the ideals of the traditional woman. After all, her public platform *exemplifies* what the historian Barbara Welter calls "true womanhood." The true American woman lived her life according to four main principles: purity, piety, submissiveness, and domesticity (1976). LaHaye clearly operates out of a sense of "purity" when she promotes sexual abstinence programs for teens, opposes condom advertisements on television, lobbies against Planned Parenthood speaking to teenagers, opposes sex education, and chastises non-married women for engaging in sexual intercourse. Additionally, she opposed the Equal Rights Amendment on the grounds that women would have to serve in the military—an opposition grounded in her belief that the women would be sexually distracting to the "real" soldiers.

LaHaye also promotes piety in her public advocacy. Almost every piece of direct mail encourages her supporters to pray, to humble themselves before God, and to work to create a society where biblical tenets guide public policy. She argues that only godly men ought to be allowed to hold public office.

Beverly LaHaye also meets Welter's third quality of the true woman—submissiveness. Although she is the leader of a national political organization, she believes that it is the proper role of women to be submissive to their husbands. She goes so far as to say that it is impossible for a woman to be both a Christian and a feminist because the Bible requires that women be submissive and that feminists refuse to accept this godly mandate ("Group Opposes 'Militant Feminism,' " 1985).

Welter's categorization of the true woman's "domesticity" is equally pertinent to LaHaye, as were the first three categories. All of LaHaye's arguments about the necessity for women to be mothers and stay-at-home housewives bolsters her similarity to Welter's traditional, true woman. LaHaye recognizes that some women must work out of financial necessity, but primarily attributes working women's motives to material greed or big government's greed: "In a two-parent, two-income household, two-thirds of the average working mother's salary goes toward increased taxes" (Lightman, 1995).

When I argue that Beverly LaHaye's embrace of traditional sex roles is at odds with her rhetorical persona, I do not mean to imply that traditional women are, by definition, unpatriotic, incapable of supporting militarism, or are pacifists. Whether we point to the role of women in Nazi Germany, Jean Bethke Elshtain's (1987) concept of the "ferocious few," the writing of Virginia Woolf in *Three Guineas* (1938) or bell hooks in *Feminist Theory from Margin to Center* (1984), there is no shortage of evidence that traditional women embrace their country's militarism. Beverly LaHaye, too, has been an ardent advocate for the military policies of every contemporary Republican president. She has supported each major weapons system proposed during the Reagan and Bush administrations, and backed U.S. policy in El Salvador, Nicaragua, Libya, Panama, Lebanon, the Persian Gulf, and the Middle East. In spite of all this evidence, I believe there is a significant difference between a traditional woman's full support of her country's militarism and such a woman speaking as if she were the commander-in-chief, that *she* sets military policy, and that other like-minded women are *soldiers* who implement her orders.

Beverly LaHaye's rhetorical persona as a military general and her promotion of traditional sex roles for women can be seen as being at odds with one another. Her negative judgment of "real" female soldiers is also inconsistent with the kinds of arguments she uses to motivate her supporters. These inconsistencies, however, seem not to trouble either Beverly LaHaye or her 600,000 "ground troops." Although it appears to be irrelevant to CWA, this chasm between image and reality is important because it allows us an opportunity to see the extent to which warism has infiltrated American discourse. That is, we have evidence attesting to the preeminence of the war talk trope in, seemingly, one of the most *unexpected* places—the discourse of a submissive, domestic woman. Even if LaHaye's war talk is inconsistent with the ideals she holds about traditional women, it is entirely in keeping with Christian history and traditions.

Perhaps the most compelling explanation for LaHaye's war talk is to suggest that her discourse draws upon or imitates the long tradition of Christians who do battle with Satan. One need only point to a handful of historical events where Christians have supported and participated in wars with "Satan's emissaries," the Inquisition, the genocidal practices against Pagans and Native Americans, and the Salem, Massachusetts, witch trials. Throughout the ages, Christians have loaned their intellectual and philosophical talents to war making, best exemplified by just-war theories and their applications to a wide variety of wars. Believers have also bolstered the relationship between Christianity and armed conflict by pointing to relevant passages in the Scriptures and exalting war in hymns such as "Onward Christian Soldiers." Thus, LaHaye's war talk ought to be seen as a strategic and persuasive appeal to her audience of female Christians precisely because she draws upon this long and venerable history of battling Satan and evil.

LaHaye's war talk is particularly adapted to the needs and beliefs of a fundamentalist Christian audience of traditional *women*. Her discourse about war is usually cast as a defensive action taken by concerned mothers and grandmothers who can no longer sit passively when "all they value and cherish is under attack" (n.d., ca. November 1991).

It is difficult for feminists to dismantle LaHaye's warist discourse because she so imbues it with religious meaning. One way she accomplishes this is by constantly defining the organization's battles as spiritual wars, moral wars, or cultural wars. An example is provided by the case of pornography in the U.S., which LaHaye describes as a "deeper war raging in society which pits the forces of Satan and darkness against the forces of Good and Light" (n.d., ca. December 1989). Curiously, LaHaye never describes these "wars" as what they really are: *political* disagreements among the citizens of a single country. This distinction is critical because one may still talk, debate, and negotiate with an opponent with whom one disagrees without trying to kill them. But the action of declaring war indicates that the time for talking and negotiating is over until one or both sides suffers enough losses to justify talking (and disagreeing) again. By defining her fellow citizens as warring combatants, there is little need for rhetorical restraint. After all, there can be no negotiation, no mediation, and no power-sharing with an enemy you believe truly is Satanic.

We may view Beverly LaHaye's war talk as inconsistent with her feminine ideology, and thereby reflecting the sheer pervasiveness of warist discourse in this society. Or we may view her war talk as entirely consistent with her religious heritage, and thereby demonstrating both the pervasiveness of warist thought as well as unnecessarily complicating political disagreements. That such disparate interpretations are equally persuasive points to a significant finding: there is no "essential" traditional woman, just as there is no "essential" Christian ideology. The ubiquity and centrality of the war talk trope in LaHaye's public discourse can be seen as reflecting the reality that *anti-feminists* are as capable as feminists in rejecting limited definitions imposed by others. Just as there are feminisms, there are anti-feminisms. We may wish that our ideological adversaries were consistent in their words and deeds, but that will not help us to oppose their warist policies.

War-based, metaphorical discourse is dangerous to all kinds of people, but Beverly LaHaye's war talk is particularly dangerous to feminists and peace activists. Even though some skeptics might argue that it is "just talk" or "mere rhetoric," I believe it is threatening because it simultaneously prepares us for war and desensitizes us to what "real" war is like.

LaHaye's metaphorical wars are like the concept of the "surgical strike" popularized by Ronald Reagan: they delude us into thinking that war is quick, clean, precise, and that we can control its outcome. LaHaye never talks about what war is really "about": dirt, blood, shit, rape, agony, grief, insanity, pain, loss, boredom, violence, fear, and death. By creating a sanitized vision of war to motivate women for political activity, LaHaye encourages her supporters to blind themselves to the variety of potential solutions to political controversies. Instead, she trains them to look first to the most extreme solutions—objectifying, demonizing, and then metaphorically killing those with whom they disagree.

Ellen Goodman observes that our elected officials leap to war talk because it seems to be the only way to motivate an otherwise apathetic audience to care about the day-to-day decisions and difficulties associated with modern American society. Beverly LaHaye's war talk operates in a very similar manner, except that she fails to admit that her declared wars are also *political* in nature and concern the distribution of power, wealth, resources, and status in society—the classic definition of the "material" world above which fundamentalist Christians are supposed to rise. By defining political controversies as moral, spiritual, and cultural wars, she inures her audience with the perception that their wars are different, better, and more justifiable than the ones the world already knows. Ironically, LaHaye relies on a theory of sexual difference to motivate female audience members to think and act in ways identical to male politicians and military planners. Thus, her rhetoric both draws upon and perpetuates a warlike mentality.

Beverly LaHaye's anti-feminist war talk is more than "just talk." It is the *substance* of a concerted campaign to redefine the feminist project as evil and destructive. It threatens feminists because it invites society to see us as demonridden adversaries whose ideas can only be defeated by symbolically or physically annihilating us. The 1989 wounding of thirteen Canadian women, and the execution of fourteen female students by Marc Lepine, a rageful, male classmate, have been written off as the actions of a deranged man. His words, though, belie this interpretation. As he separated his male classmates from his female colleagues at Ecole Polytechnique prior to his shooting rampage, he said: "I want the women. You are all feminists. I hate feminists" (Regenstreir, 1989). Like the celebrated Lepine case, the recent murders of doctors and abortion-clinic employees in Florida and Massachusetts can also be written off as the act of "utterly insane" individuals who are ostensibly unaffected by a warist, anti-feminist environment, and are "in no way typical" of the majority of anti-feminist men. These same headline-grabbing events can also be seen as the physical manifestation of LaHaye's "call to arms" in the raging, cultural war.

In a broader sense, war talk (anti-feminist or otherwise) is dangerous because it keeps us in a permanent state of fear-based agitation. There is no shortage of evidence about the violent quality of America's youth. Are these young people doing anything other than acting out a pervasive social message that the way adults deal with disagreement is through physically threatening or killing one's adversary?

I do not claim a causal link between the writings and utterances of Beverly LaHaye, the metaphoric military general, and the deaths of female engineering students in Canada or abortion clinic workers. LaHaye's war talk provides an illustration of a much broader societal tendency to define our disagreements with one another in the most extreme, objectifying, and terrifying terms possible. That one of the most traditionally feminine political leaders in America would find it to be one of her most motivating rhetorical techniques suggests the importance and centrality of the war talk trope. It suggests also that war talk is part and parcel of Christian history and our warring society. Exposing and challenging the assumptions of this language everywhere one finds it is a "do-able" step that feminist and peace activists can take in working toward a more just and peaceful world.

NOTES

1. Kenneth Burke would undoubtedly accept the idea of war as the *conceptual* opposite or "negation" of peace. His thinking is not so bifurcated, though, especially on the topics of war and peace. He writes: "You may, if you will, imagine a spectrum with absolute war at one end and absolute peace at the other, and with all acts in time considered to be lying somewhere along the intervening series of gradations, according to the varying proportions of the two ingredients. But this alone would be too thorough a mode of reduction to represent the many colors of action as they are realistically experienced. . . . But in the ordinary brands of pacifism, peace is but an ideal, a general direction towards which one should incline when plotting a course" (1969). It is unclear whether he would have accepted common distinctions between positive peace and negative peace.

2. I use the term "trope" in the classic, Aristotelian sense of a word or phrase that serves as a figure of speech.

3. LaHaye says that CWA is larger than NOW, the National Women's Political Caucus, and the League of Women Voters, combined. This claim and the size of Concerned Women for America are hotly contested by the group's adversaries: "Ann Stone, head of Republicans for Choice, estimates that CWA has at most 120,000 members . . . Eleanor Smeal, president of the Fund for a Feminist Majority also questions the CWA numbers. 'Their numbers aren't real' . . . 'If you ever gave to them or signed anything, you're counted. If NOW counted that way, we'd have multimillions' " (McDonald, 1992:5C).

4. Tim LaHaye is a conservative, political activist in his own right. He was influential in organizing the New Right social movement and is currently president of Family Life Seminars.

5. Feminists called a boycott against Idaho potatoes in 1990. According to the *Concerned Women for America Magazine*: "During late March, in an attempt to pressure Idaho Governor Cecil

Andrus to veto the most restrictive abortion bill to ever pass a state senate, the feminists declared war on the Idaho potato farmer. Simply put, the militant feminists held Idaho's farmers and their families hostages" (Feminists Take Aim, 1990).

REFERENCES

The holy bible. (1952). Camden, NJ: Thomas Nelson.

Burke, K. (1969). *A grammar of motives.* Berkeley, CA: University of California Press.

Cady, D. L. (1989). *From warism to pacifism: A moral continuum.* Philadelphia, PA: Temple University Press.

Campbell, K. K. (1989). *Man cannot speak for her: Volume 2.* Westport, CT: Greenwood Press.

Christiansen, A. E., & J. McGee. (1994). Beverly Davenport LaHaye: Spokeswoman for traditional values. In K. K. Campbell (ed.), *Women public speakers in the United States, 1925–1993: A biocritical sourcebook.* Westport, CT: Greenwood Press.

Cohn, C. (1987, Summer). Sex and death in the rational world of defense intellectuals. *Signs, 12,* 687–718.

———. (1993). Wars, wimps, and women: Talking gender and thinking war. In M. Cooke & A. Woollacott (eds.), *Gendering war talk.* Princeton, NJ: Princeton University Press.

Concerned Women for America. (1986). *1979–1986: The CWA story* (brochure). Washington, DC: Author.

Concerned Women for America. (1986). *Who is Beverly LaHaye? Questions and answers* (brochure). Washington, DC: Author.

Cone, E., & L. Scheer. (1993, February). Queen of the right. *Mirabella,* 86–93.

Cooke, M., & A. Woollacott (eds.). (1993). *Gendering war talk.* Princeton, NJ: Princeton University Press.

Cordray, R. (1985, September 27). Women urged to speak softly but with clout. *Washington Times,* n.p.

Diamond, S. (1989). *Spiritual warfare: The politics of the Christian right.* Boston: South End Press.

Eicher, D. (1987, August 19). Concerned Women for America. *Denver Post,* 2A.

Elshtain, J. B. (1987). *Women and war.* New York: Basic Books.

Elshtain, J. B., & S. Tobias (eds.). (1990). *Women, militarism, and war: Essays in history, politics, and social theory.* Savage, MD: Rowman and Littlefield.

Enloe, C. (1988). *Does khaki become you?: The militarization of women's lives.* London: Pandora/Harper/Collins.

———. (1989). *Bananas, beaches and bases: Making feminist sense of international politics.* London: Pandora/Harper/Collins.

———. (1993). *The morning after: Sexual politics at the end of the Cold War.* Berkeley, CA: University of California Press.

Feminists take aim at Idaho potato farmer to push pro-death agenda. (1990, May). *Concerned Women for America Magazine,* 9.

Goodman, E. (1989, September 12). Once again, it's off to war we go. Minneapolis *Star Tribune,* A14.

Griffin, S. (1992). *A chorus of stones: The private life of war.* New York: Doubleday.

Group opposes "militant feminism." (1985, April 27). *Washington Post,* n.p.

hooks, bell. (1984) *Feminist theorizing from margin to center.* Boston, MA: South End Press.

Jeffords, S. (1989). *The remasculinization of America: Gender and the Vietnam War.* Bloomington, IN: Indiana University Press.

LaHaye, B. (n.d.). Promotional letter.

———. (n.d., ca. 1988). Direct mail letter.

———. (n.d., ca. 1989, December). Direct mail letter.

———. (n.d., ca. 1991, September). Direct mail letter.

———. (n.d., ca. 1991, November). Direct mail letter.

———. (n.d., ca. 1992, October). Direct mail letter.

———. (n.d., ca. 1992, December). Direct mail letter.

————. (n.d., ca. 1994, July). Direct mail letter.

————. (1994, July). Reclaimed or destroyed? *Family Voice, 82,* 3, 26.

Lightman, D. (1995, January 18). GOP pushes tax break as easing load on women. Hartford *Courant,* A1.

McDonald, M. (1992, November 18). The biggest women's group you've never heard of. Dallas *Morning News,* 5C.

President Reagan addresses CWA convention. (1987, November). *Concerned Women for America Magazine,* 10.

Regenstreir, G. (1989, December 8). Mass murder victims to be buried on Monday, Montreal mourns. *Reuter Library Report,* 1.

Rosenberg, S. D. (1993). The threshold of thrill: Life stories in the skies over southeast Asia. In M. Cooke & A. Woollacott (eds.), *Gendering war talk.* Princeton, NJ: Princeton University Press.

Ruddick, S. (1989). *Maternal thinking.* Boston: Beacon Press.

Wilson, A. (1993, September 4). Conservative estimate: Beverly LaHaye is the most powerful woman in the new religious right. Houston *Chronicle,* 1.

Woolf, V. (1938). *Three Guineas.* New York: Harcourt Brace.

Woman as Caretaker:
An Archetype That Supports
Patriarchal Militarism

LAURA DUHAN KAPLAN

In this essay, I argue against a species of feminist peace theory which unfolds as follows: Women's psychological development prepares them to be connected caretakers. Men's psychological development prepares them to be individuated competitors. The prevalence of this masculine mentality is a major psychological cause of war. Therefore, war can be averted by promoting the feminine mentality. Elements of this view can be found in the writings of Jo-Ann Pilardi (1983), Robert Litke (1985), Birgit Brock-Utne (1985), James E. Morriss and Joan M. Boyle (1989), Nel Noddings (1989), Sara Ruddick (1989), Paula Smithka (1989), Susan Griffin (1990, 1992), and others.

I shall argue against the theory I have outlined above on two grounds. (1) By adopting a strict dualism between feminine and masculine development, the theory may *reinforce* rather than overcome the patriarchal dualism that constitutes the self by devaluing the other. (2) By holding caretaking as a model of virtue, the theory may obscure the role caretakers often play in supporting war and warriors, thereby *discouraging* women from examining the part they play in maintaining and reproducing a warist society.

Militarism has been defined as the commitment of social resources to the waging of war (Reardon 1985; Johnson 1994). The term "patriarchy" is understood by feminists to refer to a society in which men dominate women and justify their domination through devaluation. More recently, feminists' understanding of "patriarchy" has broadened to include societies in which power elites dominate and devalue the powerless (see, for example, Warren 1991). I use the term "patriarchal militarism" in order to highlight several features of militarism.

Hypatia vol. 9, no. 2 (Spring 1994) © by Laura Duhan Kaplan

First, war is considered by many men to be a creative masculine act (Hein 1984), and, as such, the commitment of social and economic resources to war is a male project. Second, militarism is sold to the public by male power elites who assert that those who are different must be dominated for both their own and the domi-nator's good (Cady 1991; Johnson 1994). Third, the constitution of women by men as "devalued others" serves as a model for training and inspiring masculine warriors to devalue and distance themselves from enemies (Daly 1978).

In this essay, I argue that the archetype of "woman as caretaker" supports patriarchal militarism because it is used by male warriors in the service of the war effort and because it builds on a gender opposition created by patriarchy to contain women. In the first section, I argue that peace theories that celebrate the archetype of woman as caretaker fail to question adequately the devaluation of others which justifies patriarchal militarism. In the second section, I argue that under patriarchy the commitment of social resources to war by men includes the co-optation of women's caretaking efforts.

THEORETICAL CONSIDERATIONS: THE CONCEPT OF WOMAN AS CARETAKER AFFIRMS DUALISTIC HIERARCHICAL THINKING

The type of peace theory which sees hope for peace in the model of the woman as caretaker acknowledges that it is mostly men who threaten, begin, ana-lyze, strategize, fight, and negotiate the ends of destructive wars, and that these activities are honored in the archetype of the masculine warrior. This type of theory aims to honor and extend the work, denigrated under patriarchy as merely preservative and not creative, done by women who care for young, old, sick, or distraught family members and friends. The archetype is an inspiration for many different kinds of praxis: raising male as well as female children who honor care-taking (Pilardi 1983), teaching care rather than competition in school (Brock-Utne 1985), organizing antiwar demonstrations in the name of caretaking (Rud-dick 1989), and engaging in self-reflection about our feminine and masculine ideals and actions (Griffin 1992).

The theory suggests that feminine women have a unique contribution to make to ethical education and consciousness raising. It refers, sometimes implic-itly and sometimes explicitly, to the conception of the ethics of care articulated by Carol Gilligan (see Forcey 1994). Gilligan suggests that many women em-phasize responsibilities to others with whom they have relationships over abstract principles of justice, and argues that this emphasis represents a mature and valid approach to morality (Gilligan 1982). For the insight that affiliation is a femi-nine style of relating to others, Gilligan credits Nancy Chodorow's account of feminine and masculine gender identity development. I shall present Chodorow's description of gender identity development as a basis for (1) understanding the notion of masculinity against which peace theories that emphasize "woman as caretaker" are reacting and (2) evaluating the extent to which the notion of femininity to which these peace theories appeal can serve as a corrective to that masculinity.

Chodorow begins with the socioeconomic observation that, typically, Western middle-class mothers care for infants and children full-time, while fathers work outside the home and often see little of their children. Mothers, Chodorow claims, tend to identify more strongly with infant daughters than with infant sons because mothers remember their own infancy and anticipate their daughters' future motherhood. This unconscious identification, along with an awareness of a dichotomous system of gender identity and a desire to perpetuate it, causes mothers to seek closer relationships with their daughters and more distant relationships with their sons. Typically a daughter's affiliation with and imitation of her mother continues uninterrupted throughout childhood without any jarring realization of discontinuity to necessitate a resolution of psychological conflicts (contrary to what Freud postulated in his theory of the Electra complex). Not experiencing this temporary break, the daughter's experience of human relations in early childhood is one of affiliation. The core of feminine gender identity becomes an awareness of oneself as intrinsically connected with others. The daughter is thus prepared to create and maintain a family. The boy, however, is pushed away by his mother and, through various other social channels as well, becomes cognitively aware of his gender difference from her.

Unfortunately, the boy cannot easily affiliate with and imitate his father, because father is not available. Therefore the boy constructs a masculine gender identity through alternative means. Because his mother represents that which he may not become, he constitutes her as "Other," devaluing in her and repressing in himself everything he considers part of her feminine gender identity. The boy's experience of human relations in early childhood is one of individuation by alienation. The core of masculine gender identity becomes an awareness of oneself as separated from others by unbridgeable differences and hierarchies. Sons are thus prepared for the competitive world of work outside the closeness of family (Chodorow 1974).

As a psychoanalyst, Chodorow is concerned by pathologies caused by some women's extreme dependence on their mothers or daughters and some men's extreme alienation from and devaluation of others. In order to weaken the dynamics causing women's extreme affiliation and men's extreme disaffiliation, Chodorow suggests shared parenting by fathers and mothers within nuclear families. Girls could create diverse relationships with more than one adult caretaker and role model, while boys could have a close relationship with a male role model and not need to devalue mother and femininity in order to create a gender identity.

It is easy to see how Chodorow's description of masculine gender identity could be attractive to feminist peace theorists trying to understand the causes of and cures for war; just read the final sentence of the paragraph before last as "Sons are thus prepared for the competitive world of war outside the closeness of family." If separation from mother, and therefore from others, leads to an aptitude for war, then one might speculate that affiliation with mother and others could lead to a mode of relating which does not result in war. And this is precisely how some peace theorists have made use of Chodorow's ideas. For example, peace theorist Jo-Ann Pilardi suggests that states define themselves in opposition to other states, and argues that this self-definition, which is realized through war, is the result of modeling international relations on masculine gender identity development. Implicitly assuming that the development of states will mirror the development of the people who constitute them, Pilardi offers a solution to the problem of war which was originally articulated by Chodorow as a solution to the self-destructive extremes of self-denying affiliation and other-denying separation. Pilardi suggests changing the dynamics of early childhood development so that boys need not constitute themselves by devaluing and rejecting mother (Pilardi 1983). Peace theorist and ecofeminist Susan Griffin relies on the isomorphism of a person's private and public lives to suggest that devaluation of the feminine leads to war. Griffin believes that a loss of awareness of "the matrix of connections that defines all being" enables men to make war. She identifies this awareness with a feminine consciousness. Men have blocked their awareness of connection by defining women as "other." This behavior reflects men's unwillingness to recognize the feminine aspects of themselves. A man's restoration of his feminine side must begin with an examination of the psychic webs that constitute his life; he must give particular attention to the lessons learned from family dynamics (Griffin 1990, 1992).

I do not believe that the concept of femininity which underlies these theories can save Western culture from the (so-called) masculine practice of devaluing the other. It cannot overcome what ecofeminist Val Plumwood calls the "dualistically constructed dichotomy." Such a dichotomy "polarizes difference and minimizes shared characteristics, construes difference along lines of superiority/inferiority, and views the inferior side as a means to the higher ends of the superior side" (Plumwood 1991). As Chodorow pointed out, patriarchy reproduces itself by constructing masculinity and femininity as a "dualistic dichotomy." And this dichotomy between masculinity and femininity can lead to war, either through psychology (by repressing feminine affiliative qualities, as Griffin suggests) or politics (by serving as a model for international relations, as Pilardi suggests).

Therefore, I think that a feminist peace theory begins by questioning the categories of masculinity and femininity, rather than by formulating solutions within this dichotomous world view. From that perspective, I argue more pointedly that peace theories that emphasize the image of woman as caretaker do not challenge conceptions of femininity which have served to silence women; that these theories accept hierarchical thinking about gender but invert the hierarchy, placing femininity on top; and that these theories do not adequately challenge devaluation of the other. I also make suggestions about the direction in which a feminist peace theory might move in order to challenge the creation of oppressive hierarchies among people.

Marilyn Frye (1983) rejects the biological dualism that lays the foundation for dualistic theories of gender identity. She argues that no sharp biological distinction between male and female exists. Rather there is a continuum along which people's possession of primary and secondary sexual characteristics (including the formation of reproductive organs) can be arranged. However, social conventions under patriarchy require that males and females be treated with different degrees of respect. Therefore, in a patriarchal society, most persons adopt forms of masculine or feminine dress, address, movement, livelihood, et cetera in order to proclaim clearly which gender they belong to so that they can be treated appropriately (Frye 1983). Caretaking is a form of relating to others which involves feminine forms of spending time (by deferring one's needs to those of others), making a living (in crucial but not well-paid professions such as nursing and teaching), and addressing others (with particular emphasis on listening carefully). Women who conceptualize their peace praxis under the heading "woman as caretaker" are reminding others of their femininity, and hence of the need not to respect their perspective, as they enter the political sphere. Although they call for warriors to respect and respond to their perspective, the respect is rarely forthcoming because gender stereotypes are used to announce the relative social value of persons, activities, and perspectives (Thiede and Duhan [Kaplan], 1991). Women's call for the revaluation and extension of caretaking will not be heard until the artificial dichotomizing of people into diametrically different groups has been effectively challenged.

Challenging the practice of gender stereotyping may be understood philosophically as challenging patriarchal conceptions of personal identity. And such a reconceptualization of the foundation of personal identity may be necessary for peace theory. Caroline Whitbeck (1989) labels as "masculist ontology" any theory that defines what it is to be a person by celebrating what it deems to be masculine characteristics (e.g., a healthy egoism, participation in culture, development of the mind and spirit) and rejecting what it deems to be feminine characteristics (e.g., altruism, affinity with nature, development of the body). Whitbeck notes that some feminist theories of personal identity simply celebrate the feminine way of being over the masculine. These feminist theories inherit the dualism of "masculist ontology," constituting the self in opposition to a reified, devalued "other." Whitbeck's alternative is to suggest that because we are related to others in complex ways, we constitute our identities relative to others in various complex and subtle ways. Typically, we notice both our similarities to and differences from others. Applying Whitbeck's ideas, I argue that some pacifist women who claim the title of caretaker are affirming what they seek to avoid: marginalization of the other, which leads to the divisions between people on which wars are predicated. If Whitbeck is correct in her description of dualistic and nondualistic theories of personal identity, then it is not the extension of feminine caretaking which holds a hope for peace. Instead it is the possibility that humanity can be aware, even in the face of fear, tragedy and propaganda, that we are both similar to and different from our enemies as well as our friends.

Cultivating this awareness may require some difficult recognitions of how feminine women who connect with others are similar to masculine men who devalue others. Elizabeth V. Spelman has pointed out that Chodorow's focus on gender dualism as the primary instance of hierarchical thinking is overly simplistic. As early as we learn gender identity, says Spelman, we learn class and race identity. All three of these identities are embedded in and reinforce a complex and overlapping network of social hierarchies. Entire families, including the women and children in them, are located at various matrices in these networks, and most people work both socially and psychologically to maintain their positions. Women as well as men create a sense of self partially by devaluing the real and imagined characteristics of members of other groups. Therefore, to say that women are affiliated with others while men are alienated from others is simply false. Spelman goes so far as to accuse some feminists of deliberately avoiding issues of race and class oppression in the hope that if these are not discussed, no voices will demand social justice, the institution of which of course requires sacrifice (Spelman 1988). From Spelman's perspective on race, class, and gender, revaluing women's traditional role as caretaker may be a beginning to challenging the devaluation of others which enables warriors to carry out their work. But it should be regarded *only* as a beginning. Other persons, practices, and perspectives whose marginalization is used to legitimate their domination must also be revalued, and the human tendency toward devaluation of others must be understood and addressed. Encouraging constructive relations among ethnic, racial, and class groups is crucial to making peace.

The actual tactics of war support my application of Spelman's point to peace theory. Wars are rarely understood by leaders or citizens as wars of men against women, despite Chodorow's point that men constitute women as other. Rather, wars are sold by politicians and bought by citizens as wars of one nation against another, one ethnic group against another, or one religious sect against another. And women buy into these distinctions with all they entail, just as men do.

Here I do not mean to ignore the fact that the tactics of war include the brutalization of women by men. Susan Brownmiller (1976) has documented that extensively, and the recent news about the Bosnian Serbs' organized program of the rape of Muslim women, for the dual purposes of military "recreation" and "ethnic cleansing," testifies to the continuing reality and brutality of these tactics. This case, and many others like it, support Spelman's observations, as ethnic hatred and sexual domination fuel one another.

If, as Karen J. Warren (1991) has claimed, all types of oppressive hierarchical thinking are related, then women who celebrate the archetype of the caretaker as a route to peace are affirming the general process of creating and maintaining harmful, oppositional, artificial dichotomies between people. On this view, the best hope for peace in the future may be the dismantling of all systems and structures of domination and subordination, and the psychological and conceptual forces that keep them in place. For now, the best hope may be to notice the essential connection between the maintenance of oppressive structures and gender oppression. Then the question becomes, "To what extent does the gender-stereotyped image of woman as caretaker help reinforce or help overcome these systems of oppression, and to what extent is that image embedded in patriarchal militarism?"

PRACTICAL CONSIDERATIONS: CARETAKING WOMEN
MAY SUPPORT WAR EFFORTS

If the archetype of woman as caretaker follows patriarchal classifications of persons, then it would make sense that, in practice, caretakers play patriarchally defined roles. As the classification of persons under patriarchy supports militarism, it would make sense that playing the role of caretaker under patriarchy supports militarism as well, in at least two concrete ways. First, a caretaker may find herself in a relationship with responsibilities to a warrior, and her understanding of her role as caretaker may require her to fulfill those responsibilities. Second, caretaking is often enacted within public institutions, by women in the roles of (for example) teacher or nurse. In a militarized society, these institutions come to serve military aims as well.

Caretaking is understood by Carol Gilligan as a set of ethical commitments that emphasize relationships and responsibilities over abstract universal principles of justice (Gilligan 1982). Caught in a conflict between the concrete, immediate, and personal responsibility to a present, needy warrior and the universal responsibility to protect faceless, nameless strangers, a caretaker may be more likely to choose the immediate commitment. Nel Noddings understands caretaking as a relationship between specific persons in which the one caring is motivationally displaced in the one cared for (Noddings 1984). On this understanding, a caretaker may want to oppose war, but may think she must say to her cared-for warrior, "I want what you want," and come to believe it. The classic examples of co-opted caretakers are the wives of warriors (see, for example, Bartky 1990), who, torn in loyalties between their responsibilities to their husbands and their husband's victims, choose their husbands.

From the perspective of an ethics of justice, early modern feminist author Mary Wollstonecraft speaks negatively of such women, suggesting that they are no better than the warriors they care for. Wollstonecraft rejects the ideal, celebrated by some of her contemporary educational theorists, of the coquettish woman educated for the sole end of pleasing a husband. Such a woman, says Wollstonecraft, is only "half a person." She has "manners but no morals." Curiously, in order to illuminate her analysis of the ideal of the coquettish woman, Wollstonecraft likens the coquettish woman to a military man: both have "manners but no morals." Both suffer from a lack of education, not having learned the general principles of rationality which enable a person to act in accordance with a humanistic morality. Both know only their limited personal experience, although the soldier's travels enable him to affect a shallow worldliness (Wollstonecraft [1792] 1990).

A woman need not be pledged to support a warrior in order for her caretaking to serve the practice of war. When institutions that perform caretaking functions are militarized, those who work within them serve military aims. War is a complex activity, requiring the support of families, industries, and schools. These institutions must function before wars, to train soldiers; during wars, to feed, clothe, and arm active soldiers and to nurse and replace wounded soldiers; and after wars to reeducate and reintegrate veterans for peace while training the next generation of soldiers. Most opportunities women have to serve as unpaid or paid caretakers will be within one of these institutions, and so, wittingly or unwittingly, caretaking women will contribute to the war effort.

Jean Elshtain's location of the archetype of the female caretaker in the Christian just war tradition suggests that a woman cannot nurture in a militarized society without unwittingly supporting war. The just war tradition, says Elshtain, constituted men as "just Christian warriors, fighters, and defenders of righteous causes." Women were constituted as "weepers, occasions for war, and keepers of the flame of nonwarlike values" who "cannot effectively fight the mortal wounding of sons, brothers, husbands, fathers" (Elshtain 1985; Duhan [Kaplan] 1990). By "keeping the flame of nonwarlike values," i.e., by caretaking, women may be playing a militarist rather than an anti-military role. Betty Reardon's analysis of the connection between the growth of militarism and sexism also suggests that the archetype of the caretaking woman is exploited, if not created, for making war. Under patriarchy, men reserve the right to make war for themselves. As more and more governmental and industrial institutions come to serve military aims, the exclusion of women from decision-making positions in those institutions becomes more important to men (Reardon 1985). The ideal of the caretaking woman helps exclude women from public institutions by reminding women that their first responsibility is to family. The ideal helps co-opt women's resistance to war by convincing women that their immediate responsibility to ameliorate the effects of war takes precedence over organized public action against war.

The decision to serve privately or publicly as a caretaker in wartime cannot be an easy decision for women who are aware of the human costs of war. A woman's decision may weave a psychologically painful web around her, as there is no way for her to care for those damaged by war without supporting war. She may choose, then, to suppress her awareness of the damage caused by war. The case of Mrs. Boyle, who cared for British Brigadier General Hugh Trenchard during World War II, as told by Susan Griffin (1992), offers an example. Griffin tells this story in order to reveal General Trenchard's suppression of his own femininity, but, as is typical of stories told by Griffin, this story also has much to reveal about Mrs. Boyle. It illustrates one way (a worst case scenario, perhaps) in which a commitment to caretaking can lead a woman to reinforce the subordination of women, the fragmentation of self, and the glorification of war as an act of masculine creativity, all of which characterize patriarchal militarism. I mean for the story to be suggestive, rather than representative.

Toward the end of World War II, British Brigadier General Trenchard becomes seriously ill and Mrs. Boyle, a Red Cross worker whose late husband was a friend of General Trenchard's, cares for him. During the days that she nurses him, he speaks, deliriously, half-asleep, of his guilt and uncertainty over all the men he has ordered into death. When he regains his health, he never speaks of his confession. Neither does Mrs. Boyle. She feels close to him, now knowing "the real man" and thematizing this knowledge as her secret prize. Out of kindness to him, she tells herself, she will not mention his uncertainties to him (Griffin 1992).

Mrs. Boyle seems to believe that her future husband's self-esteem depends on the maintenance of his confident warrior's persona: it is "out of kindness" (Griffin's words) that she hides from General Trenchard his own self-questioning. Apparently, Mrs. Boyle's self-esteem depends on her ability to maintain General Trenchard's self-esteem: she views her knowledge of his uncertainty as her "secret prize" (Griffin's words again). Mrs. Boyle positions herself as a subordinate in what psychologist Jean Baker Miller calls a relationship of "permanent inequality." In such a relationship, subordinates often survive by learning more about dominants than the dominants themselves know, and using this knowledge to flatter dominants into treating them well (Miller 1976). Mrs. Boyle's caretaking is practiced at the cost of suppressing fundamental truths which question her husband's masculine persona. Betty Reardon writes that this "suffocation of the true self" in the name of gender roles is a type of "social conditioning [which] . . . oppress[es] us all" and which is a psychological model for the enactment of violence between persons (Reardon 1985).

CONCLUSION

In this essay, I have tried to show how both peace theories about caretakers and the actual practice of caretaking can fail to call into question fundamental concepts of patriarchal militarism. Also, I have suggested an alternative emphasis for feminist peace theory, the dismantling of all oppressive hierarchies as a first step toward peace. I recognize that caretakers think of themselves as valuing rather than devaluing others. However, I believe that the notion of caretaking is so tainted by patriarchal evaluations of femininity that its ability to challenge the fundamental tenets of patriarchal militarism (the appropriation of war-making and war-ending by men, the domination of other persons, and the devaluation of women) is severely limited.

REFERENCES

Bartky, Sandra Lee. 1990. *Femininity and domination: Studies in the phenomenology of oppression.* New York: Routledge.

Brock-Utne, Birgit. 1985. *Educating for peace: A feminist perspective.* New York: Pergamon Press.

Brownmiller, Susan. 1976. *Against our will: Men, women, and rape.* New York: Bantam Books.

Cady, Duane. 1991. War, gender, race, and class. *Concerned Philosophers for Peace Newsletter* 11 (2): 4–10.

Chodorow, Nancy. 1974. Family structure and feminine personality. In *Woman, culture and society,* ed. Michelle Zimbalist Rosaldo and Louise Lamphere. Stanford: Stanford University Press.

Daly, Mary. 1978. *Gyn/ecology: The metaethics of radical feminism.* Boston: Beacon Press.

Duhan [Kaplan], Laura. 1990. Feminism and peace theory: Women as nurturers vs. women as public citizens. In *In the interest of peace: A spectrum of philosophical views*, ed. Kenneth Klein and Joseph Kunkel. Wakefield, N. H.: Longwood Academic.

Elshtain, Jean Bethke. 1985. Reflections on war and political discourse: Realism, just war, and feminism in a nuclear age. *Political Theory* 13(1): 39–57.

Forcey, Linda. 1994. Women as peacemakers: Contested terrain for feminist peace studes. In *In the eye of the storm: Philosophy of peace and regional conflict*, ed. Laurence A. Bove and Laura Duhan Kaplan. Amsterdam: Rodopi.

Frye, Marilyn. 1983. *The politics of reality: Essays in feminist theory*. Freedom, CA: Crossing Press.

Gilligan, Carol. 1982. *In a different voice: Psychological theory and women's development*. Cambridge: Harvard University Press.

Griffin, Susan. 1990. Curves along the road. In *Reweaving the world: The emergence of ecofeminism*, ed. Irene Diamond and Gloria Feman Orenstein. San Francisco: Sierra Club Books.

———. 1992. *A chorus of stones: The private life of war*. New York: Doubleday.

Johnson, David E. 1994. The concepts of militarism and regional conflicts. In *In the eye of the storm: Philosophy of peace and regional conflict*, ed. Laurence A. Bove and Laura Duhan Kaplan. Amsterdam: Rodopi.

Litke, Robert. 1985. Consciousness, gender, and nuclear politics. In *Nuclear war: Philosophical perspectives*, ed. Michael Allen Fox and Leo Groarke. New York: Peter Lang.

Miller, Jean Baker. 1976. *Towards a new psychology of women*. Boston: Beacon Press.

Morriss, James E., and Joan M. Boyle. 1989. Patriarchy, aggression and the politics of war. Paper presented at the Second Annual Meeting of Concerned Philosophers for Peace.

Noddings, Nel. 1984. *Caring: A feminist approach to ethics and moral education*. Berkeley: University of California Press.

———. 1989. *Women and evil*. Berkeley: University of California Press.

Pilardi, Jo-Ann [Fuchs]. 1983. On the war path and beyond: Hegel, Freud, and feminist theory. *Hypatia* 1, published as a special issue of *Women's Studies International Forum* 6(6): 565–72.

Plumwood, Val. 1991. Nature, self and gender: Feminism, environmental philosophy, and the critique of rationalism. *Hypatia* 6(1): 3–27.

Reardon, Betty. 1985. *Sexism and the war system*. New York: Teachers College Press.

Ruddick, Sara. 1989. *Maternal thinking: Toward a politics of peace*. New York: Ballantine.

Smithka, Paula. 1989. Nuclearism and sexism: Overcoming their shared metaphysical basis. In *Issues in war and peace: Philosophical perspectives*, ed. Joseph Kunkel and Kenneth Klein. Wolfeboro, N. H.: Longwood Academic.

Spelman, Elizabeth V. 1988. *Inessential woman: Problems of exclusion in feminist thought*. Boston: Beacon Press.

Thiede, Barbara, and Laura Duhan [Kaplan]. 1991. Mothers and peace activism: Do women have a special responsibility for making peace? Paper delivered at the Southeastern Women's Studies Association Meeting.

Warren, Karen. 1991. Toward a feminist peace politics. Paper presented at a meeting of Concerned Philosophers for Peace.

Whitbeck, Caroline. [1984] 1989. A different reality: Feminist ontology. In *Women, knowledge and reality: Explorations in feminist philosophy*, ed. Ann Garry and Marilyn Pearsall. Boston: Unwin Hyman.

Wollstonecraft, Mary. [1792] 1990. *A vindication of the rights of women*. In *A Wollstonecraft anthology*, ed. Janet Todd. New York: Columbia University Press.

Men in Groups:
Collective Responsibility for Rape

LARRY MAY and ROBERT STRIKWERDA

As teenagers, we ran in a crowd that incessantly talked about sex. Since most of us were quite afraid of discovering our own sexual inadequacies, we were quite afraid of women's sexuality. To mask our fear, of which we were quite ashamed, we maintained a posture of bravado, which we were able to sustain through mutual reinforcement when in small groups or packs. Riding from shopping mall to fast food establishment, we would tell each other stories about our sexual exploits, stories we all secretly believed to be pure fictions. We drew strength from the camaraderie we felt during these experiences. Some members of our group would yell obscenities at women on the street as we drove by. Over time, conversation turned more and more to group sex, especially forced sex with women we passed on the road. To give it its proper name, our conversation turned increasingly to rape. At a certain stage, we tired of it all and stopped associating with this group of men, or perhaps they were in most ways still boys. The reason we left was not that we disagreed with what was going on but, if this decision to leave was reasoned at all, it was that the posturing (the endless attempts to impress one another by our daring ways) simply became very tiresome. Only much later in life did we think that there was anything wrong, morally, socially, or politically, with what went on in that group of adolescents who seemed so ready to engage in rape. Only later still did we wonder whether we shared in responsibility for the rapes that are perpetrated by those men who had similar experiences to ours.[1]

Catharine MacKinnon has recently documented the link between violence and rape in the war in Bosnia. Young Serbian soldiers, some with no previous sexual experience, seemed quite willing to rape Muslim and Croatian women as their reward for "winning" the war. These young men were often encouraged in these acts by groups of fellow soldiers, and even sometimes by their commanding officers. Indeed, gang rape in concentration camps, at least at the beginning of the war, seems to have been common (Post et al., 1993) The situation in Bosnia is by no means unique in the history of war (Brownmiller 1993, 37). But rape historically has never been considered a war crime. MacKinnon suggests that this is because "Rape in war has so often been treated as extracurricular, as just something men do, as a product rather than a policy of war" (MacKinnon 1993, 30).

War crimes are collective acts taken against humanity; whereas rape has almost always been viewed as a despicable "private" act. In this paper we wish to challenge the view that rape is the responsibility only of the rapists by challenging the notion that rape is best understood as an individual, private act. This is a paper about the relationship between the shared experiences of men in groups, especially experiences that make rape more likely in western culture, and the shared responsibility of men for the prevalence of rape in that culture. The claim of the paper is that in some societies men are collectively responsible for rape in that most if not all men contribute in various ways to the prevalence of rape, and as a result these men should share in responsibility for rape.

Most men do very little at all to oppose rape in their societies; does this make them something like co-conspirators with the men who rape? In Canada, a number of men have founded the "White Ribbon Campaign." This is a program of fund-raising, consciousness raising, and symbolic wearing of white ribbons during the week ending on December 6th, the anniversary of the murder of 14 women at a Montreal engineering school by a man shouting "I hate feminists." Should men in U.S. society start a similar campaign? If they do not, do they deserve the "co-conspirator" label? If they do, is this symbolic act enough to diminish their responsibility? Should men be speaking out against the program of rape in the war in Bosnia? What should they tell their sons about such rapes, and about rapes that occur in their home towns? If men remain silent, are they not complicitous with the rapists?

We will argue that insofar as male bonding and socialization in groups contributes to the prevalence of rape in western societies, men in those societies should feel responsible for the prevalence of rape and should feel motivated to counteract such violence and rape. In addition, we will argue that rape should be seen as something that men, as a group, are collectively responsible for, in a way which parallels the collective responsibility of a society for crimes against humanity perpetrated by some members of their society. Rape is indeed a crime against humanity, not merely a crime against a particular woman. And rape is a crime perpetrated by men as a group, not merely by the individual rapist.

To support our claims we will criticize four other ways to understand responsibility for rape. First, it is sometimes said that only the rapist is responsible since he alone intentionally committed the act of rape. Second, it is sometimes said that no one is responsible since rape is merely a biologically oriented response to stimuli that men have little or no control over. Third, it is sometimes said that everyone, women and men alike, contribute to the violent environment which produces rape so both women and men are equally responsible for rape, and hence it is a mistake to single men out. Fourth, it is sometimes said that it is "patriarchy," rather than individual men or men as a group, which is responsible for rape.[2] After examining each of these views we will conclude by briefly offering our own positive reasons for thinking that men are collectively responsible for the prevalence of rape in western society.

I. THE RAPIST AS LONER OR DEMON

Joyce Carol Oates has recently described the sport of boxing, where men are encouraged to violate the social rule against harming one another, as "a highly organized ritual that violates taboo."

> The paradox of the boxer is that, in the ring, he experiences himself as a living conduit for the inchoate, demonic will of the crowd: the expression of their collective desire, which is to pound another human being into absolute submission. (Oates 1992, 60)

Oates makes the connection here between boxing and rape. The former boxing heavyweight champion of the world, Mike Tyson, epitomizes this connection both because he is a convicted rapist, and also because, according to Oates, in his fights he regularly used the pre-fight taunt "I'll make you into my girlfriend," clearly the "boast of a rapist." (Oates 1992, 61)

Just after being convicted of rape, Mike Tyson gave a twisted declaration of his innocence:

> I didn't rape anyone. I didn't hurt anyone—no black eyes, no broken ribs. When I'm in the ring, I break their ribs, I break their jaws. To me, that's hurting someone. (St. Louis Post Dispatch, March 27, 1992, 20A)

In the ring, Tyson had a license to break ribs and jaws; and interestingly he understood that this was a case of hurting another person. It was just that in the ring it was acceptable. He knew that he was not supposed to hurt people outside the ring. But since he didn't break any ribs or jaws, how could anyone say that he hurt his accuser, Desiree Washington? Having sex with a woman could not be construed as having hurt her, for Tyson apparently, unless ribs or jaws were broken.

Tyson's lawyer, attempting to excuse Tyson's behavior, said that the boxer grew up in a "male-dominated world." And this is surely true. He was plucked from a home for juvenile delinquents and raised by boxing promoters. Few American males had been so richly imbued with male tradition, or more richly rewarded for living up to the male stereotype of the aggressive, indomitable fighter. Whether or not he recognized it as a genuine insight, Tyson's lawyer points us toward the heart of the matter in American culture: misbehavior, especially sexual misbehavior of males toward females, is, however mixed the messages, something that many men condone. This has given rise to the use of the term "the rape culture" to describe the climate of attitudes that exists in the contemporary American male-dominated world (see Griffin 1971).

While noting all of this, Joyce Carol Oates ends her *Newsweek* essay on Tyson's rape trial by concluding that "no one is to blame except the perpetrator himself." She absolves the "culture" at large of any blame for Tyson's behavior. Oates regards Tyson as a sadist who took pleasure in inflicting pain both in and out of the boxing ring. She comes very close to demonizing him when, at the end of her essay, she suggests that Tyson is an outlaw or even a sociopath. And while she is surely right to paint Tyson's deed in the most horrific colors, she is less convincing when she suggests that Tyson is very different from other males in our society. In one telling statement in her essay, however, Oates opens the door for a less individualistic view of rape by acknowledging that the boxing community had built up in Tyson a "grandiose sense of entitlement, fueled by the insecurities and emotions of adolescence" (Oates 1992, 61).

Rape is normally committed by individual men; but, in our view, rape is not best understood in individualistic terms. The chief reasons for this are that individual men are more likely to engage in rape when they are in groups, and men receive strong encouragement to rape from the way they are socialized as men, that is, in the way they come to see themselves as instantiations of what it means to be a man. Both the "climate" that encourages rape and the "socialization" patterns which instill negative attitudes about women are difficult to understand or assess when one focuses on the isolated individual perpetrator of a rape. There are significant social dimensions to rape that are best understood as group-oriented.

As parents, we have observed that male schoolchildren are much more likely to misbehave (and subsequently to be punished by being sent to "time out") than are female schoolchildren. This fact is not particularly remarkable, for boys are widely believed to be more active than girls. What is remarkable is that school teachers, in our experience, are much more likely to condone the misbehavior of boys than the misbehavior of girls. "Boys will be boys" is heard as often today as it was in previous times. (See Robert Lipsyte's [1993] essay about the Glen Ridge, New Jersey rape trial where the defense attorney used just these words to defend the star high school football players who raped a retarded girl.) From their earliest experience with authority figures, little boys are given mixed signals about misbehavior. Yes, they are punished, but they are also treated as if their misbehavior is expected, even welcome. It is for some boys, as it was for us, a "badge of honor" to be sent to detention or "time out." From older boys and from their peers, boys learn that they often will be ostracized for being "too goody-goody." It is as if part of the mixed message is that boys are given a license to misbehave.

And which of these boys will turn out to be rapists is often as much a matter of luck as it is a matter of choice. Recent estimates have it that in the first few months of the war "30,000 to 50,000 women, most of them Muslim" were raped by Serbian soldiers (Post et al., 1993, 32). The data on date rape suggest that young men in our society engage in much more rape than anyone previously anticipated. It is a serious mistake in psychological categorization to think that all of these rapes are committed by sadists. (Studies by Amir show that the average rapist is not psychologically "abnormal" [cited in Griffin 1971, 178].) Given our own experiences and similar reports from others, it is also a serious mistake to think that those who rape are significantly different from the rest of the male population. (Studies by Smithyman indicate that rapists "seemed not to differ markedly from the majority of males in our culture" [cited in Scully 1990, 75].) Our conclusion is that the typical rapist is not a demon or sadist, but, in some sense, could have been many men.

Most of those who engage in rape are at least partially responsible for these rapes, but the question we have posed is this: are those who perpetrate rape the *only* ones who are responsible for rape? Contrary to what Joyce Carol Oates contends, we believe that it is a serious mistake to think that only the perpetrators are responsible. The interactions of men, especially in all-male groups, contribute to a pattern of socialization that also plays a major role in the incidence of rape. In urging that more than the individual perpetrators be seen as responsible for rape, we do not mean to suggest that the responsibility of the perpetrator be diminished. When responsibility for harm is shared it need not be true that the perpetrators of harm find their responsibility relieved or even diminished. Rather, shared responsibility for harms merely means that the range of people who are implicated in these harms is extended. (More will be said on this point in the final section.)

II. THE RAPIST AS VICTIM OF BIOLOGY

The most recent psychological study of rape is that done by Randy Thornhill and Nancy Wilmsen Thornhill (1992), "The Evolutionary Psychology of Men's Coercive Sexuality." In this work, any contention that coercion or rape may be socially or culturally learned is derisively dismissed, as is any feminist argument for changing men's attitudes through changing especially group-based socialization. The general hypothesis they support is that

> sexual coercion by men reflects a sex-specific, species-typical psychological adaptation to rape: Men have certain psychological traits that evolved by natural selection specifically in the context of coercive sex and made rape adaptive during human evolution. (363)

They claim that rape is an adaptive response to biological differences between men and women.

Thornhill and Thornhill contend that the costs to women to engage in sex ("nine months of pregnancy") greatly exceed the costs to men ("a few minutes of time and an energetically cheap ejaculate"). As a result women and men come very early in evolutionary time to adapt quite differently sexually.

> Because women are more selective about mates and more interested in evaluating them and delaying copulation, men, to get sexual access, must often break through feminine barriers of hesitation, equivocation, and resistance. (366)

Males who adapted by developing a proclivity to rape and thus who "solved the problem" by forcing sex on a partner, were able to "out-reproduce" other more passive males and gain an evolutionary advantage.

In one paragraph, Thornhill and Thornhill dismiss feminists who support a "social learning theory of rape" by pointing out that males of several "species with an evolutionary history of polygyny" are also "more aggressive, sexually assertive and eager to copulate." Yet, in "the vast majority of these species there is no sexual training of juveniles by other members of the group." This evidence, they conclude, thoroughly discredits the social learning theory and means that such theories "are never alternatives to evolutionary hypotheses about psychological adaptation" (364). In response to their critics, Thornhill and Thornhill go so far as to say that the feminist project of changing socialization patterns is pernicious.

> The sociocultural view does seem to offer hope and a simple remedy in that it implies that we need only fix the way that boys are socialized and rape will disappear. This naive solution is widespread. . . . As Hartung points out, those who feel that the social problem of rape can be solved by changing the nature of men through naive and arbitrary social adjustments should "get real about rape" because their perspective is a danger to us all. (416)

According to the Thornhills, feminists and other social theorists need to focus instead on what are called the "cues that affect the use of rape by adult males" (416).

The evolutionary biological account of rape we have rehearsed above would seemingly suggest that no one is responsible for rape. After all, if rape is an adaptive response to different sexual development in males and females, particular individuals who engage in rape are merely doing what they are naturally adapted to do. Rape is something to be controlled by those who control the "cues" that stimulate the natural rapist instincts in all men. It is for this reason that the Thornhills urge that more attention be given to male arousal and female stimulation patterns in laboratory settings (375). Notice that even on the Thornhills' own terms, those who provide the cues may be responsible for the prevalence of rape, even if the perpetrators are not. But Thornhill and Thornhill deny that there are any normative conclusions that follow from their research and criticize those who wish to draw out such implications as committing the "naturalistic fallacy" (see 407).

In contrast to the Thornhills, a more plausible sociobiological account is given by Lionel Tiger. Tiger is often cited as someone who attempted to excuse male aggression. In his important study he defines aggression as distinct from violence, but nonetheless sees violence as one possible outcome of the natural aggressive tendencies, especially in men.

> Aggression occurs when an individual or group see their interest, their honor, or their job bound up with coercing the animal, human, or physical environment to achieve their own ends rather than (or in spite of) the goals of the object of their action. Violence may occur in the process of interaction. (Tiger 1984, 158–59)

For Tiger, aggression is intentional behavior which is goal-directed and based on procuring something which is necessary for survival. Aggression is a " 'normal' feature of the human biologically based repertoire" (159). Violence, "coercion involving physical force to resolve conflict" (159), on the other hand, is not necessarily a normal response to one's environment, although in some circumstances it may be. Thus, while human males are evolutionarily adapted to be aggressive, they are not necessarily adapted to be violent.

Tiger provided an account that linked aggression in males with their biological evolution.

> Human aggression is in part a function of the fact that hunting was vitally important to human evolution and that aggression is typically undertaken by males in the framework of a unisexual social bond of which participants are aware and with which they are concerned. It is implied, therefore, that aggression is 'instinctive' but also must occur within an explicit social context varying from culture to culture and to be learned by members of any community. . . . Men in continuous association aggress against the environment in much the same way as men and women in continuous association have sexual relations. (Tiger 1984, 159–60)

And while men are thus predisposed to engage in aggression, in ways that women are not, it is not true in Tiger's view that a predisposition to engage in violent acts is a normal part of this difference.

Thornhill and Thornhill fail to consider Tiger's contention that men are evolutionarily adapted to be aggressive, but not necessarily to be violent. With Tiger's distinction in mind it may be said that human males, especially in association with other males, are adapted to aggress against women in certain social environments. But this aggressive response need not lead to violence, or the threat of violence, of the sort epitomized by rape; rather it may merely affect non-coercive mating rituals. On a related point, Tiger argues that the fact that war has historically been "virtually a male monopoly" (81) is due to both male bonding patterns and evolutionary adaptation. Evolutionary biology provides only part of the story since male aggressiveness need not result in such violent encounters as occur in war or rape. After all, many men do not rape or go to war; the cultural cues provided by socialization must be considered at least as important as evolutionary adaptation.

We side with Tiger against the Thornhills in focusing on the way that all-male groups socialize their members and provide "cues" for violence. Tiger has recently allied himself with feminists such as Catharine MacKinnon and others who have suggested that male attitudes need to be radically altered in order to have a major impact on the incidence of rape (see the preface to the second edition of *Men In Groups*). One of the implications of Tiger's research is that rape and other forms of male aggressive behavior are not best understood as isolated acts of individuals. Rather than simply seeing violent aggression as merely a biologically predetermined response, Tiger places violent aggressiveness squarely into the group dynamics of men's interactions—a result of his research not well appreciated.

In a preface to the second edition of his book, Tiger corrects an unfortunate misinterpretation of his work.

> One of the stigmas which burdened this book was an interpretation of it as an apology for male aggression and even a potential stimulus of it—after all, boys will be boys. However I clearly said the opposite: "This is not to say that . . . hurtful and destructive relations between groups of men are inevitable. . . . It may be possible, as many writers have suggested, to alter social conceptions of maleness so that gentility and equivocation rather than toughness and more or less arbitrary decisiveness are highly valued." (Tiger 1984, 191)

If Tiger is right, and the most important "cues" are those which young boys and men get while in the company of other boys and men, then the feminist project of changing male socialization patterns may be seen as consistent with, rather than opposed to, the sociobiological hypotheses. Indeed, other evidence may be cited to buttress the feminist social learning perspective against the Thornhills. Different human societies have quite different rates of rape. In her anthropological research among the Minangkabau of West Sumatra, Peggy Reeves Sanday has found that this society is relatively rape-free. Rape does occur, but at such a low rate—28 per 3 million in 1981–82 for example—as to be virtually nonexistent (Sanday 1986, 85; also see Sanday 1990, and Lepowsky). In light of such research, men, rather than women, are the ones who would need to change their behavior. This is because it is the socialization of men by men in their bonding-groups, and the view of women that is engendered, that provides the strongest cues toward rape. Since there may indeed be something that males could and should be doing differently that would affect the prevalence of rape, it does not seem unreasonable to continue to investigate the claim that men are collectively responsible for the prevalence of rape.

III. THE RAPIST AS VICTIM OF SOCIETY

It is also possible to acknowledge that men are responsible for the prevalence of rape in our society but nonetheless to argue that women are equally responsible. Rape is often portrayed as a sex crime perpetrated largely by men against women. But importantly, rape is also a crime of violence, and many factors in our society have increased the prevalence of violence. This prevalence of violence is the cause of both rape and war in western societies. Our view, that violence of both sorts is increased in likelihood by patterns of male socialization which then creates collective male responsibility, may be countered by pointing out that socialization patterns are created by both men and women, thereby seemingly implicating both men and women in collective responsibility for rape and war.

Sam Keen has contended that it is violence that we should be focusing on rather than sex or gender, in order to understand the causes and remedies for the prevalence of rape. According to Keen,

> Men are violent because of the systematic violence done to their bodies and spirits. Being hurt they become hurters. In the overall picture, male violence toward women is far less than male violence toward other males . . . these outrages are a structural part of a warfare system that victimizes both men and women. (Keen 1991, 47)

Keen sees both men and women conspiring together to perpetuate this system of violence, especially in the way they impart to their male children an acceptance of violence.

Women are singled out by Keen as those who have not come to terms with their share of responsibility for our violent culture. And men have been so guilt-tripped on the issue of rape that they have become desensitized to it. Keen thinks that it is a mistake to single out men, and not women also, as responsible for rape.

> Until women are willing to weep for and accept equal responsibility for the systematic violence done to the male body and spirit by the war system, it is not likely that men will lose enough of their guilt and regain enough of their sensitivity to accept responsibility for women who are raped. (Keen 1991, 47)

Even though women are equally responsible for the rape culture, in Keen's view, women should be singled out because they have not previously accepted their share of responsibility for the creation of a violent society.

Keen is at least partially right insofar as he insists that issues of rape and war be understood as arising from the same source, namely the socialization of men to be violent in western cultures. We agree with Keen that rape is part of a larger set of violent practices that injure both men and women. He is right to point out that men are murdering other men in our society in increasing numbers, and that this incidence of violence probably has something to do with the society's general condoning, even celebrating, of violence, especially in war.

Keen fails to note though that it is men, not women, who are the vast majority of both rapists and murderers in our society. And even if some women do act in ways which trigger violent reactions in men, nevertheless, in our opinion this pales in comparison with the way that men socialize each other to be open to violence. As Tiger and others have suggested, aggressive violence results primarily from male-bonding experiences. In any event, both fathers and mothers engage in early childhood socialization. Men influence the rape culture both through early childhood socialization and through male-bonding socialization of older male children. But women only contribute to this culture, when they do, through individual acts of early childhood socialization. For this reason Keen is surely wrong to think that women share responsibility *equally* with men for our rape culture.

In our view, some women could prevent some rapes; and some women do contribute to the patterns of socialization of both men and women that increase the incidence of rape. For these reasons, it would not be inappropriate to say that women share responsibility for rape as well as men. But we believe that it is a mistake to think that women share equally in this responsibility with men. For one thing, women are different from men in that they are, in general, made worse off by the prevalence of rape in our society. As we will next see, there is a sense in which men, but not women, benefit from the prevalence of rape, and this fact means that men have more of a stake in the rape culture, and hence have more to gain by its continued existence.

In general, our conclusion is that women share responsibility, but to a far lesser extent than men, for the prevalence of rape. We do not support those who try to "blame the victim" by holding women responsible for rape because of not taking adequate precautions, or dressing seductively, etc. Instead, the key for us is the role that women, as mothers, friends and lovers, play in the overall process of male socialization that creates the rape culture. It should come as no surprise that few members of western society can be relieved of responsibility for this rape culture given the overwhelming pervasiveness of that culture. But such considerations should not deter us from looking to men, first and foremost, as being collectively responsible for the prevalence of rape. The women who do contribute to aggressive male-socialization do so as individuals; women have no involvement parallel to the male-bonding group.

IV. THE RAPIST AS GROUP MEMBER

Popular literature tends to portray the rapist as a demonic character, as the "Other." What we find interesting about the research of Thornhill and Thornhill is that it operates unwittingly to support the feminist slogan that "all men are rapists," that the rapist is not male "Other" but male "Self." What is so unsettling about the tens of thousands of rapes in Bosnia is the suggestion that what ordinary men have been doing is not significantly different from what the "sex-fiends" did. The thesis that men are adapted to be predisposed to be rapists, regardless of what else we think of the thesis, should give us pause and make us less rather than more likely to reject the feminist slogan. From this vantage point, the work of Tiger as well as Thornhill and Thornhill sets the stage for a serious reconsideration of the view that men are collectively responsible for rape.

There are two things that might be meant by saying that men are collectively responsible for the prevalence of rape in western culture. First, seeing men as collectively responsible may mean that men as a group are responsible in that they form some sort of super-entity that causes, or at least supports, the prevalence of rape. When some feminists talk of "patriarchy," what they seem to mean is a kind of institution that operates through, but also behind the backs of, individual men to oppress women. Here it may be that men are collectively responsible for the prevalence of rape and yet no men are individually responsible. We call this nondistributive collective responsibility. Second, seeing men as collectively responsible may mean that men form a group in which there are so many features that the members share in common, such as attitudes or dispositions to engage in harm, that what holds true for one man also holds true for all other men. Because of the common features of the members of the group men, when one man is responsible for a particular harm, other men are implicated. Each member of the group has a share in the responsibility for a harm such as rape. We call this distributive collective responsibility (see May 1992, Ch. 2). In what follows we will criticize the first way of understanding men's collective responsibility, and offer reasons to support the second.

When collective responsibility is understood in the first (nondistributive) sense, this form of responsibility is assigned to those groups that have the capacity to act. Here there are two paradigmatic examples: the corporation and the mob (see May 1992, Chs. 2 and 4). The corporation has the kind of organizational structure that allows for the group to form intentions and carry out those intentions, almost as if the corporation were itself a person. Since men, qua men, are too amorphous a group to be able to act in an organized fashion, we will not be interested in whether they are collectively responsible in this way. But it may be that men can act in the way that mobs act, that is, not through a highly organized structure but through something such as like-mindedness. If there is enough commonality of belief, disposition and interest of all men, or at least all men within a particular culture, then the group may be able to act just as a mob is able to respond to a commonly perceived enemy.

It is possible to think of patriarchy as the oppressive practices of men coordinated by the common interests of men, but not organized intentionally. It is also productive to think of rape as resulting from patriarchy. For if there is a "collective" that is supporting or creating the prevalence of rape it is not a highly organized one, since there is nothing like a corporation that intentionally plans the rape of women in western culture. If the current Serbian army has engaged in the systematic and organized rape of Muslim women as a strategy of war, then this would be an example of nondistributive responsibility for rape. But the kind of oppression characterized by the prevalence of rape in most cultures appears to be systematic but not organized. How does this affect our understanding of whether men are collectively responsible for rape?

If patriarchy is understood merely as a system of coordination that operates behind the backs of individual men, then it may be that no single man is responsible for any harms that are caused by patriarchy. But if patriarchy is understood as something which is based on common interests, as well as common benefits, extended to all or most men in a particular culture, then it may be that men are collectively responsible for the harms of patriarchy in a way which distributes out to all men, making each man in a particular culture at least partially responsible for the harms attributable to patriarchy. This latter strategy is consistent with our own view of men's responsibility for rape. In the remainder of this essay we will offer support for this conceptualization of the collective responsibility of men for the prevalence of rape.

Our positive assessment, going beyond our criticism of the faulty responses in earlier sections of our paper, is that men in western culture are collectively responsible in the distributive sense, that is, they each share responsibility, for the prevalence of rape in that culture. This claim rests on five points: (1) Insofar as most perpetrators of rape are men, then these men are responsible, in most cases, for the rapes they committed. (2) Insofar as some men, by the way they interact with other (especially younger) men, contribute to a climate in our society where rape is made more prevalent, then they are collaborators in the rape culture and for this reason share in responsibility for rapes committed in that culture. (3) Also, insofar as some men are not unlike the rapist, since they would be rapists if they had the opportunity to be placed into a situation where their inhibitions against rape were removed, then these men share responsibility with actual rapists for the harms of rape. (4) In addition, insofar as many other men could have prevented fellow men from raping, but did not act to prevent these actual rapes, then these men also share responsibility along with the rapists. (5) Finally, insofar as some men benefit from the existence of rape in our society, these men also share responsibility along with the rapists.

It seems to us unlikely that many, if any, men in our society fail to fit into one or another of these categories. Hence, we think that it is not unreasonable to say that men in our society are collectively responsible (in the distributive sense) for rape. We expect some male readers to respond as follows:

> I am adamantly opposed to rape, and though when I was younger I might have tolerated rape-conducive comments from friends of mine, I don't now, so I'm not a collaborator in the rape culture. And I would never be a rapist whatever the situation, and I would certainly act to prevent any rape that I could. I'm pretty sure I don't benefit from rape. So how can I be responsible for the prevalence of rape?

In reply we would point out that nearly all men in a given western society meet the third and fifth conditions above (concerning similarity and benefit). But women generally fail to meet either of these conditions, or the first. So, the involvement of women in the rape culture is much less than is true for men. In what follows we will concentrate on these similarity and benefit issues.

In out discussion above, we questioned the view that rapists are "other." Diane Scully, in her study of convicted rapists, turns the view around, suggesting that it is women who are "other." She argues that rapists in America are not pathological, but instead

> that men who rape have something to tell us about the cultural roots of sexual violence. . . . They tell us that some men use rape as a means of revenge and punishment. Implicit in revenge rape is the collective liability of women. In some cases, victims are substitutes for significant women on whom men desire to take revenge. In other cases, victims represent all women. . . . In either case, women are seen as objects, a category, but not as individuals with rights. For some men, rape is an afterthought or bonus they add to burglary or robbery. In other words, rape is "no big deal". . . . Some men rape in groups as a male bonding activity—for them it's just something to do. . . . Convicted rapists tell us that in this culture, sexual violence is rewarding . . . these men perceived rape as a rewarding, low-risk act. (Scully 1990, 162–63)

It is the prevalent perception of women as "other" by men in our culture that fuels the prevalence of rape in American society.

Turning to the issue of benefit, we believe that Lionel Tiger's work illustrates the important source of strength that men derive from the all-male groups they form. There is a strong sense in which men benefit from the all-male groups that they form in our culture. What is distinctly lacking is any sense that men have responsibility for the social conditions, especially the socialization of younger men which diminishes inhibitions toward rape, that are created in those groups. Male bonding is made easier because there is an "Other" that males can bond "against." And this other is the highly sexualized stereotype of the "female." Here is a benefit for men in these groups—but there is a social cost: from the evidence we have examined there is an increased prevalence of rape. Men need to consider this in reviewing their own role in a culture that supports so much rape.

There is another sense in which benefit is related to the issue of responsibility for rape. There is a sense in which many men in our society benefit from the prevalence of rape in ways many of us are quite unaware. Consider this example:

> Several years ago, at a social occasion in which male and female professors were present, I asked off-handedly whether people agreed with me that the campus was looking especially pretty at night these days. Many of the men responded positively. But all of the women responded that this was not something that they had even thought about, since they were normally too anxious about being on campus at night, especially given the increase in reported rapes recently.[3]

We men benefitted in that, relative to our female colleagues, we were in an advantageous position vis-a-vis travel around campus. And there were surely other comparative benefits that befell us as a result of this advantage concerning travel, such as our ability to gain academically by being able to use the library at any hour we chose.

In a larger sense, men benefit from the prevalence of rape in that many women are made to feel dependent on men for protection against potential rapists. It is hard to overestimate the benefit here for it potentially affects all aspects of one's life. One study found that 87% of women in a borough of London felt that they had to take precautions against potential rapists, with a large number reporting that they never went out at night alone (Radford 1987, 33). Whenever one group is made to feel dependent on another group, and this dependency is not reciprocal, then there is a strong comparative benefit to the group that is not in the dependent position. Such a benefit, along with the specific benefits mentioned above, support the view that men as a group have a stake in perpetuating the rape culture in ways that women do not. And just as the benefit to men distributes throughout the male population in a given society, so the responsi- bility should distribute as well.

V. CONCLUSIONS

When people respond to conflict with violence, they coerce one another and thereby fail to treat one another with respect as fellow autonomous beings. Rape and murder, especially in war, victimize members of various groups simply because they are group members. These two factors combine to create a form of dehumanization that can warrant the charge of being a crime against humanity. What makes an act of violence more than just a private individual act in wartime is that killing and rape are perpetrated not against the individual for his or her unique characteristics, but solely because the individual instantiates a group characteristic, for example, being Jewish, or Muslim, or being a woman. Such identification fails to respect what is unique about each of us.

Our point is not that all men everywhere are responsible for the prevalence of rape. Rather, we have been arguing that in western societies, rape is deeply embedded in a wider culture of male socialization. Those who have the most to do with sustaining that culture must also recognize that they are responsible for the harmful aspects of that culture (see Porter 1986, 222–23). And when rape is conjoined with war, especially as an organized strategy, then there is a sense that men are collectively responsible for the rapes that occur in that war,[4] just as groups of people are held responsible for the crimes of genocide, where the victims are persecuted simply because they fall into a certain category of low-risk people who are ripe for assault.

Rape, especially in times of war, is an act of violence perpetrated against a person merely for being an instantiation of a type. Insofar as rape in times of war is a systematically organized form of terror, it is not inappropriate to call rape a war crime, a crime against humanity. Insofar as rape in times of peace is also part of a pattern of terror against women to the collective benefit of men, then rape in times of peace is also a crime against humanity (see Card 1991). Rape, in war or in peace, is rarely a personal act of aggression by one person toward another person. It is an act of hostility and a complete failure to show basic human respect (see Shafer and Frye 1977). And more than this, rape is made more likely by the collective actions, or inactions, of men in a particular society. Insofar as men in a particular society contribute to the prevalence of rape, they participate in a crime against humanity for which they are collectively responsible.

The feminist slogan "all men are rapists" seems much stronger than the claim "all men contribute to the prevalence of rape." Is the feminist slogan merely hyperbole? It is if what is meant is that each time a rape occurs, every man did it, or that only men are ever responsible for rape. But, as we have seen, each time a rape occurs, there is a sense in which many men could have done it, or made it less likely to have occurred, or benefitted from it. By direct contribution, or by negligence or by similarity of disposition, or by benefitting, most if not all men do share in each rape in a particular society. This is the link between being responsible for the prevalence of rape and being responsible, at least to some extent, for the harms of each rape.

The purpose of these arguments has been to make men aware of the various ways that they are implicated in the rape culture in general as well as in particular rapes. And while we believe that men should feel some shame for their group's complicity in the prevalence of rape, our aim is not to shame men but rather to stimulate men to take responsibility for re-socializing themselves and their fellow men. How much should any particular man do? Answering this question would require another paper, although participating in the Canadian White Ribbon Campaign, or in anti-sexism education programs, would be a good first step.[5] Suffice it to say that the status quo, namely doing nothing, individually or as a group, is not satisfactory, and will merely further compound our collective and shared responsibility for the harms caused by our fellow male members who engage in rape.[6]

Notes

1. This paragraph is based on Larry May's experiences growing up in an upper middle class suburban U.S. society. While our experiences differ somewhat in this respect, these experiences are so common that we have referred to them in the first person plural.

2. There is a fifth response, namely, that women alone are somehow responsible for being raped. This response will be largely ignored in our essay since we regard it as merely another case of "blaming the victim." See Scully (1990) for a critical discussion of this response. Undoubtedly there are yet other responses. We have tried to focus our attention on the most common responses we have seen in the literature on rape.

3. In his fascinating study of the climate of rape in American culture, Timothy Beneke also reports as one of his conclusions that the fear of rape at night "inhibits the freedom of the eye, hurts

women economically, undercuts women's independence, destroys solitude, and restricts expressiveness." Such curtailments of freedom, he argues, "must be acknowledged as part of the crime" (Beneke 1982, 170).

4. The European Community's preliminary investigation into the reports of widespread Bosnian rapes of Muslim women by Serbian soldiers concluded that "Rape is part of a pattern of abuse, usually perpetrated with the conscious intention of demoralizing and terrorizing communities, driving them from their homes and demonstrating the power of the invading forces. Viewed in this way, rape cannot be seen as incidental to the main purpose of the aggression but as serving a strategic purpose in itself" (*St. Louis Post-Dispatch*, January 9, 1993, 8A).

5. We would also recommend recent essays by philosophers who are trying to come to terms with their masculinity. See our essay on friendship as well as the essay by Hugh LaFollette in our anthology *Rethinking Masculinity* (1992).

6. We would like to thank Virginia Ingram, Jason Clevenger, Victoria Davion, Karen J. Warren, Duane Cady and Marilyn Friedman for providing us with critical comments on earlier drafts of this paper.

REFERENCES

Beneke, Timothy. 1982. *Men on rape*. New York: St. Martin's Press.
Brownmiller, Susan. 1993. Making female bodies the battlefield. *Newsweek* (January 4): 37.
Card, Claudia. 1991. Rape as a terrorist institution. In *Violence, terrorism, and justice*, ed. R. G. Frey and Christopher Morris. New York: Cambridge University Press.
Griffin, Susan. 1971. Rape: The all-American crime. *Ramparts* (September): 26–35. Reprinted in *Women and values: Readings in feminist philosophy*, ed. Marilyn Pearsall. Belmont, CA: Wadsworth, 1986.
Keen, Sam. 1991. *Fire in the belly*. New York: Bantam Books.
LaFollette, Hugh. 1992. Real men. In *Rethinking masculinity*, ed. Larry May and Robert Strikwerda. Lanham, MD: Rowman & Littlefield.
Lepowsky, Maria. 1990. Gender in an egalitarian society. In *Beyond the second sex*, ed. Peggy Reeves Sanday and Ruth Gallagher Goodenough. Philadelphia: University of Pennsylvania Press.
Lipsyte, Robert. 1993. An ethics trial: Must boys always be boys? *The New York Times* (March 12): B-11.
MacKinnon, Catharine A. 1993. Turning rape into pornography: Postmodern genocide. *Ms.* (July/August): 24–30.
May, Larry. 1987. *The morality of groups*. Notre Dame, IN: University of Notre Dame Press.
———. 1992. *Sharing responsibility*. Chicago: University of Chicago Press.
Oates, Joyce Carol. 1992. Rape and the boxing ring. *Newsweek* (February 24): 60–61.
Peterson, Susan Rae. 1977. Coercion and rape: The state as a male protection racket. In *Feminism and philosophy*, ed. Mary Vetterling-Braggin, Frederick Elliston, and Jane English. Totowa, NJ: Littlefield, Adams: 360–371.
Porter, Roy. 1986. Does rape have a historical meaning? In *Rape: An historical and social enquiry*, ed. Sylvana Tomaselli and Roy Porter. Oxford: Basil Blackwell.
Post, Tony et al. 1993. A pattern of rape. *Newsweek* (January 4): 32–36.
Radford, Jill. 1987. Policing male violence, policing women. In *Women, violence and social control*, ed. Jalna Hanmer and Mary Maynard. Atlantic Highlands, NJ: Humanities Press.
Sanday, Peggy Reeves. 1986. Rape and the silencing of the feminine. In *Rape: An historical and social enquiry*, ed. Sylvana Tomaselli and Roy Porter. Oxford: Basil Blackwell.
———. 1990. Androcentric and matrifocal gender representation in Minangkabau ideology. In *Beyond the second sex*, ed. Peggy Reeves Sanday and Ruth Gallagher Goodenough. Philadelphia: University of Pennsylvania Press.
Scully, Diana. 1990. *Understanding sexual violence*. Boston: Unwin Hyman.
Shafer, Carolyn M., and Marilyn Frye. 1977. Rape and respect. In *Feminism and philosophy*, ed. Mary Vetterling-Braggin, Frederick Elliston, and Jane English. Totowa, NJ: Littlefield Adams.

Strikwerda, Robert, and Larry May. 1992. Male friendship and intimacy. *Hypatia* 7(3): 110–25. Reprinted in *Rethinking masculinity*, ed. Larry May and Robert Strikwerda. Lanham, MD: Rowman & Littlefield, 1992.

Thornhill, Randy, and Nancy Wilmsen Thornhill. 1992. The evolutionary psychology of men's coercive sexuality. *Behavioral and Brain Sciences* 15: 363–75.

Tiger, Lionel. [1969] 1984. *Men in groups* 2nd ed. New York: Marion Boyars Publishers.

An Alternative to Pacifism?
Feminism and Just-War Theory

LUCINDA J. PEACH

Introduction

Women have traditionally been excluded from involvement in war. War has been considered almost exclusively a male enterprise: fought by men, with and against other men, for male-defined purposes and ends. Culturally, traditional ideas about gender roles identify men with war and soldiering, and women with peace and mothering. Women remain largely absent from ethical and policy debates regarding when to go to war, how to fight a war, and whether resorting to war is morally justifiable. In recent years, several feminists have challenged this traditional genderized dichotomy between war and peace, as well as the validity of the male-conceived theories that assess the morality of war. In this paper, I evaluate feminist criticisms of one of these male-generated theories, that of just-war.[1]

After having no discernible impact on foreign policy analysis of any armed conflict for many years, just-war theory suddenly gained national prominence and recognition in relation to the Persian Gulf War. The theory developed over many centuries in Christian theology and international law into a set of criteria designed to determine when, and to what extent, limited participation in armed conflict may be moral. Just-war theorists generally share with pacifists a basic presumption opposing war as morally wrong (see Miller 1991, 117; Cady 1989). However, whereas pacifist perspectives share a firm belief that war is never a moral means to achieve potentially just goals, those subscribing to just-war theory are open to being persuaded that war may be morally justified in certain circumstances. Both of these positions contrast with the views of "warists" or "war realists," who consider morality to be irrelevant, inapplicable, or ineffective in relation to war (see Cady 1989, xi-xii).[2] In our gender-structured society,

Hypatia vol. 9, no. 2 (Spring 1994) © by Lucinda J. Peach

warism has been the culturally dominant and presumptively correct view (see Cady 1989, chap. 1).

There are undoubtedly myriad problems with attempting to generalize a "feminist perspective" about just-war theory, given the variety of different feminist perspectives about the morality of war. Popular conception and actual practice alike align women with peace and pacifism, not with a position that accepts war as potentially moral. For example, women have been and continue to be more actively involved than men in peace movements.[3] Recent public opinion polls indicate that women are more oriented to peaceful resolution of disputes than are men, reflecting an average 15 to 20 percent "gender gap" on the issue of military involvement and the use of force (see Gallagher 1993; Branscombe and Owen 1993; Baxter and Lansing 1983, 56–57, 196).[4] Women's social protest movements have achieved significant political leverage from their identification as "naturally" more peaceful than men, based on their relationship to childbearing and childrearing (see Ruddick 1989; Pierson 1988; Swerdlow 1989).

But despite the historical and ideological alignments between women (and feminists) and peace, not all women, even feminist women, are pacifists.[5] Political scientist Jean Bethke Elshtain, for instance, expressly denies that she is a pacifist, arguing that some wars have been necessary and that it is not possible to transcend "collective violence in defense of the state" (Elshtain 1987, 257). Feminist theorist Sara Ruddick aligns herself more with pacifism, especially in denouncing just-war theory for its legitimation of certain forms of violence. However, she argues that "threatened peoples [may] not have alternative nonviolent ways of protecting what they love and getting what they need" (Ruddick 1989, 139). Ruddick and Elshtain agree with St. Augustine, an early Christian Church Father who is considered to be the "founder" of just-war theory within the Christian tradition (see Kehoe 1986, 156), that war may be an element necessary to peace, rather than completely separate from it (Ruddick 1989, 137; Elshtain 1987, 253).

Even those women who do characterize themselves as pacifists may have radically diverse reasons for doing so, some of them drawing on just-war reasoning (see Cady 1989, chap. 4; Miller 1991, 104–105). Further, as Elshtain discusses, the notion of women's innate or natural orientation to peace and pacifism needs to be questioned as a product of a gender system that serves to maintain men as strong warriors and women as weak and passive peacemakers, thereby perpetuating war rather than bringing peace. These factors suggest that a feminist appraisal of the just-war theory is an important component of feminist theorizing about war and peace.

Only a few feminist scholars have yet explicitly addressed just-war theory. Nonetheless, there have been a few significant feminist critiques of various elements found in just-war thinking. For example, Elshtain and Ruddick have both pointed to some specific deficiencies with traditional just-war thinking and have proposed alternative frameworks for analyzing the morality of war. In this article, I argue that many of the feminist criticisms that have been waged against traditional just-war theory are well taken. Notwithstanding the validity of these "deconstructive" efforts, however, to date no adequate constructive feminist alternative has been proposed. Rather than reject and/or replace traditional just-war theory, I argue, feminist principles and insights can and should provide a much needed reconceptualization and revitalization of the application of just-war criteria.

I begin with a brief background of just-war theory, including three classic contrasting approaches: those of Augustine, Reinhold Niebuhr, a mid-twentieth-century Protestant theologian, and Michael Walzer, a contemporary secular social and political theorist. Although by no means exhaustive of the complete spectrum of just-war ideas, these three views do exemplify some of the more significant strands and influences, both theological and secular, historical and contemporary, of the tradition. I then discuss significant ways in which traditional just-war thinking is deficient from a feminist perspective. I use Elshtain's and Ruddick's alternative approaches to the morality of war to illustrate how feminist efforts to replace just-war theory have been inadequate thus far. In the final part of the article, I outline how feminist perspectives and insights can provide a framework for revitalizing the application of just-war theory.

THE JUST-WAR TRADITION

The many variants of just-war theory which have been developed over the past millennium differ in the specific criteria used to determine the morality of war (both in general and in relation to particular conflicts), the burden of evidence necessary to satisfy those criteria, and the relation between criteria and their relative weight.[6] Nonetheless, there is general agreement that just-war analysis entails two sets of criteria: one governing the morality of *going to* war (the *jus ad bellum*), the other the actual *conduct* of war (the *jus in bello*). There is also significant agreement that the *jus ad bellum* criteria include some or all of the following:

1. a just cause (self-defense or defense of others);
2. right authority (determination to go to war is made by the appropriate governing officials);
3. right intention (must be to reestablish peace);
4. proportionality (between means employed in fighting and ends or goals to be achieved);
5. relative justice (in acknowledging that no participant in war has absolute justice on their side);
6. last resort (all other alternatives for conflict resolution have been exhausted); and
7. a reasonable hope for success.

There is also substantial consensus that the *jus in bello* criteria require:

1. "discrimination" between combatants and noncombatants and the permissibility of intentionally killing only the former, thus according noncombatants immunity; and

2. "proportionality" of means and ends in relation to particular battles and strategies such that the benefits of going to war or conduct of a particular strategy or mission within the war must outweigh its harms.

Because many of these criteria are quite vague and general in scope, their application has resulted in significantly different determinations regarding the morality of particular wars, including the recent Persian Gulf conflict (see Sizemore 1992; Johnson and Weigel 1992; Geyer and Green 1992; Decosse 1992).

Augustine concluded that Christian participation in killing is permissible when: (1) the cause is just; (2) appropriate authority (in his case, the monarch) determines that undertaking war is necessary to prevent or punish injustice; and (3) the intention is to restore peace (see Hartigan 1966, 199). In Niebuhr's view, justice—a moral good necessary for life in a sinful world—requires Christians to participate in war to defend innocent victims of aggression and secure freedom for the oppressed (Niebuhr and Dun 1955, 77).

In contrast to these theological approaches, Walzer's secular theory presumes that the defense of human rights is the only legitimate reason for war (Walzer 1977, 72). His just-war approach makes the criteria of just cause central, and downplays the moral significance of the traditional criteria of proportionality and last resort (Walzer 1982, 548), even though he admits that "every military history is a tale of violence and destruction out of all relation to the requirements of combat" (Walzer 1977, 130). All three of these approaches are subject to significant feminist criticisms.

FEMINIST CRITICISMS OF JUST-WAR THEORY

Feminist criticisms of just-war theory are clustered around several concerns: its relation to realism; its failure to insist that all criteria have been satisfied in accordance with rigorous standards, especially in relation to attempting nonviolent alternatives; its tendency to abstraction and to dichotomize reality in accordance with gendered distinctions; and the priority it accords to the state and to state authority vis-a-vis the individual. I will evaluate each of these criticisms in turn.

Realism. Realism is the political perspective that human nature makes war inevitable and unavoidable. Realism influences just-war thinking by creating a presumption that resort to war may be necessary.[7] Realist attitudes thus enhance the possibility that a just-war analysis will result in the conclusion that the use of armed force is justified. Augustine's and Niebuhr's theologically based perspectives are both realist in viewing war as a necessary remedy for human sinfulness.[8] Although Walzer explicitly intends his theory of human rights to provide an alternative to realism, he also tends to fall into realist modes of thought, evidenced by his failure to give more than cursory and pessimistic consideration to alternatives to war (see Walzer 1977, 329–35).

Many feminist scholars have criticized the realist elements of international relations theory in general, and just-war thinking in particular (see Ruddick

1989, 1987, and 1983; Tickner 1991; Grant and Newland 1991). In Ruddick's view, the realist paradigm misrepresents human beings as "primarily centers of dominating and defensive activity trying to achieve a stable autonomy in threatening hierarchies of strength" (Ruddick 1989, 183). Both she and Elshtain condemn realism's pessimism about human nature and blindness to the possibility of thinking in any terms other than war (Ruddick 1989, 136, 150; Elshtain 1985, 40–41).[9]

For Elshtain, traditional just-war theory is not problematic so much because it is itself realist as because it is anachronistic and no longer able to provide meaningful limits to war in a world governed by realist assumptions (Elshtain 1985, 47). Given the contemporary conditions of war, which include changes in the nature of political bodies, international relations, and "the totalistic deadliness of weapons" (Elshtain 1985, 46), just-war theory continually gets co-opted by the realist paradigm (Elshtain 1987, 166–67). As an example, she cites Walzer's reliance on viewing Nazism as an "immeasurable evil" to justify the overriding of *in bello* restraints during the British saturation bombing of German cities in World War II. She also points out how he uses the threat of nuclear war to justify a continuing "supreme emergency" that legitimates the immoral use of deterrence strategy (Elshtain 1985, 46).[10]

Ruddick and Elshtain's criticisms accord with those of other feminist thinkers who challenge the realist view of human nature as a male notion about men (see Grant and Newland 1991; Grant 1991, 9; Tickner 1991). Elshtain specifically attributes just-war theory's restriction of the range of "symbolic and narrative possibilities" for thinking about conflict to realism's "suppression of female-linked imagery" (Elshtain 1987, 88; Elshtain 1985, 41). Whether or not one accepts such claims that prevailing conceptions of human nature are male-biased, or that women have different natures or roles (either culturally or biologically constructed), these feminist perspectives persuasively suggest that realism provides an unduly limited view of human nature, one which can conceive of war as the only solution to conflict.

Failure to Consider Alternatives to War. The "last resort" criteria of just-war theory requires that meaningful alternatives to armed force have been tried and failed before resort to armed force can be morally justified. But in line with their realist orientation, many just-war theorists fail to consider alternatives to war fully (see Ruddick 1987; McMahon 1991). Augustine's just-war theory lacks any exhortation that nonviolent methods of restoring peace be attempted prior to the use of armed force. Niebuhr's realist and theological presuppositions underlie his conclusion that pacifism is not a feasible alternative to armed force. In his view, no form of pacifism is adequate to deal with human self-interest and the will to power (Niebuhr 1940, 5, 25; see Miller 1991, 107).[11]

Among contemporary just-war theorists, the last resort criterion is often ignored or viewed, as Walzer does, as a "prudential" matter to be left to the discretion of government officials (see *Tikkun* 1991). Because Walzer considers nonviolent resistance to be dependent upon adherence to just-war principles by those with the means and the will to use violence, he gives only minimal consideration to pacifist alternatives to war. He is cynical about the effectiveness of nonviolent approaches to conflict resolution, arguing that they can only succeed if a number of preconditions exist, including the willingness—always uncertain—of the aggressor to abide by the war convention (Walzer 1977, 330–35). Where such preconditions do not exist, nonviolence "collapses into violence directed at oneself" (Walzer 1977, 332).

The U.S. Catholic bishops are distinctive among contemporary just-war theorists in seriously considering the possibility of nonviolent alternatives to war and the escalation of conflicts. Their statement in *The Challenge of Peace* includes proposals for a nuclear freeze, weapons reductions, arms control, and political and economic policies to enhance human rights and dignity (NCCB 1983). In addition, the bishops consider peace to be a duty, not merely "an optional commitment" (136). They are thus more progressive than most just-war theorists in having a vision that reaches toward peace, and not just the next war. Yet Walzer criticizes the Catholic bishops for their emphasis on the requirement of last resort, claiming that it is "an endlessly receding possibility, invoked mostly by people who would prefer never to resist aggression with force. After all, there is always something else to do, another diplomatic note, another meeting" (Walzer 1991, 14; see *Tikkun* 1991, 40). Thus, despite his purported opposition to realism, Walzer ultimately does not take the possibility of alternatives to war any more seriously than Augustine or Niebuhr.

Ruddick opposes this tendency among just-war theorists to reject the morality of nonviolent resistance as an alternative to war (Ruddick 1989, 174–75). Elshtain recognizes that the lack of any enforcement mechanism to insure that contact and attempts at negotiated settlement have been attempted before armed force may be utilized makes just-war theory subject to being manipulated as a prop for the promotion of "armed civic virtue" rather than as a constraint on war (Elshtain 1992, 43). The failure of most just-war theorists to seriously contemplate alternatives to war is thus radically deficient from the perspective of pacifist feminists and others opposed to a knee-jerk militaristic response to civil strife.

Abstract Thought. The media and the military's portrayal of the Persian Gulf War—a conflict Walzer concludes was a just war—as a video game using "smart bombs" to perform "precision" or "surgical" strikes against "strategic targets" rather than as the use of deadly weapons resulting in the bloody slaughter of thousands of human beings, civilians as well as soldiers, illustrates the kind of abstract thinking about war that feminists accuse just-war theorists of engaging in (see Elshtain 1992; Sizemore 1992, 947). Just-war theorists tend to couch their analyses in terms of hypotheticals rather than with reference to actual conflicts. For example, Niebuhr's work deserves Elshtain's criticism that just-war theorists fail to provide either specific, concrete guidelines for determining when war is moral or narratives to illustrate whether past wars have been just or not (e.g., Elshtain 1987, 159, 248–49; Elshtain 1985, 50).

In contrast with this tendency of prevailing just-war approaches to ignore how the criteria would apply to actual wars, a number of feminist theories stress the importance of the concrete and particular over the universal and abstract (see Gilligan 1982; Noddings 1984; Ruddick 1987, 93–97; Ruddick 1989, 139). Feminist analyses specifically reveal how abstraction in the application of just-war theory has resulted in: (1) a neglect of the horrors of war and its effects on individual bodies; (2) a perception of the enemy as "Other"; and (3) a fixation on principles of justice and rights rather than the needs and interests of specific persons in particular conflicts.

Ruddick perceives the abstractness of just-war theory as controlling "our perceptions of war, turning our attention from bodies and their fate to abstract causes and rules for achieving them" (Ruddick 1989, 150). Nancy Hartsock finds that the tendency to ignore actual bodies has been prevalent in militaristic thinking throughout the history of Western philosophical thought, despite the fact that warrioring is a bodily activity (see Hartsock 1982). For example, in Augustine's overall theological perspective, the self and the body have only a relative and temporary value as parts of earthly existence. The evil of war thus does not inhere in physical death, which will befall everyone sooner or later, but rather in vices such as "love of violence," "revengeful cruelty," and "lust for power" (Holmes 1969, 64), desires that are antithetical to eternal life in the heavenly City of God (Augustine 1984, 877).[12]

Nonetheless, Elshtain finds in Augustine "an exemplary alternative" to modern just-war theorists because he emphasizes suffering and regret rather than the abstract and rationalist tenor of modern approaches "that stress legalities, rights, and the power of human reason" (Elshtain 1987, 129, 132). The "modern" attitude is illustrated by the "technostrategic" discourse of nuclear defense professionals. Carol Cohn describes the "utter absence of the burning, explosive, flesh-tearing, radiation poisoning, life-annihilating devastation of nuclear war" in their rhetoric (Cohn 1989b, 156). The absence of such descriptions results in an ability to abstract nuclear weapons from the horrible reality of suffering they have the capacity to cause, and to legitimate the neglect of human bodies and lives (Cohn 1989a, 119, 135; Cohn 1989b).[13]

Carol Gilligan suggests that this capacity for abstraction also enables the denial of suffering because it replaces actual lives with hypothetical people (Gilligan 1977, 511). Many feminists counter the inattention just-war theorists give to the horrors of war by emphasizing the enormous suffering of actual individuals which war entails, not only during actual hostilities (e.g., Ruddick 1989, 157) but also by the military-industrial complex that prepares for and perpetuates wars (see, e.g., Chapkis 1981, 36; Reardon 1985; Brock-Utne 1985; Stephenson 1986, 86). As a contrast to abstract just-war thinking, Ruddick describes maternal thinking as generating "a sturdy antimilitaristic conception of the body" in which birth is privileged over death (Ruddick 1987, 216).

Another feminist criticism of the abstract character of much just-war theorizing is its portrayal of hostile forces as a one-dimensionally evil "Other."[14] As "Other," the opposition can be perceived as inferior and "killable" alien beings, rather than as other humans sharing similar needs and desires. Although Walzer recognizes the role that this perception of the enemy as less than human plays in enhancing the willingness of human beings to kill one another (see, e.g.,

Walzer 1977, 139–43), he fails to see the far-reaching implications of this for the possibility of negotiating alternatives to armed conflict, or for assessing the morality of particular conflicts.

Along with other militarist thinking, Ruddick condemns just-war theory's dependence on a conception of " 'enemies' abstract enough to be killable" (Ruddick 1989, 150), a conception in which "human bodies are subordinated to abstract causes, [and] different bodies are organized around abstract labels of civilian or soldier, 'the enemy' or ally, us or them" (146). Moral theorist Nel Noddings considers this problem to be more prevalent among men than women, since females are socialized in a way which emphasizes relationality and connection more than separation and autonomy (Noddings 1989, 202).

A third aspect of abstraction that has troubled feminists about just-war thinking is its privileging of abstract concepts of rights and justice over and above those of love and caring (e.g., Gilligan 1982; Noddings 1984). For Augustine, war is just when necessary to counter injustice and restore peace, regardless of the relative equities in the conflict (Augustine 1984, 862). For Walzer, going to war is only justified in order to defend rights to life and liberty (Walzer 1977, 135). And in the normal course, the practice of war is just only when it does not violate human rights (135). Elshtain specifically criticizes Walzer's theory of rights as a foundation for determining the morality of war, contending that the application of a rights-based approach to the bombings of Hiroshima is "impoverished" and "inadequate to describe what happened on those dreadful days" (Elshtain 1985, 47).[15]

Many feminists reject such an emphasis on rights and justice as relying on male-derived and biased conceptions that fail to accord with the way human beings are actually constituted (e.g., Shanley 1983, 360; Shaughnessy 1988, 11). Feminist legal theorist Joan Shaughnessy argues that a focus on rights fails "to recognize that people do not exist in isolation, but rather within a complex, imperfect social structure" (Shaughnessy 1988, 12). According to Gilligan, moral theories based on individual rights and justice promote relations of separation rather than connection. Separation is more likely to lead to alienation, and ultimately to war, since the origins of aggressiveness lie in the failure of connection. In her view, whereas "male" approaches are based on rights and justice, "female" approaches proceed on the basis of nonviolence (Gilligan 1982, 173–74). Again, even if one does not accept the gendered aspects of these criticisms, they nonetheless suggest that the tendency to abstract thinking among just-war theorists makes the resort to armed force more likely.

Dichotomized Thinking. Although not in the criteria themselves, the application of just-war theory reflects a dualistic hierarchy of values privileging male over female, the "spiritual" over the "earthly," and the "State" over the "Individual." This dualism is readily evident in Augustine's validation of practices in the earthly sphere which he condemns in the heavenly (including war), on the basis that these spheres constitute "two cities" governed by different sets of laws (see Augustine 1984, 877–78). Like Augustine, Niebuhr privileges the individual's relationship with an abstract, transcendent God over relationships with other persons. Noddings characterizes this tendency as fostering separation and lack of connection between persons (see Noddings 1989, 200–201, 204).

Feminists have also argued that such dualism privileges abstract spiritual conceptions over practical earthly ones, and devalues the significance of "this world" and its inhabitants (see, e.g., McFague 1987). Ruddick, for example, believes that the tendency to abstraction in just-war theory is fueled by Christianity's eschatological focus, which separates the "inner" spiritual life from the "outer" material one (Ruddick 1989, 134–36). Elshtain also objects to the dualisms of "good and evil" and "just and unjust" in official just-war rhetoric, which she claims is unable to restrain judges from becoming executioners under conditions of total war (Elshtain 1987, 157).

One of Elshtain's main criticisms of just-war theory is its dualistic discourse of gender, which designates women as "beautiful souls" in opposition to the just Christian (male) warrior (Elshtain 1985, 45). This gendered split operates to constitute women as "civic cheerleaders", a "collective Other" in opposition to which men can be virilized as warriors (Elshtain 1985, 42–43). This split continues to operate in contemporary just-war theory, including that of the U.S. Catholic bishops (see Segers 1985, 642). Elshtain also criticizes the way just-war theory dichotomizes war and peace because it leads to a conception of peace as simply the absence of war rather than a "chastened patriotism" which would restrain thinking in warist terms. As Cohn notes, such attitudes about peace tend to confirm rather than belie the warist presumption that peace is "soft-headed" (Cohn 1989b, 128).

Relationship of the Individual to Authority. One hierarchalized dichotomy in particular that all three just-war theories discussed here reflect is a privileging of the state over the individual, which justifies allowing the innocent to die for the "social good." Both Augustine and Niebuhr place a premium on social order and political stability. For Augustine, this counsels passive obedience to secular authority (Augustine 1984, 870). For Niebuhr, social order may sometimes outweigh the obligation to pursue justice, because "contemporary war places so many moral values in incalculable jeopardy" (Niebuhr and Dun 1955, 78; Niebuhr 1956, 44).

Although Walzer purports to give primacy to individual rights, there is a tension in his just-war theory between the rights of individuals and the rights of community. State's rights—to territorial integrity and political sovereignty—can sometimes legitimately override individual rights in defense of communities (Walzer 1977, 253). His theory allows an exception to the ordinary protection of individual rights for cases of "supreme emergency," when an imminent grave emergency to one's own people exists, as well as in the case of individual soldiers, who, Walzer argues, give up their rights when they enlist or agree to be conscripted.

The privileging of authority in just-war theory also increases the risk that individuals will be viewed only instrumentally, as means sacrificed to the end of the state's winning the war (see Davis 1987, 475). This is especially evident in Augustine's view that the decision to undertake war is one for the monarch, not the individual soldier. Civil disobedience and selective conscientious objection are illegitimate (see Langan 1984, 31). Similarly, in Walzer's view, since soldiers lose their human rights "simply by fighting" (Walzer 1977, 136), soldiers are a kind of "other" who can be freely sacrificed. This objectification makes it easier to justify taking the lives of soldiers, whether through wholesale slaughter of enemy troops, or the use of large numbers of one's own soldiers sacrificed kamikaze style, and may actually risk the expansion and escalation of hostilities.

Feminists are critical of such privileging of the state. Ruddick criticizes just-war's "unquestioning obedience as a virtue" (Ruddick 1989, 114). Similarly, Elshtain proposes that the discourse of "armed civic virtue" dominating just-war thinking needs to be replaced with a "politicized" discourse that "questions and is suspicious of authority" (Elshtain 1987, 258). Feminists have noted that conservative attitudes advocating maintenance of the status quo—evident in much traditional just-war thinking—are often used to perpetuate unequal social relations, especially in respect to women and racial minorities.

Further, some feminist moral theories are founded on interpersonal relations between individuals, suggesting a greater concern for individual welfare than for social order and stability. In Noddings's theory of caring, for example, responsibilities to close relatives are primary, followed by an expanding, lessening degree of obligation toward those who are related less directly, through "circles and chains of caring" (see Noddings 1984; Gilligan 1982). These feminist critiques suggest that just-war theory's general emphasis on the good of the social order at the expense of individuals is misplaced.

These criticisms of just-war theory demonstrate that it does not provide a satisfactory method for determining the morality of war for many feminists, at least as it has been applied traditionally. Yet, as the following discussion reveals, feminist efforts to provide alternative approaches are also inadequate.

FEMINIST ALTERNATIVES TO JUST-WAR THEORY

To date, there have been two notable nonpacifist feminist alternatives to just-war theory: Elshtain's proposed "revitalized civic discourse" and Ruddick's "maternal peace politics." Elshtain proposes to reduce armed conflict by eliminating the paradigm of "armed civic virtue" that underlies realist and just-war approaches. This involves "devirilizing" war discourse (e.g., Elshtain 1985, 55) and retrieving "female-linked imagery." It requires formulating an alternative discourse which can "problematize war narratives" and move beyond "the grand narrative of armed civic virtue" (Elshtain 1987, 251),[16] with its gendered dichotomy of males as warriors and females as noncombatant peacemakers (Elshtain 1985, 50). In Elshtain's estimation, this would give "men and women the opportunity to share risks as citizens, to take up nonviolence as a choice, not a given" (Elshtain 1987, 257).

It is not evident how Elshtain's proposed "revitalized civic discourse" would be an improvement on just-war decision-making about the morality of U.S. involvement in recent conflicts. Women's exemplary military performance in the Gulf War certainly broke down many traditional gender stereotypes about women's ability to perform as soldiers under combat conditions, thus undermining the paradigm of armed civic virtue as an exclusively male domain. Yet breaking down this gender dichotomy does not seem to have altered the macho attitudes that led to U.S. involvement in the Gulf, or resulted in the indiscriminate killing of retreating Iraqi soldiers. Nor has it led to an enhanced role for women in policy-making in more recent conflicts, such as the war in Bosnia.

Thus, in the end, Elshtain's own proposal fails at the level of effecting practical decision-making. In addition, Elshtain fails to specify clearly how she would amend, supplement, or replace just-war theory, given her recognition that both just-war theory and realism have limited usefulness (Elshtain 1987, 248–49). Indeed, in her more recent work, she seems to embrace traditional just-war theory more completely and uncritically than earlier (cf., e.g., Elshtain 1991b, 134, with Elshtain 1987), offering it as a necessary antidote to the lack of in-depth moral theorizing about war by feminists.

Ruddick acknowledges that just cause for war may exist and some battles may be necessary, but she contends that "there are entirely or principally nonviolent ways of fighting them that are at least as effective as violence" (Ruddick 1983, 475–76). Ruddick's proposed alternative to just-war theory is a "maternal politics of peace" based on "maternal thinking." Maternal thinking is constituted by the virtues of "maternal practice": preservative love, fostering nurturance, and training conscience and its latent peacefulness (Ruddick 1989, 40–56, 137).[17] It requires that "peacemakers must invent myriad nonviolent actions and then name, describe and support them" (139), including nonviolent resistance (174–75). It also requires an ongoing attention to human suffering (157).

There are a number of fundamental problems with Ruddick's proposal. First, although it avoids the realist trap of undue pessimism about human nature, it tends to fall into the opposite extreme of idealistically depicting mothers as basically caring toward their offspring, selflessly caring more for their children than for themselves, and presuming that nonmothers have similar caring capacities. Second, although she denies that her theory of maternal thinking is based on essentialist conceptions about women's biological natures (see Ruddick 1989, 40–41, 157), her argument that women are more suited to promote peace than are men tends in this direction by resting on women's capacity for, and experience of, being mothers (see Code 1991, 91–93).

Ruddick's views tend to replicate the essentialist and dichotomizing tendencies in the work of "cultural" or "difference" feminists, who argue that relations of caring for others give women a "different moral voice" (e.g., Gilligan 1982; Noddings 1984). Ruddick asserts that such differences make females "naturally" more oriented to peace than war. Dichotomizing tendencies that Ruddick condemns in traditional just-war theory appear in her own contention that maternal practice promises distinctive resources for nonviolent alternatives to war because of the "*prima facie* opposition between maternal and military work," that "mothering begins in birth and promises life" whereas "military thinking is characterized by its justification of organized, deliberate death" (Ruddick 1987, 247;

Ruddick 1989, 148).[18] Elshtain is critical of this type of move to "devirilize male discourse" by replacing it with a "feminized" one, arguing that "both embody dangerous distortions" (Elshtain 1987, 258).

Third, Ruddick's approach fails to develop its implications fully or in concrete terms and thereby demonstrate its feasibility. Her theory remains as abstract as the just-war tradition that she rejects. Her most specific claim is that "the practice of mothering taken as a whole" contributes to peace politics the qualities of attentiveness, realism and a positive attitude toward change (Ruddick 1989, 220). Contrary to her own theoretical principles, however, she fails to provide concrete, particular, non-abstract examples of when or how this nonviolent approach has or could succeed. She generally fails to provide an adequate connection between the private sphere of maternal practices involving relationships with one's own children and the public sphere of international relations between antagonistic, and often culturally alien, nation-states (Ruddick 1987, 57, 178, 254; see also Code 1991, 92–93).

Ruddick's proposed "maternal peace politics" also proves deficient when applied to the real life experience of the Bosnian conflict. When former friends and neighbors who lived together peacefully for years turn to rape and kill one another based on ethnic and religious differences, it is difficult to see how a "practice of mothering" could resolve the conflict. Nor can Ruddick's idealistic optimism about the power of maternal thinking to avert violent methods of resolving conflicts be viewed as reasonable in the light of some of the U.S.'s past military interventions, including the two world wars.

This discussion suggests that neither Ruddick nor Elshtain have developed an alternative to just-war thinking which remedies the deficiencies in the tradition without contributing new problems. Ruddick and Elshtain do not hold an exclusive claim on feminist alternatives to traditional just-war theory. Nonetheless, the deficiencies in their attempts to replace traditional criteria suggest that the way to deal with traditional approaches may not be to eliminate them but to revise how they are applied.

A FEMINIST REVITALIZATION OF JUST-WAR THEORY

The feminist criticisms discussed do not suggest a need to develop radically new or different criteria for assessing the morality of engagement in armed conflict from those offered by traditional just-war theory. Rather, they are more focused on altering the *way* the traditional criteria have been applied in specific situations. To that end, feminist criticisms and counterproposals suggest a number of specific proposals for modifying the *practice* more than the *theory* of the just-war approach to armed conflict. These proposals are based on the positive dimensions of the just-war criteria already discussed rather than representing completely novel approaches.

As an initial matter, feminist criticisms suggest that just-war theory should not be premised on realist assumptions. This includes theologically derived conceptions of original sin and analogously pessimistic secular appraisals of human nature. Such negative conceptions tend to squelch consideration of alternatives to war. However, unduly idealistic appraisals of human (particularly female) nature by some feminists such as Noddings and Ruddick are also inaccurate and unproductive. Prudence dictates that the long history and habit of human warmaking must not be forgotten either.

Such a reconceptualized understanding of human nature would have at least two desirable consequences for just-war theory. Including females as well as males in "human nature" (see Tickner 1991, 37; Ruddick 1989; Elshtain 1987) would enable just-war theorists to consider the nonviolent historical practices and sentiments of women, leading to an understanding which would assume that the nature of human beings makes war neither inevitable nor completely unnecessary. In addition, such a revised understanding of human nature would permit greater opportunities for attempting nonviolent alternatives to armed conflict, without precluding consideration of the possibility that resort to war might be necessary.

A second major implication of feminist criticisms is that just-war theorists should pay more serious attention to pacifist arguments. As Cady has suggested, pacifism and just-war thinking are not radically opposed, but represent two different positions along the same continuum (Cady 1989, 35–37). The influence of pacifist perspectives would strengthen application of several just-war criteria. First, it would make "last resort" more significant in just-war deliberations, resulting in a greater effort to exhaust all reasonably effective alternatives to the use of armed force. Given their insistence on attending to the suffering of particular others, feminist applications of "last resort" might result in interpreting the preferability of alternatives to war in accordance with whether they result in less harm to the innocent (see McMahon 1991).

The emphasis on collaboration in much feminist theory could also be creatively applied to the development of new international or multinational frameworks for assessing if and when resort to armed force is morally necessary. However, these alternatives must be considered with an awareness of Walzer's admonition that the "last resort" may *never* be reached, since *some* alternative always remains theoretically available, thus effectively making this criteria function to transform just-war theory into a form of pacifism.

A just-war theory chastened by pacifist influences would also involve strengthening the force accorded to the "proportionality" and "reasonable hope for success" requirements. This would entail replacing abstract and dualistic thinking with a more casuistical attention to context and particularity, what Elshtain characterizes as "the living textures within which limited human beings think and act" (Elshtain 1987, 189). As Alan Geyer recognizes, the U.S.'s involvement in the Persian Gulf War "no longer looks so justifiable once one begins examining in detail whether the facts warranted" the conclusion to go to war (Geyer 1991, 135).

In keeping with feminist concerns with bodies and individual suffering, application of "proportionality" and "reasonable hope for success" would require a more comprehensive examination of the potential long-term consequences of contemplated intervention. Such considerations should highlight the impact on civilians. This includes not only their survival, but also the quality of their lives and relationships, particularly if the environment and/or vital links to food, water, and basic services are damaged or destroyed during the conflict. It also requires an assessment of the long-term prospects for peace and security in the surrounding region. As Elshtain and others have pointed out, just-war principles were heedlessly bandied about during the Gulf War to provide a justification for U.S. involvement, without careful attention to the many areas of uncertainty and ambiguity that existed (Elshtain 1992, 42).

A more nuanced approach to just-war theory would also give more attention to the requirements of "right intention" and "relative justice" than has been done in the past. Niebuhr's caution against self-righteousness is echoed by Ruddick's recognition that "being on the side of the good can foster a repressive self-righteousness that legitimates killing or, alternatively, condemns violence without attending to the despair and abuse from which it arises" (Ruddick 1989, 135). Elshtain similarly predicts that our "warlike way of thinking" cannot be altered until we abandon "grand teleologies of historical winners and losers," "triumphalist accounts of our victories," and "absolute moralisms" as part of our identities (Elshtain 1987, 256). Feminist concern for relationships could help temper these tendencies in just-war thinking.

In addition, feminist calls for a more particularized, contextualized, and individualized approach to war would involve a breakdown (or at least a radical reconfiguration) of the dichotomies between male and female, combatant and noncombatant, soldier and citizen, ally and enemy, and state and individual which have dominated just-war thinking. Rather than relying on traditional dichotomies, a feminist application of just-war criteria should emphasize the effects of going to war on the lives of the particular individuals who would be involved, whether soldier or civilian, enemy or ally, male or female.

A feminist application of just-war criteria in a situation like that of Bosnia, for example, would require military strategists to focus more closely on the relations between the warring factions than has been the case. Rather than concluding simply that intervention is inappropriate because none of the participants is completely innocent, a feminist analysis of the conflict would examine the relative equities of the parties, the balance of power, the history and cultures of the region, the specific conduct of each of the parties which led to and has maintained hostilities, the degree to which each party has complied with the war convention, including its treatment of innocent civilians, the prospects for a long-term settlement of hostilities through the use of armed intervention, the environmental impact of such intervention on the region, and so on. In particular, a feminist appraisal would consider the rape of Bosnian Muslim women by Serbian men as a serious war crime rivaling that of deliberately injuring or killing innocent civilians. Such a fine-grained analysis and attention to human suffering would likely result in a determination that armed intervention, or at least additional military support for the Bosnian Muslims would be morally justified, despite a sturdy presumption against violence.

Finally, a feminist approach to just-war theory would entail reformulated understandings of the proper relationship between the individual and the state. It would consider both the impact of war on individuals as well as the obligations of both men and women to defend the nation. It should provide a formulation with which the merits of a particular military engagement may be assessed by the individual soldiers and civilians involved in it as well by the relevant "authorities." In keeping with Elshtain's criticisms, it would include a reassessment of women's exemption from military combat and draft registration, as well as established laws governing conscientious objection and civil disobedience.

CONCLUSION

Feminist critiques have provided important challenges to several aspects of traditional just-war theory. The discussion of the just-war approaches of Augustine, Niebuhr, and Walzer from a feminist perspective reveals how weak and limited this tradition's vision of alternatives to war often is, how distorted by realist and gender-biased assumptions, how abstract and life-denying its application can be. Yet, despite proficiency at pinpointing a number of significant problems with traditional just-war thinking, prominent feminist alternatives proposed to date are themselves deficient in a number of respects.

In addition, feminist criticisms and alternatives do not indicate any inherent deficiencies in the just-war criteria themselves. They focus on the underlying assumptions and problematic application of the theory, not the validity or appropriateness of the criteria. Feminist principles suggest several ways in which traditional approaches to just-war theorizing can be improved, leading to a more careful and considered appraisal of when the use of armed force is morally justified. Unless or until a feasible feminist alternative to the just-war criteria is developed, feminists should work to revitalize, rather than undermine, this long-standing approach to the morality of war.

NOTES

In addition to thanking this volume's editors, Duane Cady, Karen J. Warren, and copy editor Teresa Jesionowski, the author would like to thank the Indiana Center for Global Peace and World Change for my funding as a MacArthur Scholar (1991–92); the Center's director, John Lovell, my Project Advisor, D'Ann Campbell, and fellow MacArthur Scholars, especially Todd Sullivan; doctoral advisor Richard B. Miller; and colleague Jason Beduhn for many helpful comments and suggestions.

1. By "feminist," I generally mean a critical perspective on the patriarchal and sexist dimensions of society oriented to improving the status of women.

2. These various perspectives on war can be conceptualized as located on a single continuum running from absolute pacifism on one side, through warism on the other, with various forms of pacifism, just-warism, and war realism aligned next to one another in between (Cady 1989, 35–37).

3. The association of women with peace and peace-movements is a long-standing one, extending back as far as the classical Greeks and Romans. See, e.g., Elshtain (1987, 139); Berkman (1990); Costin (1983). Many women's groups organized in the early twentieth century had peace as a significant aspect of their agendas, including the Women's Peace Union and the Women's International League for Peace and Freedom (WILPF). In recent decades, women have continued to take the lead

in mobilizing peace organizations worldwide. See Alonso (1993); Swerdlow (1989); Hunter (1991); Howes (1993); Reardon (1985, 86–87, 181).

4. Polls taken in relation to U.S. involvement in the Persian Gulf War indicate that this gap appears to be growing. In December, 1990, men were about equally divided regarding whether the United States should attack Iraq, whereas women opposed military action by 73 percent to 22 percent. Women similarly opposed surgical air strikes by 63 percent to 29 percent. Research indicates that men in many western countries tolerate aggressive stands on international and domestic public policy issues more readily than do women (Brock-Utne 1985, 33).

5. Cady points out that pacifism is sometimes rejected because it is wrongly identified as "passivism," a passive and inactive response to aggression (Cady 1989, 11–12). Some women may reject pacifism based on the official views of a cultural, social or religious group, as was the case with the National Council of Catholic Women's support for just-war doctrine between the two world wars (MacCarthy 1978, 27). Other women have rejected pacifism on realist grounds (Elshtain 1985, 42).

6. Just-war principles are described and analyzed by a number of just-war theorists, notably in recent years by Paul Ramsey (1968), Michael Walzer (1977), William O'Brien (1981), James Turner Johnson (1981, xxii), and Richard Miller (1991, 13–15).

7. Duane Cady characterizes this presumption as "warism," which he describes as leading to the abuse of certain just-war criteria, especially the *in bello* principles of discrimination and proportionality (Cady 1989, 66–69).

8. For Augustine, war is both the consequence of sin as well as a remedy for sin (see Miller 1991, 21). For Niebuhr, war is a necessary "lesser of two evils" in a sinful world, a reality that cannot be eradicated in the earthly realm, "a world in which egoism, collective and individual, will never be completely overcome" (Niebuhr 1933, 257). Niebuhr thus rejects, as contrary both to the New Testament and experience, views of "rationalists" who believe in the essential good of human beings (Niebuhr 1940, 6).

9. Richard Miller also criticizes the tendency of just-war theory to consider only war and not peace (Miller 1991, 122).

10. Despite Elshtain's rejection of the pacifist label, this criticism accords with the view of technological or nuclear pacifists, who reject the notion of limited war as feasible in the light of the destructive potential of modern weaponry (see Cady 1989, chap. 4).

11. Their exclusive focus on the individual ethic of the love commandment ignores the sociopolitical duty to promote justice and is socially irresponsible (Niebuhr 1956, 31, 76). Niebuhr criticizes pacifism based on nonviolent resistance of the sort advocated by Gandhi and Martin Luther King, Jr. as a biblically heretical and disingenuous effort to found on love what actually amounts to power politics involving coercion (Niebuhr 1940, 10–11). However, Niebuhr does validate nonresistant pacifism of sectarian perfectionists as providing an important moral voice that may temper the tendencies of militarists to allow justice to eclipse love (Niebuhr 1940, 5, 25; see Miller 1991, 107).

12. In the City of God, "there will be no animal body to 'weigh down the soul' in its process of corruption; there will be a spiritual body with no cravings" (Augustine 1984, 878).

13. Ruddick considers such technostrategic rationality as "only an extension, albeit a stunning one, of the abstractness that characterizes military discourse as a whole" (Ruddick 1989, 146).

14. Miller also discusses this view in just-war theory (1991, 59, 71, 235). Noddings suggests that this ability to construct killable enemies results from our projection of evil onto others without seeing how we are implicated (Noddings 1989, 193–99). Elshtain similarly argues that both realism and pacifism promote polarizing "masculine" tendencies that deny the violence inside ourselves and project it outward onto "the Other" (1985, 51).

15. Not all of Walzer's just-war thinking is similarly abstract and universalizing, however. He recognizes that the rules of war are not universally applicable because morality is always connected to a culture's tradition and history. Moral rules are necessarily shaped by reference to that community's particular, concrete experience of war (Walzer 1977, 24). However, this more particularist aspect of Walzer remains in tension with the centrality he accords to individual rights founded on abstract and generalized notions of justice.

16. Carol Cohn also turns to discourse as a way of destabilizing and interrupting prevailing approaches to war, claiming that deconstruction provides an important means of challenging the he-

gemony of strategic discourse as "the only legitimate language for publicly discussing nuclear policy" (Cohn 1989a, 137; see Cohn 1989b, 154–55).

17. In Ruddick's definition, mothering is not exclusive to women but includes any person who is responsible for and significantly involved in caring for the lives of children (Ruddick 1989, 40).

18. In this regard, Ruddick tends to slide from a recognition that the traditional identification of women with peace is a myth to an unsupported assertion that "women's distinctive peacefulness" has the potential to become "a reliable resource for peace" (Ruddick 1983, 479).

References

Alonso, Harriet. 1993. *Peace as a women's issue: A history of the United States movement for world peace and women's rights*. Syracuse: Syracuse University Press.

Augustine. 1984. *City of God*. Trans. Henry Bettenson. London: Penguin Books.

Baxter, Sandra, and Marjorie Lansing, ed. 1983. *Women and politics: The visible majority*. Ann Arbor: University of Michigan Press.

Berkman, Joyce. 1990. Feminism, war, and peace politics: The case of World War I. In *Women, militarism and war: Essays in history, politics and social theory*, ed. Jean Bethke Elshtain and Sheila Tobias. Savage, Md.: Rowman & Littlefield Publishers, Inc.

Branscombe, Nyla, and Susan Owen. 1993. Gun ownership among American women and its consequences for social judgment. In *Women and the use of force*. See Howes.

Brock-Utne, Birgit. 1985. *Educating for peace: A feminist perspective*. New York: Pergamon Press.

Brock-Utne, Birgit. Julianne Traylor, and Aas Solveign, eds. 1986. *Women and Peace: A report from a conference*. Oslo: International Peace Research Institute.

Cady, Duane. 1989. *From warism to pacifism: A moral continuum*. Philadelphia: Temple University Press.

Chapkis, Wendy, ed. 1981. *Loaded questions: Women in the military*. Amsterdam: Transnational Press.

Code, Lorraine. 1991. Review essay: Will the 'good enough' feminists please stand up? *Social Theory and Practice* 17(10): 85–104.

Cohn, Carol. 1989a. Sex and death in the rational world of defense intellectuals. In *Feminist theory in practice and process*, ed. Micheline Malson, Jean O'Barr, and Susan Westphal-Wihl. Chicago: University of Chicago Press.

———. 1989b. Emasculating America's linguistic deterrent. In *Rocking the ship of state: Toward a feminist peace politics*, ed. Adrienne Harris and Ynestra King. Boulder: Westview Press.

Costin, Lela. 1983. Feminism, pacifism, nationalism, and the United Nations Decade for Women. In *Women and men's wars*, ed. Judith Stiehm. Oxford: Pergamon Press.

Davis, G. Scott. 1987. Warcraft and the fragility of virtue. *Soundings* 70: 475–93.

DeCosse, David, ed. 1992. *But was it just? Reflections on the morality of the Persian Gulf War*. New York: Doubleday.

Elshtain, Jean Bethke. 1985. Reflections on war and political discourse: Realism, just war, and feminism in a nuclear age. *Political Theory* 13(1): 39–57.

———. 1987. *Women and war*. New York: Basic Books.

———. 1991a. Feminism and war. *Progressive* 55(9): 14–16.

———. 1991b. Ethics in the women's movement. *Annals of the American Academy of Political and Social Science* 515: 126–39.

———. 1992. Just war and American politics. *Christian Century* 109(2): 41–44.

Gallagher, Nancy. 1993. The gender gap in popular attitudes toward the use of force. In *Women and the use of force*. See Howes.

Geyer, Alan. 1991. Just war and the burdens of history. *Christian Century* 108(5): 134–35.

Geyer, Alan, and Barbara Green. 1992. *Lies in the sand: Justice and the Gulf War*. New York: Westminster/John Knox.

Gilligan, Carol. 1977. Concept of the self and of morality. *Harvard Educational Review* 47(4): 481–517.

———. 1982. *In a different voice: Psychological theory and women's development*. Cambridge, MA: Harvard University Press.

Grant, Rebecca. 1991. The sources of gender bias in international relations theory. In *Gender and international relations*. See Grant and Newland.

Grant, Rebecca, and Rebecca Newland. 1991. *Gender and international relations*. Bloomington: Indiana University Press.

Hartigan, Richard. 1966. Saint Augustine on war and killing: The problem of the innocent. *Journal of the History of Ideas* 27(2): 195–204.

Hartsock, Nancy. 1982. Prologue to a feminist critique of war and politics. In *Women's views of the political world of men*, ed. Judith Stiehm. Dobbs Ferry, N.Y.: Transnational Publishers, Inc.

Holmes, Arthur, ed. 1969. *War and Christian ethics*. Grand Rapids, MI: Baker Books.

Howes, Ruth, and Michael Stevenson, eds. 1993. *Women and the use of force*. Boulder, CO: Lynne Reinner Publishers.

Hunter, Anne E., ed. 1991. *Genes and gender VI: On peace, war, and gender: A challenge to genetic explanations*. New York: Feminist Press.

Johnson, James Turner. 1981. *Just war tradition and the restraint of war: A moral and historical inquiry*. Princeton: Princeton University Press.

Johnson, James Turner, and George Weigel. 1992. *Just war and the Gulf War*. Washington, D.C.: Ethics and Public Policy Center.

Kehoe, Alice. 1986. Christianity and war. In *Peace and war: Cross-cultural perspectives*, ed. M. L. Foster and Richard Rubenstein. New Brunswick, CT: Transaction Books.

Langan, John. 1984. The elements of St. Augustine's just-war theory. *Journal of Religious Ethics* 12(1): 19–38.

MacCarthy, Esther. 1978. Catholic women and war: The National Council of Catholic Women, 1919–1946. *Peace and Change* 5(1): 23–32.

McFague, Sallie. 1987. *Models of god*. Philadelphia: Fortress Press.

McMahon, Jeff. 1991. The Gulf War and the traditional theory of the just war. Paper presented at Indiana University, Bloomington, October 1991.

Miller, Richard B. 1991. *Interpretations of conflict: Ethics, pacifism and the just-war tradition*. Chicago: University of Chicago Press.

National Conference of Catholic Bishops (NCCB). 1983. *The challenge of peace: God's promise and our response*. Washington, D.C.: United States Catholic Conference, Inc.

Niebuhr, Reinhold. 1932. Must we do nothing? *Christian Century* (March 30): 415–17.

———. 1933. Why I leave the F.O.R. *Christian Century* (January 3): 254–59.

———. 1940. Why the Christian Church is not pacifist. In *Christianity and power politics*. New York: Charles Scribner's Sons.

———. 1956. *An interpretation of Christian ethics*. Cleveland: Meridian Books.

Niebuhr, Reinhold, and Angus Dun. 1955. God wills both justice and peace. *Christianity and Crisis* 15(June 13): 75–78.

Noddings, Nel. 1984. *Caring: A feminine approach to ethics and moral education*. Berkeley: University of California Press.

———. 1989. *Women and evil*. Berkeley: University of California Press.

O'Brien, William. 1981. *The conduct of just and limited war*. New York: Praeger Publishers.

Pierson, Ruth Roach. 1988. "They're still women after all": Wartime jitters over femininity. In *Women and the military system*, ed. Eva Isaksson. New York: St. Martin's Press.

Ramsey, Paul. 1968. *The just war: Force and political responsibility*. New York: Charles Scribner's Sons.

Reardon, Betty. 1985. *Women and the war system*. New York: Teachers College Press.

Ruddick, Sarah. 1983. Pacifying the forces: Drafting women in the interests of peace. *Signs* 8(3): 471–89.

———. 1987. Remarks on the sexual politics of reason. In *Women and Moral Theory*, ed. Eva Kittay and Diana Meyers. Stonybrook, New York: Rowman & Littlefield Publishers, Inc.

———. 1989. *Maternal thinking: Towards a politics of peace*. Boston: Beacon Press.

Segers, Mary. 1985. The Catholic bishops' pastoral letter on war and peace: A feminist perspective. *Feminist Studies* 11(3): 619–47.

Shanley, Mary. 1983. Afterword: Feminism and families in a liberal polity. In *Families, politics and public policy*, ed. Irene Diamond and Mary Shanley. New York: Longman.

Shaughnessy, Joan. 1988. Gilligan's travels. *Law and Inequality* 7: 1–27.

Sizemore, Russell. 1992. Reflections on the Gulf War. *Christian Century* 109(30): 945–47.

Stephenson, Carolyn. 1986. Pacifism and the roots of feminism in the United States, 1830–1930: Individual linkages. In *Women and peace*. See Brock-Utne 1986.

Swerdlow, Amy. 1989. Women strike for peace. In *Rocking the ship of state: Toward a feminist peace politics*. See Harris and King.

Tickner, J. Ann. 1991. Hans Morgenthau's principles of political realism: A feminist reformulation. In *Gender and international relations*. See Grant and Newland 1991.

Tikkun editors. 1991. On just wars: An interview with Michael Walzer. *Tikkun* 6(1):40–42.

Walzer, Michael. 1977. *Just and unjust wars*. New York: Basic Books, Inc.

———. 1982. Response to Lackey. *Ethics* 92: 547–48.

———. 1991. Perplexed. *New Republic* (January 28): 13–15.

Washburn, Patricia. 1993. Women in the peace movement. In *Women and the use of force*. See Howes.

Feminist Justice and the Pursuit of Peace

JAMES P. STERBA

The pursuit of peace is not usually associated with feminist justice. In the international arena, the usual focus for the pursuit of peace is the use of force, with realists, just-war theorists, and pacifists disagreeing over if, when, and to what extent the use of force can be legitimate. To most people concerned with such questions, feminist justice has been only marginally related, at best, to the pursuit of peace. In this paper I will argue that this is not the case. I contend that the achievement of feminist justice is centrally related to the pursuit of peace such that one cannot consistently pursue peace without pursuing feminist justice as well. I begin by setting out a plausible account of feminist justice, and I then show how feminist justice is required for the pursuit of peace.

THE IDEAL OF FEMINIST JUSTICE

Contemporary feminists almost by definition seek to put an end to male domination and to secure women's liberation. To achieve these goals, many feminists support the political ideal of a gender-free or androgynous society.[1] According to these feminists, all assignments of rights and duties are ultimately to accord with the ideal of a gender-free or androgynous society. Since a conception of justice is usually thought to provide the ultimate grounds for the assignment of rights and duties, I refer to this ideal of a gender-free or androgynous society as "feminist justice."

But how is this ideal to be interpreted? A gender-free or genderless society is a society in which basic rights and duties are not assigned on the basis of a person's biological sex. Being male or female is not the grounds for determining what basic rights and duties a person has in a gender-free society. But this is to characterize

Hypatia vol. 9, no. 2 (Spring 1994) © by James P. Sterba

the feminist ideal only negatively. It tells us what we need to get rid of, not what we need to put in its place. A more positive characterization is provided by the ideal of androgyny. Putting the ideal of feminist justice more positively in terms of the ideal of androgyny also helps to bring out why men should be attracted to feminist justice.

In a well-known article, Joyce Trebilcot (1977) distinguishes two forms of androgyny. The first form postulates the same ideal for everyone. According to this form of androgyny, the ideal person "combines characteristics usually attributed to men with characteristics usually attributed to women." Thus, we should expect both nurturance and mastery, openness and objectivity, compassion and competitiveness from each and every person who has the capacities for these traits.

By contrast, the second form of androgyny does not advocate the same ideal for everyone but rather a variety of options from "pure" femininity to "pure" masculinity. As Trebilcot points out, this form of androgyny shares with the first the view that biological sex should not be the basis for determining the appropriateness of gender characterization. It differs in that it holds that "all alternatives with respect to gender should be equally available to and equally approved for everyone, regardless of sex" (72).

It would be a mistake, however, to distinguish sharply between these two forms of androgyny. Properly understood, they are simply two different facets of a single ideal. For, as Mary Ann Warren has argued, the second form of androgyny is appropriate only "with respect to feminine and masculine traits which are largely matters of personal style and preference and which have little direct moral significance" (Warren 1982, 178–79). However, when we consider so-called feminine and masculine *virtues*, it is the first form of androgyny that is required because, then, other things being equal, the same virtues are appropriate for everyone.

We can even formulate the ideal of androgyny more abstractly so that it is no longer specified in terms of so-called feminine and masculine traits. We can specify the ideal as requiring no more than that the traits that are truly desirable in society be equally open to both women and men, or in the case of virtues, equally expected of both women and men.

There is a problem, of course, in determining which traits of character are virtues and which traits are largely matters of personal style and preference. To make this determination, Trebilcot has suggested that we seek to bring about the second form of androgyny, where people have the option of acquiring the full range of so-called feminine and masculine traits (Trebilcot 1977, 74–78). But when we already have good grounds for thinking that such traits as courage and compassion, fairness and openness are virtues, there is no reason to adopt a laissez-faire approach to moral education. Although, as Trebilcot rightly points out, proscribing certain options would involve a loss of freedom, nevertheless we should be able to determine at least with respect to some character traits when a gain in virtue is worth the loss of freedom. It may even be the case that the loss of freedom suffered by an individual now will be compensated for by a gain of freedom to that same individual in the future once the relevant virtues have been acquired.

So understood, the class of virtues will turn out to be those desirable traits that can be reasonably expected of both women and men. Admittedly, this is a restrictive use of the term "virtue." In normal usage, the term "virtue" is almost synonymous with the term "desirable trait."[2] But there is good reason to focus on those desirable traits that can be justifiably inculcated in both women and men, and, for present purposes, I refer to this class of desirable traits as virtues.[3]

Unfortunately, many of the challenges to the ideal of androgyny fail to appreciate how the ideal can be interpreted to combine a required set of virtues with equal choice from among other desirable traits. For example, some challenges interpret the ideal as attempting to achieve "a proper balance of moderation" among opposing feminine and masculine traits and then question whether traits like feminine gullibility or masculine brutality could ever be combined with opposing gender traits to achieve such a balance (see, e.g., Morgan 1982, 256–57). Other challenges interpret the ideal as permitting unrestricted choice of personal traits and then regard the possibility of Total Women and Hells Angels androgynes as a reductio ad absurdum of the idea (see, e.g., Daly 1978, xi). But once it is recognized that the ideal of androgyny cannot only be interpreted to require of everyone a set of virtues (which need not be a mean between opposing extreme traits), but can also be interpreted to limit everyone's choice to desirable traits, then such challenges to the ideal clearly lose their force because they only work against objectionable interpretations of androgyny.

Actually the main challenge raised by feminists to the ideal of androgyny is that the ideal is self-defeating in that it seeks to eliminate sexual stereotyping of human beings at the same time that it is formulated in terms of the very same stereotypical concepts it seeks to eliminate.[4] Or as Warren has put it, "Is it not at least mildly paradoxical to urge people to cultivate both 'feminine' and 'masculine' virtues, while at the same time holding that virtues ought not to be sexually stereotyped?" (Warren 1982, 181).

One response to this challenge contends that to build a better society we must begin where we are now, and where we are now people still speak of feminine and masculine character traits. Consequently, if we want to refer easily to such traits and to formulate an ideal with respect to how these traits should be distributed in society, it is plausible to refer to them in the way that people presently refer to them, that is, as feminine or masculine traits.

Another response, which attempts to avoid misunderstanding altogether, is to formulate the ideal in the more abstract way I suggested earlier so that it no longer specifically refers to so-called feminine or masculine traits. So formulated, the ideal requires that the traits that are truly desirable in society be equally open to both women and men, or in the case of virtues, equally expected of both women and men. So formulated the ideal would, in effect, expect that men and women have in the fullest sense an equal right of self-development.[5] The ideal requires this because an equal right to self-development can be effectively guaranteed only by equally expecting the same virtues of both women and men and by making other desirable traits equally available to both women and men.

So characterized, the ideal of androgyny represents neither a revolt against so-called feminine virtues and traits nor their exaltation over so-called masculine virtues and traits.[6] Accordingly, the ideal of androgyny does not view women's liberation as *simply* the freeing of women from the confines of traditional roles, thus making it possible for them to develop in ways heretofore reserved for men. Not does the ideal view women's liberation as *simply* the revaluation and glorification of so-called feminine activities like housekeeping or mothering or so-called feminine modes of thinking as reflected in an ethic of caring. The first perspective ignores or devalues genuine virtues and desirable traits traditionally associated with women, while the second ignores or devalues genuine virtues and desirable traits traditionally associated with men. By contrast, the ideal of androgyny seeks a broader-based ideal for both women and men that combines virtues and desirable traits traditionally associated with women with virtues and desirable traits traditionally associated with men. Nevertheless, the ideal of androgyny will clearly reject any so-called virtues or desirable traits traditionally associated with women or men which have been supportive of discrimination or oppression against women or men. In general, the ideal of androgyny substitutes a socialization based on natural ability, reasonable expectation, and choice for a socialization based on sexual difference.

Of course, in proposing to characterize feminist justice in terms of the ideal of a gender-free or androgynous society, I recognize that not all feminists start off endorsing this ideal. Christina Sommers, for example, has attracted attention recently by distinguishing liberal feminism, which she endorses, from androgynous feminism, which she opposes (see Sommers 1989, 82–105; 1990, 66–74; 1991, 5–19). But as one gets clearer and clearer about the liberal feminism that Sommers endorses, one sees that it begins to look more and more like the androgynous feminism that she says she opposes. There is nothing surprising about this, however. We cannot have the genuine equal opportunity for men and women which Sommers wants without reforming the present distribution of gender traits. Women cannot be passive, submissive, dependent, indecisive, and weak and still enjoy the same opportunities enjoyed by men who are aggressive, dominant, independent, decisive, and strong. So I contend that liberal feminism and androgynous feminism go together because genuine equal opportunity requires the feminist ideal of a gender-free or androgynous society.

It also seems that those who claim that we cannot escape a gendered society are simply confused about what a gender-free society would be like (Wolgast 1980). For they seem to agree with those who favor a gender-free or androgynous society that the assignments of roles in society should be based on (natural) ability, rational expectation, and choice. But what they also hold is that some of these assignments will be based on sex as well because some of the natural abilities that people have will be determined by their sex. But even assuming this is the case, it wouldn't show that society was gendered in the sense that its roles in society are based on sex *rather than* on (natural) ability, rational expectation, and choice. And this is the only sense of gendered society to which defenders of feminist justice would be objecting.[7] So once the notion of a gender-free society is clarified, there should be widespread agreement that the assignments of roles in society should be based on (natural) ability, rational expectation, and choice. The ideal of androgyny simply specifies this notion of a gender-free society a bit further by requiring that the traits that are truly desirable in society be equally open to (equally qualified) women and men, or in the case of virtues, equally expected of (equally capable) women and men.

Of course, insofar as natural abilities are a function of sexual difference, there will be differences in the desirable traits and virtues that women and men acquire even in a gender-free or androgynous society. And some contend that these differences will be substantial (Moir and Jessel 1991). But given that we have been slow to implement the degree of equal opportunity required by the ideal of a gender-free or androgynous society, it is difficult to know what differences in desirable traits and virtues, if any, will emerge that are both sex-based and natural-ability-based. What we can be sure of is that given the variety and types of discrimination employed against women in existing societies, a gender-free or androgynous society will look quite different from the societies that we know.

APPLYING THE IDEAL

One locus for the radical restructuring required by the ideal of a gender-free or androgynous society is the family. Here two fundamental changes are needed. First, all children, irrespective of their sex, must be given the same type of upbringing consistent with their native capabilities. Second, mothers and fathers must normally also have the same opportunities for education and employment consistent with their native capabilities.[8]

Yet at least in the United States this need to radically modify traditional family structures to guarantee equal opportunity confronts a serious problem. Given that a significant proportion of the available jobs are at least 9 to 5, families with preschool children require day-care facilities if their adult members are to pursue their careers. Unfortunately, for many families such facilities are simply unavailable. In New York City, for example, more than 144,000 children under the age of six are competing for 46,000 full-time slots in day-care centers. In Seattle, there is licensed day care space for 8,800 of the 23,000 children who need it. In Miami, two children, three and four years old, were left unattended at home while their mother worked. They climbed into a clothes dryer while the timer was on, closed the door and burned to death (New York Times, Nov. 25, 1987).

Moreover, even the available day-care facilities are frequently inadequate, either because their staffs are poorly trained or because the child/adult ratio in such facilities is too high. At best, such facilities provide little more than custodial care; at worst, they actually retard the development of those under their care (New York Times, Nov. 25, 1987; see also Moen 1992). What this suggests is that at least under present conditions, if preschool children are to be adequately cared for, frequently one of the adult members of the family will have to remain at home to provide that care. But because most jobs are at least 9 to 5, this will require that the adult members who stay at home temporarily give up pursuing a career. However, such sacrifice appears to conflict with the equal opportunity requirement of feminist justice.

Now families might try to meet this equal opportunity requirement by having one parent give up pursuing a career for a certain period of time and the other give up pursuing a career for a subsequent (equal) period of time. But there are problems here too. Some careers are difficult to interrupt for any significant period of time, while others never adequately reward latecomers. In addition, given the high rate of divorce and the inadequacies of most legally mandated child support, those who first sacrifice their careers may find themselves later faced with the impossible task of beginning or reviving their careers while continuing to be the primary caretaker of their children (see Weitzman 1985). Furthermore, there is considerable evidence that children will benefit more from equal rearing from both parents (Dinnerstein 1977; Chodorow 1978; Gornick 1975). So the option of having just one parent doing the child-rearing for any length of time is, other things being equal, not optimal.

It would seem, therefore, that to truly share child-rearing within the family what is needed is flexible (typically part-time) work schedules that allow both parents to be together with their children for a significant period every day. Now some flexible job schedules have already been tried by various corporations (*New York Times*, Nov. 27, 1987). But if equal opportunity is to be a reality in our society, the option of flexible job schedules must be guaranteed to all those with preschool children. Current estimates show that married full-time career women spend an average of 3.8 hours per day on housework while married full-time career men spend an average of 0.7 hours per day (Brock-Utne 1985, 6–7). Obviously, this will have to change if we are to achieve the ideal of a gender-free or androgynous society.

A second locus of change required by the ideal of a gender-free or andogynous society is the distribution of economic power in the society. In the United States, the percentage of women in the labor force has risen steadily for three decades, from 35 percent (of those aged sixteen or more) in 1960 to 58 percent in 1992 (see *New York Times*, Oct. 6, 18, 19, 1992; see also Moen 1992). Roughly 72 percent of women were employed in 1990, including more than 58 percent of mothers with children under the age of six and 53 percent of mothers with children under the age of one.

Yet in 1991 women employed full-time still earned $.70 for every dollar men earned, up from the $.60 for every dollar that held from the 1960s through the 1980s. Although the earning gap also improved slightly during this period for people of color, the earning gap is greater for minority women than it is for white women. African American women earn $.59 for every dollar men earn; Native American women earn $.47. Earnings do increase with education for all workers, but women and men of color earn less than white men at every level of education. For example, women with four years of college education earn less on average than men who have not completed high school.

Sometimes women and men working in the same job category have different incomes. For example, while female secretaries earned a median wage of $278 per week in 1985, the median wage for male secretaries was $365 (see Okin 1989, chap. 7). More frequently, however, women and men tend to be employed in different job categories which are paid differently. According to one study done a few years ago in the state of Washington, women employed as clerk-typists earned less than men employed as truck drivers or warehouse workers. In another study done in Denver, women employed as nurses earned less than men employed as tree cutters. While in each of these cases, the women earned about 20 percent less than the men, the women's jobs when evaluated in terms of skill, responsibility, effort, and working conditions were given equal or higher scores than the men's jobs with which they were compared. Clearly, denying women the opportunity to earn the same as men do for equal or comparable work is a basic injustice in our society, and it will be a very costly one to correct (Jacobs and Steinberg 1990).

It is sometimes assumed that the problem of unequal pay for comparable work will be solved once women move into male-dominated occupations (Hackett 1985). Unfortunately, as the feminization of certain occupations occurs, we are seeing a subsequent drop in pay for men. For example, as the percentage of women bartenders increased 23 points, the men's pay dropped 16 percent, and as the percentage of women pharmacists increased 12 points, male pay fell 11 percent (*Rapid City Journal*, Oct. 20, 1992). So the discrimination against women in the economic arena is a far more entrenched problem than is sometimes thought.

The problem assumes even greater proportions when we consider the world at large. According to a United Nations report, although women are responsible for 66 percent of all work produced in the world (paid and unpaid), they receive only 10 percent of the salaries.[9] The same report shows that men own 99 percent of all the property in the world, and women only 1 percent. Clearly, we have a long way to go to achieve the equality required by feminist justice.

It is also important to recognize that the equality required by feminist justice cannot be achieved on men's terms. It is not an equality in which men's values prevail and women's values are lost. As an example of what needs to be avoided, consider the integration of girl and boy scouts into the same troop in Norway (Brock-Utne 1985, 100–101). Before integration, many women had been troop leaders of the girl scouts, but after the integration, almost all troops were led by men and the former women leaders had become assistant leaders. In addition, an analysis of the activities in the former girl scouts compared to the activities of the former boy scouts revealed that the activities of the girls were of a more cooperative nature than those of the boys. The boys had activities in which they competed more against each other or against other groups of boys. After integration, the competitive activities of the boys became the activities of both girls and boys. The cooperative activities of the girls were abandoned. The integration was made on the boys' terms. But feminist justice is not a one-way street. If it is to be achieved, each person who is capable must be expected to have the virtues that are now typically associated with women (e.g., nurturance, caring, sensitivity, compassion) as well as virtues that are now typically associated with men (e.g., self-reliance, courage, decisiveness).

A third requirement of the ideal gender-free or andogynous society is the elimination of the overt violence perpetrated against women in our society. "The home is actually a more dangerous place for the American woman than the city streets," according to former Surgeon General Antonia Novello. "One-third of the women slain in the U.S.," she continues, "die at the hands of husbands and boyfriends" (New York Times, Oct. 17, 1991). In addition, women in the United States live in fear of rape. Forty-four percent of women are raped, according to a recent study, and almost 50 percent of male college students say they would commit rape if they were certain that they could get away with it (MacKinnon 1987; Young 1992). Women also experience sexual harassment (85 percent of women in the federal workplace are sexually harassed, and two-thirds of women in the military, according to recent studies), and not infrequently they are beaten by their own husbands and lovers (between a quarter and a third of women are battered in their homes by husbands and lovers) (MacKinnon 1987; Women's Legal Defense Fund 1991). One-third of all women who require emergency-room hospital treatment are there as a result of domestic violence (English 1992). Thirty-eight percent of little girls are sexually molested inside or outside the family (MacKinnon 1987). Because most of these crimes are minimally prosecuted in our society, to be a woman in our society is to be a person who can be raped, battered, sexually harassed, or sexually abused, as an adult or as a child, and little, if anything, will be done about it. So the condition of women in U.S. society is actually that of being subordinate to men by force.

To see that this problem is not confined to the United States, S. Opdebeeck reports that 40 percent of Belgian women between thirty and forty years old experienced some form of physical and/or sexual family violence (Opdebeeck 1992). Bert Young notes that wife assault is the leading cause of homicide in Canada (Young 1992). Obviously, this subordination of women must end if we are to achieve the ideal of a gender-free or androgynous society.

FROM FEMINIST JUSTICE TO PEACE

Once we appreciate the widespread changes that are required to achieve feminist justice, its connection to the pursuit of peace should be apparent.

First of all, to achieve peace we must put an end to the overt violence against women which takes the distinctive form of rape, battering, sexual harassment, and sexual abuse. This overt violence is in every way as destructive as the other forms of violence we oppose in our pursuit of peace. So we cannot in consistency fail to oppose this form of violence done to women in our society. According to one cross-cultural study of ninety-five societies, 47 percent of them were free of rape (Miedzian 1991, 74). What this shows is that it is possible to eliminate, or at least drastically reduce, overt violence against women.

One way to help bring about this result is to ban hard-core pornography that celebrates and legitimizes rape, battery, sexual harassment, and the sexual abuse of children, as the Supreme Court of Canada has just recently done (*Donald Victor Butler v. Her Majesty the Queen*). Catharine MacKinnon has argued that pornography of this sort causes harm to women by increasing discriminatory attitudes and behavior in men toward women which take both violent and non-violent forms (MacKinnon 1987).

Another way to decrease overt violence against women is to de-emphasize violent sports like boxing and football.[10] To see why this would help, all one needs to do is consider the evidence. For example, an exhaustive study of heavyweight prizefights held between 1973 and 1978 and subsequent homicide statistics showed that homicides in the United States increased by 12.46 percent directly after heavyweight championship prizefights. In fact, the increase was greatest after heavily publicized prizefights (Phillips 1983, 560–68). In addition, in a study of twenty-four cases of campus gang rapes, nine of them were by athletes, and in an investigation of sexual assaults on college campuses which included interviewing over 150 campus police, it turned out that football and basketball players were involved in 38 percent of the reported cases (Miedzian 1991, 203–4). There is also a 40 percent increase of batterings by husbands and boyfriends associated with the yearly Super Bowl football game. In the Chicago area, a local radio station has gone so far as to recommend that women "take a walk" during the game so as to avoid assault in their homes.[11]

Still another way to help reduce violence against women is to teach conflict resolution, child care, and the history of peacemaking in our schools. Several schools have experimented with teaching conflict resolution and child care to grade and high school children with impressive results, especially for boys (Sabo 1985, chaps. 6 and 7). The history of peacemaking could provide our children with a new and better set of models than the history of war-making has done (Cady 1989, chap. 1; Brock-Utne 1989, 162–63).

Second, the pursuit of peace requires that we put an end to structural as well as overt violence, and the inequalities suffered by women in their families and in the economic arena constitute well-entrenched forms of structural violence against women.[12] This structural violence, which requires full-time career women to do at least five times more housework than full-time career men, and also requires that women do 66 percent of the work done in the world, while receiving only 10 percent of the salaries and owning only 1 percent of the property, disadvantages women just as surely as they are disadvantaged by overt violence. So given that we are concerned in our pursuit of peace to eliminate overt violence, we must be concerned to eliminate structural violence against women as well. This will normally require an equal sharing of child-rearing and housekeeping tasks within families, and it will require programs of affirmative action and comparable worth.

Affirmative action is needed to place qualified women in positions they deserve to occupy because of past discrimination. Without affirmative action, the structural violence of past discrimination will not be rectified. Only with affirmative action can the competition for desirable jobs and positions be made fair again given our history of past discrimination. There are even cases in which affirmative action candidates are the most qualified, but those who select them, because of their prejudice, see the candidates only as simply qualified—not as the most qualified candidates (Ezorsky 1991).

Comparable worth is needed because without it women will not receive the salaries they deserve on the basis of their work. They will do work that is judged equal or comparable to the work that men are doing in male-dominated occupations, but without comparable worth, they will be paid less than the men are being paid. Paying for comparable worth programs will not be easy. A settlement in the state of Washington granted nearly $500 million to women workers in order to achieve pay equity (Paul 1989, 83). Even larger settlements are anticipated as Canada begins to implement extensive comparable worth programs (*Financial Post*, March 3, 1990).

Third, to achieve peace we must recognize the connection between the forms of violence we oppose in the international arena and the overt and structural violence done to women. The simple truth is that the former is rooted in the latter (Reardon 1985, chap. 3). This is because violence in the international arena arises when nations view each other as competitive, aggressive, and unwilling to cooperate, the same traits that tend to be fostered exclusively in men in a society characterized by widespread overt and structural violence against women. By contrast, the traits of openness, cooperativeness, and nurturance, which promote peaceful solutions to conflicts, tend to be fostered exclusively in women who are effectively excluded from positions of power in a society characterized by widespread overt and structural violence against women. Consequently, if we are to eliminate violence in the international arena, we must also eliminate the overt and structural violence done to women.[13] Only in this way will our leaders have the traits of openness, cooperativeness, and nurturance which will enable them to maintain peace in the international arena. Men will acquire these traits through equal sharing of child-rearing and housekeeping tasks. Women will retain these traits through an equal sharing of child-rearing and housekeeping tasks, while acquiring other traits required for personal development and leadership that have hitherto been reserved for men.

Fourth, people generally, and men in particular, first learn about violence and become skilled in its practice in their own families. They see violence and to a greater or lesser degree accept its legitimacy in the families in which they have been brought up, and they continue it in the families they themselves form. According to one study, one quarter of adult men and one in six adult women said that they could think of circumstances in which it would be all right for a husband to hit his wife or a wife to hit her husband. Eighty-six percent of those polled said that young people need "strong" discipline (Gelles and Straus 1988). Surely, closing down violence's first school is at least as important as correcting its later manifestations between political groups.[14]

Last, when those opposed to violence in the international arena champion the cause of feminist justice, they will benefit from a new surge of support from women. Adding the cause of feminist justice to one's political agenda can create new allies for one's cause within the oppressed group itself. "Women of the world unite," or better, "Feminists of the world unite" is not a bad rallying cry for those seeking social and political change. Or as former Prime Minister Prunskiene of Lithuania remarked before she resigned her post, "I am the only woman of rank in the government. And sometimes I look around me and think that the shape of democracy and the process of democracy might be well served if there were more women involved." Certainly the sight of the all-male U.S. Senate Judiciary Committee unable to conduct fair hearings on Anita Hill's charge that Clarence Thomas sexually harassed her convinced many voters in the subsequent elections that more women had to occupy positions of power in the U.S government.[15]

I have argued in this paper that the achievement of feminist justice is centrally related to the pursuit of peace, so that those who oppose violence in international arenas must, in consistency, oppose violence against women as well. I have argued that one cannot consistently oppose violence in international relations while engaging in violence in personal relations. The pursuit of justice in political relations, I contend, requires the pursuit of justice in personal relations, and this requires the acceptance of the feminist ideal of a gender-free or androgynous society. In brief, to pursue peace we must pursue feminist justice as well.

NOTES

1. See, for example, Ferguson (1977, 45–69); Warren (1982, 170–86); Kaplan and Bean (1976); Dworkin (1974, part 4); Gould (1983, 3–18); Gould (1984, 20–34); Lindsey (1990); Friedman (1991, 75–90). For some feminists who oppose the ideal of androgyny, see Daly (1978; 1982); Elshtain (1981).

2. On this point, see Pincoffs (1986, Ch. 5).

3. Of course, I cannot provide a full account of how these virtues are to be justifiably inculcated,although I make some specific recommendations later in the paper.

4. See Erchler (1980, 69–71); Beardsley (1982, 197–202); Daly (1975, 20–40); Raymond (1975, 57–66).

5. The equal right to self-development defended here is prima facie, and it needs to be weighed against other rights, such as an equal right to welfare. See Sterba (1988, 127–28).

6. For a valuable discussion and critique of these two viewpoints, see Young (1985, 173–83).

7. Moreover, given that the basic rights that we have in society, e.g., a right to equal opportunity, are equal for all citizens and are not based on our differing natural abilities, these rights are not even in this derivative sense based on sex.

8. The reason for qualifying this claim is that mothers and fathers, unlike children, may legitimately waive their right to equal opportunity when the reasons are compelling enough.

9. Report on the World Conference of the United Nations Decade for Women, Copenhagen, 14–30 July, 1981.

10. Violent sports are those in which the participants inflict a lot of (physical) harm on each other.

11. WBBM, January 31, 1993. Playing football also impacts negatively on the life expectancies of football players themselves. The average life expectancy of National Football League players in the United States is 54, nearly twenty years below the overall male mean. See Sabo (1985, 1–30).

12. Structural violence is the violation of people's fundamental rights as the result of the very structure of existing social, economic, and cultural institutions. See Gatung (1985, 414–31).

13. Of course, I am not denying that violence in the international arena also supports overt and structural violence done to women. I am simply claiming a certain causal priority here.

14. Of course, it may be possible to rid oneself of violence in the personal arena while still endorsing and participating in the unjustified use of violence in the international arena. But this can only be done by putting considerable strain on one's psychic resources as the phenomenon of doubling certainly attests. On this point, see Lifton (1986).

15. The unfairness of the hearings was evidenced by the fact that Anita Hill was not able to prevent intensive examination of her private life whereas Clarence Thomas was able to declare key areas of his private life as off-limits, and by the fact that Thomas was able to characterize the attack on him as motivated by the stereotypes of black men as male studs and rapists, whereas Hill became functionally white. See Fraser (1993).

References

Beardsley, Elizabeth Lane. 1982. On curing conceptual confusion. In *Femininity, masculinity and androgyny*, ed. Mary Vetterling-Braggin. Totowa, N.J.: Rowman and Littlefield.

Brock-Utne, Birgit. 1985. *Educating for peace*. New York: Pergamon.

———. 1989. *Feminist perspectives on peace and peace education*. New York: Pergamon.

Cady, Duane. 1989. *From warism to pacifism*. Philadelphia: Temple University Press.

Chodorow, Nancy. 1978. *Mothering: Psychoanalysis and the sociology of gender*. Berkeley: University of California Press.

Daly, Mary. 1975. The qualitative leap beyond patriarchal religion. *Quest* 1(1): 20–40.

———. 1978. *Gyn-ecology: The meta-ethics of radical feminism*. Boston: Beacon Press.

Dinnerstein, Dorothy. 1977. *The mermaid and the minotaur*. New York: Harper and Row.

Dworkin, Andrea. 1974. *Women hating*. New York: Dutton.

Elshtain, Jean Bethke. 1981. Against androgyny. *Telos* 5(1): 85–101.

English, Dierdre. November, 1992. Through the glass ceiling. *Mother Jones*, 17(1): 49–52,73.

Erchler, Margrit. 1980. *The double standard*. New York: St. Martin's Press.

Ezorsky, Gertrude. 1991. *Racism and justice*. Ithaca: Cornell University Press.

Ferguson, Ann. 1977. Androgyny as an ideal for human development. In *Feminism and philosophy*, ed. Mary Vetterling-Braggin et al. Totowa: Littlefield Adams.

Fraser, Nancy. 1993. Reflections on the confirmation of Clarence Thomas. In *Morality in Practice*, 4th ed., ed. James P. Sterba. Belmont, CA: Wadsworth Publishing Co.

Friedman, Marilyn. 1991. Does Sommers like women? *Journal of Social Philosophy* 22(1): 75–90.

Gatung, Johan. 1985. Twenty-five years of peace research. *Journal of Peace Research* 22 (4): 414–31.

Gelles, Richard and Murray Straus. 1988. *Intimate violence*. New York: Simon and Schuster.

Gornick, Vivian. 1975. Here's news: Fathers matter as much as mothers. *Village Voice* (October 13).

Gould, Carol. 1983. Privacy rights and public virtues: Women, the family and democracy. In *Beyond domination*, ed. Carol Gould. Totowa: Rowman and Littlefield.

———. 1984. Women and freedom. *The Journal of Social Philosophy* 15(1): 20–34.

Hackett, Clifford. 1985. Comparable worth: Better from a distance. *Commonweal* (May 31).

Jacobs, Jerry and Ronnie Steinberg. 1990. Compensating differentials and the male-female wage gap. *Social Forces* 69(2): 56–68.

Kaplan A. G. and J. Bean, eds. 1976. *Beyond sex-role stereotypes*. Totowa: Littlefield and Adams.

Lifton, Robert Jay. 1986. *The Nazi doctors*. New York: Basic Books.

Lindsey, Linda. 1990. *Gender roles*. Englewood Cliffs: Prentice-Hall.

MacKinnon, Catharine. 1987. *Feminism unmodified*. Cambridge: Harvard University Press.

Miedzian, Myriam. 1991. *Boys will be boys*. New York: Doubleday.

Moen, Phyllis. 1992. *Women's roles*. New York: Auburn House.

Moir, Anne and David Jesse. 1991. *Brain sex*. Secaucus: Carol Pub.

Morgan, Kathryn Pauly. 1982. Androgyny: A conceptual critique. *Social Theory and Practice* 9(3): 78–95.

Okin, Susan. 1989. *Justice gender and the family.* New York: Basic Books.

Opdebeeck, S. 1992. Determinants of leaving an abusing partner. Presented at the Second World Congress on Violence and Human Coexistence. Montreal. July 12–17.

Paul, Ellen. 1989. *Equity and gender.* New Brunswick: Transaction Publishers.

Phillips, David. 1983. The impact of mass media violence on U.S. homicides. *American Sociological Review.* 47(4): 560–68.

Pincoffs, Edmund. 1986. *Quandaries and virtue.* Lawrence: University of Kansas Press.

Raymond, Janice. 1975. The illusion of androgyny. *Quest* 2(2): 57–66.

Reardon, Betty. 1985. *Sexism and the war system.* New York: Columbia Teachers College.

Report on the world conference of the United Nations Decade for Women. 1981. Copenhagen, (July): 14–30.

Sabo, Don. 1985. Sport, patriarchy and male identity. *The Arena Review* 5(1): 1–30.

Sommers, Christina. 1989. Philosophers against the family. In *Person to person,* ed. George Graham and Hugh LaFollette. Philadelphia: Temple University Press.

———. 1990. Do these feminists like women? *Journal of Social Philosophy* 21(1): 66–74.

———. 1991. Argumentum ad feminam. *Journal of Social Philosophy* 22(1): 5–19.

Sterba, James P. 1988. *How to make people just.* Totowa: Rowman and Littlefield.

Trebilcot, Joyce. 1977. Two forms of androgynism. In *Feminism and philosophy,* ed. Mary Vetterling-Braggin, Frederick Ellison, and Jane English. Totowa: Rowman and Littlefield.

Warren, Mary Ann. 1982. Is androgyny the answer to sexual stereotyping? In *Femininity, masculinity, and androgyny,* ed. Mary Vetterling-Braggin et al. Totowa: Rowman and Littlefield.

Weitzman, Lenore. 1985. *The divorce revolution: The unexpected social and economic consequences for women and children in America.* New York: Free Press.

Wolgast, Elizabeth. 1980. *Equality and the rights of women.* Ithaca: Cornell University Press.

Women's Legal Defense Fund. 1991. *Sexual harassment in the workplace.*

Young, Bert. 1992. Masculinity and violence. Presented at the Second World Congress on Violence and Human Coexistence, Montreal. July 12–17

Young, Iris. 1985. Humanism, gynocentrism and feminist politics. *Hypatia* 3, published as *Women's Studies Intentional Forum.* 8(3): 173–83. Reprinted in *Hypatia reborn* (Indiana University Press, 1990).

Notes on Contributors

CAROL J. ADAMS is the author of *The Sexual Politics of Meat: A Feminist-Vegetarian Critical Theory*, which won the first Continuum Women's Studies Award. She is the editor of *Ecofeminism and the Sacred* and the author of *Neither Man Nor Beast: Feminism and the Defense of Animals*. Her book on woman-battering will be published this year as part of Fortress Press's Creative Pastoral Care Counseling Series. With Josephine Donovan she recently finished editing *Animals and Women: Feminist Theoretical Explorations*.

BARBARA ANDREW is a doctoral candidate in philosophy at the State University of New York at Stony Brook. She is writing a dissertation on moral agency in feminist ethics.

ALISON BAILEY is an assistant professor of philosophy and women's studies at Illinois State University. She is the author of *Posterity and Strategic Policy: A Moral Assessment of Nuclear Policy Options*. Her teaching and current research interests include feminist epistemology, peace politics, and issues related to racism and the political construction of racial categories. She has worked briefly with the Sumo Indians on the Rio Bocay in Nicaragua and with Central American refugees in the United States.

BAT-AMI BAR ON is an associate professor of philosophy and women's studies at the State University of New York at Binghamton. She is the editor of *Engendering Origins* and *Modern Engenderings*. Though she strays into other areas, the primary focus of her work is sociopolitical and ethical issues and theory, especially and specifically as these arise in relation to everyday violence and abuse. She is working on a book about these issues.

DUANE L. CADY is a professor of philosophy at Hamline University. His teaching and research interests are in history of philosophy, ethics, social and political theory, and aesthetics. He is the author of *From Warism to Pacifism: A Moral Continuum* and coauthor of *Humanitarian Intervention: Just-War vs. Pacifism*. He has worked with Southeast Asian refugees since 1975 and, more recently, with Bosnian student refugees. He is a past president of Concerned Philosophers for Peace.

JANE CAPUTI teaches in the American Studies Department at the University of New Mexico in Albuquerque. Her latest book is *Gossips, Gorgons, and Crones: The Fates of the Earth*, a feminist analysis of the cultural and metaphysical implications of the invention of nuclear technology. Her earlier book is *The Age of Sex*

Crime, an analysis of the sexual politics of serial murder. She also worked with Mary Daly on *Webster's First New Intergalactic Wickedary of the English Language*.

ADRIENNE E. CHRISTIANSEN is an assistant professor of communication studies at Macalester College. Her scholarly publications have analyzed the rhetoric of the early women's rights movement, the contemporary conservative movement, and American AIDS activism. She is currently writing a book called *Right Wing War*.

DEANE CURTIN is a professor of philosophy at Gustavus Adolphus College. His primary research interests concern the ethics of international conflict over the environment. He speaks widely about the impact of agricultural change, threats to biodiversity, and the impact of GATT on indigenous peoples. His book, tentatively titled *Worlds Apart: Seeking Global Environmental Justice*, is forthcoming from Indiana University Press. He has published articles in *Environmental Ethics*, *Hypatia*, and *Philosophy East and West*, and coedited *Cooking, Eating, Thinking: Transformative Philosophies of Food*.

LAURA DUHAN KAPLAN is an assistant professor of philosophy and interim coordinator of women's studies at the University of North Carolina at Charlotte, where she teaches philosophy, women's studies, and a variety of interdisciplinary humanities courses. She is coeditor (with Laurence F. Bove) of *In the Eye of the Storm: Philosophy of Peace and Regional Conflicts* and is a member of Concerned Philosophers for Peace. She is currently writing on the phenomenology and ethics of self-reflection and, as a new mother, is learning a great deal about the "self."

LARRY MAY teaches philosophy at Washington University in St. Louis. He is the author of *The Morality of Groups* and *Sharing Responsibility*. He has edited the anthologies *Collective Responsibility* and *Applied Ethics: A Multicultural Approach*, as well as an anthology on masculinity with Robert Strikwerda. He is currently completing a book entitled *Integrity, Solidarity and Socialization*. He continues to work on issues in feminism and male experience.

WILLIAM ANDREW MYERS is a professor of philosophy at the College of St. Catherine. He studies the ways structures of detachment show up in various fields, including the sciences, moral and political philosophy, aesthetics, and literature. A founding member of the International Society for Universalism, he is also a printmaker and book artist.

LUCINDA J. PEACH is an attorney currently completing a doctorate in religious studies at Indiana University, Bloomington. She received her M.A. in Religious Studies from Indiana University, her J.D. from New York University School of Law, and her B.A. from the University of Massachusetts, Amherst. Her dissertation is a feminist analysis of liberal and communitarian approaches to issues of religious pluralism and moral identity as they relate to abortion law-making. She has published in *Legal Studies Forum, Journal of Law and Religion,* and *Hamline Journal of Law and Public Policy* (forthcoming). As a MacArthur Scholar she researched and published an article for the Indiana Center for Global Change and World Peace on the ethics of women in combat.

CHEYNEY RYAN is a philosopher and playwright who teaches and is codirector of the peace studies program at the University of Oregon. He is a cofounder of Teatro Nuestro, a California-based theater group that performs (primarily in Spanish) throughout the western states. His most recent articles are on topics ranging from philosophy of economics to feminist legal theory to film. His play, "La Perla," was recently featured at San Francisco's Solo Mio Festival and will soon be produced in New York.

JAMES P. STERBA is a professor of philosophy at the University of Notre Dame, where he teaches political philosophy and applied ethics. He has written more than a hundred articles and published twelve books, including *How to Make People Just; Morality in Practice* (4th ed.); *The Ethics of War and Nuclear Deterrence; Justice: Alternative Political Perspectives* (2nd ed.); *Contemporary Ethics; Feminist Philosophies; Earth Ethics;* and *Social and Political Philosophy: Classical Western Texts in a Feminist and Multicultural Perspective.* He is the president of the North American Society for Social Philosophy and a past president of Concerned Philosophers for Peace.

ROBERT STRIKWERDA teaches philosophy at Indiana University, Kokomo. He is the author of numerous articles in philosophy of social science and moral philosophy. With Larry May he coedited *Rethinking Masculinity.* He continues to work on issues in feminism and masculinity.

KAREN J. WARREN is an associate professor of philosophy at Macalester College. Her main research interests are in feminism and environmental philosophy. She conducts workshops and publishes curricular materials in critical thinking for students and teachers grades K–12. She has edited a special issue of *Hypatia* on ecological feminism, edited two anthologies on ecological feminism, coedited a textbook, *Environmental Philosophies,* and is finishing a book, *Ecological Feminist Philosophy.*

Index

Abbas, Mahmoud, 33
Accad, Evelyne, 51n.24
Affirmative action, 219–20
Africa: women's indigenous agriculture in, 57, 64, 65–66n.11
Agent Orange, 62
Agriculture: women's indigenous and politics of Green Revolution, 54–65
Ahimsa: Indian concept of, 63
Alberstein, Chava, 40–41
Al-Radi, Nuha, 114
Amnesty International, 48
Anderson, Benedict, 49–50n.5
Androgyny: and ideal of feminist justice, 212–15, 218
Animal rights movement, 77, 78
Animals: feminist perspective on abuse of women, children, and pets, 68–83
Anorexia nervosa, 81
Antifeminism: war as metaphor in gender politics of new right, 152–62
Antigone (Sophocles), 125–26
Arendt, Hannah, 112
Argentina: peace activism of women in, 8
Aristotle, 79
Ascione, Frank R., 73, 82
Asia: women's indigenous agriculture in, 57. *See also* India
Atomic Cafe (film, 1982), 136
Atomic Energy Commission, 140
Augustine, St., 193, 195, 196, 198, 199, 200–201, 207n.8
Authority: and just-war theory, 200–201

Baier, Annette, 77
Bailie, Tom, 140–41, 142–43
Baltimore, David, 62
Bass, Ellen, 149
Bauman, Zygmunt, 49
Beaumont, Florence, 16
Belgium: domestic violence in, 218
Bell, Quentin, 123
Benbenishti, Meyron, 38
Beneke, Timothy, 189–90n.3
Berrigan, Daniel, 19–20
Bhopal, India, 1984 chemical disaster in, 62
Binur, Yoram, 36–37
Biological determinism: and human/animal dualism, 79; and theories of gender identity, 168–69; and theories of rape, 179–82. *see also* Socialization

Biological diversity: and indigenous agriculture, 58–59; Third World as source of plant genetic material, 61
Biomedical ethics: connection between sexual abuse and anorexia nervosa, 81
Blume, E. Sue, 139
Body: Christian mystical thinking and, 28, 31n.25. *See also* Disembodiment
Bordo, Susan, 100
Borlaug, Norman, 54, 56, 62
Bosnia, war in: and systematic rape of Muslim women, 6, 175–76, 178–79, 184–85, 205
Boustany, Nora, 82
Boyle, Joan M., 165
Branch Davidian cult, 135
Brocke-Utne, Birgit, 165
Brown, Wendy, 79, 102
Browne, Angela, 70, 71
Brownmiller, Susan, 6, 82, 170
Burke, Carol, 7
Burke, Edmund, 129, 131n.11
Burke, Kenneth, 153, 162n.1
Burstow, Bonnie, 70
Burtt, Edwin A., 10
Bush, Barbara, 115
Bush, George, 139, 145, 149
Butler, Judith, 131n.10

Cady, Duane, 3, 54–55, 59, 153, 204, 207nn.5,7
Caldecott, Helen, 10
Canada: White Ribbon Campaign against rape, 176, 189; domestic violence in, 218; ban on violent pornography, 219; comparable worth programs in, 220
Capitalism: and feminist standpoint theory, 92
Caputi, Jane, 84n.9
Caretaker: woman as and patriarchal militarism, 165–73
Carson, Clayborne, 23
Catholic Church: influence of Day on attitudes toward war in, 17; Day's decision to join, 24; and just-war theory, 197, 200
Catholic Peace Fellowship, 18–19
Catholic Worker Movement, 17
Chabousson, F., 56
Chandler, Zala, 101, 102
Chavez, Cesar, 17
Children: feminist philosophical perspective on abuse of women, pets, and, 68–83. *See also* Incest; Motherhood and mothering; Sexual abuse

Chile: politics of food aid to, 60

Chipko movement (India), 8, 14n.9, 64, 66n.11

Chodorow, Nancy, 127, 131n.8, 166–68, 169–70

A *Chorus of Stones: The Private Life of War* (Griffin, 1982), 109–13

Christianity: metaphors of war in gender politics of fundamentalist, 154–62; and just-war theory, 192, 193, 195, 200. *See also* Catholic Church

Civil Rights Movement, 23

Civil War, American, 107

Class: and maternal voices in Ruddick's text, 95–96. *See also* Hierarchy; Peasants

Clausewitz, Carl von, 3

Code, Lorraine, 77

Cohn, Carol, 9, 10, 134, 152, 198, 200, 207–208n.16

Collins, Patricia Hill, 76, 95, 98–100

Comparable worth programs, 220

Conceptual frameworks: and connections between women and peace, 2–4; oppression and patriarchal, 12, 13

Concerned Women for America, 154–62

Conroy, Pat, 144

Cooke, M., 152

Cope-Kasten, Vance, 10

Crenshaw, Kimberlé, 75

Culture: relation between Jewish-Israeli and Palestinian, 37; shared responsibility of men for prevalence of rape, 175–89

Cypress, Sandra Messinger, 51n.24

Dalit theology (India), 64

Davenport, Diana, 137

Day, Dorothy, 17–30

Day-care centers, 215–16

Desert Bloom (film, 1986), 138–39

Developmentalism: women's indigenous agriculture and politics of Green Revolution, 54–65

Difference: national identity and context of, 34, 35; gender roles and ideal of androgynous society, 215. *See also* Diversity

Dinnerstein, Dorothy, 127, 131n.8

Discrimination: and just-war theory, 194; economic against women, 216–17; and affirmative action, 219–20

Disembodiment: and technology of war, 106–17

Diversity: and feminist maternal peace politics, 100–102; additive approach to, 104n.12. *See also* Difference

Domestic violence: and ideal of gender-free society, 218. *See also* Sexual abuse; Violence, against women

Domination: and connection between feminism and peace, 2–4; women's indigenous agriculture and politics of Green Revolution, 54–65; and public/private dualism, 79–80; and

Woolf's and Wollstonecraft's critiques of the family, 119

Doniger, Wendy, 83

Dvorchak, Robert, 74

Dyson, Freeman, 108

Easlea, Brian, 134

d'Eaubonne, Françoise, 7

Ecofeminism: as grassroots political movement, 7; on global consequences of sexism and patriarchy, 12–13; and patriarchy as dysfunctional system, 14n.11

Economics: gender and distribution of power, 216; and reduction of structural violence against women, 219–20

Education: Wollstonecraft and Woolf on women's, 120–21, 129; and reduction of violence against women, 219

Eichmann, Adolph, 112

Eisenhower, Dwight, 140

Eliot, George, 21

Elkana, Dalia, 48

Elshtain, Jean Bethke, 116, 127, 131nn.7,9, 159, 172, 193, 196, 197–206, 207nn.10,14

Empirical connections: between feminism and peace, 4–6

Engelsman, Joan Chamberlain, 70

Enloe, Cynthia, 83

Environment: and disproportionate effects of war on women and children, 4; patriarchy and abuse of, 12; Green Revolution and warist ideology of, 59–63; abuse of and violence against women, 80

Epistemology: feminist philosophical perspective on abuse of women, children, and pets, 76–78

Espanioli, Nabila, 51n.23

Fascism: Woolf's critique of patriarchal family and, 120, 126, 127, 130

Faludi, Susan, 88

Family: denials and avoidance of truth in, 116; Wollstonecraft's and Woolf's critiques of domination in, 119, 126, 130; secrecy and sexual abuse in, 142–46; equal opportunity and changes in structure of, 215–18; reduction of violence in, 220. *See also* Domestic violence; Motherhood and mothering

Fanon, Franz, 50n.13

Fathering: incest and nuclearism, 133–50

The Feminine Mystique (Friedan, 1963), 135

Feminism: and discussions of peace in mainstream philosophy, 1–13; Alice Hertz's self-immolation in protest of Vietnam War and Day's nonviolent commitment to peace, 16–30; and reformation of national identity in Jewish-Israeli-Palestinian context, 33–49; women's indigenous agriculture and politics of Green Revolution, 54–65; philosophical perspective on abuse of women, children, and pets, 68–83; and Ruddick's maternal peace politics, 88–102; and Griffin's analysis of war technology, 106–17; and critiques of war by Woolf and Wollstonecraft, 118–30; and connection between incest and nuclearism, 133–50; patriarchal militarism and image of woman as caretaker, 165–73; and just-war theory as alternative to pacifism, 192–206; ideal of justice and pursuit of peace, 211–21. *See also* Antifeminism; Liberal feminism; Radical feminism; Socialist feminism

Feminist standpoint theory (FST): and Ruddick's maternal peace politics, 89, 90, 92–95, 100–102; and women's experiences, 102–103n.5

Ferguson, Ann, 49n.4

Fermi, Enrico, 109–10, 111, 112

Flapan, Simha, 50n.15

Forbidden Planet (film, 1956), 146–47

Foster, Lynne A., 84n.7

Franco, Jean, 51n.24

Franco-Prussian War of 1870, 107

Fraser, Sylvia, 72

Frederickson, DeLora, 84n.8

French Revolution, 119

Freud, Sigmund, 124

Fried, Michael, 31n.14

Friedan, Betty, 135

Friendship: and women's national identities, 34, 46–47

Frye, Marilyn, 27, 59, 168

Frye, Northrop, 31n.25

Ganley, Anne L., 70, 71

Gelhorn, Martha, 113, 114

Gender: social construction of, 2; and definition of motherhood, 103n.8; and additive approach to diversity, 104n.12; and critiques of war by Wollstonecraft and Woolf, 118–30; and war as metaphor in politics of new right, 152–62; and just-war theory, 200; and ideal of feminist justice, 212–15, 218. *See also* Women

Geyer, Alan, 204

Gilligan, Carol, 166, 171, 198, 199

Gilman, Sander, 76

Goodman, Ellen, 153, 157, 161

Gordon, Haim, and Rivca Gordon, 47

Gould, Catherine, 81

Gowdy, Barbara, 138

Green Belt Movement (Africa), 64, 65–66n.11

Green Revolution: women's indigenous agriculture and politics of, 54–65

Griffin, Susan, 10, 106–17, 165, 168, 172–73

Groups: male socialization and prevalence of rape in western societies, 175–89

Groves, Gen. Leslie, 145

Guatemala: sexual violence against women by military, 6; Green Revolution in, 64–65

Guha, Ramachandra, 65n.10

Hamilton, Cynthia, 7

Harding, Sandra, 103n.5

Hart, Gary, 9

Hartsock, Nancy, 90, 92, 95, 101, 198

Hazardous waste: politics of disposal, 4–5

Hegel, Georg, 50n.13

Herbicides. *See* Pesticides

Herman, Judith, 148

Hertz, Alice, 16–30

Hierarchy: and oppressive conceptual frameworks, 3, 79; Wollstonecraft and Woolf on gender, and, 121–23; and concept of woman as caretaker, 166–70

Hill, Anita, 74, 75, 76, 221, 222n.15

Hi-Man, Si, 43

Himmler, Heinrich, 109, 110, 111, 112–13

History: association of women with peace, 6–7, 206–207n.3, 208n.18; revisionist of Israel, 50n.15

Hoagland, Sarah, 84n.2

Hood, Elizabeth, 103n.6

hooks, bell, 83, 101, 103n.10, 159

Howard, Sir Albert, 57–58

Hudson, Pamela S., 81

Human nature: and just-war theory, 203–204

Hunter/gatherer paradigm: as sexist myth, 57

Hunting: and violence against women, 80

Identity: and Day's theory of nonviolent commitment, 26–29; reformation of national in Jewish-Israeli-Palestinian context, 33–49; and theory of aspectual self, 49n.4; sexuality and national, 51n.24; feminist peace politics and maternal, 95–102; and Woolf's critique of patriarchal culture, 127–28; Chodorow's theory of gender, 166–68, 169–70; biological dualism and gender, 168–69

Incest: and nuclearism, 133–50

India: Chipko movement, 8, 14n.9, 64, 66n.11; women's indigenous agriculture and politics of Green Revolution, 55–65; violence against women in, 65n.8

Individual: and authority in just-war theory, 200–201

Infanticide: female in India, 65n.8

International relations: and gender identity, 168; feminist critiques of, 195–96; and overt or structural violence against women, 220, 221

Intifada, Palestinian, 39–41, 45, 46

Israel: national identity in Jewish-Palestinian context, 33–49

Jackson, Wes, 58

Jaggar, Alison, 103n.5

Jankowski, Celene, 30n.1

Jefferson Proving Ground (Indiana), 5
Jewish identity: in Israeli-Palestinian context, 33–49
Joan of Arc, 21
Johnson, Lyndon, 60
Justice: and just-war theory, 199; feminist ideal of and pursuit of peace, 211–21
Just-war theory, 192–206

Kaibab Paiutes, 4
Kappeler, Susanne, 83
Kawar, Amal, 33–34, 35–36, 37–38, 39, 45, 47, 49n.3
Keen, Sam, 183–84
Kelley, Marylia, 143
Kierkegaard, Søren, 26
King, Martin Luther, Jr., 22, 31n.16
Klejment, Anne, 23
Knowledge: concept of embodied in Griffin's analysis of war technology, 106; as power in patriarchal tradition, 147
Kollwitz, Kathe, 109

LaFollette, Hugh, 190n.5
LaHaye, Beverly Davenport, 152
LaHaye, Tim, 162n.4
Language: connection between feminism and peace, 8–10; national identity and, 34–35; war as metaphor in gender politics of new right, 152–62
LaPorte, Roger, 19, 20, 25, 26
Lawrence, Ernest, 10
Lebanon: relationship of sexuality and violence in literature of, 51n.24
Leichner, P., 81
LeMay, Gen. Curtis, 144–45
Levins, Richard, 56, 63
Levinson, David, 83
Lewontin, Richard, 60
Liberal feminism: and androgynous feminism, 214
Liberation (magazine), 17
Liberation theology (Central America), 64
Lifton, Robert Jay, 10, 141, 144–45, 150n.1
Lipsyte, Robert, 178
Litke, Robert, 165
Lloyd, Roseann, 148–49
Lugones, María, 27, 50n.7
Lunde, Donald T., 84n.9

Maathi, Wangari, 65n.11
McDaniel, Jay, 82
MacIntyre, Alasdair, 102n.4
MacKinnon, Catharine, 69, 78, 147, 175–76, 182, 219
Las Madres de la Plaza de Mayo (Argentina), 8
Mai, Nhat Chi, 30
Manhattan Project, 134, 145
Marcus, Jane, 120
Markusen, Eric, 144–45

Marx, Karl, 50n.13
Marxism: and feminist standpoint theory, 92
Mary (Wollstonecraft, 1788), 118–19
Maternal Thinking (Ruddick, 1989), 89
May, Larry, 51n.26, 189n.1
Menchú, Rigoberta, 6, 8, 64–65
Merton, Thomas, 18–19, 20, 23, 26
Mexico: nation-building literature of, 51n.24; resistance to Green Revolution in, 60
Micronesia: nuclear testing in, 136–37
Mies, Maria, 61
Militarism: patriarchy and, 12–13; and image of woman as caretaker, 165–73
Military: toxic chemicals and hazardous waste disposal, 5–6; and sexual harassment, 7, 218; sexist-naturist language in, 8–10; women in Israeli, 47
Mill, John Stuart, 55
Miller, Alice, 112
Miller, David, 30n.2
Miller, Jean Baker, 173
Miller, Richard, 207nn.9,14
Minangkabau of West Sumatra, 182
Morality: shame and agency in, 47–49; interpersonal relations and feminist theories of, 201
Moral Mothers, 88
Morrison, Norman, 16, 17, 25, 26
Morrison, Toni, 37
Morriss, James E., 165
Motherhood and mothering: Day's writings on, 24–26; and Ruddick's feminist peace politics, 88–102, 202–203, 208nn.17,18; gender and definition of, 103nn.8,10; Woolf on gender roles and, 122, 126–28; and gender identity, 167–68; family structure and, 215–18
Murphy, Patricia A., 138
Muste, A. J., 17

Narveson, Jan, 30n.10
National Council of Catholic Women, 207n.5
National identity: reformation of in Jewish-Israeli-Palestinian context, 33–49; feminist scholarship on, 49n.3; and sexuality, 51n.24
Native Americans: and politics of hazardous waste disposal, 4–5; nuclear testing on ancestral lands of, 104n.13
Nature: Green Revolution and, 59–60, 61–63; technology and distancing from, 112. See also Environment; Naturism
Naturism: and language of military and of nuclear weapons, 8–10; definition of, 13n.5
Navajo, 4
Netz, Royal, 50n.19
Niebuhr, Reinhold, 195, 196, 197, 199–200, 205, 207nn.8,11
Nobel Peace Prize, 8, 64
Noddings, Nel, 165, 171, 199, 200, 201
Nonviolence: Day's peace politics and concept of, 17–30

Noske, Barbara, 83

Novello, Antonia, 218

Nuclearism: and incest, 133–50; use of term, 150n.1

Nuclear weapons: sexist-naturist language in, 8–10; testing of and exposure to radioactive fallout, 104n.13, 115, 136–37

Oates, Joyce Carol, 177–78

O'Connor, June, 18, 27

Oedipus Complex: Woolf's critique of, 124–25

Okin, Susan Moller, 80

Omolade, Barbara, 101, 102

Opdebeeck, S., 218

Oppenheimer, J. Robert, 134, 147

Oppression: and conceptual frameworks, 2, 3; canon on formative effects of, 50n.13; Woolf and Wollstonecraft on war and women's, 123–26, 130

Oren, Yoseph, 51n.29

Other: perception of women as and prevalence of rape, 187

Pacifism: continuum of degrees of, 4; women's indigenous agriculture as ecological, 63–64; and passivism, 64, 207n.5; feminism and just-war theory as alternative to, 192–206

Palestine: and national identity in Jewish-Israeli context, 33–49

Palestinian Liberation Organization (PLO), 33, 40, 44, 46

Palmer, Parker, 110

Parker, Andrew, 51n.24

Pateman, Carole, 78–79

Patriarchy: as oppressive conceptual framework, 2, 3, 4; as dysfunctional social system, 11–13, 14nn.10,11; and Wollstonecraft's and Woolf's critiques of family, 119; Woolf on fascism and, 120, 126, 127, 130; connection between incest and nuclearism, 133–50; militarism and image of woman as caretaker, 165–73; and collective male responsibility for rape, 177, 185–86

Pauling, Linus, 140

Peace: feminism and discussions of in mainstream philosophy, 1–13; Alice Hertz's self-immolation in protest of Vietnam War and Day's nonviolent commitment to, 16–30; and reformation of national identity in Jewish-Israeli-Palestinian context, 33–49; women's indigenous agriculture and politics of Green Revolution, 54–65; feminist philosophical perspective on abuse of women, children, and pets, 68–83; Ruddick's feminist maternal politics of, 88–102; and Griffin's analysis of war technology, 106–17; gender and critiques of war by Woolf and Wollstonecraft, 118–30; connection between incest and nuclearism, 133–50; war as metaphor in gender politics of new right, 152–62; patriar-

chal militarism and image of woman as caretaker, 165–73; feminism and just-war theory, 192–206; and feminist justice, 211–21. See also Pacifism

Peasants: and politics of Green Revolution, 64

Percy, Walker, 113

Peres, Shimon, 33

Persian Gulf War, 4, 114, 192, 197, 202, 204, 205, 207n.4

Pesticides: politics of Green Revolution and, 56, 57, 62, 63, 65n.9

Phelps, Timothy M., 74

Philosophy: feminist and discussions of peace in mainstream, 1–13; feminist on abuse of women, children, and pets, 68–83; and Ruddick's analysis of maternal thinking, 89

Pilardi, Jo-Ann, 165, 168

Pine Ridge Reservation (South Dakota), 5

Planet of the Apes (film, 1968), 146

Plato, 34

Plumwood, Val, 27, 168

Politics: connection between feminism and peace, 7–8; Day on problem of sustaining nonviolent, 23–26; of Israeli debate on Palestinians, 41–42; feminist philosophical perspective on abuse of women, children, and pets, 78–80, 82–83; Ruddick's feminist-maternal approach to peace, 88–102; war language of new right, 152–62; and ideal of feminist justice, 221

Pope-Lance, Deborah J., 70

Popular culture: nuclear family and violence in, 135–36, 146–47

Pornography: and violence against women, children, and animals, 72; sexual harassment and, 74; race and, 76; banning of violent, 219

Power: and oppressive conceptual frameworks, 3; and connection between incest and nuclearism, 142–46; knowledge as, in patriarchal tradition, 147; gender and economic, 216–18

Practicalist conception of truth (PCT): and Ruddick's feminist maternal peace politics, 89, 90–92, 93–95, 102

The Prince of Tides (Conroy), 144

Privilege: and oppressive conceptual frameworks, 3. See also Hierarchy

Psychology: connections between feminism and peace, 10–13; Woolf's analysis of tyranny, 124–28

Public policy: and violence against women, children, and pets, 80–81

Public/private distinction: and violence against women, children, and pets, 78–80

Quakers: and antiwar movement in Vietnam era, 17

Race: and politics of hazardous waste disposal, 4–5; racism and additive approach to diver-

Race—(*continued*)
sity, 13n.2, 104n.12; pornography and, 76; and models of maternal practice, 98–100; and feminist maternal peace politics, 100–102; and economic inequity, 216–17

Radical feminism: Woolf and, 131n.3

Randal, Jonathan, 82

Rape: war in Bosnia and, 6, 175–76, 178–79, 184 85, 205; collective male responsibility for, 175–89; cross-cultural studies of, 218–19

Rawls, John, 44

Raymond, Janice, 34

Reagan, Ronald, 9, 136–38, 154, 161

Realism: and feminist criticism of just-war theory, 195–96

Reardon, Betty, 172

Regan, Tom, 78

Reichley, Jim, 155

Relational epistemology, 77–78

Renan, Ernest, 49n.1

Resistance: Day's concept of nonviolent commitment and, 20–23; Woolf and Wollstonecraft on gender and styles of, 128–29

Ressler, Robert K., 74

Rickover, Admiral Hyman B., 134

Rights: and just-war theory, 199, 200

Ritual abuse: and violence against women, children, and animals, 73–74

Rivera, Diego, 24

Roberts, Nancy, 18

Rockefeller Foundation, 56

Root, Maria P., 81

Rose, Elizabeth, 73

Rosenberg, Stanley, 152

Rubin, Elaine, 47

Ruddick, Sara: on birth experience, 31n.21; on public/private dualism and violence, 79; feminist maternal peace politics of, 88–102, 127, 165; on just-war theory, 193, 197–203, 205, 207n.13, 208nn.17,18; on international relations, 196

Rukeyser, Muriel, 24, 25

Rush, Florence, 142

Russell, Diana, 70–71, 142, 147

Said, Edward, 38

Sakharov, Andrei, 134

Salomon, Charlotte, 109

Sanchez, Carol Lee, 150

Sanday, Peggy Reeves, 182

Sapiro, Virginia, 131n.2

Savannah River Plant (South Carolina), 144

Science: politics of Green Revolution and, 62. *See also* Technology

Scully, Diane, 187, 189n.2

Seaborg, Glenn, 134

Self-esteem: and gender roles, 173

Self-immolation: of Alice Hertz in protest of Vietnam War, 16–30

Separatism: Woolf on as strategy of resistance, 128–29

Serbia. *See* Bosnia, war in

Sexism: in language of military and of nuclear weapons, 8–10; additive approach to, 13n.2; Woolf and Wollstonecraft on hierarchy and, 123

Sexual abuse: anorexia nervosa and, 81; secrecy and, 142–46; prevalence of, 218

Sexual harassment: military and, 7, 218; of women in Israel, 46; and pornography, 74; and inequality in workplace, 218

Sexuality: and national identity, 51n.24

Shame: moral agency and, 47–49

Shapira, Anita, 50n.15

Shaughnessy, Joan, 199

Shipler, David K., 51n.25

Shiva, Vandana, 8, 61, 62

Shoshone Nation, 104n.13

Shulman, Seth, 5

Silber, David, 74

Singer, Peter, 78

Six Day War (1967), 41, 42, 43, 44

Sloan, G., 81

Smeal, Eleanor, 157, 162n.3

Smith, Amanda, 7

Smithka, Paula, 165

Smuts, Jan, 107

Socialist feminism: Wollstonecraft and, 131n.3

Socialization: of men and collective responsibility for rape, 175–89; gender roles and ideal of androgyny, 214

Socrates, 50n.19

Somalia: disproportionate impact of war on women, children, and the elderly, 6

Somatophobia: connections between abuse of women and animals, 69, 75, 83

Sommers, Christina, 214

Sophocles, 125–26

Spelman, Elizabeth, 69, 75, 97, 103n.7, 104n.12, 169–70

Spivak, Gayatri, 30n.4

Spoljar, Zorica, 6

Sports: and violence against women, 80, 219

Spretnak, Charlene, 9, 12

Standpoint theory. *See* Feminist standpoint theory

Stanley, Autumn, 57

Steiner, George, 131n.7

Stone, Ann, 162n.3

Strikwerda, Robert, 51n.26

Student Nonviolent Coordinating Committee, 23

Suicide: self-immolation as, 19–20, 26, 30n.11

Sullivan, Gerald, 30n.1

Summers, Lawrence, 59, 65n.6

Symbolism: and connections between feminism and peace, 8–10

Szilard, Leo, 134

Tailhook scandal, 7, 9
Technology: biotechnology revolution in agriculture, 56–57; and distancing or denial of war, 106–17. *See also* Green Revolution; Nuclear weapons; Science
Teenage Caveman (film, 1958), 146
Therese of Lisieux, 21, 22, 24–25, 31n.15
Theweleit, Klaus, 131n.4
Third World: women's indigenous agriculture and politics of Green Revolution, 54–65
Thomas, Clarence, 222n.15
Thornhill, Randy, and Nancy Wilmsen Thornhill, 179–82, 184, 185
Three Guineas (Woolf, 1938), 118–19, 120, 128, 129, 130
Tiger, Lionel, 181–82, 185, 187
Timerman, Jacobo, 42
Toxic Wastes and Race in the United States (Commission for Racial Justice of the United Church of Christ 1987), 5
Trebilcot, Joyce, 212
Trenchard, Hugh, 108, 109, 110, 115, 172
Tri-Valley CARE, 143
Truth. *See* Practicalist conception of truth
Tyson, Mike, 177–78

Union Carbide: 1984 chemical disaster in Bhopal, India, 62

Vachss, Alice, 72, 82
Value dualisms: and oppressive conceptual frameworks, 3, 79; patriarchal militarism and image of woman as caretaker, 165–73; and just-war theory, 199–200
Vegetarianism: violence against animals and, 68, 84n.4; relational epistemology and, 77; biomedical ethics and, 81
Vietnam War, and antiwar movement, 16–30
A Vindication of the Rights of Woman (Wollstonecraft, 1792), 119, 129–30
Violence, against women: and patriarchy, 12; and politics of Green Revolution, 54; in India, 65n.8; feminist philosophical perspective on, 68–83; antifeminism and, 161–62; collective responsibility of men for rape, 175–89; and ideal of gender-free society, 218; strategies to decrease, 219–21; definition of structural, 222n.12. *See also* Domestic violence; Rape
Von Braun, Werner, 109, 110–11

Walker, Lenore, 70
Walzer, Michael, 195, 196–97, 198–99, 200, 204, 207n.15

War: concept and logic of domination and, 2–3; continuum of degrees of, 4; distancing and denial in modern technology of, 106–17; gender and critiques of by Wollstonecraft and Woolf, 118–30; and language of gender politics of new right, 152–62; and image of woman as caretaker, 171–73; and collective responsibility of men for rape, 188–89; and just-war theory, 192–206. *See also* Nuclearism; Pacifism; Peace; Warism
Warism: definition of, 13n.4; and developmentalism, 55; Green Revolution and environmental ideology of, 59–63; and just-war theory, 207n.7
Warren, Karen J., 3, 27, 68, 69–70, 79–80, 170
Warren, Mary Ann, 212, 213
Weart, Spencer, 145
Weil, Simone, 22, 28, 31n.17
Welter, Barbara, 158
Whitbeck, Caroline, 169
Whitman, Walt, 28
Willhoite, Pam, 84n.8
Winternitz, Helen, 74
Wittgenstein, Ludwig, 90, 102n.1
Wollstonecraft, Mary, 118–30, 171
Woman and Nature: The Roaring Inside Her (Griffin, 1978), 109, 110
Women: accounts of peace in mainstream philosophy and contributions of, 1–13; Day's view of, 25; peace movement and harassment of in Israel, 46; indigenous agriculture of and politics of Green Revolution, 54–65; feminist philosophical perspective on abuse of children, pets, and, 68–83; patriarchal militarism and image of as caretaker, 165–73; historical association of with peace, 206–207n.3, 208n.18. *See also* Gender; Sexism; Violence, against women
Women in Black (Palestinian), 45–46
Women's International League for Peace and Freedom (WILPF), 206n.3
Women's Peace Union, 206n.3
Woolf, Virginia, 118–30, 159
Woollacott, A., 152
World War I, 107–108
World War II, 108–109

Young, Bert, 218

Zaroulis, Nancy, 30n.1
Zinn, Maxine Baca, 103–104n.12
Zionism, 37